SWAHILI FOR STARTERS

A Practical Introductory Course

SWAHILI FOR STARTERS
A Practical Introductory Course

JOAN MAW

Emeritus Reader in Swahili in the
University of London,
School of Oriental and African Studies

OXFORD
UNIVERSITY PRESS

OXFORD

UNIVERSITY PRESS

Great Clarendon Street, Oxford OX2 6DP

Oxford University Press is a department of the University of Oxford.
It furthers the University's objective of excellence in research, scholarship,
and education by publishing worldwide in

Oxford New York

Athens Auckland Bangkok Bogotá Beunos Aires Calcutta
Cape Town Chennai Dar es Salaam Delhi Florence Hong Kong Istanbul
Karachi Kuala Lumpur Madrid Melbourne Mexico City Mumbai
Nairobi Paris São Paulo Singapore Taipei Tokyo Toronto Warsaw

and associated companies in Berlin Ibadan

Oxford is a registered trade mark of Oxford University Press
in the UK and in certain other countries

Published in the United States
by Oxford University Press Inc., New York

First published as *Twende!* 1985

First published in paperback 1999

British Library Cataloguing in Publication Data

Data available

Library of Congress Cataloging in Publication Data
Maw, Joan
Swahili for starters: a practical introductory course.
Includes index.
1. Swahili language—Text books for foreign speakers—
English. I. University of London. School of Oriental
and African Studies. II. Title.
PL8702 M335 1985 496´.392824.21 85–15257

ISBN 0–19–823783–9 (Pbk.)

3 5 7 9 10 8 6 4 2

Typeset by Joshua Associates Ltd., Oxford
Printed in Great Britain
on acid-free paper by Biddles Ltd
www.Biddles.co.uk

I dedicate this book to 'my friends pictured within', and to Mrs Nancy Holt, without whom it might never have got finished.

Foreword

Swahili for Starters, formerly *Twende!,* is an excellent course book for introducing an aspiring learner of Swahili to the spoken and written forms of the language. Language courses are peculiarly subject to fashion: 'structural', 'situational', 'functional', 'notional', and now 'communicative'. These terms have all in their time been used to reassure the diffident learner that the course he is embarking on is the fresh fruit of the latest thinking in applied linguistics. Dr. Joan Maw's practical Swahili course has no need of such specious recommendations, although it does in fact ingeniously integrate all these approaches.

The course has a firm structural base; at each stage the criteria which determine the introduction of new items have been kept firmly in mind: each item must be immediately useful for communication and also appropriately placed in the book's grammatical sequence.

Most of the material in the Units is first presented in dialogue form. The Units follow each other in a well-thought-out, gradual and logical manner. The situations which are the basis for the conversations in most units are all 'taken from life' and not made up by the author. The attitudes and the sense of priorities they reveal, as Dr. Maw suggests, may often seem droll or surprising to the non-African learner, but they are normal to the Swahili speaker. If the foreign learner can understand them, and the social context from which they derive, then he is half-way to learning the language.

Word classes and their grammatical usage are introduced gradually and in a deliberate manner within the context of the dialogue. Each Unit is composed of a dialogue, a list of all new words and utterances with their English glosses, and relevant grammatical and sociolinguistic notes pertaining to the cultural context of the particular situational domain of language use introduced by the dialogue. I find this approach both interesting and easy to follow from the point of view of the learner as it avoids dwelling directly on heavy structural aspects of the language. The course is certainly meant to be as close to a natural contextual learning of the language as could be devised in book form. Pronunciation exercises are introduced at convenient intervals in a simple straightforward manner in the context of actual utterances of the language, with each sound being practised in the various word environments in which it occurs. Each unit has practice and revision exercises occurring at convenient places. The Units are accompanied by tapes which have been carefully recorded by speakers of the language, thus providing further help with pronunciation, intonation and the general mode of speech interaction.

The course being to a large extent in dialogue form and the many games and group exercises, may suggest that it is best suited to a class or group of students, but the course could effectively be used by a learner working alone. The course is particularly appropriate for learners who intend to spend time in Swahili-speaking areas, because

it aims at teaching a student to interact in a natural environment.
Dr. Joan Maw's academic, professional and personal experience have
successfully combined to produce a course book of this unusual range.
Apart from being a general linguist, she has taught languages,
including Swahili, at various levels. Furthermore she has spent a good
amount of time in East Africa among Swahili-speaking people, often
freely interacting with them in various social contexts. Finally her
modesty, love of the language and sympathetic understanding of the
cultural background of Swahili speakers have made an immense
contribution to her achievement in the writing of this book.

Professor Mohamed H. Abdulaziz
University of Nairobi 1983

Acknowledgements

I wish to thank all the people who have helped, advised, and encouraged me in writing this book: Professor M. H. Abdulaziz, who has kindly written a foreword; Mr John Kelly who made many helpful suggestions; Mr George Perren who was enthusiastic; my many friends in Africa and at the School of Oriental and African Studies, especially Sh. Y. A. Omar; Mr P. K. Muoka; Mr Stuart Hirst and my students, who have acted as guinea-pigs; and Ms Jean Waring who has done endless photocopying.

In the work of updating this book (formerly *Twende!*) as *Swahili for Starters*, I wish to acknowledge the helpful comments made by Professor Jim Igoe of the University of Boston, USA, many of whose suggestions I have incorporated.

The following bodies are thanked for permission to reproduce copyright material.

Equator Sound Studios, Nairobi, for the words of the songs *Malaika* and *Hakuna Mwingine*.

East Africa Publishing House, Nairobi, for the extract from *Naushangilia mlima wa Kenya* by Jomo Kenyatta.

Institute of Kiswahili Research, University of Dar es Salaam for *Mwanasesere* by Naila S. Kharusi.

Kenya Literature Bureau for the extract from *Muyaka* by M. H. Abdulaziz.

Contents

Introduction

This course is intended for the person who wants to learn Swahili in a social context. A language is more than grammar and vocabulary. It is also an expression of the way of life of the people who speak it, and a reflection of how they see the world. Learning a new language involves a great feat of memory, and to my mind learning grammar and vocabulary is not only difficult, it is also boring — which makes it still more difficult — if it is attempted without reference to the people who speak the language. We need to know not merely 'how to say it in Swahili' but *what* to say in Swahili, *when* to say it, what the Swahili speaker *means* by what he says, and what impression *we* are giving by what we say — what the Swahili speaker thinks we mean! To give a very simple illustration, there is a word in Swahili, *karibu*. It can mean 'near', 'approach', 'welcome', 'come in'. It can be used to invite someone — to come into the house, for example, or combined with other words to invite someone to sit down, have tea, have a meal, and so on. But by many speakers it will also be used in a social situation on parting. Goodbyes will have been said and then, as the guest is actually leaving, the host may say '*karibu*'. If the guest does not know the meaning of this word used in this situation he may think he is being pressed to stay longer and may even do so. This is *not* what the host meant. *karibu* in this situation means 'You're always welcome', 'I'm glad you came', 'Come again', and so on.

To give a more complex illustration: it is well known that the late President Kenyatta of Kenya was referred to as *Mzee* 'old man', and that this was a term of respect. It is generally believed by Europeans that Africans (and others) have a respect for age which Europeans do not have. There may be some truth in this (though it may be part of a sort of 'Golden Age' myth), but certainly old people in Zanzibar or Mombasa will tell you, 'Young people have no respect these days, not like when *I* was young' — exactly the same complaints as can be heard in Europe or America. Similarly, young people may sometimes complain that their elders are old-fashioned and out of touch. But the natural social system requires that older people care for the young and are in turn cared for. If you call a Swahili *mzee* he is likely to return *mwanangu* 'my child', confirming the potential social relationship between you. *Mzee* is a term of respect for power and influence, not of sentimentality. Further, the *mzee* is expected to care for the subordinate, otherwise he is not worthy of respect; and the subordinate should show respect or he is not worthy of patronage. So in Swahili to call someone *mzee* is not only to express respect for his knowledge, power and influence, it is also to suggest that he might exert it on your behalf. And to call someone *mwanangu* is to express benevolence and the expectation of future support. Perhaps there *is* more respect for sheer longevity among people with a shorter expectation of life and a tradition of oral history. Religion plays a part, and so do the social pressures felt in small traditional static communities. But times change, social organisation changes, political and economic pressures bring different ways of life. The rate of change is very rapid in

East Africa these days, and attitudes that depend on social and economic circumstances may change with them. Of course personal relationships will always evoke emotions of love, gratitude, envy, hostility, and
so on. These also may be expressed through language. One may choose
to call someone *mzee* or *mwanangu* out of affection and the desire to
foster a close relationship. But with a different intonation or voice quality
the same words could express contempt. All this is part of language
use; part of the meaning of the words *mzee* and *mwanangu* is how they
are used to express social attitudes and/or personal relationships.
Unless one acquires some insight into the social and cultural background
of the users of the language one can hardly be said to know it, and one
will certainly not be able to operate it except on a very superficial level.
This course attempts to supply some such insights, as well as to teach
the language.

Who, then, are the Swahili? This is by no means an easy question to
answer. In this book I refer at times to 'a traditional Swahili community',
and by that I mean people who today live on the coast of East Africa
(Kenya and Tanzania) or the off-shore islands, call themselves Swahili,
probably have some admixture of Arab blood, are Muslims, speak
Swahili as their first language, and live in a traditional manner. But the
matter is complex. For example in Mombasa, there are well-known clans
or families, and those who belong to these clans consider themselves to
be true Swahili. But other people may call themselves Swahili whom the
members of the clans do not recognise as such, or only marginally as
such! Conversely, there are people fulfilling one or more of the criteria
mentioned above who are not Swahili, or do not consider themselves to
be, or who are not considered by others to be. At different times in
history, different criteria have been applied — mainly by outsiders — to
define the Swahili. These days some people would even describe themselves as Swahili *and* something else, for example many Digo (a coastal
tribe) would describe themselves as both Digo and Swahili. Many Digo
have become Muslims, and for them Swahili is equated with Islam.

Genetically the Swahili seem to be a coastal Bantu people who over time
intermarried to some extent with Arabs from Saudi Arabia. From early
historical accounts the Swahili were always great travellers, up and
down the coast and across the Indian Ocean. The name Swahili comes
from an Arabic word meaning 'coast'. Swahili-speaking communities still
live along the East African coast, from Mogadishu in Somalia down to
Mozambique. Very early in their history, the Swahili were an urbanised
people. Besides present-day towns along the coast, there are also ruins
of former towns, long abandoned for various reasons. Houses, palaces
and mosques were built of stone or coral rock, the houses several
storeys high, and with running water and drainage systems everywhere.
The inhabitants of these towns were rich, trading and land-owning. They
had contacts overseas from earliest times and must have led sophisti-
cated and luxurious lives. Poetry flourished especially in the Northern
towns, much of which has been handed down orally or copied out many
times in the Arabic script, nowadays transliterated into Roman. Economically and politically, the Swahili as the link between East Africa and the
outside world were very powerful.

During the nineteenth century regular caravan routes into the interior of Africa were developed, with more or less permanent staging-posts and developing trading centres up-country. These settlements remained as communities of Swahili speakers even when the trading died out, such towns as Tabora, Ujiji, Bujumbura, and settlements in Zambia and Zaire. Of course a good deal of intermarriage with local people along these trade routes took place, so that although patrilineal descent was generally what counted, still *who* the Swahili were got more diluted.

What the Swahili *language* is may be somewhat clearer. It is a Bantu language, on linguistic evidence being spoken on the Coast before the tenth century. It has an admixture of Arabic items of vocabulary (mainly learned words), and more recently other loan words, mainly from English. Its structure remains Bantu, and it has a very rich vocabulary.

Traditionally there were always various geographical coastal dialects of Swahili, at least fifteen, grouped differently by different descriptive linguists. It is of course theoretically difficult to say when a dialect shades off into a distinct language. The Swahili spoken in the trading posts also began to change and take on characteristics of the surrounding languages. The best described of these dialects is that spoken in Zaire.

During the second half of the nineteenth century, European missionaries began to join the explorers and trading caravans, and to set up mission stations. Many of these missionaries worked on Swahili, producing dictionaries and grammars. Some of them used Swahili as a lingua franca, although others began to study and use other local languages. The problem from the missionaries' point of view, however, was that in some areas there were large numbers of languages each spoken by a relatively small number of people, so that the effort involved in producing grammars and dictionaries, translating the Bible, and producing books for the schools they set up, was very great. For many therefore, the idea of using Swahili as a lingua franca was very attractive, and its use spread.

From the beginning of the twentieth century, the various colonial administrations had to have more or less deliberate language policies. The Germans in Tanganyika decided to use Swahili as the language of administration; and as education expanded, more textbooks were produced, and newspapers began to appear in Swahili, mainly produced by missionaries. Under the British administration after the 1914-18 war, Swahili was used as the medium of instruction in Primary schools, although English was used in Secondary schools. After Independence, the use of Swahili was expanded still further as a unifying force, and it is now the national language of Tanzania.

In Kenya, Swahili was widely used under the colonial administration, and it has been increasingly used especially in towns which have attracted a mixed population. But the presence of large groups of other language speakers, principally the Kikuyu and the Luo, encouraged the use of these languages in Primary schools rather than Swahili. Since Independence, Swahili has been made an official language, but although its use is clearly spreading, it is as a lingua franca, and does not seem so far to be replacing other local languages in the affections of their speakers, nor English as the language of higher education and commerce.

Swahili is also used in Uganda as a lingua franca, but for a long time was not very popular as it was associated in people's minds with the slave trade, and Islam — many Ugandans being early converts to Christianity — and also with the army, where it was used from an early stage. It suffered perhaps from a further disadvantage that, there being no first language speakers in Uganda, the simplified forms used for trading and giving orders struck people as inferior. It is said that since the use of Tanzanian troops in Uganda following the downfall of the Amin regime, Swahili is enjoying an increase in popularity.

With the growing use of Swahili throughout East Africa for administration and education came the need for standardisation. From an early stage, two different forms of the language were used by different sets of missionaries. One, Kimvita, was a more Northerly dialect, spoken in the Mombasa area of Kenya, and the other, Kiunguja, was the dialect of Zanzibar town, which was also spoken widely in up-country Tanganyika. Not only were different dialects being used, but also there were different spelling traditions — mainly based on the spelling conventions of the first language of the missionaries, French, German, or English — which needed to be standardised for the sake of uniformity in textbooks and so on. Each of the two dialects had strong claims; the Northern dialects had a long literary and poetic tradition, but the Zanzibar dialect was already used over a wide geographical area, and it was this dialect which was chosen. The Interterritorial Language Committee was set up in 1930, and did a great deal of work in standardising the language and encouraging the production of text books and other literature. The direct successor to the language section of that committee is now incorporated into the work of the Institute of Swahili Research, at the University of Dar es Salaam, while the literary successor is the East African Literature Bureau. It is a fact though, that since Independence and the subsequent break-up of the East African Federation, the two countries where Swahili is most widely spoken, Kenya and Tanzania, have become more distinct ideologically, politically and economically. Indeed the borders between these two countries were closed for some years. Also the language policies of these two countries are rather different, Tanzania laying official emphasis on the use and more deliberate development of Swahili, Kenya having a rather more *laissez-faire* attitude, while still officially encouraging its use. This means that the language and especially the vocabulary in political, economic, and scholarly subjects in these two countries seems to be showing more and more divergence.

It is perhaps a paradox that, while in modern times the use and knowledge of Swahili is spreading rapidly not only throughout East Africa, but also in Universities to West and Central Africa, Europe, Asia, the Far East, and America, the descendants of the original Swahili people themselves have declined in economic and political power. Perhaps, although their language was originally spread by economic and political power, it is now so acceptable to many Africans precisely because it is *not* associated with such power, and thus represents no threat. The literary and linguistic interest and the beauty of the language remain, and Swahili is more than ever the gateway to understanding between Africa and the rest of the world.

In this course-book the standard form of the language is taught. This form is now used throughout East Africa for official communications, newspapers, text books, and modern literature — with of course continuous slight variations and fashions in usage and vocabulary. It is also generally used on radio and television, though again, dialect and popular forms may intervene. It is the most widely understood form of the language, so that the foreigner speaking this form will be understood even if he gets replies in a different dialect form, say, on the North Kenya coast, or in rural Zanzibar, or in a sub-standard form from a waiter in a Nairobi bar, for example. This is the problem with a standard form of any language; practically everybody writes it, almost everybody understands it, and rather few speak it all the time! Most Swahili speakers, like most English speakers, recognise the standard language and can speak it, but may also use a dialect or a modified standard form in different social situations. The foreigner will at first have only one form at his disposal, and this had better be the standard form because he can use it in the widest range of situations.

The characters of the Swahili speakers in this course are all drawn from life, and they illustrate the wide range of speakers of the language these days. Some represent the traditional coastal communities, e.g. Bibi Hadija, Sh. Yahya. But people with traditional backgrounds do not necessarily remain in them: Professor Athumani is a distinguished member of the international academic community. Philip and Jimmy represent speakers of other African languages who use Swahili in their daily work lives, but probably not at home. Toon and Jemima represent a mixed marriage: Toon is European, not English, and Jemima is Kenyan, not Swahili. They do not know each other's first languages, but they both know English and Swahili. They use Swahili in their working lives, and have chosen to use it at home, so that for their children, Swahili is the first language. Bwana Harris is an Englishman, new to Africa, trying to understand the Swahili language and the people. Bibi Maw is myself, an outsider, long engaged in learning and teaching Swahili.

The situations used in the course are ones in which the foreign learner is most likely to find himself or herself involved. Most foreigners need Swahili for daily activities, getting about, and social contact. At first, at least, the Swahili speakers they mostly meet are officials, people in various service positions, and people who live a modern town life, superficially at least not very different from that in any town in the world. Many of these people speak at least some English. Later the foreigner may meet people who live more traditional lives in the towns and villages of the coast — fishermen, sailors, housewives, farmers. These people may know hardly any English, if any at all. The more deeply one becomes involved in Swahili-speaking communities, the more necessary it is to be sensitive to the culture and ways of thought of one's hosts, in order to feel comfortable and not to give offence. I have therefore chosen situations which reveal something of the differences between the ideas of the European characters in the book and the various Swahili-speakers they encounter. Some of these ideas would be common to many East

Africans, and are not specific to Swahili speakers. The situations therefore should be studied not only from the language-learning point of view,
but also for the ideas they illustrate.

In order to put the language and situations still more into context, I have
included a section in each Unit with more background describing aspects
of the life-style and ideas of many East Africans and the elusive Swahili. I
have tried to keep a balance between describing something of the traditional society and aspects of life in the modern melting-pot.

Not much is said in the course about literature. Traditional Swahili
literature mainly consists of poetry, heavily influenced by Islam. The
earliest known manuscript is dated 1728. Much of this literature has now
been transliterated and published. It is not easy: it is mostly written in
one of the northern dialects, like all poetry it has special language conventions, its Islamic references require a study of Islam, and some
knowledge of Arabic is a help with obscure vocabulary. More modern
poetry is highly allusive and requires special study. But even today,
poetry-writing is highly popular, and many newspapers have regular
pages of poetry contributed by readers. Prose writing is a more modern
development, the earliest extant writings being accounts of the lives of
prominent people or groups, probably taken down from dictation. Such
are *Habari za Wakilindi*, a history of the Shambala people, first published
in 1905 but referring to events in the previous century; *Uhuru wa
Watumwa*, concerning the freeing of slaves in East Africa; and *Tippu
Tip*, the autobiography of a famous caravan leader active in the nineteenth century. Modern prose writing includes most popular forms:
plays, detective novels, legends, love stories — some of it titillating and
most of it moralising. Newspapers and periodicals abound, mostly
hastily written with an eye to immediate effect rather than high style. I
think it would be true to say that Swahili prose writing is still in its
infancy. This introductory course can only provide a slight taste of all this
richness and variety.

So this course is meant to do more than teach you Swahili; it is meant, if
you will, to introduce you to an aspect of Africa. By looking at another
language and culture we also learn something about our own. Perhaps
this book will be a contribution to greater future understanding and cooperation. I hope so.

Using the Book

Each unit begins with a section for the voice — generally conversation, but some pronunciation sections, relating of anecdotes, a few literary passages, and some music. The student is recommended always to read these sections aloud several times. They are also recorded on an accompanying tape which may be purchased from the Publications Department, School of Oriental and African Studies, Thornhaugh Street, Russell Square, London WC1H 0XG. However, the book itself is complete without the tape. If the student has the tape available, he can use this as he wishes, listening, speaking with the tape, stopping the tape to repeat sections, stopping the tape to respond. If he does not wish to use the tape, or it is not available, it is helpful if possible to practise aloud, or with another student, or with a teacher. Special pronunciation exercises are included, but apart from these the student should not, after the first few Units, practise words in isolation. Groups of words, clauses, or sentences should be practised as a whole. This is how natural speech occurs; furthermore the best way to retain new vocabulary is to learn it in a known context.

New vocabulary is gradually introduced, at first before each spoken passage. But soon it follows the passage, and the student should try to guess the meaning of new vocabulary in the context, before looking it up below. This is how new words are naturally encountered; moreover the effort of trying to understand will aid retention of the item. And what pleasure when you guess right! The vocabulary items are given a 'gloss'; this is the nearest equivalent in English for the use of that word in that passage. Of course a word has many meanings, the range of which you will begin to acquire in time. The curious student may begin to look them up in the dictionary. But a word of warning: use Swahili-English dictionaries if you will, but English-Swahili can be very misleading because they are aimed at the Swahili speaker. One of the oldest but still the best is the *Standard Dictionary* by F. Johnson (Nairobi, Oxford University Press) in two volumes, English-Swahili and Swahili-English.

Leaving aside the Units dealing mainly with pronunciation, the second section of each Unit explains the grammatical points encountered in the first section. These are graded as far as possible, so that the student encounters first the structures that will enable him to communicate right from the beginning. Of course at first he will only be able to communicate simple ideas. More complex communication demands more complex grammar; and this is gradually built up through the course. Occasionally it has been found necessary to include grammatical forms for the sake of natural conversation in a Unit without explaining them fully at the time. The student is asked to be patient with these few prefigurings. Again, this is the kind of thing that occurs in natural language learning. The explanation, when it comes, will be the more revealing. (The impatient student can look up the whole grammar in advance in a standard grammar book — the best is the one by E. O. Ashton — or using the index can look ahead in this course.) Generally speaking I think the student will find enough to work on within each Unit.

The third section of each Unit consists of exercises which can be written or spoken. It is hoped that these exercises have been constructed so that there are not many possible alternative responses, and so that the student can always expect to get them right. I think we learn by our successes, not by our failures. A key is given at the back of the book. There is hardly ever anything that looks like translation. Translation is a special art, and I do not find it a good teaching aid. Cudgelling one's brains for the Swahili word for something — for which most likely there is no exact equivalent anyway — does not strike me as a useful exercise. When doing an exercise, the student should try to switch his mind into using the Swahili he knows, and work on expanding that. These sections also contain games and puzzles. I beg the adult learner or the teacher not to neglect these games as childish. It is difficult with restricted grammar and vocabulary to get sufficient varied conversation practice. The games are intended to force the student to use his Swahili resources in an interesting and controlled environment, for a purpose. Playing games is also fun, and using language in pleasurable situations will help it to stick.

The first section of each Unit reflects situations which a foreigner is likely to encounter. The conversation in those situations will often reveal an attitude to the situation quite different from what the foreigner might expect. The last section of each Unit reflects and enlarges on these attitudes and the social background that produces them. I attach great importance to these sections, since they put the language into a wider context.

Quite a few Swahili proverbs and sayings are also included. These are not just linguistic curiosities, although quite often they share with poetry a specially succinct or picturesque use of the language. But they are used in everyday Swahili conversation and they often sum up an attitude or concentrate an accepted truism of the society.

A student can use this course to suit himself. If he or she is not interested in learning to speak, he need not practise the first sections, use the tapes, nor do the pronunciation exercises. He can read the passages and go straight on to the grammatical explanations. If he wishes *only* to speak, he can concentrate on the first sections and not study the second. If he wishes to write he can write out the exercises in the third sections; if not, he can do them orally. If he wants to know about the people who already speak this language, there is something for him in the last sections. If not, he can ignore them.

Of course I myself think that all these aspects of language learning are equally important and, really, interdependent. I once knew a Polish scholar who had learned English solely in order to read linguistics articles, he had never heard it spoken nor paid any attention to how it should be spoken. Therefore when he read it to himself he mentally pronounced it as if it were Polish. It was almost impossible to communicate with him orally. I suppose he never read articles concerned with the phonetics of English! But I think such single-minded people are rare. Most of us want to become as competent as possible in every way. I hope this course will assist you to do that. *Twende!* — 'Let's go!'

▷ indicates material recorded on the tape

Please note that in a few places the words on the tape differ slightly from those in the text. This is especially so where prices in the text have been updated.

Unit 1   Fungu la kwanza
Hujambo? 'How are you?'

I

(a) *hujambo?* — the first word of greeting, addressed to one person. Means something like 'How are you (singular)?' 'Nothing wrong with you, I hope'.
sijambo — response to *hujambo*. 'I am well.' 'Nothing wrong with me'.
bwana — polite term of address to a man, 'sir'. (Occasionally used between women equals.)
bibi — polite term of address to a woman, 'madam'.

▷ Hujambo?
sijambo

bwana   bibi

(b) You should always address people by title or by name, not with the bare greeting word.

bwana and *bibi* can be combined with proper names, whether 'Christian' or surname, e.g. *Bibi Joan* or *Bibi Maw*. (Written abbreviations are *Bw.* and *Bi.* 'Mr' and 'Ms'.)

▷ Bibi: Hujambo, bwana.
Bwana: Sijambo, bibi.

Bwana: Hujambo, bibi.
Bibi: Sijambo, bwana.

Bi. M.:   Hujambo, Bwana Harris.
Bw. H.:   Sijambo, Bibi Maw.

Bi. J.:   Hujambo, Bwana Mohammed.
Bw. M.:   Sijambo, Bibi Joan.

(c) *mama* — literally 'mother', but also used as a term of polite address to a woman whom you judge to be worthy of being a mother! Warmer than *bibi*.
baba — literally 'father'; used to a man under the same circumstances as *mama* to a woman. But see also section IV.
mzee — 'old man' — a term of respect. President Kenyatta of Kenya was known as *Mzee*.

▷ mama   baba   mzee

(d)   Greet the people in the pictures:

You have been greeted by the following people. Respond:

(e)   You cannot simply respond to a greeting, you must return it. The following dialogues show you how.

wewe — 'you (singular)'. Only used for emphasis.
je? — an interrogative exclamation 'eh?'. Can come initially or finally in an utterance.
mimi — 'I, me', only used for emphasis.

> Baba: Hujambo, mama.
> Mama: Sijambo, baba. Wewe, je?
> Baba: Mimi sijambo.

na — 'and'.
sana — an intensifier, 'very/very much'.

> Bibi: Hujambo, mzee.
> Mzee: Sijambo bibi. Na wewe hujambo?
> Bibi: Mimi sijambo sana.

sijui — 'I don't know (about).'
asante — 'thanks', but not much used for actual thanking. Here it means something like 'that's all right then', 'good', 'glad to hear it'.

> Bi. M.:   Hujambo, Bwana Harris.
> Bw. H.:   Sijambo Bibi Maw. Sijui wewe.
> Bi. M.:   Mimi sijambo sana, bwana.
> Bw. H.:   Asante, bibi.

(f)   It is polite to make enquiries about other people. This is how:

hajambo? — 'is he/she well?'. 'Nothing wrong with him/her, I hope?'
hajambo — 'he/she is well'. 'Nothing wrong with him/her'.
watoto — 'children'.
hawajambo? — 'are they well?', 'Nothing wrong with them, I hope?'
hawajambo — 'they are well', 'Nothing wrong with them.'

> Mimi: Mzee hajambo?
> Wewe: Hajambo.

Mimi: Bwana hajambo?
Wewe: Hajambo.

Mimi: Bibi Maw hajambo?
Wewe: Hajambo.

Mimi: Mama hajambo?
Wewe: Hajambo.

Mimi: Baba hajambo?
Wewe: Hajambo.

Mimi: Watoto hawajambo?
Wewe: Hawajambo.

(g)   Enquire about the people in the pictures:

(h)   Dialogue practice:

Mama: Hujambo, mzee.
Mzee: Sijambo mama. Na wewe, je?
Mama: Mimi sijambo sana.
Mzee: Watoto hawajambo?
Mama: Hawajambo.
Mzee: Asante, mama.

Mama: Hujambo, baba.
Baba: Sijambo, mama. Sijui wewe.
Mama: Mimi sijambo, baba.
Baba: Je, bwana* hajambo?
Mama: Hajambo.
Baba: Na watoto, je?
Mama: Watoto hawajambo.
Baba: Asante sana.

*bwana here means '(your) husband'.

wote — 'all (people)', 3rd person plural 'all of them'

Bw.H: Hujambo, Bwana Philip.
Bw.P.: Sijambo, Bwana Harris. Na wewe hujambo?
Bw.H.: Sijambo sana. Mama* hajambo?
Bw.P.: Hajambo, bwana. Mzee hajambo?
Bw.H.: Hajambo. Na watoto, je?
Bw.P.: Hawajambo. Wote hawajambo.

mama here implies 'your mother'.

(i)   *wanafunzi* — 'students, pupils'.
      mwalimu — 'teacher'. A prestigious title — ex-President Nyerere of
      Tanzania is called *Mwalimu,* not only because he was once a teacher,
      but as a title of respect.
      nyinyi — 'you (plural)'. Only used for emphasis.
      sisi — 'us, we'. Only used for emphasis.

▷   wanafunzi   mwalimu

      nyinyi (pay special attention to pronunciation of *ny*)
      sisi

(j)   *hamjambo?* — 'are you-all well?', 'You (plural) have no problems, I
      hope?'
      hatujambo — 'we are well', 'we have no problems'.
      asanteni — 'thank you-all' (*asante+ni*), 'Right, you lot'.

▷   Mwalimu: Hamjambo, watoto?
      Watoto: Hatujambo, mwalimu. Wewe, je?
      Mwalimu: Mimi sijambo.

      Watoto: Hujambo, mwalimu.
      Mwalimu: Sijambo, watoto. Na nyinyi hamjambo?
      Watoto: Hatujambo, mwalimu.

      Wanafunzi: Hujambo, mwalimu.
      Mwalimu: Sijambo, wanafunzi. Sijui nyinyi.
      Wanafunzi: Sisi hatujambo.
      Mwalimu: Asanteni.

▮▮

(i)   The words *hujambo* and *sijambo* are almost like verbs, and are in the
      negative. *hu-* is negative second person singular (you), and *si-* is negative
      first person singular (I). *jambo* means something like 'matter for con-
      cern'. So this greeting and response mean something like 'there's
      nothing the matter with you, I hope' (*hujambo*), 'No, there's nothing
      wrong with me' (*sijambo*). Similarly, *hajambo* as a query means 'Nothing
      wrong with him/her?' (third person singular) and as a response confirms

that nothing is wrong. *hatujambo* — first person plural (we/us) 'nothing wrong with us'; *hamjambo* — second person plural (you) 'nothing wrong with you lot' (normally a query); and *hawajambo* as a query 'nothing wrong with them?' — third person plural (they/them), and as a response confirms that nothing is wrong. So we have the paradigm:

singular	**plural**
1 (I) sijambo	(we) hatujambo
2 (you) hujambo	(you) hamjambo
3 (he/she) hajambo	(they) hawajambo

Notice that there is no distinction in Swahili grammar between masculine and feminine, so *hajambo* means either *he* or *she* is alright, according to the context.

You may have noticed *sijui* 'I don't know (about)' in the third dialogue in (e). The *si-* is the same as in *sijambo*. *ju-* is a verb root meaning 'know', and *-i* is a negative suffix. This will be dealt with later.

(ii) A number of personal pronouns, *mimi* 'I/me', *wewe* 'you (singular)', *sisi* 'us/we', and *nyinyi* 'you (plural)' have been met with. There is also *yeye* 'he/him, she/her', and *wao* 'they/them'. The full paradigm may be laid out as follows:

singular	**plural**
1 mimi	sisi
2 wewe	nyinyi
3 yeye	wao

Verbs, however, normally include a morpheme (part of a word) which indicates person, e.g. *hatujambo* contains *-tu-* which means 'we' (1st person plural), *hamjambo* contains *-m-* 'you' (2nd person plural), *hawajambo* contains *-wa-* 'they' (third person plural), so separate personal pronouns are not needed grammatically. To say *sisi hatujambo* is to repeat the person, i.e. to say 'we, we are well', 'as for us, we are well'. These personal pronouns, then, are only used in Swahili for emphasis or contrast, e.g. *mimi sijambo, sijui wewe* 'I'm alright, but how about *you*?'

(iii) '**all**'. The word *wote* is 3rd person plural; we could also say (*sisi*) *sote* 'all of us' and (*nyinyi*) *nyote* 'all of you'.

(iv) Note that the subject normally precedes the verb, e.g. *watoto hawajambo* 'the children are well'. In greetings this would almost invariably be the case.

(v) Note that the vocative (person addressed) usually comes last, e.g. *hujambo, bwana*? 'how are you, sir?'. But you might call out to someone *bwana, hujambo*? 'Hey there sir, how are you?'.

(vi) Note that questions expecting the answer yes (or no) have the same grammatical form as statements, e.g. *baba hajambo* can mean *either* 'is (your) father well?' *or* '(my) father is well'. In most contexts — as here in greetings, the distinction is plain, since one would not mention the state of father's health if one had not been asked. The distinction between question and statement *can* be made by intonation if necessary, but where there is a possibility of ambiguity, the interrogative particle *je?* is normally used to make it clear that a question is being asked: *Je, baba hajambo?*

III

(k) How would you greet:

    an old man
    a class of students
    your boss
    a market-woman
    a group of children.

How would you respond to a greeting from:

    your boss's wife
    your father
    a teacher
    Miss Maw.

How would you ask about someone's:

    father
    mother
    husband
    children
    aged relative
    students.

(l) Invent some dialogues of your own. If working in a group, practise them with others. Try impromptu greetings and responses.

(m) Fill in the blanks:

    'I have no problems'   _____ jambo
    'Has she problems?'   _____ jambo
    'We have no problems'   _____ jambo
    'They have no problems'   _____ jambo
    'Have you-all problems?'   _____ jambo
    'Have you any problems?' _____ jambo

(n) How would you say:

    '*I* have no problems, what about *you*?'
    '*He* has no problems, what about *them*?'
    '*We* are all right, what about *you lot*?'

(o) In greetings, does the Subject normally come before or after the Verb?
    Where does the Vocative (person addressed) come in the clause?
    How do you make yes/no questions in Swahili?

IV

It is very important in Swahili culture to greet people properly. You cannot get away with a smile or a mumbled word as in English. Indeed, if you simply smile at someone in the street without speaking he may think you are laughing at him. But people like to be greeted, and it is considered rude to ignore them. Further, it is very important to address people by name or by some title of respect. You must also make enquiries about their family (even if you do not know them), or about other matters such as work; and you must respond to such enquiries yourself. These are formal enquiries and responses, but they are very important in establishing a relationship. It would constitute a social gaffe in English to respond to 'How do you do' or 'Good morning' with anything other than an echo of the first expression, whatever one may later go on to discuss. Similarly in Swahili when asked 'How are the children?' the reply is 'Well', not 'I haven't any' or 'They've got the measles'! These formal greetings and enquiries should not be cut short. Sometimes, especially away from the coast, you may hear people shout simply *Jambo!* This is an abbreviated and informal greeting, like 'Hi!' and is used jocularly, or sometimes to foreigners who are presumed not to know the correct forms.

There are also constraints. We have seen that the word *bwana* is used as a polite form of address to a man. It may also mean 'husband', so that if you ask a woman *bwana hajambo?* it normally means, 'How is your husband?'. Similarly, *bibi*, a polite form of address to a woman, may also mean 'wife', and if a man should speak of his wife, he may well refer to her as his 'bibi'. But although one may ask a woman how her husband is, it would not be correct form to ask a man how his wife is (especially if the enquirer is himself a man). That would be to show too close a personal interest. When, therefore, you ask a man *Watoto hawajambo?*, *watoto* (literally 'children') is taken to mean 'dependents', and therefore by implication includes the wife (or wives) at home.

Although what has been said about the terms *mama* and *baba* in section I (b) generally holds good, it should be noted that among Swahili speakers of the old aristocracy, these terms (except when used for 'mother' and 'father') are applied to people considered to be of a lower social status. It might be tactful, therefore, to address people as *bibi* and *bwana* until one is sure of the usage among the group one is mixing with. (In Tanzania, especially in Zanzibar, the term *ndugu* ('brother/sister') is also used since the revolution as a general term of address, mostly by the younger generation, see also note in Unit 10.)

As in any culture, there are conventions about who speaks first. Generally, in Swahili, the person of lower status greets the person of higher status. There are greetings expressing the extreme, for example, a small child or a school-pupil may say to an elder *shikamoo* (lit. 'I clasp your feet'), to which the response is *marahaba* ('thanks'). A stranger entering a village should greet the people sitting on their verandahs, who will then welcome him to their village. It is important to observe these conventions, otherwise, for example, the visitor (you) will feel unwanted because nobody speaks and everyone looks unwelcoming, and the villagers will feel offended because you are wandering about in their territory without even having the decency to make yourself known to them! Of course in towns you are not going to greet everyone in the street; even so it is impolite not to stop and exchange greetings with people you know, however slightly. Behaviour which seems to the Briton businesslike and brisk may well strike the Swahili as unfriendly and brusque.

Note that in some areas (especially Tanzania) people of your own age and status *may* be addressed as *dada* (elder sister) or *kaka* (elder brother), but be careful if they are not of the same sex as you. It could be interpreted as a come-on. *Bibi* and *bwana* are safer until you get to know them.

Habari? 'What's new?'

I

(a) *habari* — 'news', generally plural.
asubuhi — 'morning'.
mchana — 'daytime'.
usiku — 'night'.

▷   habari

asubuhi   mchana   usiku

(b) *za* — 'of'. *Habari za asubuhi?* 'What's the news of this morning?'
nzuri — 'good'.
tu — 'only, simply'; *nzuri tu* — 'just fine'.

▷   Mimi: Habari za asubuhi?
Wewe: Nzuri.

Mimi: Habari za mchana?
Wewe: Nzuri.

Mimi: Habari za usiku?
Wewe: Nzuri tu.

(c) *leo* — 'today'.
siku — 'day(s), 24 hrs'.
nyingi — 'many'.
tangu — 'since'.
juzi — 'the day before yesterday', 'recently'.

▷   leo
siku nyingi
tangu juzi

(d) *habari za siku nyingi?* 'What's new in the long time (since I saw you)!'

▷   Mimi: Habari za leo?
Wewe: Nzuri.

Mimi: Habari za siku nyingi?
Wewe: Nzuri tu.

Mimi: Habari za tangu juzi?
Wewe: Nzuri tu.

(e) *kazi* — 'work'.
nyumbani — 'at home'. Here means 'people at home, your folks'.
safari — 'journey'. Originally a sea voyage, now used for any travel.

▷ kazi  nyumbani safari

(f) *salama* — 'peaceful, safe, safety'.
zako — 'your' (news).

▷ Mimi: Habari za kazi?
Wewe: Nzuri tu.

Mimi: Habari za nyumbani?
Wewe: Salama.

Mimi: Habari za safari?
Wewe: Salama tu.

Mimi: Habari zako?
Wewe: Nzuri sana.

(g) Ask the news of the times/occasions pictured.

▷

▷ (h) Mama: Hujambo, mzee.
Mzee: Sijambo, mama. Na wewe, je?
Mama: Mimi sijambo. Habari za siku nyingi?
Mzee: Nzuri tu. Habari zako?
Mama: Salama. Habari za nyumbani?
Mzee: Nzuri. Watoto hawajambo?
Mama: Hawajambo.
Mzee: Asante.

Bibi: Hujambo, bwana.
Bwana: Sijambo, bibi. Sijui wewe.
Bibi: Mimi sijambo sana. Habari za tangu juzi?
Bwana: Nzuri tu. Habari zako wewe?
Bibi: Salama tu. Mzee hajambo?

Bwana: Hajambo sana. Na watoto, je?
Bibi: Watoto hawajambo.
Bwana: Asante.

Bw.P.: Hujambo, Bibi Maw.
Bi.M.: Sijambo Bwana Philip. Hujambo wewe?
Bw.P.: Sijambo sana. Habari za tangu juzi?
Bi.M.: Salama tu. Habari zako?
Bw.P.: Habari nzuri tu. Je, Bwana Harris hajambo?
Bi.M.: Hajambo tu.
Bw.P.: Asante.

II

(i) The intensifier *sana* 'very/very much' can be attached to adjectives or verbs, e.g. *nzuri sana* 'very good', *hajambo sana* 'he is very well'. Note that it follows the item it modifies.

(ii) Qualifiers also almost all follow the item they qualify, e.g. *habari zako* 'your news'.

(iii) The subject *may* follow the verb, for special emphasis, e.g. *hujambo wewe*, but here there is also some emphasis on the *hujambo*, so that the whole thing means something like '*How* are *you?*'

(iv) There is no need for a word for 'is/are' when equating two ideas, especially in spoken Swahili, e.g. *habari nzuri tu* 'the news (is) just fine'.

(v) Note the words *za* 'of' and *zako* 'your' associated with *habari*. The *z*- is a marker of agreement (concord). This will be dealt with later.

III

(i) How would you greet someone:
> in the afternoon
> when you have not met for ages
> before breakfast
> when you saw them only yesterday
> after supper
> when you saw them two days ago.

How would you enquire about someone's:
> trip abroad
> household
> job
> father.

Give two ways of saying that all is well.

(j) Go through the dialogues in (h) noting new combinations of items, e.g. *habari zako wewe?* 'what's *your* news?'. Do the qualifiers (adjectives) come before or after the words they qualify?

(k) Ask for *news* about the people in the pictures:

(l) Write dialogues of your own, using structures from Units 1 and 2. If possible, practise them with a partner. Try impromptu greetings and responses.

IV

Notice that the initial response to requests for news about anything is always 'good'. In the following unit we shall see how to indicate a less than perfect state of affairs.

You may have noticed a similarity between the word *siku* 'day, 24 hours' and *usiku* 'night, night-time'. It is as if the Swahili counts nights, as we once did in English, cf. the word 'fortnight', and older 'sennight' (week). Do not confuse the word *siku* meaning the period of 24 hours with the word *mchana* 'daytime'. 'He stayed for two days' would be *siku*; 'He stayed all day' would be *mchana*.

Unit 3 Fungu la tatu
Lakini . . . 'But. . . .'

I

(a) *lakini* — 'but'
mvua — 'rain'
pole — an expression of condolence, 'I'm sorry to hear that', 'what a pity'.

▷ lakini
mvua (be careful about the pronunciation of this word)
pole

▷ (b) Baba: Hujambo, mzee.
Mzee: Sijambo, baba, sijui wewe.
Baba: Mimi sijambo sana. Habari za siku nyingi?
Mzee: Nzuri tu. Habari zako?
Baba: Habari nzuri. Watoto hawajambo?
Mzee: Hawajambo. Habari za safari?
Baba: Nzuri, lakini mvua nyingi*.
Mzee: Pole.
Baba: Asante.

mvua nyingi — 'much rain' 'it rained a lot' (cf. *siku nyingi* 'many days' 'a long time').

(c) *gani?* — interrogative word 'what sort of?'
ndiyo — here a strong form of copula 'that really is'
maisha — 'life'
ee — a sound expressing agreement, 'mm', 'yeh'.
kweli — 'true', 'truly, really'.
haya — an introductory word, 'er', 'well then', 'O.K.'
kwa heri — 'goodbye', 'farewell', 'all the best', said to one person.

▷ (d) Bwana: Hujambo, mama.
Mama: Sijambo, bwana, na wewe je?
Bwana: Sijambo tu. Habari gani?
Mama: Salama tu. Habari zako wewe?
Bwana: Nzuri, lakini kazi nyingi!
Mama: Ndiyo maisha, bwana!
Bwana: Ee, kweli.
Mama: Haya, kwa heri, bwana.
Bwana: Kwa heri, mama.

(e) *poleni* — i.e. *pole+ni*. 'I'm sorry for you folks'.
kwa herini — i.e. *kwa heri+ni*. 'Goodbye folks'.
kuonana — 'to see one another', 'to meet'.
kwa heri ya kuonana — 'Goodbye for now', 'See you again'.

▷   pole
           poleni (notice the stress is now on *le*)
           kwa heri
           kwa herini (notice the stress is now on *ri*)
           kuonana
           kwa heri ya kuonana

▷   (f)   Mwalimu: Hamjambo, watoto.
           Watoto: Hatujambo, mwalimu.
           Mwalimu: Habari gani za kazi?
           Watoto: Nzuri, lakini kazi nyingi sana.
           Mwalimu: Poleni.
           Watoto: Asante.
           Mwalimu: Haya, kwa herini watoto.
           Watoto: Kwa heri mwalimu, kwa heri ya kuonana.

    (g)   *kusomesha* — 'to teach', 'teaching'.
           lo! — an expression of surprise, 'Goodness!'
           kubwa — 'big, large'.

▷   kusomesha
           lo!
           kubwa

    (h)   *kazi ya kusomesha* . . . 'the job of teaching . . .
           kusomesha Kiswahilli kweli . . .' teaching Swahili (is) really . . .

▷   Baba: Hujambo, mwalimu.
           Mwalimu: Sijambo, baba. Na wewe, je?
           Baba: Mimi sijambo. Habari zako?
           Mw.:   Nzuri tu. Zako, je?
           Baba: Salama. Habari za kazi?
           Mw.:   Nzuri tu, lakini nyingi sana.
           Baba: Pole sana. Kazi gani?
           Mw.:   Kazi ya kusomesha Kiswahili.
           Baba: Lo! Kusomesha Kiswahili kweli kazi kubwa.
           Mw.:   Ee.

    (i)   *kusoma* — 'to learn/read'.
           oho! — expression of polite surprise, 'I see!'
           mkali — here means 'stern, cross'.
           nimeshapoa — formal reply to *pole*, 'I am already better'.

▷   kusoma
           oho!
           mkali (take care with the pronunciation of *m+k*)
           nimeshapoa

    (j)   Bw.P.:   Hujambo, Bwana Harris.
           Bw.H.:   Sijambo, Bwana Philip. Sijui wewe.
           Bw.P.:   Mimi sijambo sana. Habari gani?
           Bw.H.:   Nzuri tu, lakini kazi nyingi sana.
           Bw.P.:   Pole, bwana. Kazi gani?
           Bw.H.:   Kazi ya kusoma Kiswahili.

Bw.P.:   Oho! Kazi ya kusoma Kiswahili!
Bw.H.:   Ndiyo*, na mwalimu mkali sana.
Bw.P.:   Pole sana, bwana.
Bw.H.:   Asante, bwana. Nimeshapoa.

*ndiyo here means 'that is so'.

II

(i)   Word stress in Swahili is on the penultimate (next to last) syllable. (There
      are a very few exceptions to this rule, consisting of some loan words.)
      The rule holds even where words are extended, e.g. asante has stress
      on sa, asanteni has stress on te. Similarly pole (on po), poleni (on le);
      kwa heri (on he), kwa herini (on ri).

(ii) Note further examples of qualifiers following their 'head', e.g. kazi nyingi
      'a lot of work/jobs', kazi kubwa 'a big job'; mvua nyingi 'a lot of rain'. It is
      not necessary in Swahili for a noun to be present, e.g. in dialogue (h) we
      have nyingi sana 'very much', referring back to kazi in the previous
      speaker's question. We also have zako referring back to habari in the
      previous utterance. This would correspond to English 'yours' as opposed
      to 'your'.

(iii) The infinitive form of the verb (or verbal noun) has now occurred several
      times: kusoma 'to read/learn, reading/learning', kusomesha 'to teach,
      teaching', kuonana 'to see one another, to meet'. Note the prefix ku- in
      each example. You may also notice the root som- in the verbs kusoma
      and kusomesha. These verbs are related, kusomesha meaning 'to make
      (someone) learn/read', i.e. 'to teach'. kusomesha is the so-called causa-
      tive form of the verb kusoma. This topic will be dealt with later.

(iv) Note that we have now had -a combined with three prefixes:

      (1) za as in habari za nyumbani
      (2) ya as in kazi ya kusoma Kiswahili
      (3) kwa as in kwa heri.

      It was mentioned earlier that habari in Swahili is generally plural, and in
      example (1) it is so. This plurality is shown only by the prefix z- in za 'of'.
      kazi in example (2) is singular, however, and this is only shown by the
      prefix y- in ya 'of'. habari singular could exist, meaning 'a bit of news',
      and then 'of' would be ya, e.g. habari ya mwalimu 'an item of news
      about the teacher'. Conversely, kazi could be plural, 'jobs', so that kazi za
      mwalimu would mean 'the duties of the teacher', 'the teacher's duties'.
      habari and kazi are just two examples of a large class of nouns in Swahili
      which have the same form for singular and plural. They may be com-
      pared with 'sheep' in English, where the form of the word itself does not
      change, but we can tell whether singular or plural is meant from other
      words occurring with it, e.g. 'this sheep' (singular), 'these sheep' (plural);
      'the sheep are in the corn' (plural), 'the sheep is in the corn' (singular).

So we have:

kazi ya mwalimu
habari ya mwalimu } singular, and:

kazi za mwalimu
habari za mwalimu } plural.

kwa in *kwa heri* consists of *kw+a*, and refers to place. This will be dealt with later, but see also note in section IV.

(v) *ndiyo* expresses agreement 'that is so', and may be used alone. It may also be used as a strong form of copula ('is/am/are/was/were'). So we could say *kazi kubwa sana* 'the job (is) very great', or, more strongly *kazi ndiyo kubwa sana* 'the job really is enormous'.

III

(k) How would you say goodbye to:

a group of students
the teacher
Mr. Harris
Philip

How would you say:

Be seeing you!
Too bad, mate!
That's life!
O.K.!
(I'm) snowed under with work!
(It's) raining cats and dogs!
The news is excellent!
(That's) true!
What's *your* news?
(My) father's full of energy!
The trip (was) fantastic!
I'm better already!
Learning Swahili is a huge task!
The teacher is a right b_____!

(l) Write responses to complete the dialogues. If working alone, try to check your work from the texts in Section II. Practise speaking.

Wewe: Hujambo, mama.
Mama: _____
Wewe: Mimi sijambo sana.
Mama: _____
Wewe: Hajambo.
Mama: _____

          Hujambo, mwalimu.
Mwalimu: _____

Hatujambo sana. Habari za kazi?

Mwalimu: _____

Pole.

Mwalimu: _____

Kwa heri, mwalimu.

Mwalimu: _____

Hujambo, mzee.

Mzee: _____

Sijambo tu. Habari za siku nyingi?

Mzee: _____

Nzuri tu. Watoto hawajambo?

Mzee: _____

Salama. Haya, kwa heri, mzee.

(m) Write stimuli to complete the dialogues. Check your work from the texts in section II. Speak your dialogues.

_____

Sijambo sana. Sijui wewe.

_____

Nzuri tu. Habari za nyumbani?

_____

Hawajambo. Na mzee, je?

_____

Haya, asante.

_____

Hatujambo, mama. Na wewe, je?

_____

Nzuri, lakini mvua nyingi.

_____

Asante.

_____

Kwa heri ya kuonana.

_____

Sijambo, bwana. Na wewe hujambo?

_____

Salama. Habari zako?

_____

Pole sana, lakini ndiyo maisha bwana.

_____

Haya, kwa heri, bwana.

(n) What is the difference between *kazi nyingi* and *kazi kubwa*? Besides *mvua nyingi* we could also say *mvua kubwa*. What do you think would be the difference?

(o) Give three ways of agreeing with someone in Swahili.

(p) How is 'to' in the infinitive verb (e.g. 'to read') expressed in Swahili?

IV

Life is not always perfect, so you may actually have some bad news to convey, especially to someone you know. But even so, the initial response to a greeting or enquiry must still always be reassuring. Only then can you add the real stuff. Similarly in English to the greeting 'How are you?' you may reply, 'Fine, but my back has been playing me up lately,' — in other words, you are not 'fine' at all!

In taking leave of someone you wish them well. *heri* means 'happiness', 'blessedness', 'good fortune', and the *kw-* in *kwa* refers to (unspecified) place. In saying *kwa heri*, then, you are wishing that other person may be going to some place of good luck or blessing. It is somewhat like 'farewell' in English, or 'Go in peace'. *kwa heri ya kuonana* means 'to the blessed place of seeing one another' i.e. 'I wish we may meet again', 'Till we meet again'. This expression is not informal, as 'be seeing you' is in English; it is proper.

Pole and *nimeshapoa* are related. You may notice the *po* they have in common. This *po* as a verb root is to do with the idea of cooling. Many illnesses in Africa are fevers; when things get better one cools down, or calms down. To say *pole* to someone is thus to wish them a recovery from whatever troubles them, as you would wish the temperature of a feverish patient to come down. To say *nimeshapoa* 'I am already cool' is to say 'Thank you, your wishes have made me better', 'All the better for your good wishes'.

'Words' like *ee, oho!, lo!, haya*, and so on are very important to communication between individuals even though they do not convey facts. What they convey is information about the speaker's attitude, which is often far more important. They should therefore not be neglected. Moreover, if you sprinkle them around in your own speech — in suitable circumstances, of course — you will find them very useful, not only in assisting communication, but also in giving you time to think how to put your next piece of information correctly!

Revision Exercises   Units 1, 2, 3.

(a) Choose the right stimuli to complete the conversations:
   Stimuli:
   1 Nzuri tu. Habari za kusoma?
   2 Hujambo, bibi.
   3 Poleni. Kwa herini, watoto.
   4 Hajambo sana. Haya, kwa heri, bibi.
   5 Nzuri tu. Habari za watoto?
   6 Hamjambo watoto.

Conversations:

Bwana: _____
    Hatujambo, bwana. Habari za asubuhi?
Bwana: _____
    Nzuri tu, lakini mwalimu mzee sana.
Bwana: _____
    Kwa heri, bwana.

Mama: _____
    Sijambo, mama. Habari za siku nyingi?
Mama: _____
    Hawajambo tu. Na bwana hajambo?
Mama: _____
    Kwa heri ya kuonana.

(b) Choose the right responses to complete the conversations:

Responses:
1 Haya.
2 Salama tu. Lakini kazi kubwa sana.
3 Asante, mwalimu.
4 Sijambo Bwana Philip. Habari za kazi?
5 Sijambo, mama. Sijui wewe.
6 Hatujambo, mwalimu. Habari za safari?
7 Asante, mama. Nimeshapoa.
8 Mvua nyingi sana, lakini kazi tu!
9 Wote hawajambo. Mzee hajambo?

Conversations:

    Hujambo, Bibi Maw?
Bi.M.: _____
    Kazi nyingi sana. Habari za watoto?
Bi.M.: _____
    Hajambo sana.
Bi.M.: _____

    Hamjambo, wanafunzi.
Wanafunzi: _____
    Nzuri tu. Habari za nyumbani?
Wanafunzi: _____
    Poleni.
Wanafunzi: _____

    Hujambo, mzee.
Mzee: _____
    Mimi sijambo sana. Habari za mvua?
Mzee: _____
    Pole, mzee.
Mzee: _____

Matamshi — Pronunciation

I

(a)   **d**   **b**   **g**

▷   daa   baa   gaa
    dee   bee   gee
    dii   bii   gii
    doo   boo   goo
    duu   buu   duu

(b)   The following are all words in Swahili, but use them simply as pronuncia-
      tion practice. Concentrate only on the sound in question. Try to listen and
      imitate *without* looking at the spelling. The gloss is a rough guide to *one*
      meaning of the word.

▷   damu   'blood'   shada   'bunch'   dada   'sister'
    dini   'religion'   radi   'lightning'   didimia 'sink' v.
    dema   'fish-trap'   dede   'pulley'
    dola   'State'   fida   'ransom' v.   dodo   'small breast'
    dumu   'vase'   shudu   'oil-cake'   dudu   'insect'

    bata   'duck'   saba   'seven'   baba   'father'
    bila   'without'   bibi   'madam'
    beza   'scorn'v.
    boma   'hedge'   robo   'quarter'   bibo   'cashew apple'
    bure   'useless'   hebu   'behold'   sababu   'reason'

    bwana   'sir'   kubwa   'big'
    bweha   'jackal'

    gani   'what sort'   piga   'hit' v.   gaagaa   'roll about'
    gema   'gash'v.
    giza   'darkness'
    goti   'knee'   mzigo   'load'   gogo   'log'
    gumu   'hard'   njugu   'peanut'   gugu   'weed'

II

The sounds represented by the letters *b, d, g,* and *j* as normally pronounced in Swahili are different from English. In Swahili there is a
momentary sucking *in* of breath for the production of these sounds. (In
phonetic terms, they are *implosives*.) What happens is that the vocal
cords come together closing the glottis, at the same time as, say, the lips
come together for a 'b'. Then the glottis is lowered, causing rarefaction
of the air between the glottis and the lips. Then when the lips part for the
'b', air enters the vocal tract from the outside. This makes a rather
'hollow' sound. The following face diagrams show the sequence of
movement (imagine a head cut in two, front to back).

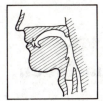 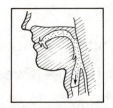 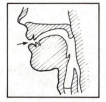

To make these sounds it may be sufficient to imitate the speaker. If not, try first with your lips together closing the 'back of the throat' (glottis) as if to make some effort, or as if about to cough. This will give you the sensation which is closing the glottis. Then, with the glottis and the lips still closed, try to suck in, or think of yawning. This will cause you to make a small sound in the throat, and looking in a mirror you may see your 'Adam's apple', if you are a man, moving down and up. (You can also feel the movement by putting your hand on your neck.) Then, making this sucking effort, let the lips part suddenly, and with luck you will produce a 'sucked-in' *b*. You might find a *d* easier at first. Try the same process. Then try g. Once you follow these sounds with a vowel, the air-stream reverts to normal. Try at first making the consonant sounds without thinking about following them with any particular vowel. Then proceed, following the tape, as seems easiest to you.

III

▷   (c)   Words containing different implosives:

debe	'can'	dege	'big bird'
dubu	'bear'	dogo	'small'
daba	'fool'	Digo	a tribe
adabu	'manners'		
bado	'not yet'	boga	'pumpkin'
baada	'after'	bega	'shoulder'
badala	'instead'	bagua	'separate' v.
bidii	'effort'		
abudu	'worship' v.	buga	'cadge'
gudi	'dock'	gubika	'cover' v.
godoro	'mattress'	goboa	'pick over' v.
gwaride	'parade'		

IV

Many Swahili speakers have another language as their mother-tongue, and their first language may well influence their pronunciation of Swahili. Also, as with all widely-spoken languages, there are dialects and regional varieties of the language. The pronunciation advocated in this course is that of speakers from the East African coast, for whom Swahili is their first language. Their type of pronunciation is accepted by many as a model. But in East Africa you may well hear other varieties.

Matamshi — Pronunciation

I

▷ (a) **j**
   jaa
   jee
   jii
   joo
   juu

jana	'yesterday'	haja	'need'	jaji	'judge'
jela	'gaol'				
jino	'tooth'	taji	'crown'	Ujiji	a town
joto	'heat'	fujo	'commotion'		
juzi	'recently'	mkwaju	'walking-stick'	juju	'Gog'

II

j in Swahili, like *b, d*, and *g*, is also pronounced as an implosive. But there are other differences from the sound in English represented by the letter *j*. Firstly, in Swahili, *j* is pronounced with the tip of the tongue down, behind the lower front teeth, and the body of the tongue against the hard palate (roof of the mouth). (In English, the *tip* of the tongue is raised for the first part of *j*.) This Swahili tongue position is similar to the position for the nasal sound represented by *gn* in the French word *agneau* 'lamb'. If necessary, practise this *j* sound by holding the tip of your tongue down the end of a biro. Secondly, once the sound has been made, in Swahili the tongue moves quickly away from the hard palate, without the fricative (zh) sound that can be heard in the English pronunciation. The following diagram shows the tongue position for the Swahili *j*.

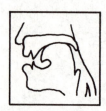

In Swahili, all sounds represented by the letters *b, d, g*, and *j* are implosive *except* in cases where they are preceded by a nasal consonant (*m* or *n* in spelling), unless that nasal consonant happens to constitute a syllable in itself. So, for example, in the word *hujambo*, the *j* is implosive but the *b* is not, because it is preceded by the nasal (*m*). However, in the word *mbu* 'mosquito', the *b*, although preceded by a nasal (*m*), is implosive because the nasal here constitutes a separate syllable. Fortunately, words such as this are few, and the learner should concentrate on the implosive sounds, since they do not occur in English. Where, in Swahili, *b, d, g,* or *j* are preceded by a nasal and are not implosive, they are pronounced as in English. (For many Swahili speakers, the implosive forms of *b, d, g* and *j* are particularly pronounced at the beginning of stressed syllables, less so in unstressed portions.)

III

▷   (b)   Words containing *j* and another implosive consonant:

jadi   'pedigree'   jibu   'reply'   jagi   'jug'
juhudi 'try hard'   jabali   'rock'   jogoo   cock
jadili   'argue'   ajabu   'surprise'
                      jibini   'cheese'

daraja 'bridge'   beja   'scorn' v.
                      Bajuni   a tribe

▷   (c)   gubigubi   'covered head to foot'
         bubujika   'bubble out'
         debwedebwe   'waterlogged'
         dibaji   'preamble'
         bibidia   'turn down lower lip in derision!'

haba na haba hujaza kibaba 'a little and a little fills the measure' (proverb)

▷   (d)   Compare the following pairs of words:

riba   'interest' : rimba   'musical instrument'
poda   'powder'   : ponda   'pound' v.
gogo   'log'   : gongo   'back'
vuja   'leak' v.   : vunja   'break' v.

    (e)   Pick out the words in Unit 1 which have a *b, d, g* or *j* in any position. Underline the letters that represent implosive sounds in these words. Practise the words with implosives.

Revision

Go over the conversations in Unit 1, concentrating at all times on the pronunciation of implosives. You will notice that although the actual number of words containing implosives is not very many, they do occur frequently (e.g. *-jambo, habari*).

Unit 6 Fungu la sita
Wapi? — Where?

I

(a) *shule* — 'school' (derived from German *schule*. The word *skuli* is sometimes heard)
hospitali — 'hospital'
soko — 'market'
duka — 'shop'
msikiti — 'mosque'
kanisa — 'church'
hoteli — 'hotel'
shamba — 'smallholding/farm', also 'country as opposed to town'
ofisi — 'office'
jiko — 'kitchen/stove'
kitanda — 'bed'
meza — 'table' (from Portuguese)

You recall asking *Habari za nyumbani? nyumbani* means '(those) at home'. *nyumba* means 'house/home'. On the same model, *shule* means 'school' and *shuleni* means 'at/in school'.

▷ nyumba nyumbani

shule shuleni

hospitali hospitalini

soko sokoni

duka dukani

msikiti msikitini

kanisa kanisani

hoteli hotelini

shamba shambani

ofisi ofisini

jiko jikoni

kitanda kitandani

meza mezani

(b) To ask where people are we need the word *wapi?* 'where?', and a connecting word 'be'. For a person we use *yuko* 'he/she is (place)'. So *baba yuko wapi?* means 'where is father?'. Notice the word-order is different from English, i.e. literally 'father is where?'.

wapi? — 'where?'
yuko — 'he/she is (place)'

▷ Mimi: Baba yuko wapi?

Wewe: Yuko sokoni.

Mimi: Bwana yuko wapi?

Wewe: Yuko ofisini.

Mimi: Mzee yuko wapi?

Wewe: Yuko shambani.

Mimi: Mama yuko wapi?

Wewe: Yuko kitandani.

Mimi: Bibi yuko wapi?

Wewe: Yuko msikitini.

(c) You may wish to ask if someone is in a particular place, e.g. *Baba yuko nyumbani?* 'Is father at home?'. If the answer is yes, you say *Ndiyo, yuko* 'Yes, he is', 'It is so, he is there'.

▷   Mimi: Mama yuko jikoni?
       Wewe: Ndiyo, yuko.

       Mimi: Mwalimu yuko shuleni?
       Wewe: Ndiyo, yuko.

       Mimi: Bwana yuko hotelini?
       Wewe: Ndiyo, yuko.

       Mimi: Bibi yuko kanisani?
       Wewe: Ndiyo, yuko.

       Mimi: Mzee yuko msikitini?
       Wewe: Ndiyo, yuko.

(d) Suppose the person is not where you expect.
       siyo — 'it is not so'
       hayuko — 'he/she is not (there)'

▷   Mimi: Mama yuko nyumbani?
       Yeye: Siyo, hayuko nyumbani, yuko sokoni.

Mimi: Mzee yuko msikitini?
Yeye: Siyo, hayuko msikitini, yuko hospitalini.

Mimi: Baba yuko   ?

Yeye: _____

Now you answer:

Mimi: Mwalimu yuko   ?

Wewe: Siyo,

Mimi: Bwana yuko ?

Wewe: Siyo,

Mimi: Bibi yuko ?

Wewe: Siyo,

(e) You may wish to know the whereabouts of more than one person.
     wako — 'they are (there)'

▷   Mimi: Watoto wako wapi?
         Yeye: Wako shuleni.

              Answer, putting the children in the pictures:
     Mimi: Watoto wako wapi?
     Wewe: Wako

     Mimi: Watoto wako wapi?
     Wewe: Wako

     Mimi: Watoto wako wapi?
     Wewe: Wako

     Mimi: Watoto wako wapi?
     Wewe: Wako

     Mimi: Watoto wako wapi?
     Wewe: Wako

     Mimi: Watoto wako wapi?
     Wewe: Wako

Mimi: Watoto wako wapi?
Wewe: Wako

Mimi: Watoto wako wapi?
Wewe: Wako

(f)   *hawako* — 'they are not (there)'

▷   Mimi: Wanafunzi wako shuleni?
            Yeye: Siyo, hawako shuleni, wako nyumbani.

Mimi: Wanafunzi wako sokoni?

Yeye: Siyo, hawako sokoni, wako kanisani.

Reply:
Mimi: Wanafunzi wako hospitalini?

Wewe: _____

Mimi: Wanafunzi wako msikitini?

Wewe: _____

II

(i) A suffix -*ni* may be added to most common nouns which can be thought of as locations to make them locative, with the meaning 'at/near/in/on' etc. The precise shade of meaning may be indicated elsewhere in the utterance, or it may be understood from the nature of the noun. For example, in *baba yuko kitandani*, *kitandani* would imply 'in bed', whereas *watoto wako mezani* would imply that they are 'at table'. If we had been speaking of, say, a cat, then we might have glossed *kitandani* as 'on the bed' and *mezani* as 'on the table'.

Proper nouns referring to geographical locations (e.g. names of towns, countries, mountains etc.) do not add -*ni*. *baba yuko Mombasa* means 'father is (at/in) Mombasa'. Some loan words (especially recent loans) do not add -*ni*, e.g. *sinema* — 'cinema', so we might say *mama yuko sinema*. (Stress on *ne*.)

(ii) *ndiyo* means 'that is so'. It can often be used where in English we use 'yes', but not always. For example, when asked *baba yuko nyumbani?* 'is father at home?' we may answer *ndiyo* 'that is so', and here *ndiyo* might be thought to mean 'yes'. But if asked *baba hayuko nyumbani?* 'Isn't father at home?', the answer *ndiyo* would still mean 'that (which you said) is so', i.e. he is not there. (The English speaker would say 'no'.)
siyo means 'that is not so', and similarly may often seem to have the same meaning as 'no'. If asked *baba yuko nyumbani?* we may answer *siyo* 'that is not so', and in English we would say 'no'. But if asked *baba hayuko nyumbani?* 'isn't father at home?' the answer *siyo* would mean 'that (which you said) is not so', i.e. he *is* there. (The English speaker would say 'yes'.)

(iii) *yuko* may be analysed as *yu-*, 3rd person singular (he/she), plus -*ko*, general place.
hayuko has a negative prefix *ha-*. Compare this with the *ha-* negative prefix in *hatujambo* etc.
wako consists of *wa-*, 3rd person plural (they), plus -*ko*. (You may also notice that *watoto* and *wanafunzi* begin with *wa-*. This is part of the language system and will be dealt with later.)
hawako has negative prefix *ha-* again. cf. *hawajambo*.

(iv) *wapi?* Note that *wapi?* 'where?' does not come first in the question as the word 'where?' does in English. In Swahili, *wapi?* follows the copula (*yuko* etc.) or verb. We could say *baba yuko wapi?* 'where is father?', or for special emphasis we could say *yuko wapi, baba?* '*where* is he, father?'. It may be worth pointing out also that the word *wapi* is always interrogative. It can *not* be used referentially (as in English 'the place where I live').

III

(g) These places do not add -*ni*. They are derived from English. What do you
     think their originals are?

     baa   stesheni polisi
     stesheni   benki
     sinema   jela
     posta

(h) Here are a few more characters:

     mlevi   — 'drunkard'

     mwizi   — 'thief'

     askari   — 'policeman', 'soldier'

     maskini   — 'poor man'

Ask the whereabouts of the following people, and give an appropriate
answer using the vocabulary in (g). e.g.

      Watoto wako wapi? Wako posta.

(i) Asked where your father is you want to reply that he is at work. What would you say?
How would you tell someone that your mother is not at home, she is travelling?

(j) With a partner, play 'spot the lady'. Take a character from (h) and three place pictures. (Draw them roughly on separate pieces of paper.) Hide the character under one picture. Then play, e.g.

Player A: Mlevi yuko wapi?
Player B: Yuko baa?
Player A, either: Ndiyo, yuko.
          or: Siyo, hayuko.
Player B may challenge if he gets the answer *siyo* and say:

   Mlevi yuko wapi, basi? (*basi* — 'then, well')

Player A must then reply and demonstrate, e.g.

   Yuko kitandani.

Each player chooses different characters and pictures. The game *must* be accompanied by the correct wording, and any mistake causes the player to lose the point. Far be it from me to encourage gambling, but 'best of ten and loser buys the coffee' can add stimulus.

IV

A well-mannered Swahili person is never abrupt. You may notice that in the conversations so far there seems a good deal of repetition. This is not put in for the sake of practice for you, it reflects actuality. Asked *Mama yuko nyumbani?* it would not be sufficient merely to reply *Ndiyo*. *Ndiyo, yuko* is the minimum, unless you want to be off-putting for some reason, and you would often hear *Ndiyo, yuko nyumbani*. W. H. Davies' sentiment 'A poor life this if, full of care We have no time to stand and stare' would appeal to many Swahili people, and they would add, 'no time to stand and chat'. What may seem to a European to be super-fluous seems to a Swahili to be the oil that helps the wheels go round. Use it: it helps socially; and also it does give you time to collect your thoughts.

In the same connection, of civilized communication, I think it is no acci-dent that the form of a yes/no question in Swahili is the same as a state-ment. The interrogator does not ask baldly for information, he puts forward a hypothesis, e.g. 'Father's at home (I presume)' *Baba yuko nyumbani?*, and the respondent either confirms or refutes the sugges-tion, 'It is as you say' or 'It is not so' (*Ndiyo*, or *Siyo*). There is no un-equivocal word for 'yes'. There is, however, a (loan) word *la* which means unequivocally 'no'. It should be used very sparingly, as it conveys the feeling of contradiction or refusal. It may be heard in an argument or quarrel, for example. A well brought up Swahili would try to avoid such a situation, although among friends there is also a sort of mock quarreling, a kind of language play or contest (somewhat similar to 'flyting' in Chaucer), where the friends try to score points off one another, and here *la* or *la-la-la-la-la* may be heard, along with ritualised insults and other

special language usages. But the circumstances of this are well understood by the participants, it can only occur within specified relationships,
and even then care must be taken, since where real feelings are
involved, what starts as a ritual joke can degenerate. The foreigner may
enjoy hearing such exchanges but should be very wary of indulging in
them himself. There is a special verb, *kutania*, meaning to tease in this
special way, and a person who is in this special relationship with another
is his *mtani*. If a person oversteps the mark in a discussion, he may be
rebuked by being accused of *kutania: unanitania, bwana* 'you are teasing
me (as you have no right to do), sir'.

Note that in some areas, especially where Swahili is a second language,
and also among some younger 'with it' speakers, the word *hapana* (lit.
'there is not') is used in place of *siyo*. But many speakers would
consider *hapana* to be very strong, rather a contradiction than a simple
negation.

Unit 7 Fungu la saba
Wapi hasa? — Where precisely?

I

Pronunciation note:
Not all new words were taped separately for pronunciation in Unit 6. From this point on in the course, new vocabulary will not be practised as individual items except for specific pronunciation points. This is because, apart from special occasions, words are not normally heard in isolation, and the student should try to hear, and learn, and eventually speak, words in contexts. This is much more valuable than learning words in lists, and makes them easier to recall.

(a) *-ko* expresses general place. *-po* expresses a more precise place. *mzee yuko nyumbani* means 'the old man is at home' — he might be anywhere about, in the garden perhaps. *mzee yupo nyumbani* means 'the old man is in the house'. *yuko ofisini* means 'he is at the office': *yupo ofisini* means 'he is in the (his) office'.

yupo, wapo — 'he/she, they are in a precise place'
hasa — 'exactly, precisely'
njia — 'road'
pwani — 'coast'. This is probably historically a locative *pwa+ni*, but is now used as a fixed form.

▷   Mimi: Mama yuko nyumbani?
     Wewe: Ndiyo, yuko.
     Mimi: Yuko wapi hasa?
     Wewe: Yupo jikoni.

     Mimi: Baba yuko ofisini?
     Wewe: Ndiyo, yuko.
     Mimi: Yuko wapi hasa?
     Wewe: Yupo mezani.

     Mimi: Watoto wako hospitalini?
     Wewe: Ndiyo, wako.
     Mimi: Wako wapi hasa?
     Wewe: Wapo kitandani.

     Mimi: Bw. Philip yuko pwani?
     Wewe: Ndiyo, yuko.
     Mimi: Yuko wapi hasa?
     Wewe: Yupo Lamu. [Lamu is an old town on the coast of Kenya.]

     Mimi: Bwana Harris na Bibi Maw wako safarini?
     Wewe: Ndiyo, wako.
     Mimi: Wako wapi hasa?
     Wewe: Wako njiani tu.[†]

Mimi: Wanafunzi wako shuleni?
Wewe: Ndiyo, wako.
Mimi: Wako wapi hasa?
Wewe: Sijui hasa, wako tu.[tt]

[t] Why do we have *wako* and not *wapo* here?
[tt]*wako tu* — 'they are just somewhere about'.

(b) This telephone conversation illustrates contrasting uses of *-ko* and *-po*.

Badi — a nickname for Mohammed, the first name of Professor Athumani
a'a — 'no'
ala — expression of mild surprise, 'is that so!'
vilevile — 'likewise'
basi — 'well then'
bahati — 'luck'
mbaya — 'bad', referring to *bahati*
labda — 'perhaps'.

▷   Kiring'-kiring'   Kiring'-kiring'   Kiring'-kiring' . . .
    J.:   Hello?
    Bw.H.: Hello! Badi?
    J.:   A'a, mimi siyo Badi.* Mimi Jimmy. Nani wewe?
    Bw.H.: Oh, hujambo Jimmy. Mimi Stuart Harris.
    J.:   Ala! Hujambo, Bwana Harris. Habari za siku nyingi?
    Bw.H.: Nzuri. Habari zako?
    J.:   Salama tu. Sisi tuko tu.[t]
    Bw.H.: Haya. Professor Athumani yupo?
    J.:   Hayupo. Yuko ofisini.
    Bw.H.: Na bibi, je?
    J.:   Bibi vilevile hayupo. Yuko Mombasa.
    Bw.H.: Basi, bahati mbaya leo.
    J.:   Ee, ndiyo. Labda usiku.
    Bw.H.: Ee, ndiyo. Haya, kwa heri, Jimmy.
    J.:   Kwa heri, bwana.

*mimi siyo Badi — 'I'm by no means Badi', 'I'm not Badi at all' — compare this with the use of *ndiyo* as a strong form of the copula. *siyo* here is used as a strong negative copula.
[t]*sisi tuko tu* — 'we are just hanging about (at your service)', 'We're still around', 'Nothing's changed'.

After studying the conversation, try to decide on the reason for each instance of *-ko* or *-po*.

(c) *nani?* — 'who?'

▷   Mimi: Nani yuko stesheni?
    Yeye: Yuko mama.

    Mimi: Nani wako baa?
    Yeye: Wako mlevi na baba.

You answer:

Mimi: Nani wako posta?

Wewe: Wako na

Mimi: Nani wako stesheni polisi?

Wewe:

Mimi: Nani wako jela?

Wewe:

Mimi: Nani wako benki?

Wewe:

(d)   *uko* — 'you (singular) are (place)'
      hapa—'here, in this specific place'
      nipo—'I am (particular place)'
      huko—'you (sing.) are not (place)'
      kumbe—'Lo and behold'—surprise at some sight
      mpo — 'you (pl.) are (particular place)'

▷   A child comes in from school and calls out:

      Mtoto: Mama, uko wapi?
      Mama: Nipo hapa, jikoni.
      Mtoto: Ala, huko ofisini leo?
      Mama: A'a, niko nyumbani tu.
      Mtoto: Yuko wapi baba?
      Mama: Yuko Nairobi.
      Mtoto: Hayuko kazini?
      Mama: Siyo, yuko kazini Nairobi leo. ('Yes he is, he's working (at work)
              in Nairobi today'.)

Baba enters suddenly:

Baba: Kumbe, mpo hapa!
Mama na mtoto: Ndiyo, tupo tu.

II

(i)   *nani?* 'who?' is always interrogative. It can *not* be used referentially (as in English 'the man who came to dinner').

(ii) Besides *-ko* and *-po* for general and precise place respectively, there is also *-mo*, meaning 'right inside'. You might say *mwizi yumo nyumbani* to express that he had got in whereas he ought to be outside! But usually *-mo* would be used for something in a container, like money in a pocket, or cigarettes in a packet.

The full paradigm for *-ko* is:

	positive	**negative**
1 sing.	niko	siko
2 sing.	uko	huko
3 sing.	yuko	hayuko
1 pl.	tuko	hatuko
2 pl.	mko	hamko
3 pl.	wako	hawako

The use of first and second person with *-ko* etc. may not be very frequent. It tends to occur when (a) the parties are out of sight of each other, or (b) the situation is surprising. There are also some idomatic uses, as described in section IV.

(iii) Note the use of *siyo* as copula, in *mimi siyo Badi* 'I am not Badi'.

III

(e)   How would you:

ask who is in hospital?
ask where exactly the boss and his wife are?
tell someone that you don't know where the thief is?
say that the thief is in jail and the policeman is too?
say that perhaps the teacher is at work today?

(f)   Here is a list of countries and geographical areas, many of which you will recognise:

Afrika
Kenya
Uganda
Tanzania
Unguja (Zanzibar)
Mvita (Mombasa island)
Msumbiji (Mozambique)

Ngazija (Comoros)
Habesh (Ethiopia)
Misri (Egypt)
Afrika ya Mashariki (East Africa)
Afrika ya Magharibi (West Africa)
Afrika ya Kusini (South Africa)
Afrika ya Kaskazini (North Africa)

Ulaya (Europe)   Uarabu
Uingereza (England)   Uyahudi (Israel — 'Jew-land')
Ufaransa   Uchina
Ujerumani   Urusi
Ureno (Portugal)   Uamerika
                                        Bara Hindi (Indian continent)

Notice how many of them begin with *U-*. This is the prefix for a particular class of nouns, including names of countries. Notice also the *-ni* in the words for South and North. *kusi* means 'south wind', and *kaskazi* means 'North wind', these two winds being very important for trade up and down the coast of East Africa. *Uarabu* (Arabia) may also appear as *Arabuni*. This is the only name of a country that may have the locative *-ni* affixed to it, however,

Enter the names on the world map:

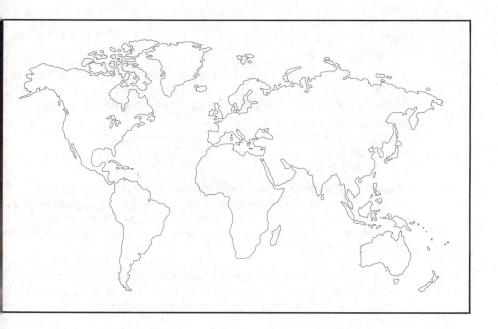

Play the game (*mchezo*): *Uko wapi?*

1st player: Niko safarini!
2nd player: Uko wapi hasa?
1st player: Bahatisha! (Guess!) (cf. *bahati* — 'luck' in Unit 7, I(b))
2nd player: Upo hapa Uingereza? (touching the chosen spot)
1st player: Sipo! (softly if far away, more loudly as the right place is approached)
             Nipo!

Count the number of guesses to find the winner.

(g) Work out the paradigms, positive and negative, for *-po* and *-mo*.

IV

(i) Place and state

The distinction between being in a place and carrying out an activity associated with place is not always made specific. For example, *yuko kazini* means he is at work and probably also working. *yuko safarini* says more about his travelling than any one spot where he may happen to be. We can of course (as in English) be more specific if need be.

Being in a state is also sometimes expressed as locative. We have seen in the telephone conversation (b) Jimmy says *tupo tu* 'we are just here'. It means 'we are around, at your service'. It is often heard in the singular, *nipo* 'here am I'. The state of readiness also requires a place copula in Swahili: *yuko tayari* means 'he is ready', and may be used with other persons, as in the following conversation:

Uko tayari?
Ndiyo, niko tayari.
Haya, basi, twende.
Haya.
(*twende* — 'let's go')

Trouble is also a state one can be in (as in English). *taabu* is 'trouble'; locative *taabani* 'fed up, tired'. Following analogies already presented, this form 'should' be *taabuni, but this is not often heard.

Habari za baba?
Nzuri tu, lakini yuko taabani.
Pole. Taabu gani?
Taabu ya kazi tu.

Difference is another state: *yuko tofauti na X* 'he is different from X'. *tofauti* — 'different'. Note the use of *na*, which often suggests association rather than addition ('with' rather than 'and'). Being involved is a state you could get right into: *mimi simo* 'I am not concerned in that affair', '*I* am not in (it)'.

God, of course, is always 'there', and not just anywhere, but in his rightful place. *Mungu yupo!* 'God's in his heaven . . .!' is used as a response, for example when hearing of someone's escape from danger, recovery from illness, etc. e.g.

Habari za somesha Kiswahili?
A'a, mimi simo, Alhamdulillahi!
Mungu yupo!
Kweli, yupo.

Alhamdulillahi — expletive from Arabic, 'God be praised'.

(ii) Gradation of terms of address

You will notice that in the telephone conversation Bwana Harris addresses the person he thinks is Professor Athumani as Badi, a nickname. This indicates of course that they are on very friendly terms. The most formal form of address is *Bwana*, *Bibi*, or other polite term such as

Mzee or *Mwalimu. Mheshimiwa* 'Your honour, respected sir' may be heard in court or in parliament; and a combination of *Bwana/Bibi* plus a designation, such as *Bwana Askari, Bibi Daktari* might be used by the anxious supplicant. To call someone by their first name alone is a sign of intimacy when it is reciprocal; power when it is not (as from an employer to an employee).

(iii) **Naming**

In a traditional Swahili community a baby is given a name when it is seven days old. A widespread tradition is for a number of names to be selected and written on pieces of paper. These are scattered on the floor and then a young child is asked to pick one up. That name is given to the baby. It may well be the name of a parent or grandparent, or someone else whom it is wished to honour or remember. It may very well be a Muslim name; or in some areas, especially in Tanzania, the name may have a meaning e.g. *Chausiku* for a child born at night (*cha usiku*), or *Tatu* for a third child. Another custom, somewhat dying out, is to call the child a title (*Bwana, Bibi, Mwinyi* — 'owner, lord') plus what seems like a Bantu name, such as *Mwinyi-kombo* 'Lord of the left-overs', i.e. someone who will live long. But these days there are also other fashions, unusual names being sought out, and foreign examples copied.

Although a certain name may be given, for various reasons a child may never be known by it. For example if it is the father's name, another may be used. The 'real' name of the person is entered on official documents (such as birth registration, marriage, death, land purchase, and so on), but may otherwise be quite forgotten by everyone else. It can happen that, if a child ails a great deal, the mother may decide that '*jina halimfai*' — the name doesn't suit him/her — and another name may be chosen.

A person is often known by three names, his/her own, followed by those of the father and grandfather. If more names are used, they go further back up the family tree, on the male side. Sometimes the word *bin* 'son (of)' or *binti* 'daughter (of)' is also used, as e.g. Shaaban bin Robert (a well-known author), or Siti binti Saad (a famous singer). Within the society a person may be referred to or addressed with a title (e.g. *Bwana, Bibi, Mwalimu, Sheikh*) plus, usually, the given name, e.g. Sheikh Yahya (who normally uses the names Yahya Ali Omar, i.e. Yahya son of Ali son of Omar); or by reference to the father, e.g. Binti Abdalla (daughter of Abdalla); or to a child, e.g. Mama Hadija (mother of Hadija). The custom of using a title plus a patronymic (e.g. Bibi Maw, Professor Athumani) is a cross-cultural one.

Revision Exercises   Units 6 and 7

(a) Ask the whereabouts of the following people, and answer.

(b)   Supply appropriate questions or answers:

_____?
Hayuko, yuko kazini.

Mzee yuko wapi?
_____.

_____?
Hawako, lakini yuko mwalimu*.

Mama yuko nyumbani?
_____.

Na baba, je?
_____.

Bwana Harris yuko?
_____.

_____?
Ndiyo, yuko, lakini yupo kitandani.

_____?
Hawako hapa, wako safarini.

Mama yuko wapi, yuko sokoni?
_____.

Wako wapi Bwana Harris na Bibi Maw[†]
Hawako hapa, _____.

Mlevi bado yuko baa?   (*bado* — 'still')
Siyo, _____.

*Notice emphatic word order here, *yuko mwalimu* means 'there *is* the *teacher* (here)'.

[†]Again, word order is emphatic, '*where* are *Bw. Harris and Bi. Maw*?'.

(c) Ask where the children are, and reply that they are in bed, thank God.

Suggest to someone that you should both go to East Africa.

Tell your mother that you are still in trouble.

Write to your father that you and your husband/wife are still here in England.

Unit 8   Fungu la nane
Matamshi — Pronunciation

I

(a) The letter *a* in Swahili represents a vowel sound somewhere between that represented by 'a' in the English word 'man' and that in 'father'. The native English learner should aim at making that same vowel wherever it may occur in the Swahili word. He/she should particularly beware of making the 'reduced' sound as heard in the first syllable of the English word 'about', or as in the last syllable of 'fella'.

▷
saa	'clock/hour/time'
taa	'lamp'
-faa	'be suitable'
-kaa	'stay' v.
-vaa	'wear' v.
-zaa	'give birth'
-twaa	'take up'*

Take particular care with the final vowels in the following:

sasa	'now'
dada	'elder sister'
kaka	'elder brother'
-lala	'sleep' v.
-tata	'tangle' v.
papa	'shark'

Take particular care with the first as well as the final vowels in the following:

alama	'sign'
adhama	'glory'
-achana	'divorce' v.
samaha	'forgiveness'
-lalama	'appeal' v.
-fanana	'resemble' v.

maana	'meaning'
baada	'after'
msaada	'help'

* The student of phonetics may wish to note that 'double' vowels (e.g. *aa*) represent two syllables in Swahili.

(b)   The letter *i* in Swahili represents a vowel similar to the English vowel
      sound in the word 'feed'. It *never* sounds like the English vowel in 'thin',
      and native English speakers should be very careful not to make that
      sound. Pay particular attention to unstressed syllables, where there is a
      temptation to use the wrong sound.

▷   -tii   'obey'
      hii   'this -class 9'

Take particular care with the final vowels in the following:

      nini   'what?'
      lini   'when?'
      hivi   'thus, in this manner'
      -zidi   'exceed'
      titi   'breast'
      pishi   a measure

Take particular care with the first as well as the final vowels in the
following:

      jibini   'cheese'
      sitini   'sixty'
      -fikiri   'think'
      bilisi   'devil'
      hirizi   'amulet'
      kipini   'handle'
      sisimizi   'sugar ant'

(c)   The letter *u* in Swahili represents a vowel rather like the one heard in the
      English word 'food'. It *never* sounds like the vowel in 'good', even when
      in unstressed syllables, and native English speakers should pay attention
      to this point.

▷   huu   'this, class 3'
      guu   'swollen leg'
      fuu   'husk'

Take particular care with the final vowels in the following:

      lulu   'pearl'
      sumu   'poison'
      huyu   'this person'
      bubu   'deaf and dumb person'
      dudu   'insect'
      kuku   'hen'

Take particular care with the first as well as the final vowels in the
following:

      uhuru   'freedom'
      ufungu   'relationship'
      ugumu   'difficulty'
      -shutumu   'scold' v.
      -shukuru   'thank' v.
      turufu   'trump (cards)'

      tutuu   'wart'
      utukufu   'fame'

(d) Words containing combinations of the vowels i, a, u.

bali	'on the contrary'
vazi	'clothing'
mali	'wealth'
wavu	'net'
shavu	'cheek'
zamu	'turn' n.
-lima	'cultivate'
hima	'hurry'
-pima	'measure' v.
simu	'telephone'
timu	'team'
mvivu	'lazy person'
-nuna	'sulk' v.
-juta	'repent'
-nusa	'smell (transitive)'
fupi	'short'
Juni	'June'
vuli	'shade'
yai	'egg'
dau	'dhow'
-lia	'cry' v.
mbiu	'buffalo horn'
-vua	'fish' v.
tui	'coconut milk'

▌▌

Spelling in Swahili is very consistent. With vowels, one letter almost always represents the same sound. (In phonetic terms, there is one symbol for each vowel phoneme, although some vowels have two distinct allophones.) We do not have the problems that exist in English, of several spellings for the same vowel sound (as in the words 'food', 'rude', 'chewed' etc.), nor the problem of one spelling representing several vowel sounds (as in the words 'food' vs. 'good').

For those interested in phonetics, the following vowel figure shows the approximate positions of the vowels i, a, u, in stressed syllables.

Primary cardinal vowels

Swahili vowels

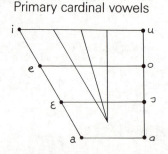
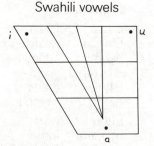

All these vowels may be somewhat centralised in unstressed syllables. Some speakers, however, use a fronted allophone of the phoneme /a/ in unstressed syllables, somewhere near Cardinal vowel 4.

III

(e) Find examples of words you already know which contain only the vowels i, a, u, or combinations of these. Arrange the words in groups and practise pronouncing them slowly and carefully. Try to listen to yourself as you do this.

IV

Native English speakers can of course make the vowel sounds *a, i*, and *u* as in Swahili, perfectly well, especially as they are not *too* different from some English vowels. The reason why English speakers find it so difficult to remember to make these sounds in unstressed syllables is because in English, whatever the spelling, the vowel sounds in such syllables are almost always the vowel as in 'thin' (e.g. 'y' as in 'beauty', 'ay' as in 'Monday', and many other spellings), or the vowel sound 'ə' which has many spellings, and never occurs in stressed syllables (e.g. 'a' in 'about', 'er' in 'butter', etc.)

Matamshi — Pronunciation

I

(a) The letter *e* in Swahili normally represents a vowel sound similar to the first part of the vowel in the English word 'grey'. This vowel in English (Received Pronunciation) is actually a diphthong, i.e. the vowel starts with an 'e' quality and moves to an 'i' quality. If you say it slowly you should be able to hear the change of sound. In the following Swahili words, try to imitate the speaker, avoiding a final 'i' sound, especially when the vowel is final in the word.

▷　mzee
　　bee　　'at your service'

Pay particular attention to the final vowels in the following:

pele　　'pimples'
sheshe　'beauty'
pete　　'ring'
teke　　'kick'
tele　　'plenty'
zeze　　a musical instrument

Pay particular attention to the first vowels in the following:

sesere　'doll'
pelele　'hyrax'
kelele　'din'

tepetepe　'many'

kekee　　'boring tool'
pekee　　'alone'

(b) The letter *o* in Swahili normally represents a sound between those in the English words 'cot' and 'coot' but is not a diphthong. Listen hard and try to imitate:

▷　choo　　'lavatory'
　　koo　　'neck'

Pay particular attention to the final vowels in the following:

somo　　'lesson'
moyo　　'heart'
tobo　　'hole'
posho　　'porridge'
kopo　　'tin can'
popo　　'bat (animal)'

Pay particular attention to the first vowels in the following:

korosho   'cashew nut'
fofofo   'dead asleep'
porojo   'chatter'

(c) When *e* is followed by a combination of a nasal consonant (m, n) plus b, d, j, or g, the quality of the vowel is more open. That is, it approximates more to the vowel in the English word 'hen'.

▷ tembo   'elephant'
    tendo   'deed'
    -penda   'love' v.
    chenga   'grain'

The following words contain both close [e] and open [ɛ] varieties of /e/:

tende   [ɛ, e]   'date (fruit)'
jembe   [ɛ, e]   'hoe'
genge   [ɛ, e]   'gang'

kengele   [ɛ, e, e]   'bell'
kengee   [ɛ, e, e]   'blade'

peremende   [e, e, ɛ, e]   'peppermint, sweet'
lengelenge [ɛ, e, ɛ, e]   'blister'

(d) Similarly, when *o* is followed by a nasal consonant plus b, d, j, or g, it has a more open quality. The sound approximates more to the vowel in the English word 'long'.

▷ komba   'galago'
    -omba   'beg'
    -ponda   'crush'
    -konda   'get thin'
    -onja   'taste' v.
    -gonga   'strike' v.

The following words contain both close [o] and open [ɔ] varieties of /o/:

kombo   [ɔ, o]   'a scraping'
songo   [ɔ, o]   'coil'
sombo   [ɔ, o]   'girdle'
tondo   [ɔ, o]   kind of snail

borongo   [o, ɔ, o]   'muddle'
korongo   [o, ɔ, o]   'crane (bird)'
kongoro   [ɔ, o, o]   'old bull'
dondoo   [ɔ, o, o]   'steinbuck'

fondogoa   [ɔ, o, o]   'smell of mouldy flour'
gorong'ondo [o, o, ɔ, o]   'leg of animal'

(e) When two or more vowels are adjacent, each must be given its full value. Each vowel in Swahili constitutes a syllable. Be careful after a vowel *e* not to let a 'y' sound intrude before the following vowel.

▷ leo
    cheo   'social position'

-lea	'bring up child'
-mea	'grow (intransitive)'
-kwea	'clamber'
kweu	'clearness'
-geuka	'change' v.
-teua	'choose'
pei dei	'pay-day'

Be careful after a vowel *o* not to let a 'w' sound intrude before the following vowel:

-oa	'marry'
-poa	'cool' v.
-toa	'take out'
boi	'boy'
hoi	'helpless'
doea	'spy' v.
-zoea	'get accustomed'
ngao	'shield'
mbao	'plank'
angalao	'although'
chuo	'institute'
kituo	'stopping-place'
mbio	'quickly'

‖

Those interested in phonetics may like to see the vowel figure with the allophones of /e/ and /o/ plotted. In each case the open allophone is the one preceding the nasal cluster.

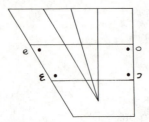

In fact there is some individual variation in the degree of openness and closeness in these vowels, both between individuals and within the speech of one individual, in different stress positions and/or influenced by the surrounding consonants. This can the more easily occur because of the unlikelihood of a phonemic clash, i.e. no vowel *o*, for example is going to get so close as to be confused with *u*, nor so open as to be confused with *a*; but between these extremes there is ample room for variation.

Many Bantu languages have seven vowels, with open and close /e/ and /o/ constituting distinct phonemes. No doubt there is some connection between this fact and the distinct allophones of these vowels in Swahili.

Swahili has virtually no diphthongs. (A few may be creeping in in loan words.)

III

(f)   Collect words from Units 1, 2, 3, 6 and 7 containing the vowel *e* and/or *o*. Arrange them in groups and practise them carefully.

Revision Exercises   Units 8 and 9; 4 and 5

(a)   Care must be taken with pronunciation when two vowels of the same quality are adjacent (e.g. aa, ee, etc.), particularly where one or the other is stressed. There is often a tendency on the part of foreign learners to shorten these vowels, especially when they occur in final position. Since the structure of Swahili words is generally CVCV . . . (consonant-vowel), double vowels of the same quality are not very frequent. *aa* is the most frequent, and in final position seems to give the most trouble to English learners.

maarifa	'information'
maagizo	'invitation'
maamuzi	'arbitration'
baada	'after'
baadhi	'several'
-kaanga	'fry' v.
taabu	'trouble'
maasi	'revolt'
-paaza	'raise, lift up'
mkaaji	'inhabitant'
msaada	'help'
-andaa	'prepare'
balaa	'calamity'
bidhaa	'trade goods'
-chakaa	'be worn out'
chokaa	'lime, chalk'
dagaa	'sardines'
fadhaa	'dismay'
jukwaa	'stage, platform'
-kataa	'refuse' v.
kichaa	'madness'
-lemaa	'be disfigured'

-shangaa   'be amazed'
tamaa   'hope'

ljumaa   'Friday'
kitambaa   'cloth'
mkandaa   'mangrove'
-tapakaa   'be scattered'
-gaagaa   'roll about'

makaakaa   'palate, roof of mouth'

There are some pairs of words distinguished only by the presence of one
or two of these vowels, e.g.

-chakaa	: chaka	'be worn out'	: 'clump of trees'
chokaa	: -choka	'chalk'	: 'be tired'
-kaanga	: kanga	'fry'	: cloths worn by women
-kataa	: -kata	'refuse' v.	: 'cut' v.
-komaa	: -koma	'be ripe'	: 'come to an end'
-shangaa	: shanga	'be amazed'	: 'beads'
-tamaa	: tama	'hope'	: 'cheek (of face)'

Other vowels to practise follow.

ii

kiini   'kernel'

nabii   'prophet'
utii   'obedience'
utalii   'tourism'

bidii	: -bidi	'diligence'	: 'be necessary'
hasikii	: siki	'he does not hear'	: 'vinegar'
sifikirii	: sifikiri	'I don't imagine'	: 'I don't think'

ee

kekee   'boring tool'
kizee   'old woman'
pekee   'unique'

harambee   'heave-ho'
kipengee   'side path'
kipokee   'in turn'

kengee	: kenge	'blade'	: 'large lizard'
niletee	: nilete	'bring (to) me'	: 'let me bring'

oo

-pooza   'fade'
jogoo   'cockerel'
jongoo   'millipede'
pomboo   'porpoise'

dondoo	: dondo	'steinbuck'	: 'tiger cowrie'
kondoo	: kondo	'sheep'	: 'afterbirth'
popoo	: popo	'areca nut'	: 'bat (animal)'

uu

uuguzi	'nursing'
uume	'penis'
uungu	'deity, godhead'
buluu	'blue'
bunguu	'large dish'
juzuu	'chapter (of Koran)'
kifuu	'empty shell'
miguu	'legs'
tambuu	'betel'
karafuu	'clove'
kitunguu	'onion'
manukuu	'a copy'
mjukuu	'grandchild'
mkumbuu	'sash, bandolier'
kijuujuu	'overall', 'superficial'
kikuukuu	'worn out'

(b) Go over the words for practice in Units 4 and 5, paying attention this time to vowel quality as well as the implosive consonants. (Use the tape as a model.)

(c) Find examples of words from units 1, 2, 3, 6 and 7 containing consonants b, d, g, and j, and combinations mb, nd, ng. Arrange them in groups according to your own system, and practise them slowly, paying attention to both vowel quality and implosive consonants.

Unit 10   Fungu la kumi
Ngapi? — How many?

I

▷ (a)

1	moja	20	ishirini
2	mbili	30	thelathini
3	tatu	40	arobaini
4	nne	50	hamsini
5	tano	60	sitini
6	sita	70	sabini
7	saba	80	themanini
8	nane	90	tisini
9	tisa (or *kenda*)	100	mia moja
10	kumi	1,000	elfu moja
11	kumi na moja	100,000	laki moja

Count from 11 to 20:
kumi na moja, kumi na mbili, _____

(b) *ni* — 'is/am/are'
tarehe — 'date';   *tarehe gani?* — 'what date?'

▷
Mimi: Leo ni tarehe gani?
Wewe: (22nd) Leo ni tarehe ishirini na mbili.

Mimi: Leo ni tarehe gani?
Wewe: (31st) Leo ni tarehe _____

Answer the date according to the numbers:
18th, 3rd, 16th, 25th, 19th.

Mimi: Leo ni tarehe gani?
Wewe: (1st) Leo ni tarehe mosi.*

Mimi: Leo ni tarehe gani?
Wewe: (2nd) Leo ni tarehe pili.†

mosi — 'first', †*pili* — 'second'

(c) Time in Swahili runs from sunset to dawn, dawn to sunset; not from midnight to midday. So when the clock shows 12, that is 6 o'clock in Swahili. (Look at the opposite number from the one the hour hand shows.)

saa — 'time', 'hour', 'watch/clock'
ngapi? — 'how many?' *saa ngapi?* here means 'what time?'
sasa — 'now'
kamili — 'exactly'

▷   Mimi: Sasa ni saa ngapi?

Yeye: Sasa ni saa sita.

Mimi: Sasa ni saa ngapi?

Yeye: Sasa ni saa saba.

Mimi: Sasa ni saa ngapi?

Wewe: Sasa ni saa _____

Mimi: Ni saa ngapi sasa?

Wewe: Sasa ni saa _____

Mimi: Ni saa ngapi sasa?

Wewe: Sasa ni saa _____ kamili

Sasa ni saa ngapi? is an neutral question.
(Ni) saa ngapi sasa? is insistent, '*What time* is it now?

robo — $\frac{1}{4}$
nusu — $\frac{1}{2}$
kasa robo — 'quarter to', 'less a quarter'.

▷   Mimi: Saa ngapi sasa?

Wewe: Sasa ni saa kumi na mbili na robo.

Mimi: Saa ngapi sasa?

Wewe: Sasa ni saa moja na nusu.

Mimi: Saa ngapi sasa?

Wewe: Sasa ni saa mbili kasa robo.

dakika — 'minute(s)'
kasoro — 'less, minus'

▷   Mimi: Saa ngapi sasa?

Yeye: Sasa ni saa moja kasoro dakika kumi.

Mimi: Saa ngapi sasa?

Yeye: Sasa ni saa tatu kasoro dakika tano.

Mimi: Saa ngapi sasa?

Wewe: Sasa ni saa kumi kasoro dakika _____

Mimi: Saa ngapi sasa?

Wewe: Sasa ni saa tatu _____

Mimi: Saa ngapi sasa?

Yeye: Sasa ni saa moja na dakika tano.

Mimi: Saa ngapi sasa?

Wewe: Sasa ni saa sita na dakika _____.

Answer the following times:

(d) *una* — 'you have'
   pesa — 'money, cash'
   nina — 'I have'

▷   Mimi: Una pesa ngapi, bwana?

   Bwana: (1s) (1s)   Nina shilingi tatu.
            (1s)

   Mimi: Una pesa ngapi, mama?

   Mama: (1s) (1s)   Nina shilingi nne
           (1s) (1s)

   Mimi: Una pesa ngapi, mzee?

   Mzee: (1s) (1s)   Nina shilingi _____.

Answer as follows:

   (1s) (1s)   (1s) (1s)
      (1s)   (1s) (1s)
   (1s) (1s)   (1s) (1s)

   Mzee: Shilingi moja ni senti ngapi, bwana?
   Bwana: Shilingi moja ni senti mia moja, mzee. Una senti ngapi?
   Mzee: Nina senti kumi tu.
   Bwana: Pole, mzee.

   Mimi: Una shilingi ngapi, bwana?
   Bwana: (10) (5)   Nina shilingi kumi na tano.

Answer with the following amounts:

   (10) (10) (5)   (10) (10)   (10) (10)
                        (10)   (10) (10)

   Bwana: Una pesa ngapi, mama?
   Mama: [20s] [20s] (5)   Nina shilingi arobaini na tano.

Bwana: Kumbe una pesa nyingi, mama!

Mama: Shilingi mbili na senti tano ni pesa nyingi? Wapi, bwana!

wapi — 'where?' in the tone of voice of the tape, means 'get lost!'

(e) *ana* — 'he/she has'
watoto wangapi? — 'how many children?'

▷   Mimi: Baba ana watoto wangapi?

Yeye: Ana watoto wawili

Mimi: Bwana ana watoto wangapi?

Yeye: Ana watoto watatu.

Mimi: Mlevi ana watoto wangapi?

Yeye: Ana watoto wanne.

Mimi: Mama ana watoto wangapi?

Yeye: Ana watoto _____.

Mimi: Mzee ana watoto wangapi?

Wewe: Ana watoto _____.

Mimi: Askari ana watoto wangapi?

Wewe: Ana mtoto mmoja tu.

Mimi: Mwalimu ana watoto wangapi?

Wewe: Mwalimu hana watoto. Mwalimu ni maskini tu.*

hana — 'he/she has not'

*maskini here means poor in children, not in money! 'Poor thing!'.

II

(i) Numbers are almost all the same, whether cardinal (one, two, three, etc) or ordinal (first, second, etc). The exceptions are only for 'one' and 'two'. In dates, the first day of the month is *tarehe mosi* (not *moja*), and the second is *tarehe pili* (not *mbili*). *siku ya pili* means 'the next day', as a rule. For the first of a series, when thinking of it as such, one would use *kwanza* (literally 'to begin'). So the first day of Creation would be *siku ya kwanza*, followed by *siku ya pili, siku ya tatu, siku ya nne*, and so on. *siku moja* is 'one day' — either when counting or when story-telling — *siku mbili* — 'two days', etc.

(ii)   *ni* is the simplest form of copula: 'is/am/are'. The negative is *si*.

Leo ni tarehe kumi?
A'a, leo si tarehe kumi, ni kumi na moja leo.
Kumbe, si Alhamisi leo? (Thursday)
Ndiyo, leo ni ljumaa. (Friday)

(iii)   *-na* may remind you (rightly) of *na* 'and, with'. If you put a personal prefix before *-na*, e.g. *ni+na*, it means 'I have'. The full paradigm is as follows:

	positive	**negative**
1st sing.	nina watoto wawili	sina pesa
2nd sing.	una watoto wawili	huna pesa
3rd sing.	ana watoto wawili	hana pesa
1st pl.	tuna watoto wawili	hatuna pesa
2nd pl.	mna watoto wawili	hamna pesa
3rd pl.	wana watoto wawili	hawana pesa

Note the third person singular agreement *a-*, negative *ha-*, and compare it with the form with *-jambo*, viz *hajambo*. Note also that *nina/sina* etc must normally be followed by an Object.

(iv)   Many nouns in Swahili do not change for singular and plural, e.g. *shilingi, siku, saa*. But we have seen that for persons there is a distinction between, e.g. *ana* 'he has' and *wana* 'they have'. Most nouns which refer to persons have different forms for singular and plural. *mlevi* 'drunkard' is singular; *watoto* 'children' is plural. 'child' is *mtoto*; 'drunkards' is *walevi*. The singular prefix for these nouns is usually *m-* (sometimes *mw-* before a vowel), and the plural usually *wa-* (sometimes *w-*. before a vowel). In grammar these nouns are referred to as 'class 1/2' nouns. Those which do not change are referred to as 'class 9/10' nouns. The numbering is for reference and comparison with other Bantu languages.

Some numbers also change to 'agree' with the nouns they qualify. Numbers 1 to 5, and no. 8 change, the rest do not. So we have:

saa moja	but	mtoto mmoja
saa mbili		watoto wawili
saa tatu		watoto watatu
saa nne		watoto wanne
saa tano		watoto watano
saa nane		watoto wanane.

Compound numbers also change, though this is not always strictly observed:

23 days: siku ishirini na tatu
23 children: watoto ishirini na watatu.

Other adjectives also agree, so *siku ngapi?* 'how many days?' but *watoto wangapi?* 'how many children?' Most agreements are regular, but a few are not; so we have *pesa nyingi* 'much money' but *watoto wengi* 'many children'. These seeming irregularities are subject to complex morpho-phonological rules as set out in formal grammars. In practice they are few in number but frequent in occurrence, so you will soon know them.

Some nouns referring to people do not change for singular and plural. These are mainly words taken from other languages, e.g. *askari*, *maskini*. Yet other nouns, those for some family relationships and those for professions have a plural in *ma-*, e.g. *bibi, mabibi; bwana, mabwana; daktari*, ('doctor') *madaktari*. But whether they change or not, all these nouns referring to people have the same concordial agreement with adjectives and most other words. e.g.

mzee mmoja   wazee wawili
askari mmoja   askari wawili
bibi mmoja   mabibi wawili

However, the vast majority of Bantu nouns for people have *m-* (*mw-*) and *wa-* (*w-*) prefixes, and the rest are soon learned in practice because they occur frequently.

III

(f)   Write the Swahili for the following numbers:
21, 32, 43, 54, 65, 76, 87, 98, 109, 1200.

(g)   Months are easy:

Januari	Julai
Februari	Agosti
Machi	Septemba
Aprili	Oktoba
Mei	Novemba
Juni	Disemba

In what month (*mwezi gani?*) is Christmas (*Kirismasi*)?
Answer: Mwezi wa _____.

In what month is Easter (*Pasaka*)? (*au* — 'or')
                         is New Year's Day (*siku ya mwaka*)?
                         is St. Valentine's day?
                         is May-day?
                         were you born?
                         will you go on holiday next?

mwezi also means 'moon'.

(h)   *mwaka* — 'year'

What year (*mwaka gani?*)
did William the Conqueror invade Britain? Mwaka wa _____
did the first world war end?

did the second world war break out?
did the French revolution start?
was this book published?
were you born?
is it now?

(i)   *Mchezo — Pesa ngapi?* Game — How much money?

Put a number of silver coins (between 1 and 5) in your hands and shake
them. Ask a friend to guess:
Nina shilingi ngapi mkononi? (*mkono* — hand)

He guesses:
Una shilingi _____ mkononi.

If he guesses right you say *Ndiyo*; then it is his turn.
If he is wrong you say *Siyo*, and tell him how many you have, simultaneously showing him. Any mistakes in Swahili or in counting must be
penalised. Play again with paper representing notes (20, 50, 100, 200,
1,000 shillings).

(j)   Here are the singulars and plurals of the nouns referring to persons we
have met so far:

mtoto	watoto
mzee	wazee
mlevi	walevi
mwanafunzi	wanafunzi
bwana	mabwana
bibi	mabibi

baba
mama
askari
maskini

mwizi	waizi/wezi/wevi
mwalimu	waalimu/walimu

The following nouns are regular. Give their plurals:

mtu — 'person'
mgonjwa — 'sick person'
mvuvi — 'fisherman'
mkulima — 'farmer'
mzungu — 'European'
mwarabu — 'Arab'

(k)   Answer the following questions in the negative, using *-na*:
Una pesa ngapi?
Sasa ni saa ngapi?   Sijui, _____
Mna watoto?
Watoto wana pesa?
Mna wanafunzi sasa?

Wanafunzi wana kazi nyingi?
Mwalimu ana watoto wangapi?

(l) Fill in the blanks:
Mimi: Hujambo, bwana.
Wewe: _____
Mimi: Mimi sijambo sana. Habari za siku nyingi?
Wewe: _____
Mimi: Salama. Habari za watoto?
Wewe: _____. Wawili wako_____
Mimi: Kumbe una watoto wangapi?
Wewe: _____. Wawili wako _____,
        Wawili _____, na mmoja _____
Mimi: Kweli Mungu yupo!
Wewe: _____

(m) Write questions to the following answers:
Ana watoto kumi na wawili.
Sasa ni saa nane kasa robo.
Nina shilingi nne na senti arobaini.
Wako wawili shuleni lakini wanane wako nyumbani.
Wapo kitandani.
Ana wanne tu.
Sijui.

IV

(i) **Time, dates, seasons**

Time for the Swahili, as for many other ancient peoples, runs from dawn to dusk. This conveniently varies little in East Africa throughout the year, and as watches and clocks are now almost universal, we can make a straight switch. Nevertheless, there are a few things to bear in mind. Traditionally the change-over from one day to the next (which with us takes place at midnight) for the Swahili takes place in the evening. So they have a sequence dark+light as their *siku*, which we may translate as 'day' only in the sense of '24 hrs'. You recall the connection between Swahili *siku* and *usiku* 'night-time'. There is an expression for 'dead of night': *usiku wa manane*. Other expressions for times of day refer to prayer periods in the Muslim day, such as *alfajiri* — 'dawn', *adhuhuri* — 'noon', *alasiri* — 'afternoon', *magharibi* — 'sunset' ('west').

Days of the week lead up to the Muslim holy day, Friday in our terms: *Ijumaa*. The week then begins:

Jumamosi — 'first day of the week' (Saturday)
Jumapili — 'second day of the week' (Sunday)
Jumatatu — 'third day of the week' (Monday)
Jumanne — 'fourth day of the week (Tuesday)
Jumatano — 'fifth day of the week' (Wednesday)
Alhamisi — 'fifth day' according to old reckoning (Thursday)
Ijumaa — (Friday)

The word for 'week' is *wiki*, but *juma* (as in *Jumamosi* etc.) was formerly used and may still be heard.

The Swahili are not so obsessed with strict time as many Europeans are, and have a much more relaxed attitude. Of course there are proper social conventions about times for performing certain functions — e.g. nobody calls on anyone in the early afternoon, when anyone with any sense will be having a siesta. The time for social calls is about 5.30. When you get used to it, it is much more comfortable to live by the seasons, the weather, and inclination than it is by a clock.

Calendar dates are used, but there is also the Muslim year since although some Swahili are Christians, many more are Muslim. Important times are of course *Ramadhani* 'Ramadan', the last month of the Mohammedan year, and a period of fasting, when no food is eaten between dawn and sunset. At this period strict Muslims do not even swallow their saliva, but spit it out. Important festivals are *Idi el fitr*, the festival at the end of Ramadan; *Idi el haji*, the commemoration of the Prophet's journey to Mecca; *Maulidi*, the Prophet's birthday; and so on. The Islamic calendar does not coincide with the Gregorian.

There are also terms for the seasons, e.g. *masika*, the greater rains (in April); *mvuli*, the lesser rains (November); *kaskazi*, the time of greatest heat (December to February) when the North wind blows; *kusi*, the coolest period (June to October), when the South wind blows; and other smaller divisions.

(ii) **Currency**

The three East African countries have separate currencies but notes and coins of the same denominations. The *shilingi* equals 100 *senti*, but *senti* are no longer current except for a 50 cent coin known as *thumuni* (literally 'an eighth' — a small coin). Sometimes coins are known by the picture on the obverse, e.g. *sungura* 'hare'. There are coins of 1, 5, and 10 shillings, and notes of 20, 100, 200, 500, and 1,000 shillings. There is a good deal of slang connected with money, as in most cultures.

(iii) **Children**

A Swahili would naturally like to have as many children as possible; but although it is a great sadness not to have children of one's own, the family system is such that everyone 'has' children. Your brother or sister's children are almost as much yours as if you had borne them, and there is much love and mutual obligation between the generations. Indeed, mother's sister is called *mama mdogo* 'little mother' and father's brother is *baba mdogo* 'little father'. Children are a blessing from God; and a particularly loving relationship holds between grand-parent and grand-child. The kind of teasing described in Unit 6 often takes place with grandparents, and between uncle and nephew. Cousins are also very close, and even cousins far removed are generally referred to as *ndugu* 'brother/sister'. In Tanzania this word is nowadays being adopted generally as 'comrade'. But there is still a difference, since to a real relative (or close friend) one would say *ndugu yangu* 'my brother/sister', whereas the Tanzanian 'comrade' usage is without the possessive, and often prefixed to a name, e.g. *ndugu Hamisi* 'comrade Hamisi'.

If asked *una watoto?* 'have you (any) children' and you have not any of your own, but this is what the questioner wants to know, you would never answer no, you would say *bado* 'not yet'. You must not give up hope, for you never know what God has in store for you. In the same way, asked whether you are married (*umeolewa?* — query to a woman) the answer must be *bado*. The questioner will then often say comfortingly *utapata* 'you will get (some, one)'.

(iv) **Idiomatic usage**. sina neno (*neno* — 'word') — 'I have no problems (nothing to say)' *hana neno* 'don't worry about him, he won't hurt you/ cause problems'.

Matamshi — Pronunciation

I

(a) The letters *ny* in Swahili represent a sound like that spelled *gn* in Italian *signora* or *ñ* in Spanish *señor*. The tongue is in the same position as for *j* in Swahili. We have met this sound in the word *nyumba*.

▷

nyayo	'footprint'
nyororo	'soft'
nyuma	'behind'
nyoka	'snake'
Nyerere	
nywele	'hair'

onyo	'warning'
onyesho	'show'
fanya	'do' v.
unyaa	'disgust'
manyoya	'fur'

nyanya	'grandmother', 'tomato'
nyonya	'suck' v.
nyanyasa	'tease'
manyunyu	'drizzle'
nyekenya	'decompose'
nyungunyungu	'porcupine' 'kind of worm'
mnyenyekevu	'humble person'

(b) The combination *ng'* in Swahili represents the same sound as spelled *ng* in the English word 'singer'. It *never* represents the *ng* in 'finger'. (That sound is spelled in Swahili *ng* without the apostrophe.)

▷

ng'ombe	'cow, cattle'
ng'ambo	'opposite bank'
ng'amua	'find out'
ng'aa	'shine' v.
ng'oo	expression of derision
ng'oa	'root out'
ng'wafua	'snatch (as a dog)'

nung'unika	'grumble'
ning'inia	'dangle'
ng'ong'ona	'gnaw'
ng'ong'a	make a secret sign of derision
ng'ang'ama	'hang on'

(c) These words contain both *ny* and *ng'*:

▷   nyang'anya   'snatch' v.
           kinyong'onyo   'wearily'
           vinying'inya   'descendants'

(d) The letter *n* before *g* represents the sound *ng+g* (i.e. as in English 'finger').

▷   nguo   'clothes'
           ngoma   'dance', 'drum'
           ngiri   'wild boar'
           ngamia   'camel'
           Ngazija   Comoro Is.
           ngoja   'wait' v.
           nguruma   'roar' v.
           nguruwe   'pig'
           nguzo   'ladder'
           ngwe   'allotment' (In this word the sound *ng'* — letter
                               n — is stressed.)

(e) When *m* precedes another consonant it normally constitutes a separate syllable, especially when in initial position. Be careful not to insert a vowel after the *m*.

▷   mtoto   'child'
           mgeni   'guest'
           mkate   'bread'
           mzigo   'load'
           Mhindi   'Indian'
           mchuzi   'gravy'
           mjomba   'mother's brother'
           mguu   'leg'
           mdomo   'lip'
           mnyonge   'abject person'

In the following words, the *m* has the stress:

           mtu   'person'
           mji   'town'
           mbu   'mosquito'
           mla   'greedy person'
           mbwa   'dog'
           mchwa   'white ant(s)'

(f) *n* may also sometimes constitute a syllable for some speakers, as in:

▷   njaa   'hunger'
           nzige   'locust'
           njia   'road, way'
           njugu   'peanut'
           ndugu   'brother/sister'

It constitutes a syllable and also takes stress, as in:

           nje   'outside'
           nne   'four'

II

(i) *ny* in Swahili represents a *palatal* nasal /ɲ/. The body of the tongue touches the hard palate and the tip of the tongue is low, behind the lower teeth. You may wish to practise holding your tongue-tip down with a pencil, as for Swahili implosive *j*. *ny* does not represent n+y (as in the English word 'opinion'). One even sometimes hears BBC announcers pronounce the name of President Nyerere as if it began like the word *night*! Please avoid that trap. The face diagram shows the tongue position for *ny*.

(ii) *ng'* in Swahili represents the velar nasal /ŋ/. Swahili spelling is more consistent than English. In English the letters *ng* represent both the sound in 'singer' and the sound in 'finger' (/ŋ/ and /g/). In Swahili, the sound as in 'singer' is spelled *ng'*; that in 'finger' is *ng*.

To be totally consistent, the sound as in English 'finger' 'ought' to be represented in Swahili as *ng'g*. In one word, *ng'ge* 'scorpion', it sometimes is so spelled. But this word also appears as *nge*; and the convention is (as in English) that the letter n before g represents the sound *ng'* (/ŋ/). So all the words in Section I (d) *could* have been spelled with initial *ng'g*. There is no need for this, however, if the convention n+g = ng'g is accepted.

(iii) The nasal consonants *m* and *n* are pronounced as in English. The only problem you are likely to have with them is when they occur in combinations which are not found in English, as in I (e) and (f).

III

(g) Go through a dictionary practising all the words with initial *n* plus another consonant, *m* plus another consonant, *ny*, and *ng'*. Contrast those having initial *ng'*- with those in *ng*-.

Unit 12   Fungu la kumi na mbili
Kupika chai — Making tea

I

(a) *kupika* — 'to cook, prepare food/drink' 'cooking, preparing etc.'
nipike? — 'shall I prepare . . .?'
pika! — 'cook!', 'prepare!'
chai — 'tea'
vipi? — 'how?'
chemsha — 'boil (something)' v.
maji — 'water'
halafu — 'then, afterwards'
tia — 'put in'
nitie? — 'shall I put in?'
majani — 'leaves' (here, *majani ya chai* — leaf tea)
vijiko — 'spoons' (here, spoonfuls)
maji ya moto — 'hot water' (*moto* — 'fire')
tunywe — 'let's drink (it)'

▷
Bw. Philip:	Nipike chai?
Bi. Maw:	Ndiyo, pika tu.
Bw.P.:	Nipike vipi?
Bi.M.:	Kwanza chemsha maji.
Bw.P.:	Haya.
Bi.M.:	Halafu tia majani.
Bw.P.:	Nitie majani vijiko vingapi?
Bi.M.:	Vijiko vitatu tu.
Bw.P.:	Haya.
Bi.M.:	Sasa tia maji ya moto.
Bw.P.:	Haya basi, chai tayari.
Bi.M.:	Tunywe tu.

Note *majani vijiko vingapi* — lit. 'leaves spoons how many?' i.e. 'how much leaf tea?' and *vijiko vitatu* — 'three spoons(ful)'.

(b) *karibu* — 'welcome, approach'
maziwa — 'milk'
ongeza — 'increase' v.
kidogo — 'a little'
sukari — 'sugar'
nikoroge? — 'shall I stir?'
koroga! — 'stir!'

▷
Bi. Maw:	Karibu chai!*
Wewe:	Asante.
Bi.M.:	Nitie chai?
Wewe:	Tia tu.

Bi.M.:   Nitie maziwa?
Wewe: Tia tu. Ongeza kidogo . . . basi.[†]
Bi.M.:   Nitie sukari?
Wewe: Tia tu.
Bi.M.:   Vijiko vingapi?
Wewe: Vijiko _____ tu. (2)
Bi.M.:   Nikoroge chai?
Wewe: Koroga tu.
Bi.M.:   Haya, chai tayari.
Wewe: Haya.

*karibu chai 'come and have some tea/will you have some tea?'
†Note that basi is used here to mean 'stop, that's enough'. If you don't
want any at all you can also say basi, or basi tu.

usitie — 'don't put in'
hutumii? — 'you don't take?' (lit. use)
situmii — 'I don't take'

▷   Wewe: Nitie chai?
     Mimi: A'a, tia maziwa kwanza.
     Wewe: Haya. . . . Nitie sasa chai?*
     Mimi: Tia tu.
     Wewe: Nitie na sukari?†
     Mimi: A'a, usitie sukari.
     Wewe: Kumbe, hutumii sukari?
     Mimi: Ndiyo, situmii.
     Wewe: Haya, chai tayari.
     Mimi: Haya.

*Note: nitie chai sasa? would have been the neutral sequence.
nitie sasa chai? means 'shall I pour the tea in now?'
†na is used here to mean 'also, too'.

(c)   aondoe — 'shall he take away/let him take away'
       vyombo — 'pots, vessels'
       naam — an expression of paying attention, 'Yes, what is it?', or 'yes, I
       see'

▷   Bi. Maw: Bwana Philip aondoe vyombo?
     Bw. Harris   Aondoe tu.
     Bi.M.:   Philip!
     Bw. Philip: Naam.
     Bi.M.:   Tuko tayari.
     Bw.P.:   Niondoe vyombo?
     Bi.M.:   Ndiyo, ondoa tu.
     Bw.P.:   Haya.

(d)   njoo — 'come on' (a unique form of imperative)
       chakula — 'food'
       mahindi — 'maize'
       chumvi — 'salt'
       do! — an expression of surprise; variant of lo!
       tule? — 'shall we eat?'

ale — 'let him eat'
baadaye — 'after that'
vizuri — 'very well' (note relationship with nzuri 'good (news)')

▷   Bi. Maw: Njoo, tupike chakula.
           Bw. Philip: Tupike chakula gani?
           Bi.M.:   Tupike mahindi.
           Bw.P.:   Haya. Nitie maji?
           Bi.M.:   Tia tu.
           Bw.P.:   Nitie mahindi?
           Bi.M.:   Tia tu.
           Bw.P.:   Basi.
           Bi.M.:   Tia na chumvi.
           Bw.P.:   Do! Nitie sasa?
           Bi.M.:   Ndiyo, tia tu. Ongeza kidogo.
           Bw.P.:   Haya. . . . Basi, mahindi tayari. Tule sasa?
           Bi.M.:   Bado. Bwana Harris ale kwanza.
           Bw.P.:   Haya. Na tule baadaye sisi?*
           Bi.M.:   Ndiyo.
           Bw.P.:   Vizuri.

*Note: putting sisi at the end instead of before the verb has the effect
of giving it more emphasis. The speaker is anxious to know when we
are going to eat!

(e)   nimalize — 'let me finish'
      unywe — 'drink!', 'you may drink'
      nilete? — 'shall I bring?'
      keki — 'cake'
      lete — 'bring!'
      nikate? — 'shall I cut?'
      kata — 'cut!'
      ule — 'eat!'
      chakula kitamu — 'the food (is) good' (lit. 'sweet')

▷   Bwana Philip: Nipike chai, bwana?
           Bwana Harris: Bado. Nimalize kazi kwanza.
           Bw.P.:   Haya.

                 . . . .
           Bw.H.:   Philip!
           Bw.P.:   Naam.
           Bw.H.:   Habari za chai?
           Bw.P.:   Nipike sasa?
           Bw.H.:   Ndiyo, pika tu.

                 . . . .
           Bw.P.:   Haya, chai tayari. Nilete sasa?
           Bw.H.:   Lete tu.
           Bw.P.:   Haya bwana, unywe.
           Bw.H.:   Haya.
           Bw.P.:   Nilete na keki, bwana?
           Bw.H.:   Ndiyo, lete.
           Bw.P.:   Nikate?
           Bw.H.:   Ndiyo, kata tu.

Bw.P.:   Haya, bwana, ule.
Bw.H.:   Asante Philip. Chakula kitamu.

(f) *hodi* — a word to call out when approaching a house, 'Can I come in?'
'Anyone at home?'
starehe — 'don't get up' 'be comfortable' 'don't disturb yourself' said on
entering a room, to the people inside.
kiti — 'chair'
nimekaa — here, 'thanks', lit. 'I'm sitting'.
nimeshiba — 'I've had enough'
nakwenda — 'I'm off'
mara hii! — 'so suddenly!' 'already?'
lazima — '(it's) necessary'

▷ Bibi Maw: Hodi!
   Bibi Hafida: Karibu.
   Bi.M.:   Hodi hodi!
   Bi.H.:   Karibu karibu. Oh, karibu Bibi Maw.
   Bi.M.:   Starehe.
   Bi.H.:   Karibu, karibu kitini.*
   Bi.M.:   Asante, nimekaa.
   Bi.H.:   Habari za siku nyingi?
   Bi.M.:   Nzuri tu. Habari za hapa?
   Bi.H.:   Salama. Karibu chai.
   Bi.M.:   Asante. . . . Chai tamu sana.**
   Bi.H.:   Niongeze?
   Bi.M.:   Basi tu, nimeshiba.
                  ....
   Bi.M.:   Haya, nakwenda sasa.
   Bi.H.:   Mara hii!
   Bi.M.:   Ee, lazima.
   Bi.H.:   Haya.
   Bi.M.:   Basi, kwa heri bibi.
   Bi.H.:   Kwa heri, bibi, kwa heri ya kuonana.
   Bi.M.:   Ee.
   Bi.H.:   Haya, karibu.
   Bi.M.:   Haya.

*Karibu ukae 'come in and sit down' may also be heard

**chai tamu sana* — 'the tea (is) very good (sweet)'

▮▮

(i) The imperative verb (singular) is simply the 'stem', i.e. without the *ku-*
infinitive prefix. So *kupika* 'to cook, cooking' has imperative *pika!* 'cook!'.
Exceptions are verbs with one-syllable stems, such as *-la* 'eat', *-nywa*
'drink'. The imperative of these verbs normally keeps the *ku-* prefix for
the sake of somewhere to put the stress. There is also a plural form of
the imperative, consisting of the 'root' ('stem' minus final vowel, e.g.
-pik-) plus *-eni*, e.g. *pikeni!* 'cook ye!', 'you-all cook!', *kuleni*, 'eat' pl.

(ii) The form of the verb with a final -e is often referred to as the subjunctive, or the '-e stem'. The verb in this form must have a subject prefix. It is used:

   (a) for an enquiry: *nipike?* 'shall I cook?'; *apike?* 'shall he cook?'; *tupike?* 'shall we cook?'
   (b) as the imperative for other than 2nd. persons: *nipike!* 'let me cook!'; *apike!* 'let him cook!' *tupike!* 'let us cook!'
   (c) to express a wish: *ufike salama!* 'may you arrive in safety'
   (d) as an alternative to the use of the *ku-* prefix for the imperative with verbs whose stems have one syllable, e.g. *kula!* or *ule!* 'eat!'; *kunywa!* or *unywe!* 'drink!'

   The full paradigm of the subjunctive form for the verb *-pika* is:

1st person singular	nipike
2nd person singular	upike
3rd person singular	apike
1st person plural	tupike
2nd person plural	mpike
3rd person plural	wapike

(iii) There is only one negative form to cover both negative commands and wishes. This has the subject prefix followed by *-si-*. The stem ends in *-e* e.g. *usipike!* 'don't cook!', *tusiende!* 'don't let's go', 'let's not go'. The full paradigm for the negative subjunctive form of the verb *-pika* is:

1st person singular	nisipike
2nd person singular	usipike
3rd person singular	asipike
1st person plural	tusipike
2nd person plural	msipike
3rd person plural	wasipike

(iv) In the *Standard Dictionary* (Johnson), verbs are quoted as *stems*, e.g. *pika* 'cook', *enda* 'go'.

(v) You may have noticed some new agreements, viz: vijiko *vi*ngapi, chakula *ki*tamu. You may also have noticed a negative verb *hutumii?* 'don't you take?' and *situmii* 'I don't take'. These points will be dealt with later.

III

(g) *kabisa* — 'completely'
   zaidi — 'more, further'
   ufike — 'may you arrive'
   ukae — 'may you stay, remain'

Bi. Maw:	Habari gani, Bwana Harris?
Bw. Harris:	Nzuri tu. Habari zako?
Bi.M.:	Salama kabisa. Habari zaidi?*
Bw.H.:	Sina habari nyingi.

Bi.M.:   Habari za safari, je?
Bw.H.:   Safari ni leo tu.
Bi.M.:   Do! Ufike salama bwana.
Bw.H.:   Asante. Ukae salama bibi.

*Note: you ask *habari zaidi?* when you want to know what the real reason for the conversation is!

(h)   *twende* — 'let's go' (this 'should' be *tuende*, but never is)

Bwana Harris: Bibi Maw, uko tayari?
Bibi Maw;   Ndiyo, nipo tu.
Bw.H.:   Haya basi, twende.
Bi.M.:   Twende wapi, bwana?
Bw.H.:   Twende sinema!
Bi.M.:   Haya, twende tu!

(i)   Answer these questions in the positive:

Nipike keki?   Ndiyo, _____ tu.
Nichemshe maziwa?
Niondoe chai?
Nitie sukari?
Ninywe maji?
Nikoroge chai?
Nile mahindi?

(j)   Answer these questions in the negative, giving an alternative:

Nitie chai?   A'a, _____ chai, _____ maziwa tu.
Nile mahindi?   _____ keki _____
Nipike kahawa? (coffee) _____ chai _____
Niondoe maziwa?   _____ maji _____
Kupika chai nitie maji
   baridi? (cold)   _____ ya moto _____
Mwalimu asomeshe
   Kiswahili?   _____ Kiingereza _____
Tule mchele? (rice)   _____ mahindi _____
Wanafunzi wanywe bia?
   (beer)   _____
Watoto wale sukari?   _____
Bi. Maw atie sukari?   _____
Bw. Philip atie maziwa
   ya moto?   _____
Bw. Harris aende Lamu?   _____

(k)   Start to make a loose-leaf grammar book of your own. Have a section for verbs. Write in the paradigms for the subjunctive (positive) of *-chemsha* and *-la*. Then the negative subjunctive (on another sheet) of *-koroga* and *-nywa*.

(l) On another leaf, write out a table for all verbs from this unit, as follows:

root	**infinitive**	**imperative**		**subjunctive**	
		(sing.	pl.)	(pos.	neg.)
-pik-	kupika	pika	pikeni	nipike	nisipike

(Note that *-let-* 'bring' has an irregular imperative *lete* 'bring!' not *leta.)
(Note also that there is a relation between *kula* 'to eat' and *chakula* 'food'.)

(m) Write a conversation for a tea-party from *hodi* to *kwa heri*.

(n) If possible, *have* a tea-party, but do not give anyone tea etc. without all using the proper words.

IV

Calling on someone, you do not knock at the door (which in any case may well be open) but call out *hodi*. People are normally delighted to have visitors, but it could be that you have called at an inconvenient moment. Even if you know that someone is in, you must not persevere if, after calling out *hodi* three separate times you get no reply. Normally, however, you will hear *karibu*. (Confusingly, you may alternatively hear *hodi* from within.) You do not at once go in. The people inside may need a few moments to pull themselves together. You call again *hodi* — *hodi*. Then they say *karibu, karibu* and appear at the door to welcome you. There are degrees of intimacy reflected in how far you are invited into the house. There is usually a small hall or passage inside the door in a Swahili house in town; in the country there may be a covered verandah in front, perhaps with chairs and small tables. If there is a verandah, this is the reception room (and you do not step onto it before calling out *hodi* and being invited further). If there is no verandah, one of the rooms leading off the side of the hallway may be used, or the hallway itself. Many reception rooms contain beds, except in rich households, and you may be invited to sit on the bed. The floor will usually be covered with mats and if so you take your shoes off in the doorway; the mats are for sitting on. It is in fact cooler to sit on the mat than up on a chair or bed. Women should be sure to cover their legs when sitting down. If your dress is short, the hostess may offer you a cloth to cover them with.

You may well be offered some refreshment, tea, or '*soda*' (bottles of sweet fizzy drinks such as Fanta or Coca-cola). In the text here we have mostly supposed drinking tea with milk and sugar as in Europe; but some households will offer strong tea already mixed with milk (condensed or evaporated), sugar and spices. It would not be polite to refuse; on the other hand you may notice that someone slips out to buy the 'soda', and that the children look longingly at you, or that non-one else is drinking. You can just as well ask for water (*naomba maji*), which is anyway a great gift in a hot country and will not involve your hosts in cash outlay.

Tea, if offered, and if there is no table, is usually brought on a tray and put in the centre of the room. The host(ess) serves. If you are invited to a meal (and this must be by invitation—people who arrive at mealtimes are not highly regarded in any society), this may also be served on the mats in some households, although less traditional homes use tables. In any case you must first wash your hands; and often a small child will come with a basin and ewer to pour water over your hands, giving you soap and a towel if necessary. If you are lucky enough to be invited to a traditional meal you may be offered a spoon as a concession to a foreigner. But most people eat with the hand and it *must* be the *right* hand — also if using a spoon. (The left hand is used for cleaning yourself in the lavatory.) The right hand is always used for giving or receiving anything, and it is impolite to do otherwise. The exception is that sometimes someone may slightly bow to receive something, proffering both hands cupped, the right uppermost, held close to the chest. This is a gesture of special gratitude or subservience. It is surprising how dextrous (!) one gets with a little practice, even when buying newspapers, giving money, taking the paper, getting change and so on.

Food is often rice with some meat, fish, or vegetables as a relish. These may all be mixed together and brought in on a large dish, or they may be brought in separate dishes. It is not easy at first to eat rice or maize porridge with the fingers, but the trick is to form it into a sort of ball. Little dishes of fish or meat may be placed near you as the guest; do not make the mistake of thinking they are individual portions, and eat them all up yourself. They are meant for everyone, to help down the mass of the food. After the meal, you wash your hands again. Men and women often eat separately, but not always. Children do not normally eat with adults. The hostess will be pleased if you praise the food.

When you leave, the hosts may well say *karibu*. This is not an invitation to stay longer, and everyone would be surprised if you came back in again! Rather it means 'come again'. They *may* say *Karibu tena* (*tena* 'more', 'again'), probably influenced by English.

It is mainly women who visit each other at home. On the whole men traditionally have their social life around the mosque.

Unit 13   Fungu la kumi na tatu
Kununua mahindi — Buying maize

I

(a)   *gari* — 'car, vehicle'
anaendesha — 'he/she is driving'
tusimame — 'let us stop' (*-simama* can also mean 'stand up')
kwa nini? — 'why?' (*kwa* — 'for, with'; *nini?* — 'what?')
kwa sababu — 'because' (*sababu* — 'reason, cause')
anataka — 'he/she wants, he/she is wanting'
kununua — 'to buy'

Bwana Harris, Bibi Maw na Bwana Philip wako njiani, garini.
Bibi Maw anaendesha gari.

▷   Bwana Harris: Tusimame hapa sokoni.
Bibi Maw: Kwa nini?
Bw.H.:   Kwa sababu Philip anataka kununua mahindi.
Bi.M.:   Haya.

....

wanasimama — 'they are stopping'
nenda — 'go!'
usije — 'should you not come'
nami — 'with me'
nije? — 'shall I come?'

Wanasimama

▷   Bw.H.:   Basi Philip, nenda tu.
Bwana Philip: Kwa nini usije nami?
Bw.H.:   Nije?
Bw.P.:   Ee.
Bw.H.:   Haya, vizuri, twende.

....

wanaondoka — 'they are leaving'
kurudi — 'returning'
hakuna — 'there is no/not'
kabisa — 'totally'
kufaa — 'to be suitable' *mahindi ya kufaa* — 'suitable maize', 'maize
that will do'
penginepo — 'somewhere else'
wananchi — 'local people' (often used as a political term, literally 'the
people of the country, citizens')

Bwana Harris na Bwana Philip wanaondoka na kurudi.

▷   Bi.M.:   Habari za kununua?
Bw.P.:   Hakuna mahindi.

Bi.M.: Kumbe, hakuna kabisa?
Bw.P.: Hakuna mahindi ya kufaa.
Bw.H.: Twende penginepo.
Bi.M.: Wapi sasa?
Bw.P.: Twende soko la wananchi.
Bi.M.: Haya.

....

wanafika — 'they are arriving'
ujaribu — 'you try'
tena — 'again, further'
niende — 'let me go'
ninakuja — 'I am coming'

Wanafika soko la wananchi.

▷   Bi.M.: Basi, Philip, ujaribu tena.
     Bw.P.: Haya, niende. Njoo tu, bwana.
     Bw.H.: Nije tena?
     Bw.P.: Kwa nini usije?
     Bw.H.: Basi, ninakuja.

....

tufanye — 'shall we do'
nimechoka — 'I am tired'
jua — 'sun'

Bwana Harris na Bwana Philip wanaondoka na kurudi.

▷   Bi.M.: Habari za mahindi?
     Bw.H.: Hakuna mahindi ya kufaa.
     Bi.M.: Kumbe hakuna tena?
     Bw.P.: Ndiyo, hakuna.
     Bi.M.: Basi, tufanye nini?
     Bw.P.: Sijui.
     Bi.M.: Twende zetu.* Nimechoka sasa. Tena jua kali sana.†
     Bw.H.: ⎫
     Bw.P.: ⎭ Haya, twende.

     **twende zetu* — 'let's be off'
     †*jua kali* — 'the sun (is) hot'; *tena* here means 'moreover'

....

tazama — 'look'
huko — 'over there'
kuna — 'there are'
nazi — 'coconut(s)'
yaani — 'that is, that's to say, i.e.'
mwende — 'you (pl) go'

Wote watatu wako njiani tena.

▷   Bw.H.: Simama, simama!
     Bi.M.: Nisimame tena? Kwa nini sasa?

Bw.H.: Tazama huko. Kuna nazi.
Bi.M.: Kumbe tunataka nazi?
Bw.H.: Ndiyo, tunataka. Yaani, Philip anataka.
Bi.M.: Basi, na mwende tu.*

*'Well get on, then'.

....

tele — 'lots, in abundance'
hapa hapa — 'right here'
kikapu — 'basket'
pale — 'in that spot', 'just there'
yanafaa? — 'will it (the maize) do?'
ngoja — 'wait'

Bwana Harris na Bwana Philip wanaondoka na kurudi.

▷   Bi.M.: Habari za nazi, je?
         Bw.P.: Hakuna nazi za kufaa.
         Bi.M.: Pole, Lakini tazama hapa. Si mahindi tele hapa?†
         Bw.H.: Wapi?
         Bi.M.: Hapa hapa, kikapuni pale.
         Bw.P.: Kumbe kweli, kuna mahindi.
         Bw.H.: Yanafaa?
         Bw.P.: Ndiyo, yanafaa sana. Ngoja ninunue.‡
         Bw.H.: Haya, nunua tu.
         Bi.M.: Alhamdulillahi!

†Literally, 'Isn't there lots of maize here?' The use of the negative
implies impatience, 'Can't you see there's . . .!
‡*ngoja ninunue* — literally 'wait, let me buy (some)'. *ngoja* here is
used idiomatically, 'hang on, I'm just going to buy some', 'let me get
some', 'I'll just get some' etc.

                              II

(i)   Note various words for place: *hapa* 'here' (occurred in Unit 3). *hapa hapa*
      'right here', 'just in this spot'; *pale* — 'there', 'in that spot'; *penginepo* —
      'somewhere else', 'in another place'; *huko* 'over there'. These words and
      others will be dealt with more fully later.

(ii) Note that *kwa sababu* is normally only used when an actual, direct
      reason or cause is being put forward; and one's view of what constitutes
      a direct cause is very much a matter of culture-specific world-view.

(iii) We have had the use of *-na* with persons, e.g. *nina* — 'I have', *ana* —
      'he/she has', etc. This -na can also be prefixed by *ku-* expressing place.
      So *ku+na* means 'there is/are' (perhaps literally something like 'the
      place has', cf. *ana* 'he/she has'). Indeed, there could be a locative
      subject, e.g. *hospitalini kuna wagonjwa wengi* — 'in the hospital there
      are many patients'. This structure would be used, as in English, when
      the topic of interest was the hospital rather than the patients (cf. *wako*

wagonjwa wengi hospitalini — 'there are many patients in the hospital', a neutral word order, where the topic of interest is the presence of many patients). The negative of *kuna* is *hakuna* 'there is/are not/no'. In place there is no distinction between singular and plural.

(iv) The 'tense prefix', or 'tense sign' *-na-* may be inserted between the 'subject prefix' (*ni-, u-, a-, tu-, m-, wa-*) and the stem, to represent the present continuous tense. Thus *ni+na+nunua* means 'I am buying'. You may relate this *-na-* to the *-na* in *nina* — 'I have', 'I am associated with'. The full paradigm is:

ninanunua mahindi	I am buying maize
unanunua mahindi	you are buying maize
ananunua mahindi	he/she is buying maize
tunanunua mahindi	we are buying maize
mnanunua mahindi	you-all are buying maize
wananunua mahindi	they are buying maize

This tense sign *-na-* can not be stressed, so if a verb with a monosyllabic stem (e.g. *-la, -nywa, -ja* — 'come') is used with this tense, the morpheme *-ku-* is used (as with imperatives in unit 7) to carry the stress. So we have *ananunua* — 'he/she is buying'; but *anakula* — 'he/she is eating', *wanakunywa* — 'they are drinking' and *ninakuja* — 'I am coming' as in the text in section I, with *-ku-* inserted between the *-na-* tense sign and the verb stem.

(v) When two actions are performed in sequence and there is no close relationship (e.g. causal or resultative) perceived between them, the second verb is usually in the infinitive, and the two are linked by *na*. So we have *wanaondoka na kurudi* 'they go (are seen going) and (then later they) come back'.

(vi) *na* is also sometimes used before a subjunctive used as an imperative, when the speaker feels somewhat impatient. So in the text, *basi na mwende tu* means 'alright, get on with it, go on then'.

(vii) *nami* — 'with me'. This is derived from *na mimi*. All persons can be combined with na- in this way, viz:

nami	with me
nawe	with you (sing.)
naye	with him/her
nasi	with us
nanyi	with you (plural)
nao	with them

e.g. *njoo nami* — 'come with me'; *niende naye?* — 'shall I go with him?'; *wanasoma nasi* — 'they are studying with us'.

(viii) *twende zetu* — 'let's be off', 'let's be on our way'. *zetu* is a form of the possessive 'our, ours'. You *could* say to someone very importunate, *nenda zako* — 'be off' (*zako* is a form of second person singular possessive, 'your, yours'), but this should only be used in extreme circumstances, as it is very impolite.

(ix) The verbs *-enda* — 'go' and *-ja* — 'come'. occur very frequently, and are
      slightly irregular in form. *-enda* has infinitive *kwenda* (not *kuenda*);
      imperative *nenda* (not *enda*), *twende* (not *tuende*), *mwende* 'go ye' (not
      muende); and present continuous *ninakwenda, unakwenda* etc. (not
      ninaenda etc.). In fact this verb retains the *-kw* after all tense signs
      except *-ka-* (Unit 23). The verb *-ja* has imperative *njoo* (plural *njooni*), but
      is otherwise a regular one-syllable stem verb.

 (x) The adjective *-kali* has a number of uses. Perhaps its central meaning is
      something like fierce intensity. We have seen that *mwalimu mkali* is a
      strict teacher, even short-tempered. *Jua kali* is 'hot sun'. Applied to a
      knife, *-kali* means 'sharp', to coldness it means 'penetrating', to food it
      means 'acid', to beer it means 'strong'.

(xi) Notice that after verbs of wishing etc, the following verb is in the infini-
      tive form if the subject of both verbs is the same, e.g. *Bw.P. anataka
      kununua mahindi* (P. wants to buy some maize).

III

(b) **Kununua mahindi — Ufahamu — Comprehension**.
     Jibu maswali. Answer the questions. (Answer in complete sentences*):
     1 Bibi Maw asimame wapi?
     2 Nani anataka kununua mahindi?
     3 Nani anakwenda na Philip?
     4 Wanakwenda kufanya nini?
     5 Kuna mahindi sokoni?
     6 Pili, wanakwenda soko gani? (*pili* — 'secondly')
     7 Kwa nini Bibi Maw anataka kurudi nyumbani?
     8 Philip anataka kununua nini tena?
     9 Kuna nazi?
     10 Mahindi tele yako wapi?
     11 Philip ananunua mahindi *mwisho*ni? (*mwisho* — 'end')

*Remember that it would be considered rather abrupt in Swahili to
answer a question, especially one requesting information (as opposed to
a proposition merely requiring confirmation) by a single word, e.g. *Bibi
Maw, mahindi*; etc. To do so would imply impatience on the part of the
person answering.

(c) Pick out all the expressions of Bi. Maw in the passage that show she
     feels fed up.

▷ (d) Jibu maswali. Answer the questions.

1 Watu wanasimama wapi?   _____

2 Mtoto anakunywa nini?   _____

3 Mama ananunua nini?   _____

4 Unakwenda wapi?   _____

5 Bibi Maw anakula nini?   _____

6 Unatia nini?   _____

7 Wanafunzi wanataka nini?   _____

8 Mwalimu anasomesha nini?   _____

9 Mnatazama nini?   _____

10 Unakwenda Nairobi na nani? _____

(e) Andika maswali. Write questions.
1 _____? Ninakwenda kanisani.
2 _____? Kwa sababu ninataka kununua chai.
3 _____? Anajaribu kuendesha gari.
4 _____? Wanaondoa vyombo na keki.
5 _____? Wanafanya kazi sasa.
6 _____? Kwa sababu Bibi Maw anakuja.
7 _____? Wananchi wanataka *uhuru* ('independence')

(f) Andika majibu ya kufaa. Write suitable answers.

1 Mlevi anakwenda wapi?
2 Unafanya nini?
3 Mnasoma nini?
4 Watoto wanajaribu kufanya nini?
5 Unataka kwenda wapi?
6 Kwa nini Bwana Philip anakwenda sokoni?
7 Nani anapika chai?
8 Kwa nini watu wanataka kwenda Mombasa?
9 Mwalimu anafanya kazi gani?
10 Unakula chakula gani?

(g) Make a list in alphabetical order of the new verb stems in the passage in
section I.
Write out the paradigm of the present continuous tense of *kurud*
nyumbani — 'going back home'.

(h) **Mchezo. Game**.
Player A asks Player B: Kwa nini unakwenda sokoni bwana/bibi?
B answers: Ninakwenda sokoni kwa sababu ninataka kununua X.
    then asks Player C: Kwa nini _____.
C answers: Ninakwenda sokoni _____ X na Y.
The game continues until a player forgets or misplaces an object, or runs
out of things to buy!

IV

We have seen with respect to greetings, general conversation, answering questions, and so on, that the Swahili take their time. This is also the
case when shopping. A Swahili man or woman does not buy the first
thing he or she sees, although he/she may frequent particular traders
But buying and selling is too important and enjoyable a transaction to do
in a hurry. A prospective buyer will take immense trouble to find just
what he wants, and even when he finds it, the actual transaction may

take a good deal of time. In the incident sketched in this unit, the length of time taken was irritating to the European Bibi Maw, but not at all to Bwana Philip who was actually buying. One has to consider also that the outlay of cash is both a pleasure to be savoured and a responsibility not lightly discharged.

In towns there is often more than one market for fresh produce; in fact there is likely to be one of some sort in every district. But there is normally a big central market with permanent stalls where in the past mainly Europeans and 'Asians' (people originating in the Indian sub-continent) shopped. Other markets were mainly patronised by local Africans. Now the customers are much more mixed, but old divisions may still be reflected in the names of the markets, as here. There are also markets for cloth and clothing, hardware, basketware, pottery, and other necessities of life. Haggling may be expected (as also in many tourist shops), but it is difficult to do if you are a foreigner. In local markets it is more the case that the price is raised for strangers, whatever their ethnic origin.

Unit 14   Fungu la kumi na nne

Sokoni — At the market
Matamshi ya kiarabu — Arabic-type pronunciation

I

(a) *mwuzaji* — 'seller'; *-uza*, v. -'sell'
 mnunuzi — 'buyer': *-nunua*, v. — 'buy'
 ndizi — 'banana(s)'
 bei — 'price'
 rahisi — 'cheap' 'easy'
 ghali — 'expensive'
 kidogo — 'rather, fairly, somewhat'
 siwezi — 'I can't/I won't'; *-weza*, v. — 'be able'
 kulipa — 'to pay'
 punguza — 'reduce'
 kiasi — 'amount'
 haiwezekani — 'it's impossible' (cf. *-weza*)
 tuseme — 'let's say'; *-sema*, v. — 'say'
 nipe — 'give me' (could also mean 'let me give' in another context);
  -pa, v. — 'give'

 chukua — 'take'
 kuvunja — 'to change' (lit. 'to break')
 chenji — 'change, n'.

▷   Mwuzaji: Karibu, karibu bwana.
  Mnunuzi: Hujambo, mama.
  Mwuzaji: Sijambo, bwana. Sijui wewe.
  Mnunuzi: Mimi sijambo.
  Mwuzaji: Karibu sana bwana. Unataka kununua nini, bwana?
  Mnunuzi: Ninataka ndizi.
  Mwuzaji: Tuna ndizi nzuri sana. Tazama hapa.
  Mnunuzi: Unauza bei gani?
  Mwuzaji: Moja shilingi tatu, bwana, rahisi sana.
  Mnunuzi: Moja shilingi tatu! Kumbe ghali sana, tena sana!
  Mwuzaji: Siyo ghali bwana, rahisi kidogo.
  Mnunuzi: Mimi siwezi kulipa shilingi tatu ndizi moja, mama.
   Punguza bei.
  Mwuzaji: Basi unalipa kiasi gani bwana?
  Mnunuzi: Shilingi moja moja.
  Mwuzaji: Shilingi moja moja! Haiwezekani kabisa! Tuseme
   shilingi mbili.
  Mnunuzi: Haya. Nipe ndizi sita.
  Mwuzaji: Haya bwana. Ndizi sita, shilingi kumi na mbili. Lete pesa
   bwana.
  Mnunuzi: Haya mama. Chukua pesa. Unaweza kuvunja shilingi ishirini
  Mwuzaji: Huna chenji, bwana?

Mnunuzi: Chenji sina.
Mwuzaji: Do! Siwezi kuvunja shilingi ishirini.
Mnunuzi: Ngoja kwanza mama . . . haya, nina shilingi kumina tano. Una
          shilingi tatu?
Mwuzaji: Ndiyo, chukua bwana.
Mnunuzi: Haya, kwa heri mama.
Mwuzaji: Kwa heri, bwana, karibu.

(b) Practise these expressions:

Unauza bei gani? 'What price are you selling (at)?'
Unauza kiasi gani? 'What amount are you selling (by)?'
Moja shilingi kumi. 'One (for) ten shillings', 'ten shillings apiece'
Shilingi mbili mbili. 'Two shillings a time', i.e. for goods arranged in
    little piles, each pile costs two shillings.
Ghali sana, tena sana! '*Extremely* expensive!'
Punguza bei, bwana! 'Lower the price, friend!'
Siwezi kupunguza bei. 'I can't (sc. won't) reduce the price'
Huna chenji? 'Haven't you (any) change?'
Unaweza kuvunja noti ya shilingi ishirini? 'Can you change a twenty-
shilling note?'
Lete pesa, bwana! 'Bring out (your) money, sir'
Chukua pesa! 'Here's the money, take it'
Ongeza kidogo! 'Add a bit!' — said by the buyer at the end of the
    transaction, if he's bought a fair amount of smallish items. The seller
    should pop an extra one in automatically, but if he does not, the buyer
    can legitimately suggest it. The seller will not refuse, though he may
    do it with bad grace!

(c) If possible, with a friend practise buying and selling, using anything to
     hand — real goods, or pebbles etc. to represent them. The goods should
     first be laid out neatly in piles, or singly in front of the seller.

     If practical work is not possible, write a few transactions and practise
     speaking them out loud.

Additional vocabulary:

nyanya — 'tomatoes' (bought in piles)
viazi — 'potatoes' (bought in piles or by weight)
mahindi — 'corn cobs' (bought in piles or singly)
nazi — 'coconut(s)' (bought singly)
machungwa — 'oranges' (bought in piles)
ndizi — 'banana(s)' (bought singly or by the hand — *mkono*)
pauni — 'pound' (weight); *nusu pauni* — 'half a pound'; *pauni moja na
    nusu* — 'a pound and a half' (but also occasionally used for a 20-
    shilling note now)
kilo — is now coming in, and I have heard plural *vilo* 'kilos'.
rat(i)li is an older weight term from Arabic, 'pound'; other Arabic weights
    and measures can be found in the dictionary and may still be heard.

(d) *Pronunciation*. The word *ghali* 'expensive' begins with a sound derived
     from Arabic. In some words you will also see a spelling *kh* (as in the
     name Khamisi — also spelt Hamisi), which represents another sound

derived from Arabic, and similar to that heard in the Scottish word *loch*,
German *ach-laut*. (Phonetically this is a voiceless velar fricative.) This *kh*
sound may be acquired by practising putting the tongue in the position
for *k* and then lowering it slightly while letting the breath make a fricative
(hissing) sound between the tongue and the soft palate. However,in
Swahili the sound *kh* is a stylistic feature, used by speakers with some
knowledge of (or pretensions to) Arabic, and simple *h* can always be
substituted for it. This is not the case with *gh*, however. Some non-
native speakers of Swahili may substitute *g* for *gh*, but this is not really
acceptable. *gh* represents a voiced velar fricative, and can be practised
by putting the tongue in the position for *g* and then moving it slightly
away from the soft palate, while continuing to force the breath out,
making voice. The sound is something like gargling.

▷　ghadhabu — 'anger, fury'
　　ghafula — 'suddenly'
　　ghali — 'expensive'
　　gharama — 'expense, outlay'
　　gharika — 'flood' n.
　　ghorofa — 'storey, flat'
　　ghoshi — 'adulterate', v.
　　ghuba — 'bay, inlet'
　　ghurika — 'be vain'

　　aghalabu — 'as a rule'
　　faragha — 'privacy'
　　lugha — 'language'
　　shughuli — 'business'

II

The general negative of the verb is formed by using the negative subject
prefix (exactly as with *-jambo*), and at the same time replacing the final
vowel in the verb stem with *-i*. So we have the verb *kununua* 'to buy',
ninanunua 'I am buying', and negative *sinunui* 'I don't buy, I am not buying.' You have already learned *sijui* — 'I don't know'. In the text in
section I we had *siwezi* 'I can't', meaning 'I'm not going to. I won't!'.)
The full paradigm is:

siwezi	I can't/won't
huwezi	you (sing.) can't
hawezi	he/she can't
hatuwezi	we can't
hamwezi	you (pl.) can't
hawawezi	they can't

(*siwezi* is also sometimes used to mean 'I'm not very well' — 'I can't
(work, get up etc!)')

If a verb stem begins with a vowel, the second person plural negative
prefix is *hamw-* (not *ham-*) e.g. *-uza* 'sell' gives *hamwuzi* 'you (pl.) don't
sell'.

Notice that there is no tense sign in this general negative. If you cannot do something, this is without reference to time (in English, too). Of course you could introduce a time word, e.g. *siwezi sasa* 'I can't (do it) now', implying that at some past or future date perhaps you could do it. There are forms of the negative associated with certain tenses, which will be dealt with later.

In the general negative form, problems about stress disappear. So although in verbs with one-syllable stems in the present continuous tense we introduced *-ku-* to carry the stress, as in *ninakula* 'I am eating' (stem *-la*), in the general negative this is not necessary. The stress is on the penultimate syllable, e.g. *síli* 'I don't eat, I'm not eating', *hatúli* 'we don't eat, we're not eating'. Somewhat similarly, in the verb *-enda* 'go', we saw that *-kw-* was inserted after the tense sign, e.g. *ninakwenda* 'I am going'. In the general negative this is not required, so the form is *siendi* 'I don't go, I'm not going', *hatuendi* 'we don't go, we're not going'.

III

(e) Write out the general negative forms of the verbs *kuchukua* 'to take, carry' and *kunywa* 'to drink'.

(f) Write answers in the negative to the following questions:

Unauza machungwa leo?
Mama ananunua ndizi?
Watoto wanataka kufanya kazi?
Wanafunzi wanasoma Kiingereza?
Mnapika keki?
Unaweza kuvunja noti ya shilingi kumi?

(g) Answer in the negative, then give the alternative:

Mnauza nazi? e.g. Siyo, hatuuzi nazi, *bali** tunauza nyanya.
Unakwenda dukani? (sokoni)
Bibi Maw anapika chai? (kahawa)
Wanafunzi wanakunywa maziwa? (bia)
Watoto wanakula keki? (*mkate* — 'bread' related to *-kata* 'cut')
Unataka kwenda sinema? (nyumbani)

*bali — 'but, on the other hand'

IV

(i) Some speakers, especially on the coast, use sounds derived from Arabic; and indeed many coastal people know Arabic well. Seafaring folk have relatives on the coasts of Arabia, and the very word Swahili is said to mean 'coast'. Many Swahili children attend Koranic schools where they learn to recite the Koran in Arabic even if they do not understand it, and many still learn the Arabic script before they learn the Roman. Things Arabic still have a certain prestige and an aura of civilisation; and indeed many items of Swahili vocabulary to do with learning, religion and jurisprudence etc. are borrowed from Arabic. Many second-language speakers of Swahili who have not this Arab-influenced background may yet aim at a style of pronunciation influenced by Arabic, even though they do not know the language. Of course, as in English with the pronunciation of initial *h* among uneducated speakers, Swahili speakers aiming at a 'high-class' pronunciation may make mistakes at times.

One useful effect of the influence of Arabic is that the two sounds represented in English by the letters *th* (as in the words *thigh* and *thy*) are distinctly spelt in Swahili. *th* represents *only* the sound as in *thigh*, and *dh* the sound as in *thy*.

Sounds in Swahili which are usually derived from Arabic are spelled th, dh, gh, h. However, some sounds may have Arabic-type varieties (usually because they derive from two or more distinct sounds in Arabic). These are:

   t, s, dh, h, (kh), k(q).

A glottal stop may also be heard. The pronunciation of vowels in words where consonants are given a 'dark' or 'glottal' quality is also often affected. A few examples follow of words with 'normal' and 'Arabic' pronunciations contrasted.

▷   (h)   sultani   'sultan'
         ramadhani   'Ramadan'
         safi   'ritually clean, pure'
         tafadhali   'be so kind'
         kadhi   'judge' n.
         haki   'rights'
         habari   'news'
         hotuba   'speech'
         arusi   'wedding'
         dhiki   'distress'
         maana   'meaning'

Note that such words are normally those with strong cultural associations.

(ii)   Negative of the verb *-taka* 'want'. Note that in the negative, the meaning of this verb is very strong. We had *-taka* used in the positive in Unit 13 (*anataka kununua mahindi* — 'he wants to buy maize'). In the negative, *sitaki* may literally mean 'I don't want (it)', but socially it means 'I refuse'. It is not acceptable, for example, when offered something to say *sitaki*, as this would constitute a very brusque refusal. The most you could say would be *sipendi* 'I don't like (it)' (*-penda*- 'like', 'love'), but better, as we have pointed out, to say of food or drink, *situmii* 'I don't take (it)'.

(iii)   Note that money values and therefore prices are different in Tanzania from Kenya.

Revision Exercises

(a)   Write answers:

Nani apike chai?
Wanafunzi wale nini?

Twende wapi sasa?
Ninunue nini leo?
Watoto waende wapi?
Nisome Kiswahili leo? Ndiyo, _____
Tufanye nini sasa?

(b)   Change the questions in (a) to the present continuous tense (-*na*-) where
      it makes sense.

(c)   Write new answers to (b), using the same tense (-*na*-).

(d)   Answer in the negative, giving a reason:

Niondoe vyombo? e.g. Siyo, usiondoe vyombo kwa sababu bado
   ninakunywa chai. (*bado* with a positive verb means 'still'*).

Wanafunzi wasome Kiswahili?
Tununue viazi?
Mwende nyumbani?
Mwalimu asomeshe Kiswahili?
Wazee waende kanisani?
Nipike kahawa sasa?
Ninunue sukari nyingi?
Mama akate keki?
Tunywe chai sasa?

*So note that *bado nina pesa* means 'I still have some money', *bado sina
pesa* means 'I haven't any money yet (but hope to get some in the
future)'.

Unit 15   Fungu la kumi na tano
Kwenda Mombasa (1) — Going to Mombasa (1)

I

(a) *imefika* — 'it has arrived' — referring to *gari*
kwa boti — 'by boat'
kesho — 'tomorrow'
reli — 'rail'
mbona? — 'whyever?' — this is a very strong form of the question 'why?'.
pamoja — 'together'. This is made up of a *pa-* prefix to do with place, plus the stem *-moja*, 'one, single'
tikiti — 'ticket'

Gari ya Bwana Harris imefika Mombasa, kwa boti.

▷   Bwana Harris: Lazima niende Mombasa kesho, kuchukua gari.*
Bibi Maw.:   Bahati yako. Unakwenda kwa reli?
Bw.H.:   Ndiyo. Mbona usije nami?
Bi.M.:   Nije mimi?
Bw.H.:   Ndiyo. Twende pamoja. Lakini lazima ununue tikiti.
Bi.M.:   Haya. Ngoja nijaribu.

*to get/collect (my) car.

....

karani — 'clerk'
lini? — 'when?' — always and only a question word.
kilasi — 'class' (*daraja* 'bridge' is used in Tanzania)
nafasi — 'room' 'opportunity'
dirisha — 'window'

Stesheni, ofisini.

▷   Bi.M.: Hujambo,
(continue greetings)
Ninataka kwenda Mombasa.
Karani: Unataka kwenda lini?
Bi.M.:   Ninataka kwenda kesho.
K.:   Unataka kilasi ya kwanza au ya pili?
Bi.M.:   Ya kwanza. Kuna nafasi?
K.:   Ndiyo, kuna nafasi. Lakini kwanza ununue tikiti.
Bi.M.:   Ninunue wapi tikiti?
K.:   Pale pale, dirishani pale. Halafu urudi hapa.
Bi.M.:   Haya.

....

mkata tikiti — literally 'the ticket-cutter' — any person who sells tickets.
-tegemea — 'expect', literally 'lean on'
nauli — 'fare'
-toa — 'offer, give out' the opposite of *-tia* 'put in'
nikupe — 'let me give you, I am giving you'

Dirishani.

▷   Bi.M.:   Hujambo
                    (continue greetings)
                    Ninataka tikiti ya kwenda Mombasa kesho.
Mkata tikiti: Tikiti moja tu?
Bi.M.:   Ndiyo, moja tu.
M.t.:   Kwenda na kurudi?
Bi.M.:   Siyo, kwenda tu. Ninategemea kurudi kwa gari.
M.t.:   Haya.
Bi.M.:   Nauli ni shilingi ngapi?
M.t.:   Shilingi elfu mbili mia saba na hamsini . . . Unatoa
                    shilingi elfu tatu. Nikupe shilingi mia mbili na
                    hamsini, pamoja na tikiti.
Bi.M.:   Haya.

       ....

nimesharudi — 'I'm back again!' 'I'm already back'
nipe — 'give me'
-andika — 'write'
jina — 'name', *jina lako* — 'your name', *jina langu* 'my name', *jina lako
    nani?* — (your name who) 'what is your name?'
nambari — 'number'
behewa — 'railway carriage'
godoro — 'mattress'
mablanketi — 'blankets'
-pata — 'get'
katika — 'in'
usinilipe — 'don't pay me'
mlipe — 'pay him', *mlipe Steward* — 'pay the Steward' (attendant)'.
    This structure will be dealt with later.
treni — 'train', *gari la moshi* (smoke-vehicle) 'train'
inaondoka — 'it (train) leaves'
kila — 'every'. This word is one of the very few that precede the noun
    they qualify.

Ofisini tena. ·

▷   Bi.M.: Haya bwana, nimesharudi.
K.:   Haya mama. Nipe tikiti. Ngoja niandike jina lako. Jina lako nani?
Bi.M.: Jina langu Bibi Maw.
K.:   Sasa, nambari ya behewa lako ni B 12.
Bi.M.: Haya. Na godoro na mablanketi, je?
K.:   Godoro na mablanketi unapata katika behewa.
Bi.M.: Nilipe?
K.:   Ndiyo, lakini usinilipe mimi. Mlipe Steward. Godoro shilingi
       thelathini na mablanketi shilingi sitini.

Bi.M.:   Haya. Treni inaondoka saa ngapi?
K.:   Inaondoka saa kumi na mbili na nusu ya usiku.
Bi.M.:   Kila siku?
K.:   Ndiyo, kila siku.
Bi.M.:   Na kufika Mombasa?*
K.:   Kufika Mombasa† inafika saa mbili ya asubuhi.
Bi.M.:   Haya, asante bwana.
K.:   Haya mama, ufike salama.

*kufika Mombasa? — 'arriving in Mombasa?'
†kufika Mombasa inafika . . . — 'as for arriving in Mombasa, it . . .'.

II

(i)   The infinitive form of the verb can be used for 'intention', also after verbs
      of wishing, willing, trying, and so on, e.g. *ninataka kununua tikiti* — 'I
      want to buy a ticket'. However, if the subject of the second verb is not
      the same as that of the first, it is necessary to use the subjunctive, e.g.
      ninataka ununue tikiti — 'I want you to buy a ticket', *anataka ninunue
      tikiti* — 'he wants me to buy a ticket' etc. Either verb can be in the
      negative, e.g. *sitaki ununue tikiti* — 'I don't want you to buy a ticket', and
      nataka usinunue tikiti — 'I want you not to buy a ticket'. The difference is
      subtle but real, and can sometimes be crucial. The negative infinitive has
      -*to*- before the stem, e.g. *kutonunua* — 'not to buy'. You might say to
      your husband, *jaribu kutokunywa bia leo usiku* — 'try not to drink (any)
      beer this evening'.

      A rather idiomatic use of the infinitive for a sort of 'reference' is found in
      the last paragraph of the text: *kufika Mombasa, inafika saa mbili ya
      asubuhi* — 'as for arriving in Mombasa, it arrives at eight in the morning';
      kunywa bia, anakunywa nyingi sana — 'as for . . .'.

(ii) Note that we have an agreement *l*- with -*a* in *gari la moshi*; contrast this
      with *gari ya Bwana Harris*. The word *gari* 'vehicle' if used for something
      small has *y*- agreement. Obviously a train is big, and so *gari la moshi*
      (vehicle-of-smoke) 'train' has an *l*- agreement which often (though not
      always) gives the idea of something large and cumbersome. This will be
      dealt with more fully later.

(iii) Notice the possessive forms in *jina lako* 'your name', *behewa lako* 'your
      carriage' and *jina langu* 'my name'. More on this in unit 16.

(iv) Note the expressions *kwa boti* 'by boat', *kwa reli* 'by rail' etc. Other
      means of travel are:

      kwa basi

kwa baisikeli

 kwa lori

 kwa ndege (*ndege* also means 'bird')

 kwa miguu (*miguu* is plural, 'feet, legs').

III

(b) **Ufahamu — Comprehension**.

Kwa nini Bwana Harris aende Mombasa?
Aende Mombasa kwa basi au vipi?
Kwa nini Bibi Maw aende stesheni?
Bibi Maw anunue tikiti ya kilasi gani?
Nini nauli ya kwenda Mombasa?
Nini nauli ya kwenda Mombasa na kurudi Nairobi?
Bwana Harris na Bibi Maw warudi Nairobi kwa reli?
Wapate wapi godoro na mablanketi?
Treni inachukua* saa ngapi kufika Mombasa?

*-*chukua* — 'take', here in sense of 'take time'.

(c) Jibu maswali:

Kwenda Nairobi kutoka London uende vipi?

Kwenda Mombasa kutoka Lamu wananchi waende vipi?

Kufika stesheni polisi kutoka British Council Bwana
   Harris aende vipi?

Kufika Hurlingham (a suburb) kutoka posta watu
   waende vipi?

Polisi waende njiani vipi?

Bwana Philip afike kazini vipi?

Watu waende vipi Kisumu kutoka[†] Nairobi?

Wananchi maskini waende vipi kazini?

(In the last two questions, the effect of moving the word *vipi* from its
neutral position — final in the clause — is to give it prominence, similar
to the effect in English of stressing the word.)

[†]*kutoka* — 'from'; *kutoka* is also a verb, meaning 'to leave'.

(d)   Jibu maswali:

Bwana Philip anataka kununua nini?

Bwana Harris anataka Bibi Maw afanye nini?

Mnataka kwenda wapi?

Mnataka twende wapi?

Unategemea kufika lini?

Unategemea nije lini?

Mwalimu anataka kusoma nini?   (Swahili)
Mwalimu anataka wanafunzi wasome nini?   (English)

(e)   How would you ask: and reply:
      What the fare to Kisumu is   2,600s
      What time the train to Kisumu
        leaves   at 9 a.m.
      Where you can get a mattress   in the carriage
      How much two return tickets
        to Kisumu cost   _____
      How much mattress and blankets
        cost together   _____

(f)   Jibu maswali:
      Unataka tikiti ngapi?   (3)
      Unataka kwenda leo?   (kesho)
      Kuna nafasi leo?   (kesho)
      Gari la moshi linafika Mombasa lini?
      Jina lako nani?

(g)   Make a list of all the loan words from English you recognize in this unit.

(h)   Write a conversation buying a ticket or tickets etc. for travel to Kisumu.

IV

The construction of the railway (begun in 1895) from Mombasa to Lake Victoria was a great achievement. The engineers contended with a fantastic variety of terrain, the most spectacular being the descent of some 2000 feet into the Rift Valley; the workers contended with a tremendous variety of climate and natural enemies from tsetse flies to man-eating lions; and the problems of logistics, politics and finance were a constant headache to the directors. Economically and politically the railway has been extremely important; it also introduced a new element into the complex East African racial scene, in that most of the labourers and many others employed were Indians, many of whom, with their families, found a new life in East Africa, often as successful entre-preneurs. The capital of Kenya, Nairobi, was itself founded as a rail depot, on a flat, rather swampy area just before the railway reaches the Kikuyu Escarpment, the Eastern edge of the Rift Valley; and it would probably never have been chosen as the site for an urban centre for any other reason.

For the visitor from Europe, travel on the railway is a delightful experience. Owing to the tremendous gradients (and perhaps the age of the track and rolling-stock) the train goes very slowly, frequently stopping at small stations. The variety of the landscape is fantastic, although unfortunately between Nairobi and Mombasa much of the journey is in the dark. There are compensations, however, for the sleeping-cars and the dining-car are relics of a bygone age, solid and still comfortable though shabby. The service from the staff is delightfully courteous, and the menus seem not to have varied since the railway was completed. A journey by train in East Africa for the European is a mixture of nostalgia and novelty, an experience not to be missed.

The railway is not, however, the chief mode of travel in East Africa, partly because the lines are not extensive. There are also buses, including long-distance buses. Within towns, especially Nairobi and Dar es Salaam the municipal buses are often very crowded and difficult to get on to. In Kenya there are additionally fleets of privately-owned small vans known as *matatu* 'threes' because originally they charged a flat fare of thirty cents (three 10-cent pieces). Fares are now much higher, but *matatu* still undercut the buses, and are more mobile. The vehicles are driven with panache and the drivers compete fiercely for passengers. They also carry a fare-collector who hangs out of the back. The *matatu* sweep up to the bus stops, the driver and conductor bellowing out their destinations. They get very crowded and are often involved in accidents, though with relatively surprisingly few fatalities. Only the most intrepid foreigners use them. Long-distance buses can be very useful, but except on the most frequented routes it is often maddeningly difficult for the foreigner to discover on what day or at what time the bus you want will leave. Taxis are widely used (especially in Kenya) and people who do not own cars will often, for example, hire a taxi to take them to Nairobi from Mombasa. The driver or the passengers will try to fill up the taxi and the expense will be shared. If you go in for such a scheme, some detours may be expected as passengers are dropped or picked up at odd destinations along the route; but it is by no means an expensive way to travel. Taxis in towns, or to and from the airport, can need watching, and the fare should always be agreed in advance.

Particularly in rural areas, the bicycle is a favourite mode of transport. Motorists should take care, however, as the roads are often very uneven and the cyclist may not be very skilled. Some cyclists, indeed, will leap into a ditch when they hear a car coming, a sad indication of their low expectations of consideration by drivers.

Much travel up and down the coast is by boat. Dhows still sail to and from the islands, trading between them and with the mainland. They do take passengers, who may well be expected to help if necessary — rowing out of harbour, hauling the sails, or bailing. Accommodation is primitive and the food is basic, but the Swahili are competent sailors and there is not much danger.

Of course most people walk a great deal from necessity. Children may walk up to 15 miles a day to and from school. Walking is not generally regarded as a pleasant recreation as some Europeans find it; although people (especially men) may take a social stroll in the cool of the evening, along the Mombasa waterfront, for example.

Travel by air is quite extensive, and although expensive, it is used by surprisingly large numbers of people, perhaps because of the long distances and the difficulties of surface travel.

Note. Since the incident in section I took place, an extra train has been put on between Nairobi and Mombasa, so that there are now two trains each night, one stopping more frequently than the other. Prices also rise continually.

Kwenda Mombasa (2)
Behewa la kulalia — In the sleeping-car

I

(a)   *kuketi* — 'to sit down' *karibu uketi* is higher style than *karibu kitini*.
peke yako — 'alone, on your own'.
mwingine — 'other (person)'.
wengi — 'many (people)'.
kuvuta — 'to drag' — *kuvuta sigara* — 'to smoke (cigarettes etc.)'
kuonekana — 'to appear, seem', *inaonekana* — 'it seems'
karamu — 'party'
kulalia — 'to sleep in'
kuingia — 'to enter'

Behewa la kulalia. Bibi Maw yumo.
Bwana Harris anaingia.

▷	Bwana Harris:	Kumbe uko hapa!
	Bibi Maw:	Ndiyo, nipo tu. Karibu. Karibu uketi.
	Bw.H.:	Nimeshakaa. Uko peke yako?
	Bi.M.:	Ndiyo, hakuna mtu mwingine.
	Bw.H.:	Basi, bahati yako. Katika behewa langu wako watu wengi.
	Bi.M.:	Pole bwana.
	Bw.H.:	Tena wanakunywa bia na kuvuta sigara. Inaonekana ni karamu.
	Bi.M.:	Pole sana. Basi, karibu kwangu.*
	Bw.H.:	Haya, asante.

*karibu kwangu — 'welcome to my place'
....

kuonyesha — 'to show'
tikiti zenu — 'your (pl.) tickets'
ndiye — strong form of 'be', 3rd person singular.
kukupatia — 'to get for you'

Kandakta anaingia.

▷	Kandakta:	Hamjambo.
		(continue greetings)
		Onyesheni tikiti zenu. (Anatazama tikiti.) Wewe ndiye Bwana Harris?
	Bw.H.:	Ndiyo.
	K.:	Basi bwana, behewa lako namba ngapi?
	Bw.H.:	Namba B3, lakini wako watu wengi katika behewa langu.
	K.:	Ee, ngoja nijaribu kukupatia nafasi penginepo.
	Bw.H.:	Haya.

Kandakta anaondoka

liko — 'is' (place, agreeing with *behewa*)
kukuonyesha — 'to show you'
kukuchukulia — 'to carry for you'
mizigo — 'luggage'
kupaona — 'to see (a place)'

Kandakta anarudi.

> K.:　　　Hodi.
　　　　　(continue greetings)
　　　　　Basi bwana, una nafasi katika behewa la C20.
　Bw.H.:　Asante sana. Behewa liko wapi hasa?
　K.:　　　Njoo nikuonyeshe. Nikuchukulie mizigo?
　Bw.H.:　Bado. Twende tupaone kwanza.
　K.:　　　Haya.

Kandakta na Bwana Harris wanaondoka.

　　.......................

behewa lako — 'your carriage'
mbali — 'far'
kupita — 'to pass'
kulia — 'to eat in'
kuacha — 'to leave something', 'to leave off'
kitabu changu — 'my book'

Bwana Harris anarudi.

> Bw.H.:　Haya, nimesharudi.
　Bi.M.:　Behewa lako liko wapi?
　Bw.H.:　Liko mbali sana. Unapita behewa la kulia, halafu ni behewa
　　　　　la tatu.
　Bi.M.:　Kweli mbali kidogo.
　Bw.H.:　Nimeacha kitabu changu huko, basi.

　　.......................

magodoro — 'mattresses' (plural of *godoro*)
kutengeneza — 'to fix' (mend, make etc.)
vitanda — 'beds' (plural of *kitanda*)
kuweka — 'to put down, in, on etc'.

Steward anafika.

▷ S.:　　　Hodi
　　　　　(continue greetings)
　　　　　Nilete magodoro sasa?
　Bw.H.:　Haya, lete tu.

Steward analeta.

　S.:　　　Nitengeneze vitanda?
　Bw.H.:　Bado kidogo. Lete kwanza chai.
　S.:　　　Haya.

　　.......................

S.:   Hodi
           (continue greetings)
           Haya, bwana, chai.
Bw.H.: Haya, weka mezani.

Steward anaondoka

....

afadhali — 'it would be better'
kwako — 'your place'
ukipenda — 'if you want'
kukaribishwa — 'to be made welcome'
hata — 'even', *kama* — 'if'; *hata kama* — 'if perhaps' (even if)
kutatokea — 'there will occur'
hatari — 'danger'
kukulinda — 'to guard you'

▷   Bw.H.: Labda afadhali niende zangu, lakini hapa pana starehe*.
         Bi.M.:   Kumbe kwako mbali sana. Ukipenda kukaa hapa,
                  unakaribishwa.
         Bw.H.: Nikae?
         Bi.M.:   Karibu tu.
         Bw.H.: Basi, na hata kama kutatokea jambo la hatari usiku, mimi nipo
                  tu, nikulinde.
         Bi.M.:   Ndiyo.

hapa pana starehe 'it's peaceful (comfortable) here'
         ....

kukusaidia — 'to help you'
mlango — 'door'
kugonga — 'to knock'
kimya — 'silence'

Kandakta anarudi.
▷   K.:   Hodi.
                   (continue greetings)
                   Basi bwana, nikusaidie kuchukua mizigo?
         Bw.H.: Bado kidogo.
         K.:   Haya.

Anaondoka.
         ....

Steward anarudi.

         S.:   Hodi
                   (continue greetings)
                   Nitengeneze vitanda sasa?
         Bw.H.: Haya, tengeneza tu.

         ....

Usiku.

> Mlangoni: Gonga gonga gonga!
> Bi.M.:   Yuko mtu mlangoni!

Kimya.

....

kulia — 'to eat in'
kitabu hiki — 'this book'
kitu — 'thing'
sawa — 'all right, as it should be'; *sawasawa* — intensive of *sawa*

> Asubuhi, katika behewa la kulia. (Not all trains have this.)
Kandakta anafika.

> K.:   Habari za asubuhi?
>   (continue greetings) Hiki kitabu chako, bwana?*
> Bw.H.:   Ee, ndiyo, asante sana.
> K.:   Kila kitu sawa?
> Bw.H.:   Sawasawa kabisa.
> K.:   Haya.

Anaondoka.

Hiki kitabu chako? — 'Is this your book?'
Kitabu hiki chako? — 'Is this book yours?'
Kitabu chako hiki? — 'Is your book this one?'; 'Is it your book,
this one?'

....

hukusikia — 'didn't you hear/you didn't hear'
kugongwa — 'knocking (by someone)' (This is actually a passive form
                and will be dealt with later.)
jana — 'yesterday'
sikusikia — 'I didn't hear'
bila shaka — 'without doubt'
alitaka — 'he wanted'
kunilinda — 'to guard me'
watu hawa — 'these people'
kushikilia — 'to cling on to'
desturi — 'custom(s)'
zamani — 'long ago'

> Bi.M.:   Hukusikia kugongwa mlangoni, jana usiku?
> Bw.H.:   Sikusikia.
> Bi.M.:   Bila shaka kandakta alitaka kunilinda na hatari za usiku!*
> Bw.H.:   Kweli watu hawa wanashikilia desturi za zamani!
> Bi.M.:   Sana.

*na here means 'from'

II

(i) **Noun classes 7/8 and 5/6.**

You will have noticed some nouns with new plural forms, e.g. *kitanda*
'bed': *vitanda* 'beds'. Nouns which have *ki-* in the singular have *vi-* in the

plural. Other examples in the text are *kitu* 'thing': *vitu* 'things', and *kitabu* 'book': *vitabu* 'books'. A few words in this class have *ch-*: *vy-* as their prefixes; such nouns are those whose stems begin with a vowel, e.g. *choo* 'lavatory, toilet': *vyoo*. *chakula* 'food' (plural *vyakula*) is also in this class, which is given the numbers 7/8 in the Bantu system of class numbering; in other words, *chakula* may be said to be 'in' class 7, and *vyakula* 'in' class 8.

Another class of nouns is those whose plurals begin with *ma-*. Most of the nouns in this class have no singular prefix. So we have *godoro* / *magodoro* 'mattress / mattresses', and *behewa* / *mabehewa* 'carriage/ carriages'. A few nouns in this class have a singular prefix *ji-* or *j-*, e.g. *jicho* 'eye': *macho* 'eyes'. *jina* 'name' has plural *majina*. This class is numbered 5/6, i.e., *jina* may be said to be 'in' class 5, *majina* 'in' class 6. (It also contains most names of types of people that are not in class 1/2; e.g. *bwana* : *mabwana* ; *bibi* : *mabibi*.)

Generally speaking, nouns 'in' odd-numbered classes are singular, e.g. *mtoto*, class 1; *kitanda*, class 7; *godoro*, class 5; and those in even-numbered are plural, e.g. *watoto*, class 2; *vitanda*, class 8; *magodoro*, class 6; *but this rule is not invariable*.

(ii) **Possessives**

Possessive adjectives (my, your, etc.) correspond to the personal pronouns in Swahili. We have had *jina lako* 'your name', *behewa lako* 'your carriage', *jina langu* 'my name' and other forms. The full paradigm of possessive forms with words like *behewa* in class 5 is:

behewa langu	my carriage
behewa lako	your carriage
behewa lake	his/her carriage
behewa letu	our carriage
behewa lenu	your (pl.) carriage
behewa lao	their carriage.

You will notice that the *l-* is constant; also that *l-* has been associated with *behewa* in other contexts, e.g. *behewa la tatu* and *behewa liko mbali sana*. You will therefore deduce that the words *jina* and *behewa* belong to a class (5) that has *l-* as an agreement marker. You will also deduce that the possessive word consists of a prefix (*l-* in this case) plus the roots *-angu, -ako, -ake*, etc. Plural nouns in class 6 have possessive agreements in *y-*, notwithstanding that their own prefix is *ma-*.

Words which do not change their form from singular to plural (i.e. those in class 9/10), e.g. *kazi* 'work', you already know are associated with *y-* in the singular and *z-* in the plural (as in *kazi ya baba* : *kazi za baba*). We have also already used the form *habari zako?*. You will thus be able to deduce the forms of the possessive for words in this class.

Nouns of class 7/8 form their singulars and plurals with *ki-*, *vi-* as we have seen above in (i), e.g. *kitabu* 'book', *vitabu* 'books'. Their agreements with the possessive are *ch-* and *vy-*, since the possessive stems all begin with a vowel. e.g. *kitabu changu* 'my book'; *vitabu vyangu* 'my books'.

Possessive adjectives also function as possessive pronouns, i.e. they can be used alone without nouns, e.g. *kitabu changu* 'my book': *changu* 'mine':

Hiki kitabu chako?   '(Is) this your book?'
Ndiyo, changu.   'Yes, (it's) mine.'

Possessives can also refer to place. Thus Bibi Maw says 'Karibu kwangu' 'Welcome to my place'. The *kw-* in *kwangu* is the 'same' as *ku-* in *kuna*, *hakuna* 'there is/is not' which we have already met. *ku-* becomes *kw-* before a vowel.

(iii) **ndiye**

This is made up of *ndi-* plus *-ye* (3rd person singular). *wewe ndiye Bwana Harris?* means something like 'Bwana Harris is that you?' 'You are actually Bw. Harris, are you?'. This *ndi-*, a strong form of the copula, can be prefixed (like *na-*) to all shortened forms of the personal pronoun, viz.:

    ndimi   'it is really me'
    ndiwe
    ndiye
    ndisi
    ndinyi
    ndio.

The form with the 3rd person singular is by far the most commonly used.

(*ndiyo, siyo* may refer to the idea of class 6 and could be said to have reference to the plural of *jambo*, i.e. *mambo* 'affairs, matters, subjects, ideas' or *maneno* 'words'. The *-y-* is a marker of class 6, the *-o* is a reference marker. So *ndiyo* means something like 'that (which you said) is so'; *siyo* 'that (idea) is not so'.)

(iv) **Prepositional extensions of the verb**

Verbs in Swahili are structurally very interesting. We have seen that the final vowel in a verb is usually *-a*, but can be *-e* for the 'subjunctive', or *-i* for the 'general negative'. Before this final vowel, but after the verb root (the lexical element, the part which has meaning in the real world), so-called 'extensions' can be inserted. One of the most common is the 'prepositional' extension. Examples of verbs with this extension are found in the text:

kulalia 'to sleep in', from *kulala* 'to sleep'
-patia 'get for', from *-pata* 'to get'

You will see that the vowel *-i-* has been inserted in these cases. There is also:

-chukulia 'carry for', from *-chukua* 'carry'
where *-li-* has been inserted; and:

-shikilia 'cling on to', from *-shika* 'hold'
which is a so-called 'double' prepositional form, and has both *-i-* and *-li-* inserted.

We could also have:

kuletea 'to bring for', from *kuleta* 'to bring'
with *-e-* inserted; and:

kuondolea 'to remove for', from *kuondoa* 'to remove'
with *-le-* inserted.

From the following examples you should be able to deduce a set of rules
for forming the prepositional extension of the Swahili verb:

-fika	-fikia
-leta	-letea
-pata	-patia
-soma	-somea
-fuma 'knit'	-fumia
-sikia 'hear'	-sikilia
-pokea 'receive'	-pokelea
-twaa 'take'	-twalia
-ondoa	-ondolea
-nunua	-nunulia

The rules may be formulated thus:

(a) If the verb root ends in a consonant, the extension will be *-i-* or *-e-*; if
the root ends in a vowel, the extension will be *-li-* or *-le-*.
(b) If the last vowel in the root is *i, a* or *u*, the extension will have *i*; if the
last vowel in the root is *e* or *o*, the extension will have *e*. (This rule is
one of so-called 'vowel harmony'.)

We can summarise these rules in a grid:

root ends in   **root ends in**
consonant   **vowel**

-i-	-li-
-e-	-le-

final vowel in root i, a, u

final vowel in root e, o

The choice of vowel in prepositional forms of verbs with one-syllable
stems is not predictable, e.g. *kuja: kujia; kula: kulia*; but *kunywa:
kunywea*. These forms simply have to be learned; but there are not
many of them.

Verbs of non-Bantu origin can often be recognised by the fact that they
do not normally have a final vowel *-a*. An example is the verb *kurudi* 'to
return'. Such verbs are mostly Arabic, though there is at least one
English one: *kupasi* 'to pass' (the ball in football). Such verbs form their
prepositional extensions mainly by addition, e.g.

kurudi	kurudia
kusamehe 'forgive'	kusamehea
kusahau 'forget'	kusahaulia

There are not many such verbs; the vast majority are regular.

The meaning of the prepositional form is *normally* to do something to or
for another person (but see also unit 25). So in the above text we had:
nikuchukulie mizigo? 'shall I carry the bags for you?'

But other prepositional ideas may be conveyed, e.g.

behewa la kulalia   'carriage to sleep in (sleeping-car)'
behewa la kulia   'carriage to eat in (dining-car)'

The precise meaning of a prepositional verb (indeed of *any* word) depends on the context (though in some cases it has a special meaning which must be learnt). A double prepositional form generally has the additional effect of intensifying the meaning of the original lexis, e.g.

wanashikilia desturi   'they cling to the customs'

We may not always in English recognise the prepositional idea which is clear to a Swahili. For example, compare:

maji ya kunywa   'water for drinking/to drink/drinking-water'
with   gilasi ya kunywea   'glass for drinking (from), drinking-glass'.

In general, instruments whose use is described by this structure require the use of the prepositional extension, e.g.

sindano ya kushonea   'needle for sewing with, sewing-needle'

(v) Note in the forms:

kukupatia   'to get for you'
nikuchukulie   'let me carry for you'
nikusaidie   'let me help you'
nikulinde   'let me protect you'

the second syllable (morpheme) in each example (*-ku-*) is an 'object prefix' referring to 2nd person singular 'you'. Also the *-ni-* in

anilinde   'let him protect me'

is similarly an object prefix referring to 1st person singular (me). This phenomenon will be dealt with more fully later.

III

Ufahamu Comprehension.

(b) Jibu maswali. Answer the questions.

1 Wako watu wangapi kwanza katika behewa la Bi. Maw?
2 Kwa nini Bw. Harris hataki kukaa katika behewa lake la kwanza?
3 Watu katika behewa la Bwana Harris wanafanya nini?
4 Kwa nini Kandakta anaingia kwanza?
5 Halafu Kandakta anakwenda wapi? (*kumpatia* 'to get for him')
6 Behewa la C20 liko mbali?
7 Kwa nini Bwana Harris hataki Kandakta achukulie mizigo?
8 Bwana Harris anaacha kitabu chake wapi?
9 Kwa nini Bwana Harris anaacha kitabu chake huko?
10 Kwa nini Bwana Harris anapenda behewa la Bibi Maw?
11 Kwa nini Kandakta hataki Bw. Harris akae katika behewa la Bi. Maw?

(c) Complete the paradigms:

1 ninaingia behewa langu
   unaingia behewa lako
   etc.
2 ninanunua kitabu changu
   etc.

3 nina bahati yangu
etc.
4 ninataka kwenda zangu
etc.
5 ninamkaribisha mama kwangu 'I am inviting mother to my place'
etc.

(d) How would you tell someone to:
bring your blanket
take away his (someone else's) things
look at his (own) books
make our tea
eat our biscuits
make his (own) bed
bring their (some other people's) blankets.

(e) Jaza mapengo. Fill in the blanks:

magodoro _____ (your, pl.)
vitu   _____ (their)
kitabu   _____ (her)
kahawa   _____ (your, sing.)
majina   _____ (my)
behewa   _____ (our)
keki (pl.) _____ (your, sing.)

(f) Give the prepositional forms of the following verbs:

kuandika —	(to write for)
kufanya	(to do for)
kufika	(to turn up)
kugonga	(to knock for)
kuja	(to come to)
kujaribu	(to try out)
kukaa	(to stay for)
kuleta	(to bring for)
kulipa	(to pay back)
kungoja	(to wait for)
kununua	(to buy for)
kunywa	(to drink from)
kuongeza	(to increase for)
kupika	(to cook for)
kupita	(to pass by)
kupunguza	(to reduce for)
kusema	(to speak for)
kusimama	(to stand over, supervise)
kutaka	(to wish for)
kutengeneza	(to arrange/mend for)
kutia	(to put in for)
kutoa	(to take out for)
kuuza	(to sell for/to)

(g) Write a conversation on a bus. Additional vocabulary you may require is
     maili 'mile(s)'; *kutelemka* 'to get down/off'.

(h) You may note the expression *nakutakia kila la heri* 'I wish you every
     blessing', said on parting. Response *na wewe pia* 'You too'.

IV

The 'Conductor' on the train to Mombasa was obviously shocked at the
possibility that Bwana Harris and Bibi Maw might share a sleeping
carriage, since they were plainly not married; and indeed it is not
normally possible to book shared accommodation on the train for people
of different sexes, except for married couples. This reflects a more strict
view of what constitutes proper behaviour between the sexes,
especially in public, than is common in Europe, and also, conversely, the
presumption that no two people of the opposite sex would share a railway carriage, for example, unless there was a close physical relationship. If Bwana Harris thought the views of the sleeping-car attendant
were old-fashioned and/or unnecessarily suspicious, the attendant
thought the behaviour of Bwana Harris and Bibi Maw was improper.
From his point of view it certainly was. Indeed, many Swahili people
have a very poor view of the morals of Westerners. One must realise
that most people acquire an impression of life in Europe and the U.S.A.
from films and television, much of which suggests great affluence,
violence, and promiscuity. Even tourists, from whom much is forgiven,
often give great offence, for example, by wandering about in bikinis. Dis-
approval is not often directly expressed to the offender, who is generally
pointedly ignored, but letters to local newspapers and occasional
petitions for some kind of regulation of dress in public are an indication of
feeling.

After puberty, young Swahili people are more or less segregated.
Schools are not normally mixed, and after school girls spend most of
their spare time at home, typically busy with domestic matters or visiting
their women friends and being visited. There are some women's
organisations, but most women find their social life at home, visiting
friends and relatives, or in the many ceremonies constantly occurring —
religious ceremonies of course, and also funerals, births, and especially
weddings. Young men go out more in gangs, play football and other
games and sports; and as they get older, their social life tends to centre
more round the mosque with its discussion groups. Even at home the
sexes are somewhat segregated in practice. When the men are at
home, they and their visitors tend to be sitting in the reception room, and
the women and children in the kitchen most of the time.

Swahili women are ideally supposed to be modest and self-effacing.
When they go out they wear a black enveloping garment called a *buibui*
which covers them from head to foot and can also be drawn over the
face. Women themselves generally simply regard this as a normal
proper outer wear for adults; but a few occasionally express feelings if
pressed — one common one being that it can be a useful disguise!
Under the *buibui* many women wear western-style dresses, but some

wear the *kanga*, two brightly patterned cloths, one tied under the arms, covering the body, and the other draped over the head and shoulders. It is very comfortable to wear in the heat. Young men generally wear western clothes; older men often wear a *kanzu*, a long white garment, also very comfortable, though sometimes over a shirt and trousers, with jacket above; and a *kofia*, a small embroidered white cap.

While it may sometimes happen, it is not the normal thing for a young man and woman to go out alone, even when they are engaged. Marriages are still very much a family affair, if not actually arranged, and anxious parents seek out suitable matches for their children, and go carefully into the backgrounds of any possible partners their children may suggest. Opportunities are made for the young people to get to know one another, but generally in company.

Men and women are not demonstrative to each other in public. In fact gestures of affection in public are more common between individuals of the same sex, and should not be misunderstood by the Westerner. For example, men may sometimes be seen walking along holding hands. This is friendship and nothing more. Conversely, people (especially from the country) may walk in single file in the streets, talking quite amicably. Women habitually walk behind men, either directly behind or beside them but half a pace behind. This *may* be seen as reflecting custom in dangerous country, where the man walks ahead with the spear and the woman follows with the bundles, children etc. Among Swahilis it reflects traditional ideas of respect. This respect between the sexes is two-way in a Muslim community, though it may not have that appearance to the Westerner. A good reputation is of great importance to a Swahili man or woman, and loose sexual behaviour, or the appearance of it, is greatly frowned upon.

All this is not to say that there are not such things in East Africa as pimps and prostitutes of both sexes. There are, especially in towns. But it is probably true to say that there is a sharper distinction between the sexual and social behaviour of a 'decent' person and that of a prostitute or gigolo in many African societies than is found in some Western societies today.

Jamaa — The family
Matamshi: Mkazo — Pronunciation: stress

I

Vocabulary note

From this point on in the course, new vocabulary will be listed following the text, not preceding it. The learner should try to understand the text, guessing the meaning of the new words from the context as far as possible, before checking them below.

Try to fill in the agreements in this text. Then correct yourself from the tape.

(a) Bibi Maw pamoja na mpwa wake Daudi (David) wako njiani.
     Wanakutana na Bwana Harris.

>
Bw. Harris:	Hujambo Bibi Joan.
Bi. Maw.:	Sijambo Bwana Stuart. Habari za siku nyingi?
Bw.H.:	Nzuri tu. Habari zako?
Bi.M.:	Nzuri. Bwana Stuart, huyu ni mtoto wangu.
Bw.H.:	Ala! Mtoto -ako, eh?
Bi.M.:	Ndiyo, mtoto -angu -a kwanza. . . . Kusema kweli, ni mtoto -a marehemu kaka -angu.
Bw.H.:	Oho. Mtoto -a kaka -ako, eh? Jina -ake nani?
Bi.M.:	Jina -ake Daudi.
Bw.H.:	Hujambo Daudi. Nimefurahi sana kujuana nawe.
Daudi:	-jambo Bwana Harris. Hata mimi nimefurahi. Na wewe hujambo?
Bw.H.:	Mimi sijambo sana. Kumbe unajua jina -angu!
D.:	Ndiyo, bwana. Nimeona jina -ako mara nyingi.
Bw.H.:	Ala! Namna gani?
D.:	Ninasoma Kiswahili, na nimeona jina -ako katika kitabu -enu.
Bw.H.:	Lakini kitabu -etu bado tayari.
D.:	Ndiyo, lakini shangazi langu, Bibi Maw, -ko katika kuandika.
Bw.H.:	Ndiyo, kweli. Haya, tutaonana, Daudi.
D.:	Inshallah, bwana. Kwa heri bwana.
Bw.H.:	Kwa heri Daudi. Kwa heri Bibi Joan.
Bi.M.:	Kwa heri Bwana Stuart, kwa heri -a kuonana.
Bw.H.:	Haya, kwa herini.

Maneno mapya — new vocabulary:

mpwa — 'nephew/niece; child of sister'
kukutana — 'to meet (with)'

huyu — 'this (person)'
marehemu — 'the late, the deceased'
kaka — 'brother; elder brother'
nimefurahi — 'I am happy'
kujuana — 'to get to know'
hata mimi — 'I too' (lit. 'even I')
nimeona — 'I have seen'
mara — 'time(s)'
namna — 'sort'; *namna gani?* — 'how can that be?' 'What do
    you mean?'
shangazi — 'father's sister'
yuko katika kuandika — 'she is engaged in writing'
tutaonana — 'we shall meet again'
Inshallah — 'God willing'

II

(i) **Possessives of animates**.

Possessives of nouns in class 1/2 have prefix *w-* for both singular and plural, e.g.

mtoto wangu : watoto wangu
mtoto wako etc.

However, as we have seen, some nouns delineating people are 'in' class 5/6, e.g. *bibi*: *mabibi*. Others are 'in' class 9/10, e.g. *ndugu* 'brother(s), sister(s)'. All these nouns, confusingly, have possessives as if they were in class 9/10, i.e.

bibi yangu   ndugu yangu
mabibi zangu   ndugu zangu

though you may also *occasionally* hear *shangazi langu*, as in the text — though more as a joke than anything. And, alas for general rules, the word *bwana* has *w-*, i.e. *bwana wangu*. A few nouns for people are 'in' class 7/8, e.g. *kipofu*: *vipofu* 'blind person(s)'. These nouns are mainly names of persons with some defect. Animals are in class 9/10 in the sense that they are not distinguished as to singular and plural in the form of the noun, but they have possessive agreements as if they were people in the singular, e.g. *ng'ombe wangu* 'my cow', but often as class 10 in the plural, e.g. *ng'ombe zangu* 'my cows'.

However, all nouns naming people or animals normally have all agreements other than possessives as if they were in class 1/2, e.g.:

mtoto wako		yuko shambani?
ndugu yako	mmoja	
ng'ombe wako		anataka nini?
kipofu		

watoto wako		wako shambani?
ndugu zako	wawili	
ng'ombe zako		wanataka nini?
vipofu		

Sometimes some names of close relatives are combined with some possessives, e.g. *mamangu, mamako, mamake; babangu, babako, babake; nduguye, nduguze*. Unfortunately no rules can be given for what can occur; the student should use only those he hears and is sure of. (I have heard *nyumbake*, but am not sure how widely acceptable the form is.) The examples given below are the most common ones.

mamangu	from	mama yangu	'my mother'
mamako		mama yako	'your mother'
mamake		mama yake	'his/her mother'
babangu		baba yangu	'my father'
babako		baba yako	'your father'
babake		baba yake	'his/her father'
nduguyo		ndugu yako	'your sister/brother'
nduguye		ndugu yake	'his/her sister/brother'
nduguzo		ndugu zako	'your sisters/brothers'
nduguze		ndugu zake	'his/her sisters/brothers'
mwanangu		mwana wangu	'my child, son'
mwanao		mwana wako	'your child'
mwanawe		mwana wake	'his/her child'
wanangu		wana wangu	'my children'
wanao		wana wako	'your children'
wanawe		wana wake	'his/her children'
mumeo		mume wako	'your husband'
mumewe		mume wake	'her husband'
mkeo		mke wako	'your wife'
mkewe		mke wake	'his wife'
mwenzangu		mwenzi wangu	'my friend'

(for other forms of this word see Unit 28).

A few other words are formed on the same principle, e.g. *baadaye* 'after-wards' (Unit 12), from *baada yake* (*baada* — 'after', Unit 20); *mwishowe* 'finally', from *mwisho* 'end' + *wake*.

(ii) **Possessives with -a**

Other possessive structures are formed with *-a*, cf. *habari za asubuhi, kazi ya mwalimu*, etc. Names of people and animals normally have *w*-prefix, so we get:

    mtoto wa mwalimu
    watoto wa mwalimu
    bwana wa Bibi Hadija
    ng' ombe wa mzee
    etc.

except, as with possessives, where *y-* or *z-* is used. For example *kaka ya bibi Maw* 'Miss Maw's brother' cf. *ng'ombe za mwalimu* 'the teacher's cows'.

Nouns in other classes have agreements with *-a* as for the possessives, e.g.

    jina la mwalimu   (cf. jina lake)
    majina ya mwalimu   (majina yake)

kitabu cha mwalimu   (kitabu chake)
vitabu vya mwalimu   (vitabu vyake)
nyumba ya mwalimu   (nyumba yake)
nyumba za mwalimu   (nyumba zake)

This -a is sometimes called the '-a of relationship', and we have seen it functioning with a slightly different meaning in *kilasi ya kwanza* 'first class' etc.

(iii) **Locative nouns** (e.g. *shambani, nyumbani*) have possessive and other agreements in *p-, kw-, mw-*, according to meaning, e.g.
   nyumbani pa mzee   'right at the old man's house'
   nyumbani pake   'right at his house'
   nyumbani kwa mzee   'at the old man's house'
   nyumbani kwake   'at his house'
   nyumbani mwa mzee   'in the old man's house'
   nyumbani mwake   'in his house'

Without the noun, such possessives alone refer to place, so in the previous Unit, Bi. Maw said *karibu kwangu* 'welcome to my (place)'

(iv) **The reciprocal extension**

The verb stems -*kutana* 'meet together', -*juana* 'get to know each other', -*onana* 'see each other', derive from simple forms -*kuta* 'come across', -*jua* 'know', and -*ona* 'see'. You will see that an extension -*an*- is inserted before the final vowel of the stem. This changes the meaning of the verb to make the action mutual or reciprocal. Sometimes the meaning of a reciprocal verb may be slightly different from mere reciprocity, e.g.

kupiga 'to strike';   *kupigana* 'to fight'.

It may connote 'together', e.g. *kulana* (from *kula*) may mean 'to eat together' or 'to eat each other' according to the context. Sometimes care is needed in use, for example *kulalana* (from *kulala* 'to sleep') means 'to have sexual intercourse'. Occasionally the meaning seems quite different, e.g. *kupata* 'to get'; *kupatana* 'to agree'.

Very often the subject of a verb with a recriprocal extension is plural, e.g. *tunapendana* 'we love each other'; but if a person other than the subject is named, as in

   wanakutana na Bwana Harris 'they meet Bw. Harris'

the grammatical structure requires the linker *na* 'with'. We can have a singular subject of a reciprocal verb if another protagonist is mentioned, e.g.

   Mohammed Ali anapigana na watu wengi.

We can also say:

   Wairaki na Waajemi wanapigana sana 'The Iraqis and the Iranians are fighting hard'.

A reciprocal extension can be added to a prepositional extension, e.g.

   wanafunzi wanasomeana vitabu vyao 'the students are reading their books to one another'.

(v) **Group stress**

We have seen that each word of more than one syllable in Swahili has a stress on the penultimate syllable when the word is said in isolation. However, when words are combined in certain kinds of groups, they may lose their individual stress. In so-called 'nominal' groups, i.e. groups normally consisting of a noun plus one or more qualifiers, only one stress is normally heard, and that is on the penultimate syllable of the last word in the group. So in *mtoto wangu*, stress is only heard on *wangu*, not on *mtoto*. Other examples from the text are:

siku nyingi
namna gani
kitabu chenu
shangazi langu.

III

(b) In the following pronunciation exercise, pay particular attention to the stressing in the groups *underlined*:

> Habari za *siku nyingi?*
Wako *watu wengi* sokoni.
Leo tunafanya *kazi kubwa.*
Twende *nyumbani kwangu*, mama.
Watoto wangu wako hospitalini.
Mama ananunua *vyakula vingi.*
Mtoto wa kwanza apate keki.
Ndugu zangu wote wanasoma Kiswahili.

(c) How would you ask someone if his

parents are still

   is still

   is still

are still

(d) How would you ask who has the

 belonging to

 belonging to

 belonging to

 belonging to

 belonging to

 belonging to

(e) Fill in the blanks:

__toto (pl.) __ko __ko wapi? __ko   __a

Bwana Harris __ko wapi? __mo __ake

__anafunzi (sing.) __etu __ko wapi hasa? __po __a askari.

__zee (pl.) __angu __nakwenda __a Mhindi.

Ng'ombe (pl.) __enu __nakaa wapi? __nakaa __tu.

(f) Give the reciprocal form of the following verbs, and make up a sentence using each:

kupenda   kupata
kujua   kupita
kusomesha   kugonga

(g) Give the prepositional reciprocal forms of the following verbs, and make up a sentence using each:

kununua   kungoja
kutia   kuuza
kuleta   kupika
kupata

(h) **Mchezo: Jamaa**. Game: 'Happy Families.'

Make cards for the characters out of the following list, two families for each player. (They can be simply drawn on scraps of paper.) Display your cards to the other players, naming them, e.g.

Huyu ni Bwana Chaki. Bwana Chaki ni mwalimu.

The other members of Bwana Chaki (chalk)'s family are:

Bibi Chaki, mke wa mwalimu
Kaka Chaki, mtoto wa kiume wa mwalimu (Brother, son)
Dada Chaki, mtoto wa kike wa mwalimu (Sister, daughter)

Other heads of families suggested are:

Bwana Unga, mpishi (Flour, cook)
Bwana Mbao, seremala (Planks, carpenter)

Bwana Chupa, mlevi (Bottle, drunkard)
Bwana Bunduki, askari (Gun, policeman)
Bwana Dawa, mgonjwa (Medicine, patient)
Bwana Jembe, mkulima (Hoe, farmer)
Bwana Upepo, nahodha (Wind, ship's captain)
Bwana Chewa, mvua samaki (Rock cod, fisherman)
Bwana Fimbo, mzee (Stick, old man)
Bwana Mfuko, mwizi (Bag, thief)
Bwana Mtego, mwindaji (Trap, hunter)
Bwana Dhahabu, mtajiri (Gold, rich man)

When families have been displayed, shuffle and share out the cards. Player A asks player B for a card he needs. He must already have at least one of the family he is collecting. The aim is to collect complete families. Player A asks:

Bwana/Bibi B, una Bwana Bunduki, askari?

Player B answers either: Ndiyo, ninaye*
                  or: Siyo, sinaye*

*Notice that when no object is present, the abbreviated form -ye for third person singular is added to nina- and sina-. ninaye 'I have him/her', sinaye 'I have not got him/her' -o could also be added for 3rd person plural, e.g. anao 'he has them'.

If the answer is yes, Player A says:
    Nipe tu,

and Player B hands over the card, saying:
    Haya, chukua.

Player A says:
    Sasa ni zamu yangu tena (zamu 'turn') and asks again for another card.

If Player B has not got the card asked for, and answers:
    Siyo, sinaye,

Player A says:
    Nimeshindwa. Sasa ni zamu yako. (nimeshindwa 'I'm defeated')

The game continues until one player has got all his families, when he cries:
    Nimeshinda! 'I've won!'

All count their families, the scorer asking: Una jamaa ngapi? to each player. The game can be played as many times as liked; finally one person is acknowledged to be mshindi 'the winner'; and the rest are washindwa 'the losers'.

(i)   Use the following additional vocabulary and the family tree to answer the questions. Students working in groups can invent their own questions (and use their own family trees) to practise together.

babu	grandfather
nyanya/bibi	grandmother
mjukuu	grandchild
mume	husband

mke	wife
kaka	brother
dada	sister
mjomba	mother's brother
shangazi	father's sister
baba mdogo	father's brother ('little father')
mama mdogo	mother's sister
binamu	son of father's brother
ndugu	brother/sister
binti	daughter
mama wa kambo	step-mother

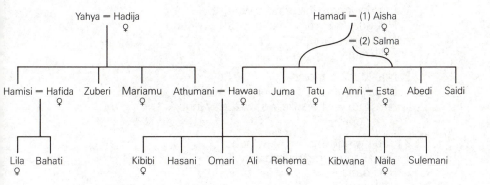

Students working alone can answer the following questions, or make up their own to answer.

Bw. Yahya ana watoto wangapi?
Bw. Hamadi ana watoto wangapi?
Bi. Aisha ana watoto wangapi?
Bi. Salma ana watoto wangapi?
Bw. Hamisi ana watoto wangapi?
Bi. Hawaa ana watoto wangapi?
Bi. Esta ana watoto wangapi?

Bi. Hadija ana wajukuu wangapi?
Bw. Hamadi ana wajukuu wangapi?
Bi. Salma ana wajukuu wangapi?

Bw. Hamisi ana ndugu wangapi?
Ana ndugu wa kiume wangapi?
Ana ndugu wa kike wangapi?

Bi. Hawaa ana binti wangapi?
Ana watoto wa kiume wangapi?

Hasani ana dada wangapi?
Naila ana kaka wangapi?

Bw. Yahya ana uhusiano* gani na Bi Hadija?
Bi. Hadija ana uhusiano gani na Bi. Mariamu?

Bi. Hafida ana uhusiano gani na Bw. Hamisi?
Bw. Hamisi ana uhusiano gani na Omari?
Bi. Mariamu ana uhusiano gani na Ali?
Bw. Juma ana uhusiano gani na Hasani?
Bi. Salma ana uhusiano gani na Bi. Tatu?
Bw. Hamadi ana uhusiano gani na Naila?
Bi. Salma ana uhusiano gani na Sulemani?
Bi. Tatu ana uhusiano gani na Kibibi?

*uhusiano 'relationship'. There is a verb kuhusu 'to concern, relate'. uhusiano is an abstract noun formed from the prepositional reciprocal form -husiana of the verb.

Mchezo — Ni nani? Who am I?

1 Mama yangu ana watoto watatu.
   Ndugu yangu mmoja ana watoto watano.
   Nina kaka mmoja.
      Ni nani?

2 Nina dada mmoja.
   Baba yangu ana dada mmoja.
   Ni mtoto wa kwanza wa wazee wangu.
      Ni nani?

3 Baba yangu ana wajukuu saba.
   Kaka yangu ana watoto wawili.
   Sina dada.
      Ni nani?

(j) Draw up a family tree of your own family, naming the relationships to you as far as possible, i.e. mimi, baba yangu, mama yangu, etc.

IV

The Swahili family. The term 'extended family' is often used for the kind of family group and its relationships that is found in many countries but not, normally, in Western Europe or North America. It means simply that family ties of rights and obligations are kept up with a wider range of relatives than in countries with so-called 'nuclear' families (parents plus children). The extended family system is most common, for obvious reasons, in countries where state social services are less developed. For the individual, the extended family system — like any other — can be alternately supportive and irksome. The difference may be that the extended family system is more difficult for the individual to escape from than the nuclear system — partly because societies where it is prevalent do not provide much alternative as a safety-net, and partly because the extended family is so extensive that one meets one's relatives virtually everywhere. The importance of family relationships may be indicated grammatically by the fact that relationship words are hardly ever used without a possessive, e.g. ndugu yangu, mume wangu. Even when speaking directly to the person concerned, one usually addresses him or her in this way. It is also noticeable that in conversation speakers normally address each other by relationship terms rather than by personal names.

Traditionally the generations tend to live together, so that a Swahili baby is born into a household containing a fairly large number of people of varying ages and degrees of relationship. At first the baby is carried about most of the time by the mother, but when he/she begins to crawl or toddle, other children — sisters or aunts or cousins — will tend to look after him/her. As the child grows older he/she will tend to play more with other children of his own age, in his own household or with the neighbours. This means that a good deal of the child's language-learning is from other children rather than from adults, and leads to special, children's usages.

As children grow up, girls and boys tend to separate, the girls staying more at home helping with domestic tasks, and the boys forming gangs. There is some overt social pressure from adults if a boy shows a tendency to prefer the company of girls at this stage, which the less extrovert boys may well do. That girls are said never to show any inclination to want to be with the boys may indicate an even stronger element of (covert) pressure! Even brothers and sisters are kept rather separate after a certain age, and develop somewhat formal relationships to all appearances, although of course there may be strong attachment.

It is the custom, in traditional Swahili families, for some trusted woman, outside the family, or at least not the mother, to instruct and help the adolescent girl at puberty. This woman, called the girl's *somo* ('teacher'), teaches her privately about the mysteries of growing up and proper adult behaviour. She becomes a very important person in the girl's life, and there is often considerable affection between them. If there are difficulties between the girl and her mother, the mother will call in the *somo* to correct the girl's behaviour. There is no comparable system for boys.

Education may also bring young people into close contact with relatives other than the parents. It may be that the parents are unable to pay fees and expenses for secondary or further education, and in this case other relatives will help. It is also quite common for even fairly young children to stay with relatives who are better-off, or who have access to schools, for instance by living in Nairobi.

It is quite common — as in other cultures — for adolescents to have a close relationship with the grandparents. This is particularly so for a boy and his grandmother, since among many Swahili there are more or less strict avoidance rules between an adolescent boy and his mother.

Thus young people grow up with close ties of affection and/or obligation to many relatives. At the same time, each relationship tends to be perhaps less complex. For the boy, for example, the grandmother is indulgent and can tease and be teased, while the mother is traditionally afforded deep respect but is somewhat distant; the father is a disciplinarian, while the mother's brother is the most likely to help financially if he can. Of course, in turn the young person will have to play his/her part in the network.

The ramifications of a family are a matter of great interest to its members. When meeting someone new, the natural point of interest is relationships. In some places, particular families traditionally inhabit particular areas, as in Mombasa, for instance, where there are twelve 'families'. Members of these families know exactly the boundaries of each family's territory, although now there are no natural boundaries since Mombasa is a maze of streets. These territories are irrespective of present ownership of land.

This strong bond between blood relatives, the rather communal care of children, and perhaps the higher death-rate among the Swahili, meant that, for example, Bibi Maw's Swahili friends accepted as absolutely natural and normal her 'adoption' of a nephew, whereas it was frequently a matter of surprise and curiosity to her European friends and acquaintances.

Mwoga — The coward

I

▷ (a) Bw. Philip: Bwana Hasani ni mwoga sana.
    Bwana Harris: Usiniambie!
    Bw.P.:   Ndiyo, kweli. Juzi juzi tu tunakwenda* Bagamoyo, na
        kwa baisikeli yangu. Mimi ninaendesha baisikeli, na
        yeye anakaa nyuma. Mara moja anasema, 'Oh,
        bwana, twende upesi, nimeona kitu msituni!'
        Anatetemeka kabisa. Ninamwambia, 'Usiogope,
        hakuna kitu,' lakini anatazama nyuma, analia,
        'Tusiende huko!' Ninamwambia, 'Usiogope bwana,
        ni nguruwe tu, hana neno.' Lakini anaendelea
        kutetemeka, karibu tunaanguka. Ninamwambia,
        'Usifanye hivyo, bwana, ni nguruwe tu. Nguruwe
        hatafuni mtu.'† Lakini anaendelea kulia, 'Twende
        upesi, pengine anakuja.' Bila shaka ni mwoga sana.
        Bado hajaweza kutembea usiku . . . Oh, hujambo,
        Bwana Hasani!
    Bwana Hasani: Sijambo Bwana Philip. Unasemaje?
    Bwana Philip: Ee, yaani, ninaeleza habari ya nguruwe mkali.
    Bw. Hasani: Usinipige kigongo, bwana, unanipiga kigongo.
    Bw. Philip: Nawe usininyoe bila ya maji, bwana.
    Bw. Hasani: Usinipige kigongo we.
    Bw. Harris: Usijali, Bwana Hasani, Bwana Philip anakutania tu.
        Usijali.
    Bw. Hasani: Kunitania anaweza kunitania, lakini asinipige kigongo!

mwoga sana — 'very cowardly' 'a great coward'
usiniambie! — 'you don't say!' lit. 'don't tell me'
juzi juzi — 'recently' (cf. *juzi* — 'day before yesterday')
nyuma — 'behind'
mara moja — 'all at once'
upesi — 'quickly'
nimeona — 'I have seen'
msitu — 'undergrowth'
-tetemeka — 'tremble'
ninamwambia — 'I say to him'
-ogopa — 'be afraid'
-lia — 'cry (out)'
nguruwe — 'pig'
-endelea — 'continue' (from *-enda* 'go' — double prepositional form)
-anguka — 'fall'
hivyo — 'thus'; *usifanye hivyo* 'don't do that (what you're doing)'
-tafuna — 'eat', lit. 'chew', so 'chomp' or other slang word here
pengine — 'perhaps' lit. '(at) another time/place'; 'sometimes'

-tembea — 'walk about'

unasemaje? — note addition of *-je?* — 'What are you saying?'; can also be used as a greeting, rather matey: 'What have you got to say for yourself?'

-eleza — 'explain, tell'

usinipige kigongo — 'don't stab me in the back' *gongo* — 'back'; *ki-* here is a sort of adverbial usage.

usininyoe bila ya maji — lit. 'don't shave me without water', i.e. don't accuse me without foundation, or, you're just getting at me.

we — *wewe*, used to a person when the speaker is irritated.

-jali — 'take notice'

anakutania — 'he is teasing you'; *kunitania* 'as for teasing me'

*The 'present continuous' (-na-) tense is used here in telling a story in an informal manner, cf. in English 'and I says to him. . .' 'then he gives me a push. . .' etc.

†*nguruwe hatafuni mtu* — in English we would probably use the plural 'pigs don't eat people'; Swahili often has the singular collective use, e.g. *mwingereza*, lit. (the) English (person) for 'the English (people)'.

II

(i) The object prefix

As well as having a prefix marking the subject, verbs in Swahili may also have a prefix marking the object. In fact they *must* normally have an object prefix if the 'object' is a person or animal. Examples in the text are *usiniambie* 'don't tell me' (u+si+ni+ambie), *ninamwambia* 'I says to him' (ni+na+mw+ambia), *anakutania* 'he is teasing you' (a+na+ku+tania). The forms of the personal object prefixes are as follows:

1st person singular	-ni-	'me'
2nd person singular	-ku-	'you' singular
3rd person singlar	-m-	'him/her' (*mw-* before vowels)
1st person plural	-tu-	'us'
2nd person plural	-wa-	'you' plural
3rd person plural	-wa-	'them'

You will notice that the 2nd and 3rd person plural forms are identical. In context it is normally clear whether 'you' or 'them' is meant. If there is a possibility of confusion, the 2nd person plural can have *-eni* substituted for the final vowel of the stem.

If a tense sign is present, the object prefix follows the tense sign. So in the text we had *ninamwambia*. Further examples:

ananipenda	'he/she loves me'
anakupenda	'he/she loves you (sing.)'
anampenda	'he/she loves him/her'
anatupenda	'he/she loves us'
anawapenda/anawapendeni	'he/she loves you (pl.)'
anawapenda	'he/she loves them'

(It is also possible to add -eni to the root for the second person *singular* too, for special effect, e.g.

> nitakupigeni   'I shall hit each of you individually'
> nitawapigeni   'I shall hit all the lot of you'

This form is not often heard, however.)

The subjunctive form can also have an object prefix, e.g. *anipe chai* 'let him give me some tea'. If the meaning is clear, the object prefix can even occur with the subjunctive without a subject prefix, e.g.

> *Iweke mezani* 'Put it (e.g. *chai*) on the table' (NOT *iweka*)
> *Mpige!* 'Hit him!' (NOT *mpiga*)

*(i.e. the simple imperative cannot have any kind of prefix. Plural would be e.g. *mpigeni!* 'Hit him, you lot!')

The infinitive form can also have an object prefix, as in the text: *kunitania* 'teasing me'. (It can never have a subject prefix, since in effect the *ku-* is already a class prefix; nor any other prefix except the negative — see Unit 20.)

The object prefix, when present, immediately precedes the verb stem.

You will notice that the forms of the object prefix are the same as the subject prefix for the 1st persons, singular and plural, and the 3rd person plural. Second persons, singular and plural, and 3rd person singular are not the same as the subject prefix. (You may like to compare this with the case of English, where 'you' is the same for subject or object, singular or plural, but the other persons have different forms, viz. I: me, he: him, she: her, we: us, they: them.)

There is also a reflexive object prefix, *-ji-*, which is the same for all classes and persons, e.g.

> anajipenda   'he/she loves him/herself'
> usijikate!   'don't cut yourself!'

Nouns of all classes have subject and object prefixes to verbs and copulas. The forms of these prefixes are the same for subject as for object for non-animate nouns, as follows:

> class 5   *li* behewa liko wapi?
> class 6   *ya* mabehewa yako wapi?
> class 7   *ki* kitabu kiko wapi?
> class 8   *vi* vitabu viko wapi?
> class 9   *i* nyumba iko wapi?
> class 10 *zi* nyumba ziko wapi?

This applies to verbs as well as copulas, e.g. in the proverb: *kidole kimoja hakivunji chawa* 'one finger won't crack a louse' (i.e. you need two—cooperation).

Object prefixes with nouns representing inanimate objects are only used when (a) the object is not named, or (b) the object precedes the verb, e.g.

> Unasoma kitabu changu? (no object prefix)

(a) Ndiyo, ninakisoma. (object prefix)
(b) Kitabu chako ninakipenda sana. (object prefix) This gives prominence to the idea of 'your book'.

Note that the subject prefix *i-* is also sometimes used for an impersonal subject, as in Unit 17 *inaonekana ni karamu* 'it seems to be a party'.

(ii) **-me- tense**

Several examples of the use of this tense have already occurred, e.g. *nimeshiba* 'I am full (of food)'. The *-me-* tense implies a completed action, which has some reference to the present, i.e. *nimeshiba* implies 'I ate in the past and am still satisfied'. *askari amefika* means 'the police-man has arrived and is still here'. So in the text we have *nimeona kitu* 'I have seen something and the impression of it is still with me'. Some-times something more like a state is implied. In Unit 13, Bi. Maw, after driving to several markets says *nimechoka* 'I am tired', i.e. 'I have got tired and am in that state now'; and when invited to sit down, the polite answer is *nimekaa* 'I am sitting/seated' (even if you are not!).

-ja- tense

We have noted elsewhere that, for example in the matter of marital status, the Swahili do not care to give a definite negative. The form used is the negative subject prefix plus *-ja-* tense sign, often, but not always, associated with the word *bado*. So an enquiry as to whether Bibi Maw is married would elicit the answer *bado*, or *bado hajaolewa*, or *hajaolewa (bado)*. Of a guest who is late, one might say *bado hajafika* 'he has not yet arrived'; asked if one has ever been to a certain place, one would never reply no, but say *(bado) sijafika* if one had not. *bado* placed after the verb suggests that the contingent event is more likely to occur soon. In the text we have *Bado hajaweza kutembea usiku* 'He daren't (yet) go out at night' — an expression of great scorn referring to a man.

It may be felt by some people that the *-me-* and the *-ja-* tenses are in some sense complementary. Some would perhaps rather refer to them as 'aspect' rather than 'tense'. I shall refer to them as 'tense' since this term seems more widely understood than 'aspect'; and in any case what matters is the use of the Swahili form rather than the descriptive terms chosen.

III

(b) **Ufahamu**. Jibu maswali:
Bwana Philip anamwogopa nguruwe?
Wewe unaogopa nguruwe?*
Nani anaendesha baisikeli?
Bwana Hasani anakaa wapi?
Bwana Hasani anatazama wapi?
Nguruwe anatafuna mtu?
Bwana Philip na Bwana Hasani wanaanguka?
Kwa nini Bwana Hasani anatetemeka?
Bwana Hasani ni mwoga?
Nani anamtania Bwana Hasani?
Nani anaeleza habari ya nguruwe?

Nguruwe ni mkali?
Mwoga ni nani, kwa kweli? Eleza.

*Here there is no object prefix because the question is general.

(c) Jaza pengo. Fill in the blanks, e.g. (yeye) *anani*saidia (mimi)

Bw. Harris __na__saidia Bi. Maw.
Bw. Philip __na__ona Daudi:
(sisi) __na__ona (wewe)
Bw. Harris na Bi. Maw __na__penda Bw. Philip.
(mimi) __na__tazama mpwa wangu. (-*tazama* here means 'look after')
(wewe) __na__pa Bi. Maw na Bw. Harris chai.
Bw. Harris __na__chukulia mzee mizigo.
Sheikh Yahya __na__saidia (nyinyi)
(nyinyi) __na__pa (sisi) chakula.
Daudi __na__pa (mimi) pesa.

Repeat, changing the verbs to the negative, e.g. *hanisaidii.*
Repeat, changing the verbs to the imperative, e.g. *anisaidie.*
Repeat, changing the verbs to the negative imperative, e.g. *asinisaidie.*

(d) Fill in the blanks and complete the exercise, reversing the subject and object:

Unawaona waalimu? Ndiyo, __na__ona, bali ha__on__ mimi.
Mwalimu anampenda mtoto?
Mwizi anatutazama?
Mwizi anawaona askari?
Askari wanamtazama mlevi?
Mnatupenda?
Mvua samaki anawafundisheni kuvua samaki? (-*fundisha* — 'teach (skill)')
Mwuzaji ananidanganya? (-*danganya* 'cheat')
Mnamjua Bwana Harris?

(e) Fill in the gaps and make parallel sentences for each noun:

▷   Vitabu __angu __mepotea.* Ume__ona? Siyo, bado __ona.
    Mtoto
    Nguruwe (pl.)
    Bibi
    Gari

    kupotea — 'to be lost'

(f) Ask where is/are the students':

▷   chairs   houses
    oranges   tea
    parents   buses

(g) Ask where is the drunkard's:

▷   pig   car
    beer   child
    bottle

(h)   Answer the following questions, to the effect that the event has not yet
      taken place:

Babake amefika nyumbani?
Dada yako amekwenda sokoni?
Mjomba wako ameingia hospitalini?
Umemwona ng'ombe wangu?
Mtoto amelala?
Wanafunzi wamemaliza kazi?
Mmekwenda Dar es Salaam?

(i)   Answer the following questions in the positive, omitting to name the
      object:

Umeona kitabu changu?
Unataka kununua viazi?
Unapenda kula keki?
Umeandika jina lako?
Umekula biskuti zote?
Umepika chai?
Umetengeneza vitanda?
Umeuza mahindi yote?

Rewrite your answers in the negative (not yet).

(j)   Make questions for the following answers:

Bado sijamwona.
Nimezinunua Mombasa.
Kwa kweli halipendi sana.
Ndiyo, ameyaandika.
Tumeiona katika duka la Mhindi.
Wamekutana nao London.
Siyo, bado hatujavila.
Nguruwe ameyatafuna yote.
Kwa sababu kimeanguka.

(k)   Answer the following questions, omitting to name the object, and giving
      a reason:

Kwa nini hujanunua viazi? Sija___nunua kwa sababu _____
Kwa nini baba mdogo hajaleta keki nyingi?
Kwa nini Bibi Maw hajapika chai?
Namna gani hamjajua Kiswahili?
Mbona wagonjwa hawajakunywa dawa?

(l)   **Mchezo**: Kutafuta. Game: 'Hunt the thimble'. Wachezaji wawili. Two
      players. On separate cards draw pictures of a cupboard (*kabati*), a box
      (*sanduku*), a bag (*mfuko*). Make a set of six smaller cards with pictures
      respectively of a book (*kitabu*), books (*vitabu*), a pen/pencil/biro
      (*kalamu*), pens (*kalamu*), a lemon (*limau*), lemons (*malimau*). Have two
      blank cards the same size.

      Player A goes out (or shuts his eyes). Player B puts one picture from the
      smaller set under one of the set of 3 cards, and blank cards under the

other two. Player A then (enters and) looks at the five remaining small cards. Player B asks:

Unatafuta nini? (-*tafuta* 'look for')

Player A answers, e.g.

Ninatafuta kitabu changu (or whichever card is missing).
Umekiona?

Player B: Ndiyo, nimekiona.

Player A: Kiko wapi, basi, kitabu changu?

Player B: Bahatisha (-*bahatisha* 'guess', cf. *bahati*)

Player A: e.g. Kimo sandukuni? (or whichever place he thinks)

Player B: Ndiyo, kimo/Siyo, hakimo.

If Player A has guessed right, he wins a point; if not, Player B wins one. Player A may challenge Player B if he wishes, saying:

Nionyeshe ('show me')

If on a challenge he finds Player B out in a lie, he cries *Mrongo we!* (You're a liar), and wins two points. If, however, Player B has not lied, he has an extra point. Players take turns at guessing.

IV

(i) The 'object prefix' is normally used whenever a person or animal is referred to as the object. If this object prefix is omitted, the effect is disparaging to the object. So, referring to an alleged thief, the prose-cuting counsel might ask a witness:

Unajua mtu huyo? 'Do you know that person?',

whereas in normal conversation the question would be:

Unamjua mtu huyo? with object prefix *m* in the verb. (*huyo* — 'that (person) referred to'.)

(ii) Swahili social life typically involves conversation. This may vary from learned discussions between men who regularly meet (often at the mosque) for the purpose, to casual chat in the street. Many ceremonies (such as those connected with marriages or funerals) involve large groups of people spending long periods together, and apart from musical entertainments, dancing or taking refreshment, much of the time is spent talking or telling stories. Story-telling is an art, and stories are not told only to children. The person who is skilled at speaking or telling stories is much admired. *ufasaha* 'eloquence' is a quality that everyone would like to possess. Written prose is a relatively new art for the Swahili, and what is produced does not have a very wide sale; but oral performance of both prose and poetry has a long history, and is highly valued.

fitina 'backbiting' is often denounced, which may suggest that it often occurs!

Unit 19   Fungu la kumi na tisa
Kudanganywa! — Cheated!
Matamshi — Pronunciation

I

(a) Saa sita ya mchana. Ofisini.

▷
Bwana Harris:	Unategemea kula wapi lanchi yako, Bibi Joan?
Bibi Maw:	Sijui, labda hotelini.
Bw.H.:	Twende nyumbani kwangu, pana starehe zaidi huko.
Bi.M.:	Haya, nitafurahi, Bwana Stuart.
Bw.H.:	Lakini kwanza twende sokoni, ninunue vyakula vingi kidogo.
Bi.M.:	Unataka kununua vyakula gani, Bw. Stuart?
Bw.H.:	Ninataka kununua mikate miwili na jibini pauni moja, pamoja na nyanya nyingi na matunda machache.
Bi.M.:	Soko lenyewe liko wapi?
Bw.H.:	Liko njiani, karibu na nyumba yangu. Uko tayari?
Bi.M.:	Ndiyo, niko tayari.
Bw.H.:	Basi, twende tu.

lanchi — 'lunch'. If Bw. Harris had known more Swahili he might have said *chakula cha mchana*.
nitafurahi — 'I shall be pleased'
mikate miwili — 'two loaves'
jibini — 'cheese' (*chizi* is also used)
matunda — 'fruit (pl.)'; *matunda machache* — 'a little fruit' (*-chache* — 'few')
soko lenyewe — 'the market itself'; the whole utterance means something like 'Where is the market, in fact?' or 'Where is that particular market?'.
karibu na nyumba yangu — 'near (to) my house'
....

Sokoni.

▷
Mwuzaji:	Bwana, bwana, nunua matunda bwana.
Bw.H.:	Matunda gani?
Mwuzaji:	Tazama bwana, mazuri sana, tena rahisi.
Bw.H.:	Unauza kiasi gani?
Mwuzaji:	Shilingi mia tatu tu bwana, mfuko mzima.
Bw.H.:	Shilingi mia tatu! Unacheza tu, bwana. Punguza bei.
Mwuzaji:	Unanunua bei gani bwana?
Bw.H.:	Shilingi hamsini labda.
Mwuzaji:	A'a, bwana, siwezi.
Bw.H.:	Basi tu, shauri lako!

mazuri — 'fine' (*matunda*); cf. *nzuri* response in greetings.
mfuko mzima — 'the whole bag'

-cheza — 'play', v., cf. *mchezo* — 'game'
shauri — 'business, affair'; *shauri lako* 'that's up to you'
....

▷ Bi.M.:   Unataka kununua nini, Bwana Stuart?
   Bw.H.:   Ana machungwa makubwa. Tazama, moja amelikata, ni
            zuri sana.
   Bi.M.:   Ee, labda. Lakini anauza kwa wingi sana. Unataka
            machungwa mengi?
   Bw.H.:   Labda, kwa sababu kila asubuhi ninakunywa maji ya
            machungwa.
   Bi.M.:   Lakini ghali mno!
   Bw.H.:   Ee, kweli.

-kubwa — 'big'
-zuri — 'fine (orange)'
kwa wingi — 'in bulk', *wingi* — 'abundance'
machungwa mengi — 'many oranges', cf. *siku nyingi, watu wengi,* etc.
mno — 'excessively'
....

Mwuzaji anarudi.
▷ Mwuzaji: Basi, bwana, shilingi mia mbili.
   Bw.H.:   Mia moja.
   Mwuzaji: Mia moja na hamsini bwana.
   Bw.H.:   Siyo, siyataki. Nenda zako tu.
   Mwuzaji: Basi bwana, thelathini na tano.
   Bw.H.:   Labda wakati wa kurudi . . . Unajua, Bibi Joan, kama kweli
             hutaki kununua, wanakupa bei nzuri zaidi.
   Bi.M.:   Ee, kweli.

wakati — 'time, point in time', *wakati wa kurudi*; lit. 'the time of returning' i.e. 'when (I) come back'
bei nzuri zaidi — 'a really good price, the best price'
....

Wananunua mikate na jibini, pamoja na nyanya, halafu wanarudi.
Bwana Harris ananunua matunda ya shilingi mia moja na thelathini.
Wanakwenda zao.
Nyumbani kwa Bw. Harris.
▷ Bw.H.:   Philip!
   Philip: Naam, bwana.
   Bw.H.:   Lete machungwa katika gari. Chukua ufunguo.
   Philip: Haya.
            (Bwana Philip analeta mfuko . . . .)
   Philip: Lakini bwana, mfukoni hamna machungwa.
   Bw.H.:   Vipi? Mna nini basi?
   Philip: Ndiyo, bwana, mna madanzi, tena makali sana. Na hayana
            maji. Tazama tu.
   Bw.H.:   Si nilinunua machungwa!

Bi.M.:   Labda mwuzaji alishika chungwa moja mkononi, lakini katika
          mfuko mna madanzi. Ni mwizi tu.
Bw.H.:   Mwizi wa kupindukia! Tumedanganywa sana!

katika gari — '(from) in the car'
ufunguo — 'key'
mfukoni hamna — 'in the bag there are no(t) (in)'
vipi — 'how can that be, what do you mean'
mna — 'there is in'
madanzi — *danzi* — a kind of sour orange
si nilinunua — 'didn't I buy . . .'
mkono — 'hand'
-pinduka — 'overturn'; *mwizi wa kupindukia* — 'an out-and-out thief'
-danganywa — 'be cheated'
....

Note that when Bw.H. asked, 'Matunda gani', meaning 'What sort of
fruit?', the hawker answered, 'mazuri sana, tena rahisi' i.e. an answer to
a different question from the one Bw. Harris was asking, but sufficiently
ambiguous to put Bw. Harris off the scent. *machungwa* and *madanzi*
look very alike from the outside.

II

(i) You will have noticed the forms *mna* and *hamna*, as in *mfukoni hamna
     machungwa* 'in the bag there are no oranges'. Place nouns can be
     subjects of the *-na* copula, like any others. In Unit 13 we had *kuna* and
     hakuna mahindi. We have also had *pana* in *hapa pana starehe* (unit 16),
     and in this text *pana starehe zaidi huko* 'there is more peace there'.
     Bwana Harris could have said *kuna starehe* . . . . . In other words, all
     three kinds of place, positive and negative, can be subject of *-na*, viz:

pana	'there is (at)'	hapana	'there is not (at)'
kuna	'there is (around)'	hakuna	'there is not (around)'
mna	'there is (in)'	hamna	'there is not (in)'

The difference between saying in Swahili:
          mfukoni hamna machungwa
     and: machungwa hayamo mfukoni
is like the difference in English between:
          in the bag there are no oranges
     or: there are no oranges in the bag
i.e. there is something else (or nothing) in there, and we are interested in
the bag and its contents;
     and: the oranges are not in the bag
i.e. the oranges are somewhere else, and we are interested in the
oranges and their whereabouts.

(Note that quite often the word *hapana* is used alone — mainly by
second-language speakers, particularly Europeans and Asians — as an
expression of strong negation, or disagreement. This usage is not
favoured in polite Swahili conversation.)

(ii) **Noun classes 3/4**.

Nouns in class 3 have a prefix m- (mw- before vowels other than u), but they are not the names of living beings. (Interesting exceptions are the two nouns mtume 'prophet' i.e. Mohammed, and mungu 'God'.) Nouns in class 4 have prefix mi- e.g.

mfuko   'bag'   mifuko   'bags'
mkate   'loaf'   mikate   'loaves'
mwavuli   'umbrella'   miavuli   'umbrellas'.

The subject and object prefixes of these nouns are u and i respectively. So we have:

mfuko uko wapi?   'where is the bag?'
mifuko iko wapi?   'where are the bags?'

The agreements with the possessive and with -a are w- and y- respectively. Thus:

Mfuko wa mwalimu (or, wake) umepotea. Umeuona?
Mifuko ya mwalimu (or, yake) imepotea. Umeiona?

(iii) **Noun class 11(14)**.

Nouns in this class consist of words which in other Bantu languages comprise two separate classes. In Swahili they have prefix u- (w- before vowels), and are often either names of countries (e.g. Uingereza 'England') or abstract (e.g. uzuri 'beauty'). In the text we have the noun wakati 'time, point in time', and wingi 'abundance'. Some concrete nouns are also included, however, e.g. uzi 'thread', wembe 'razor'. The plurals of these nouns are in class 10 as a rule (a few are in class 6), and their formation follows the rules set out in section (vi) below. They have subject/object prefix u in the singular; in the plural zi as for class 10. So we have:

wembe uko wapi?   'where is the razor?'
nyembe ziko wapi?   'where are the razors?'

The class 11(14) possessive agreement, and for -a, is w-; so that in the text we had wakati wa kurudi. Agreement in the plural is as for class 10, e.g.

Wembe wa mwalimu (or, wake) umepotea. Umeuona?
Nyembe za mwalimu (or, zake) zimepotea. Umeziona?

(iv) **Noun class 15**.

Nouns in this class are all verbal nouns (infinitives). They have subject/ object prefix ku-; and agree with possessives and -a by kw-; e.g.

   kuendesha kwake kunaniogofya 'his driving frightens me' (-ogofya 'frighten')

There are no further noun classes in Swahili, the student will be glad to know.

(v) **Adjectives**.

You will have noticed in the text a number of nouns followed by adjectives. These adjectives, like some of the numerals, normally 'agree'

with 'their' noun. There are some adjectives which are loan words and
do not change. But most do 'agree', and generally have prefixes like
those for the noun class. So in the text we had:

mfuko mzima (-zima)	'a whole bag(ful)'
mikate miwili (-wili)	'two loaves'
chungwa zuri (-zuri)	'a nice orange'
matunda machache (-chache)	'a few fruits'
madanzi makali (-kali)	'a bitter citrus-fruit'
machungwa makubwa (-kubwa)	'big oranges'

Prefixes for adjectives of all classes are as follows: (-*ekundu* 'red', 'light
brown')

1	*m-* (*mw-* before vowels)	mtoto mzuri (mwekundu)
2	*wa-* (*w-* before vowels)	watoto wazuri (wekundu)
3	*m-* (*mw-* before vowels)	mfuko mzuri (mwekundu)
4	*mi-* (*my-* before vowels)	mifuko mizuri (myekundu)
5	Ø (*j-* before vowels)	chungwa zuri (jekundu)
6	*ma-* (*m-* before vowels)	machungwa mazuri (mekundu)
7	*ki-* (*ch-* before vowels)	kitabu kizuri (chekundu)
8	*vi-* (*vy-* before vowels)	vitabu vizuri (vyekundu)
9 10	See (vi) below. (*ny-* before vowels)	nyumba nzuri (nyekundu)
11 (14).	*m-* (*mw-* before vowel)*	wembe mzuri (mwekundu)
15	*ku-* (*kw-* before vowels)	kupika kuzuri (kwenyewe) (-enyewe 'itself')
16	*pa-* (*p-* before vowels)	mahali† pazuri (penyewe)
17	*ku-* (*kw-* before vowels)	mahali kuzuri (kwenyewe)
18	*m-* (*mw-* before vowels)	mahali mzuri (mwenyewe)

* Sometimes *u-* is used with abstract nouns, e.g. *utu uzuri* (*utu* —
'manhood')
† *mahali* — 'place'

The adjectival stems -*ingi* 'many', 'much' and -*ingine* 'other' mostly are
formed predictably, but in a few cases there are slight differences
caused by the juxtaposition of certain vowels. So we have:

2	watoto wengi, wengine	wa+i > we
4	mifuko mingi, mingine	mi+i > mi
6	machungwa mengi, mengine (one can hear *mangi* sometimes)	ma+i > me
7	chakula kingi, kingine	ki+i > ki
8	vitabu vingi, vingine	vi+i > vi
16	mahali pengi, pengine	pa+i > pe

Note that adjectives in Swahili can only be modified by words such as
zaidi 'more', *mno* 'very'. There is no comparative and superlative as in
English (good: better: best). Note also that they do not need nouns; you
could say: *nimenunua mazuri* 'I've bought fine (ones)'.

(vi) **Class 9/10 agreements**.

Nouns in class 9/10 do not have different singular and plural forms, but many of the nouns in this class which are of Bantu origin do in fact have a prefix, a nasal, and it is important to recognize the conditions giving rise to this prefix in order to be able to form the correct plurals for nouns in class 11(14), and the agreements for adjectives. The rules are as follows:

(a) Nouns and adjectives whose stems have only one syllable have a nasal prefix: *m*- before labial consonants (*p, b, f, v*); *n*- (pronounced as *ng* in si*ng*) before velar consonants (*k, g*); and *n*- before all other consonants, e.g.

nouns	adjectives
mvi 'grey hair'	mpya 'new'
nge 'scorpion(s)'	
nchi 'country(ies)'	nne 'four'

Nouns in class 11(14) whose stems have only one syllable retain their u-prefix and add ny- to form their plurals in class 10, e.g.

11(14)	10
uso 'face'	nyuso 'faces'
ua 'courtyard'	nyua 'courtyards'

(b) Nouns and adjectives whose stems have more than one syllable, if they begin with a vowel or b, d, j, g, v or z (voiced plosive, affricate or fricative) have a nasal prefix.

This is *ny*- before vowels, e.g.

nouns 9/10	adjectives
nyumba	nyekundu

nouns 11(14)	nouns 10
wavu 'net'	nyavu 'nets'
wakati 'occasion'	nyakati 'occasions'

spelt *n*- but pronounced *ny* before *j, ng'* before *g*, (very few examples):

nouns 9/10	nouns 11(14)	nouns 10	adjectives
njaa 'hunger'			
ngano 'wheat'	ugimbi 'beer'	ngimbi	ngumu 'hard'

and *m*- before *b, v*, e.g.

mbegu 'seed'	ubao 'plank'	mbao 'planks'	mbaya 'bad'
mvua 'rain'			

n- before *d, z*, e.g.

ndege 'bird'	udevu 'hair of	ndevu 'beard'	ndogo 'small'
nzige 'locust'	beard'		nzuri 'fine'

Some sound changes take place; especially noteworthy are that
(1) stems beginning with *w* have *m+b*- as adjectival or plural of class 11(14) agreement e.g.:

mbili 'two'   (stem *-wili*)
mbati 'hut poles'   (singular *uwati*)

(2) stems beginning with r or l have n+d- as adjectival or plural of class 11(14) agreement, e.g.

ndefu 'long'   (stem -refu)
ndimi 'tongues'   (singular ulimi)

(c) Nouns and adjectives in classes 9/10 whose stems begin with other consonants (nasals and voiceless consonants) have no prefix. This absence of prefix will of course only be obvious in contrast situations, e.g. with adjectives, or with class 11(14) nouns with plurals in class 10; for instance:

ufunguo 'key'   funguo 'keys'
ukuta 'wall'   kuta 'walls'

In the past it was the case that the voiceless plosive consonants p, t, k, and the affricate ch were pronounced with aspiration (i.e. a brief puff of air after the pronunciation of the consonant but before the onset of the vowel), but this is being lost now, partly because Swahili nowadays is a second language for many speakers, and partly because this aspiration has never been shown in the spelling. Aspiration can also sometimes make a difference in meaning between words spelt alike. See exercise (n), section III.

III

(b) Jibu maswali:

Kwa nini Bi. Maw na Bw. Harris waende nyumbani?
Waende nyumbani gani?
Kwa nini waende kwanza sokoni?
Bw. Harris anataka kununua vyakula gani?
Soko lenyewe liko wapi? (lenyewe is a special adjectival form for class 5)
Bwana Harris anunua mikate mingapi?
Mwuzaji amekata machungwa mangapi?
Bw. Harris ananunua matunda kwa bei gani?
Bw. Harris ananunua mifuko mingapi ya matunda?
Bw. Harris ananunua machungwa matamu?
Mna machungwa mfukoni?
Bi. Maw anasema 'Ni mwizi tu'. Nani ni mwizi?
Kwa nini Bw. Harris anafikiri (-fikiri 'think') amenunua machungwa?

(c) Make a list of the nouns you have already met which you think could be in class 3/4. Give their plurals.

(d) Give the plural forms of the following:

uso mzuri   uso mmoja
uso mbaya   uso mwekundu
uso mkali   uso mrefu

(e) Give the plurals of the following nouns:

shauri, tunda, mkono, mguu, danzi, mwavuli (umbrella), upepo (wind), ushanga (bead).

(f) Answer the following questions:

Unataka kununua kitabu gani?
Unataka kununua kalamu gani?
Unataka kununua mfuko gani?
Unataka kununua mikate gani?
Unataka kununua ufunguo gani?

(g) Add two of the following adjectives to each of the nouns: Adjectives:
-refu (tall, long), -dogo (small), -kubwa (big), -kali (sharp), -zuri (nice),
-baya (nasty, bad), -ekundu (red)

Nouns: 1 mzee   _____   2 _____
            3 mfuko   _____   4 _____
            5 duka   _____   6 _____
            7 kiti   _____   8 _____
            9 nyumba   _____   10 _____
           11(14) ulimi _____

(h) Ask where the following items of yours are; e.g.

kitabu changu kiko wapi?

mkebe (tin can)
shanga
uma (fork)
mifuko
mwavuli
funguo

(i) How would you tell someone in Swahili:

not to buy the small oranges, to buy the big ones.
not to give you cold tea, to give you hot.
not to bring a few cakes, to bring them all.
not to sell the good potatoes, to sell the bad ones.
not to steal (-iba) one bag, to steal lots.
not to drink a little beer, to drink plenty.

(j) Fill in the blanks:

Mfuko __ake __zuri sana. Una__penda? Siyo __ __pend__
   ninapenda zaidi mfuko __ a _____
Kuimba (-imba 'sing') _____
Malimau _____
Ng'ombe (pl) _____
Kitanda _____
Nyumba (sing.) _____
Jina _____
Viti _____
Dada _____.

(k) Answer the following questions in the negative, giving an alternative,
e.g. Mna machungwa garini? Siyo, hamna machungwa, mna madanzi tu.

Kuna nazi sokoni? Siyo, _____

Mna waizi katika jela? Siyo, _____
Nyumbani kuna watu wengi? Siyo, _____
Hapa pana wanafunzi wa Bi. Maw? Siyo, _____
Kikapuni mna nyanya nzuri? Siyo, _____.

(l) Write a detailed shopping list giving the amounts (or numbers) and type of each article you require. Include items from as many different classes as possible. Number/amount adjectives should follow those of quality.

(m) **Mchezo — Nyumbani kwetu.** Game — At home.
For this game a dice is needed, and each player needs a pencil and paper. The aim is to draw the inside of a house including:

milango miwili
viti vitano
mikeka minne (*mkeka* 'mat')
madirisha matatu
makabati mawili
meza moja

Players throw the dice in turn, and must get a 6 to start. Getting a 6, the player says:
    nina mlango mmoja
and has a second throw, announcing what he has, and then drawing the article on his paper. To get a door he must throw a 6, a 5 for a chair, a 4 for a mat, and so on. He needs two doors, i.e. two 6s, etc. The first player to complete his house cries:
    nimejenga nyumba! (*-jenga* 'build')
and has won.

▷ (n) **Pronunciation of p, t, ch, k.**
Care must be taken to pronounce with aspiration only those consonants marked with a following tick, i.e. p', t', ch', k'.

paa	— p'aa	roof; gazelle
paka	— p'aka	apply (v.); cat
papa	— p'apa	ooze (v.); shark
panga	— p'anga	lease (v.); swords
taa	— t'aa	lamp; kind of fish
taka	— t'aka	want (v.); dirt
tende	— t'ende	elephantiasis; dates (fruit)
tundu	— t'undu	hole; large basket
katu	— wat'u	gum, glue; people
changu	— ch'angu	my; kind of fish
cheki	— ch'eki	cheque; check (v.)
chora	— ch'ora	draw (picture); kind of children's food
chungwa	— ch'ungwa	large orange; orange
mchicha	— ch'icha	spinach; residue
kaa	— k'aa	charcoal (a piece); crab
kanga	— k'anga	fry (v.); guinea-fowl
kesha	— k'esha	stay up at night; vigil
konde	— k'onde	fist; field

kata	— k'ata	ladle; coil for head when carrying load
kuku	— k'uku	large hen; hen
kucha	— k'ucha	all night; fingernails
kikuku	— kik'uku	small hen; bangle

IV

Emotion is often expressed by gestures accompanying words. The potential customer who is pestered by traders may feel annoyance to the extent that he cries *Nenda zako, bwana, nenda zako!* 'Be off!'; and this may well be accompanied by a large gesture waving the right hand in the air, at about head-height, making warding-off movements with the *back* of the hand towards the offender.

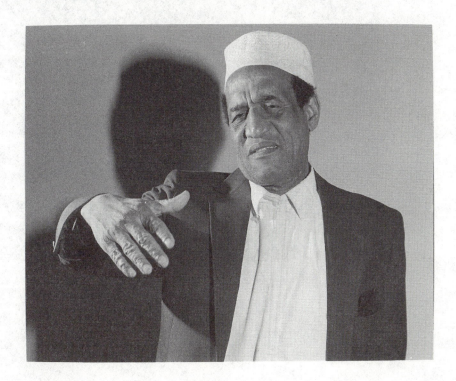

A gesture of disgust, such as might be called for on the discovery of the *madanzi* in the text, is to shrug the shoulders, drawing the upper arms in to the body, the lower arms forward towards the offending object, opening the hands, palm upwards, while exclaiming *Tazama!* 'Look at that!' The right hand alone, or both hands could be used. This gesture could also be made at a child who has misbehaved, i.e. 'Look what you've done!'

Unit 20 — Fungu la ishirini
Kutodanganywa — Not being cheated

I

(a) Bibi Maw, Bwana Harris na Bwana Philip wako pwani. Bwana Harris anaendesha gari.

> Bwana H.:   Philip anataka kununua nazi.
> Bi.M.:   Namna gani? Maanake tuna nazi mbili nyumbani.
> Bw.H.:   Ndiyo, lakini tunataka kurudi Nairobi kesho, na Nairobi
>   hakuna nazi. Kwa hiyo anataka kuzinunua nyingi hapa.
> Bi.M.:   Haya. Haya basi, simama Bwana Stuart. Kuna nazi
>   dukani pale.
> Bw.H.:   Duka lipi?
> Bi.M.:   Lile karibu na mnazi.
> Bw.H.:   Ndiyo, kweli. Nenda huko Philip uzinunue.

maanake — 'that is, i.e.' from *maana yake* 'its meaning'
kwa hiyo — 'therefore, for that reason'
lipi? — 'which? (shop)'
lile — 'that (shop)'
mnazi — 'coconut palm'
....

Philip anakwenda na kurudi, asinunue.

> Bw.H.:   Namna gani, Philip? Nazi zile, je?
> Bw. Philip: Sijanunua bwana, kwa sababu wananidai bei ghali sana.
> Bw.H.:   Kiasi gani, Philip?
> Bw. Philip: Shilingi thelathini thelathini. Endelea bwana, tujaribu
>   penginepo.

zile — 'those (coconuts)'
-dai — 'claim, demand'
....

Wanakwenda penginepo, lakini mambo ni yale yale. Njiani tena.

> Bw.H.:   Basi, tufanyeje, Philip?
> Bw.P.:   Sijui.
> Bw.H.:   Kwa nini nazi hizo ni ghali hivi, Philip?
> Bw.P.:   Ni kosa lenu. Watu wananiona katika gari. Wanaona tuko
>   pamoja. Wanafikiri mimi ni mtajiri sana, kwa hiyo
>   wanapandisha bei.
> Bi.M.:   Basi, Bwana Stuart, tumteremshe Philip, halafu twende mbali
>   kidogo, watu wasifikiri tuko pamoja.
> Bw.H.:   Haya.
> Bi.M.:   Simama, simama! Hapa pana nazi. Nenda ununue, Philip. Sisi
>   twende kununua petroli huko.
> Bw.P.:   Haya.

mambo ni yale yale — 'things are just the same', 'it's the same story'
tufanyeje — 'what shall we do?'
hizo — 'those (coconuts) mentioned'
hivi — 'thus'
kosa — 'fault' (noun or verb)
-fikiri — 'think'
-pandisha — 'raise'
-teremsha — 'put down' (someone)
....

Bibi Maw na Bwana Harris wananunua petroli. Baada ya nusu saa
Bwana Philip anafika na nazi, chungu nzima.

▷   Bw.H.: Karibu Philip, upesi, twende. Jua kali sana. Umechelewa mno.
         Bw.P.: Haya.
         Bi.M.: Ngoja nikusaidie kuweka nazi.
         Bw.H.: Umenunua nazi hizi kwa bei nzuri?
         Bw.P.: Ndiyo, bwana.
         Bi.M.: Kiasi gani?
         Bw.P.: Shilingi ishirini ishirini.
         Bw.H.: Umetosheka, Philip?
         Bw.P.: Nimetosheka sana, bwana.
         Bw.H.: Vema. Twende huyo-o-o.

baada ya — 'after' (cf. *baadaye* 'afterwards' from *baada yake*)
chungu — 'heap'; *chungu nzima* — 'a whole heap, lots'
-chelewa — 'be late'
hizi — 'these (coconuts)'
-tosheka — 'be satisfied'
vema (sometimes *vyema*) — 'good', an expression of satisfaction.
huyo-o-o — 'whee'

II

(i) **The negative infinitive** is formed by inserting *-to-* after the infinitive
prefix, as in *kutodanganywa* 'not being swindled'. This prefix *-to-* cannot
take stress, so we have:
    kula (ni) kuzuri

but   kutokula (ni) kubaya
where, as with other forms of the verb, *-ku-* is used to carry stress.

(ii) **Demonstratives**.

In Swahili there are three demonstratives, two of which refer to place
(near and far), corresponding roughly in English to 'this/these' and 'that/
those'; and the third a kind of reference, somewhat as in colloquial
English 'that-there' or 'yon'. In Swahili we have already used some place
words: *pale* 'there', *hapa* 'here', *hapa hapa* 'right here', and *huko* 'the
place referred to'. Bw. Harris said once, speaking of Bi. Maw's railway
carriage:
    Hapa pana starehe '*Here* (there) is peace'.

On another occasion he said:

Twende nyumbani kwangu. Pana starehe zaidi *huko*. 'Let's go to my place. There's more peace *there*' (referring to his house).

These words form part of a series, viz:

near	**far**	**reference**
cl. 16 hapa 'this very spot, here'	pale 'that very spot, there'	hapo 'that very spot referred to'
cl. 17 huku 'around this place, here'	kule 'around that place, there'	huko 'around that place I mean'
cl. 18 humu 'in here'	mle 'in there'	humo 'in that place referred to'

From the above examples you will be able to deduce that the 'near' words begin with *h-*
'far' words end in *-le*
'reference' words begin with *h-* and end with *-o*.

Speaking of Daudi, Bi. Maw said:

Huyu ni mtoto wangu' 'This (person) is my child'
The series for class 1, then, is:

	huyu 'this person'	yule 'that person'	huyo 'that person referred to'
cl. 2	hawa 'these people'	wale 'those people'	hao 'those people referred to'

Perhaps the student can now deduce the formation of the 'this/these' word. The vowels are 'in harmony' with the class agreement, e.g. in class 1 the *yu-* as in *yule* also appears in *huyu*, preceded by a vowel *u*; whereas in class 2 the *wa-* as in *wale* appears in *hawa* preceded by a vowel *a* to 'match'. The medial vowel in the 'reference' word is also in harmony with the class prefix vowel.

The remaining classes of demonstratives are predictably as follows:

cl. 3	huu	ule	huo
cl. 4	hii	ile	hiyo
cl. 5	hili	lile	hilo
cl. 6	haya	yale	hayo
cl. 7	hiki	kile	hicho
cl. 8	hivi	vile	hivyo
cl. 9	hii	ile	hiyo
cl. 10	hizi	zile	hizo
cl. 11	huu	ule	huo
cl. 15	huku	kule	huko
cl. 16	hapa	pale	hapo
cl. 17	huku	kule	huko
cl. 18	humu	mle	humo

Note 1 In the text we have *kwa hiyo* 'therefore, because of this' referring to class 9 used impersonally; cf. *inaonekana* 'it seems', already noted.

Note 2 In the text we also have *hivi* 'thus'. Class 8 sometimes has a sort of adverbial function, as here. We have also had *vizuri* 'well'. We could also have *vibaya* 'badly'. In unit 18 we had *hivyo*, in *usifanye hivyo* 'don't do that (you know what)!'

(iii) **Reduplication**

In the text we have *mambo ni yale yale* 'it's the same old tale'. Repeating an item intensifies the meaning. We had earlier *hapa hapa* 'right here'. *Mtu yule yule* would mean 'that very same man'. More on reduplication will be found in unit 34.

(iv) **Lengthening**

In referring to distance, a speaker may lengthen the final vowel. The longer the vowel, the further away the referent, compare: *mtu yule: mtu yuleee*; *mtu yuleeeeeeee*. In the text, Bw. Harris says *huyooo*, glossed as 'whee'. This word is a fixed form for this meaning, but may perhaps originally refer to following an animal in hunting, cf. 'there he goes', 'gone away', etc.

(v) **Which?**

The question 'which?' is formed by means of the morpheme *-pi* preceded by the class prefix as for copulas. So we have *yupi?* 'which person?', and in the text *duka lipi?* 'which shop?' The formation of this word is regular for all classes, except for class 2, where we have *wepi?* 'which people?' (possibly to distinguish it from *wapi?* 'where?')

(vi) **-je**

-je can be suffixed to a verb, making it into a question what . . .?' e.g. *tufanyeje* 'what shall we do? *anafanyaje* 'what is he doing?' In Unit 18, Bw. Hasani asked *Unasemaje* 'What have you to say?'

To suffix *-je* to a verb asks about the *quality* of the action; to prefix it to a question queries the *action itself* and expects the answer yes or no.

> cf. Unaendeleaje?   'How are you getting along?'
> Je, unaendelea? 'Are you getting on (or not)?'

(vii) **Forms of the class prefix**.

It will have become apparent that for most classes (leaving aside class 1/2 where there are also personal prefixes) each class has two sorts of prefix: one which precedes nouns, epithets (adjectives) and numerals; and the other which precedes possessives, demonstratives, copulas and verbs. e.g. class 6 has *ma-* for *macho* 'eyes', *mazuri* 'fine', *mawili* 'two'; *ya-/y-* for *yangu* 'my', *yale* 'those', *yapo* 'are in a specific place', and *yamefumba* 'are shut' (*-fumba* — 'be shut', of eyes). By some writers on Swahili the prefix for epithets and numerals is called the 'adjectival prefix', and the one for possessives etc the 'pronominal prefix'. The linguistically minded student may like to note that, within the nominal group (noun phrase) we have one shape of prefix (e.g. *ma-*) for the lexical stems, and the other (e.g. *ya-/y-*) for the grammatical stems.

(viii) **Sequence of words in the nominal group**

In a Swahili nominal group (i.e. the words that cluster round what is normally a noun) the sequence is not entirely fixed. It is not often that

more than two items are found qualifying a noun in any case. Normally
the noun is the first item in the group. The possessive, if present, always
immediately follows the noun. The other qualifiers, if present, normally
follow in the sequence (noun — possessive) — epithet — demonstrative
— numeral. However, the last three can vary in sequence. Any sequence
other than the neutral one as above, throws emphasis on the final word
in the group (provided that the intonation stays the same). So:

mtoto mrefu yule	is neutral
mtoto yule mrefu	has emphasis on *mrefu*
watoto warefu wawili	is neutral
watoto wawili warefu	has emphasis on *warefu*
watoto wale wawili	is neutral
watoto wawili wale	has emphasis on *wale*.

A very few words can come before the noun; the most frequent of these
are *kila* 'each', *kina (akina)* a collective, e.g.

kila mtoto	'each child'
akina mama	'womenfolk'
akina Juma	'Juma's lot'.

Forms of the demonstrative can also precede the noun, and often occur
in this position in spoken Swahili; less often in formal style or written
Swahili. When they occur in this position their meaning is much
weakened; they mean something like *the* in English. Usually the *-le* form
is used, e.g.
     yule bwana   'the man'.

It is also possible to say, e.g.
     wale kina mama   'the womenfolk'
and here the word order is fixed, i.e. *kina* can not precede *wale*.

III

(b) **Ufahamu**.

Kwa nini Philip anataka kununua nazi kwa wingi pwani?
Unafikiri Philip anataka kufanya nini na nazi hizo?
Kwa nini Philip hataki kununua zile nazi za kwanza?
Unafikiri Philip ni mtajiri? Eleza maana yako.
Kwa nini Bwana Harris na Bibi Maw wanakwenda gereji?
Kwa nini Bwana Harris amekasirika? (*-kasirika* 'be angry')
Kwa nini Bwana Philip hasemi sana?

(c) The reference table (blank) shows, on the left, the noun class numbers;
then allomorphs of the minimal agreement morphemes (i.e. different
forms that the noun class prefixes may have); then examples of nouns
with the different forms of the prefixes. Make a copy and fill in the
spaces for possessive, epithet (adjective), demonstrative, numeral,
place, copula, *ndi-* copula (class 1/2 only), verb subject prefix, object
prefix, 'all', 'many', 'other', *-a*, and *na-* (class 1/2 only).

Table 1 Noun class agreements

noun[2]	possessive	epithet[2]	demonstrative			numeral[2]	copula (place)		
			-le	h-	h -o		-ko	-po	-mo
1. m mzee mw mwana mwingereza mu Muumba		zuri ekundu							
2. wa wazee w wana waingereza									
3. m mfuko mw mwavuli									
4. mi mifuko (my) myavuli } miavuli }									
5. ji jicho j jino ø ua									
6. ma } macho m } meno maua									
7. ki kitabu ch choo									
8. vi vitabu vy vyoo									
9. N[1]. nyumba ø kalamu									
10. N[1]. nyumba ø kalamu									
11/ u ufunguo 14. uzuri w wembe									
15. ku kuimba kufika									
16. pa { mahali 17. ku { nyumbani 18. mu { etc.									

[1] N stands for a nasal prefix
[2] take 'adjectival' prefix

copula		verb	prefix	relative	whole/all	any	'many'[2]	'other'[2]			
ø	ndi-	s	o		-ote	-o -ote	-ingi	-ingine	-a	-enye	na-
		1 2 3									
		1 2 3									

(d)   How would you ask which:

(e)   Fill in the blanks (with zero where appropriate!):

Vitabu __le ni __ako? Ndiyo, ni __angu.
Unasoma kitabu __a mwalimu? Ndiyo nina__soma, ni __zuri sana.
Kiti h__ __nafaa? Siyo, ha__fai, ni __a zamani sana.
Ninunue nazi h__ ? A'a, usi__nunue, ha__fai.
Unapenda kula keki (pl.) __le? A'a, si__pendi __le, __na sukari
   mno; ninapenda zaidi h__, __na matunda kidogo.
Ufunguo __ako __ko wapi? __mo mfukoni __angu.
Ushanga __angu __a dhahabu __ko wapi? Sijui, sija__ona.
__ko watu __ngi katika darasa (cl. 5, 'class') __ako? Siyo, ha__ko __ngi
   __ko _____ tu.
Koti (cl.5) __angu __zuri __ko wapi? __mo kabatini __le.
Kwa nini unanunua kalamu __le ghali? Kwa sababu nina__penda, tena
   ni siku __angu __a kuzaliwa. ('birthday', -zaliwa 'be born')
Mnakula chakula __a usiku saa ngapi? Tuna__la saa _____.
Mti h__ __na matunda __ngi? Siyo, ha__na __ngi, lakini __zuri.
__ko maji __a moto katika birika? Ndiyo, __ko __ngi.

(f)   Write responses to the following questions, changing the demonstrative
      and possessor:
      Tunda hili ni lako? Siyo, __le ni _____.
      Kiti hiki ni cha Bwana Harris? Siyo, _____
      Tikiti hii ni yangu?
      Gari hii ni ya nani?
      Shilingi hizi ni zako?
      Bia hii ni ya Bibi Maw?
      Mfuko huu ni wa nani?
      Kitanda hiki ni chako?
      Minazi hii ni ya mkulima?
      Samaki hizi ni za nani?

(g)   Fill in the blanks, and answer using a demonstrative plus another
      descriptive word, e.g.
      Kitabu ki pi ni chako? Kile kizuri ni changu.
      Mtoto __pi ni __a mwalimu?
      Unataka kununa shanga __pi?

Nyumba __pi ni __a mtajiri?
Kalamu (pl.) __pi ni __a Bwana Philip?
Viti __pi ni __a shule?
Mama amekupa mfuko __pi?
Bwana Harris amenunua matunda __pi?
Bwana Philip amekula chungwa __pi?
Bwana Harris amempa Bwana Philip ufunguo __pi?

(h) Make each of the following verbal nouns negative, and put each in a
sentence:

kufika
kunywa
kununua

IV

'Them and us'.

An individual in any society will feel affinity with a number of groups, a
family, an age-group, a sex, a nation and so on. At different times one or
the other affinity may predominate; sometimes loyalties may clash.

Owing to the extended family system, the Swahili probably feel more
affinity with relatives than most Europeans do — i.e. with more relatives.
There is also strong pressure to get on with neighbours (who may of
course also be related). Even in large towns in East Africa the anonymity
and sometimes isolation of the individual which is not unknown in
Europe, would be quite impossible.

However, these ties of affinity and mutual support do not stretch far
beyond family and neighbours. Their place may be taken in the case of
strangers by laws of hospitality, but these will apply mainly to those who
have some legitimate entrée to the society, or who come with some
personal recommendation. In fact the Swahili do like visitors and guests,
and are very hospitable. Foreigners may not realise, however, that
guests become almost honorary members of the family, and thereby
acquire obligations, too. Of course, there are limits to hospitality. There is
a Swahili saying:

Mgeni wa siku tatu, mpe jembe! 'A three-day visitor, give him a hoe!', i.e.
after three days one should expect to earn one's keep.

When it comes to business or trade*, something of the same principles
applies. The relative, the neighbour, the regular customer, have claims to
better terms than the stranger. Strangers are assessed and put into cate-
gories. In the text in section I Bwana Philip was originally assessed by
the traders as 'rich', because he got out of a big car and was associating
with Europeans. So he was definitely one of 'them'. Away from those
associations he became more like 'us' and got better terms. On
occasions Swahili speakers tried to use him as a go-between, which
sometimes embarrassed him since he naturally felt loyalty to his friends
on both sides.

Of course it is universal human nature to have in-groups. It is difficult for
a stranger entering a new society, however, to recognise what groups
exist or how he himself is classified. The stranger may be anything from
honoured guest to despised outcast, from generous friend to exploitable
fool. Only time and patience can make the newcomer a sort of honorary
Swahili.

* In fact the old Swahili aristocracy do not engage much in trade, but
many Swahili-speaking people do.

Revision

Write a composition about yourself entitled *Mimi mwenyewe*. Include
answers to the following questions:

Jina lako nani?
Una umri gani? (yaani, una miaka mingapi?) (*umri* — 'age')
Una jamaa gani?
Unakaa wapi? Nyumba yako iko wapi hasa?
Unakaa pamoja na nani?
Unasoma nini? au unafanya kazi gani?
Baada ya kusoma, unategemea kufanya nini?
Unapenda kufanya nini, wakati wa mapumziko? (*mapumziko* — 'relaxa-
tion')

Unit 21   Fungu la ishirini na moja
Lini? — When?

I

(a) Jumamosi.

Bw. Harris:	Tutaonana kesho, Badi?
Professor Athumani:	Siyo, Stuart. Nitakwenda Ghana kesho.
Bw.H.:	Utarudi lini?
Pr.A.:	Nitarudi siku ya Jumatano.
Bw.H.:	Kumbe utakwenda Ghana kesho Jumapili na kurudi Jumatano!
Pr.A.:	Ndiyo.
Bw.H.:	Utachoka kabisa!
Pr.A.:	Labda. Lakini niambie, Stuart, rafiki yako ataondoka lini?
Bw.H.:	Ataondoka Ijumaa.
Pr.A.:	Basi mtaweza kuja kwangu kula chakula cha jioni Alhamisi?
Bw.H.:	Kumbe utarudi Ghana Jumatano na kuwaalika wageni Alhamisi?
Pr.A.:	Ndiyo; Jimmy atanisaidia. Njooni tu.
Bw.H.:	Basi nitamwambia, lakini sijui kama kweli tutafika.

tutaonana? — 'shall we see each other?'
rafiki — 'friend'
jioni — 'evening'
-alika — 'invite'
mgeni — 'visitor', also used for 'foreigner'

....

Jumanne.

Bi. Maw:	Bwana Stuart, Badi yuko wapi?
Bw.H.:	Yuko Ghana.
Bi.M.:	Do! Yuko Ghana! Alikwenda lini?
Bw.H.:	Alikwenda jana.
Bi.M.:	Atarudi lini?
Bw.H.:	Alisema atarudi kesho Jumatano, lakini sijui kama kweli atarudi kesho.
Bi.M.:	Bila shaka atachoka sana.
Bw.H.:	Kabisa. Tena alitualika kula chakula cha jioni Alhamisi.
Bi.M.:	Kumbe, atarudi kesho na kutualika kesho kutwa!
Bw.H.:	Ndiyo, kwa sababu utaondoka wewe Ijumaa.
Bi.M.:	Basi ulimwambia nini?
Bw.H.:	Nilimwambia kwamba sijui kama tutafika kweli.
Bi.M.:	Ulifanya vizuri.

alikwenda — 'he went'
kesho kutwa — 'the day after tomorrow'
kwamba — 'that' introducing reported speech
....

Alhamisi

▷   Bi. M.:   Badi amerudi Ghana, Bwana Stuart?
           Bw.H.:   Ndiyo, amerudi.
           Bi.M.:   Alirudi lini?
           Bw.H.:   Alirudi leo asubuhi tu. Alitaka kurudi jana lakini ndege
                    ilichelewa.
           Bi.M.:   Maskini. Bila shaka amechoka kabisa.
           Bw.H.:   Lazima. Lakini aliniambia tufike leo usiku.
           Bi.M.:   Kumbe, amefika nyumbani tu, naye anataka wageni wafike!
                    Afadhali tusiende.
           Bw.H.:   Lakini ametualika. Lazima tutakwenda.
           Bi.M.:   Basi, tunaweza kwenda, lakini tusikae sana.
           Bw.H.:   Ndiyo, tutaondoka saa tatu, apate kulala mapema.

amefika nyumbani tu — 'He's only just arrived home'
-pata — 'manage'; can also mean 'get'
mapema — 'early', 'soon'
....

Alhamisi, jioni, nyumbani kwa Professor Athumani. See section III (b).

II

(i) **Future tense**.

This is shown by the tense sign *-ta-*, as in:
atafika 'he will arrive'.

(ii) **Negative future tense**.

This is shown by the negative prefix plus *-ta-* tense sign, as in:
hatafika 'he will not arrive'.

(iii) **Past tense**.

The tense sign *-li-* is used to refer to an action in the past, without
reference to the present. Care should be taken to distinguish this from
-me-, which refers to an action in the past but with present implications.
Thus in the text, Bi. Maw's question:
Badi amerudi?
might be glossed as 'has Badi come back?', 'is Badi back?', referring
rather to a state of having got back, being back; whereas in:
alirudi lini?
'when did he get back?', Bi. Maw is now asking about a past occurrence,
not a present state.

(iv) **Negative past tense**.

This is shown by a tense sign -*ku*-, with negative prefix, e.g.
alifika 'he arrived'   *hakufika* 'he did not arrive'
This negative should be distinguished from the negative with -*ja*-
(*hajafika* — 'he has not yet arrived'). -*ja*- suggests a state, resulting from
a non-occurrence in the past, i.e. 'up to now he/she has not arrived'. -*ku*-
(as in *hakufika*) simply states that at a certain time in the past he/she did
not arrive, it implies nothing about the present.

Note. None of these tense signs can take stress, except -*ku*-. So we
have:

nitafika nyumbani	but	nitakula mkate
sitafika nyumbani	but	sitakula mkate
nilifika nyumbani	but	nilikula mkate
sikufika nyumbani	but	*sikula* mkate

(v) **Reported speech**.

Reported speech in Swahili may (or may not) be introduced by the word
kwamba, which is historically related to the verb -*ambia* 'tell'. *kwamba* is
sometimes glossed as 'that', as in 'he said that he was going out'. An
indirect question is often introduced by *kama*, which has already been
used for 'if'. It may sometimes be glossed as 'whether'. So in the text,
Bw. Harris said:
    Nilimwambia *kwamba* sijui *kama* tutafika kweli
    'I told him *that* I did not know *whether* we would really come'.
Notice that, in Swahili, there is no need to change the tense of the verb,
nor the person, in reported speech. In fact the distinction between
reported and direct speech is not made clear structurally in Swahili, since
there is no need to use *kwamba* or *kama*, and the grammar does not
change. The context usually shows whether the speech is direct or
reported, and indeed the distinction may be thought to be a somewhat
artificial one in many cases, and is perhaps a literary rather than an oral
tradition. It is possible, if felt necessary, to say:
    aliniambia hivi 'he said thus (to me)'
and then the listener is in no doubt that the actual words of the original
speaker will follow.

The introductory clause (*alisema* (*kwamba*) 'he said (that)') almost
always precedes the 'reported' clause in Swahili. i.e. the sequence
'"What do you want?" he asked' would not be natural in Swahili, though
it is sometimes found in the works of modern writers who have been
influenced by English.

III

(b) Write out a conversation suitable for Professor Athumani's Thursday
evening party.

(c) Write out the paradigm for the past tense:
nilimwona mamangu jana

(d) Write out the paradigm for the negative past tense:
sikufika nyumbani kwangu jana

(e) Write out the paradigm for the future tense:
nitakutana na rafiki yangu kesho kutwa

(f) Write out the paradigm for the negative future tense:
sitaonana na mtoto wangu tena

(g) Jibu maswali:
Utakwenda wapi wakati wa Krismasi?
Utakula chakula gani sikukuu? (*sikukuu* 'holiday')
Utampa mama yako zawadi gani ya Krismasi? (*zawadi* 'present')
Watu watafanya nini sikukuu?
Ulifanya nini jana?
Ulikwenda mahali Jumapili? (*mahali* here gloss 'anywhere')
Ulifika hapa saa ngapi leo?
Ulianza lini kusoma Kiswahili? (*-anza* 'begin', cf. *kwanza* 'first')
Ulizaliwa mwaka gani?

(h) Answer using a negative verb:
Bwana Hasani na Bwana Philip walianguka baisikeli?
Bwana Philip alimwogopa nguruwe?
Bwana Harris alinunua machungwa matamu?
Bwana Philip alinunua nazi chache?
Bibi Maw alikwenda Ghana?

(i) Answer in the negative, giving an alternative, e.g.
Bibi Maw atakufundisha Jumapili? Siyo, hatanifundisha Jumapili, bali
atalala kitandani labda.

Utasoma Kiswahili sikukuu?
Watu watakaa nyumbani siku ya mwaka mpya?
Mtamaliza kazi zenu mapema?
Utamsaidia mamako nyumbani kidogo, siku ya Krismasi?

(j) Report the conversation given between Bi. Maw and Bw. Harris in the
text, Alhamisi. You will need the verb *-uliza* 'ask (a question)'.

IV

(i) In Swahili, the distinction between past time (tense) and state may be
expressed by the choice between *-li-* and *-me-* in the 'tense sign' slot in
the verb. Compare *alinunua gari* 'he bought a car' and *amenunua gari* 'he
has bought a car'. In the first example there is no implication about
whether he still has the car or not, he simply bought one at some time in
the past. In the second he is in the condition (or state) of having bought a
car, i.e. he still has it. Often the state is conveyed in English by the use of
the auxiliary 'have/has' plus past participle, as in 'he has bought a car', or

e.g. *ameondoka* 'he has left'; but it may also be conveyed by the use of the verb 'be' plus a present participle, e.g.
  amesimama   'he is standing',
'be' plus past participle, e.g.
  amepotea 'he is lost',
or 'be' plus an adverb, e.g.
  amelala 'he is asleep'.

To use the *-na-* 'tense sign' in the last four examples would indicate a process in time, i.e.
  anaondoka 'he is leaving'
  anasimama 'he is getting up'
  anapotea 'he is getting lost, going astray'
  analala 'he is going to sleep'

Foreign learners often confuse what to the Swahili is a state with a tense. This is generally a result of interference of first language, but is sometimes a result of a different view of things. For example, 'she is wearing a lovely dress' would be:
  amevaa nguo nzuri sana
and not **anavaa . . .* , which would mean 'she is putting on . . .'.

(ii) The Swahili are great travellers. Before the days of steam there was always a lot of trade and travelling up and down the East African coast, and between Africa and Arabia. Caravans also went inland as far west as present-day Zaire. The spirit of adventure and love of travel persists today. Owing to the extended family system there is often someone one can claim relationship with, sufficient to be put up for a night or two, in the most far-flung places. Traditionally it was men who travelled, women staying at home, but nowadays women are also travelling more, visiting relatives at a distance, even sometimes working away from home. Compared with many other groups of people, the Swahili individually appear to be intrepid travellers. One of the most interesting pieces of Swahili writing is the account by one Salim B. Abakari of his travels in Europe, Russia and Siberia in 1896, called *Safari yangu ya bara Urusi na Siberia* ('My journey through inland Russia and Siberia'), reprinted in *Swahili Prose Texts*, ed. Lyndon Harries (Oxford University Press, 1965). European travellers' tales of Africa abound; a Swahili traveller's tale of Europe is more uncommon.

Unit 22 Fungu la ishirini na mbili
Nchi yetu — Our country

I

(a) **Wimbo wa Taifa la Kenya**.

▷   Ee Mungu nguvu yetu
     Ilete baraka kwetu
     Haki iwe ngao na mlinzi
     Na tukae na undugu
     Amani na Uhuru
     Raha tupate na ustawi.

     Amkeni ndugu zetu
     Tufanye sote bidii
     Nasi tujitoe kwa nguvu
     Nchi yetu ya Kenya
     Tunayoipenda
     Tuwe tayari kuilinda.

     Na tujenge Taifa letu
     Ee ndiyo wajibu wetu
     Kenya istahili heshima
     Tuungane mikono
     Pamoja kazini
     Kila siku tuwe na shukrani.

taifa — 'nation'
nguvu — 'strength'
baraka — 'blessing'
haki — 'right', 'justice'
-wa — 'be'
ngao — 'shield'
mlinzi — 'protector' from *-linda* 'protect, defend'
undugu — 'brotherhood', from *ndugu* 'brother, sister'
amani — 'peace', from *amini* 'believe', cf. 'amen'.
raha — 'comfort'
ustawi — 'prosperity'
-amka — 'awake'
bidii — 'zeal' *-fanya bidii* 'make an effort', 'exert oneself'
tunayoipenda — 'which we love (country)'
wajibu — 'duty'
-stahili — 'deserve, be worthy of'
heshima — 'respect' — a very important concept in Swahili society
-ungana — 'join' (*-unga mkono* — idiom for 'agree' e.g. *siwezi kukuunga
    mkono* 'I can't agree with you')
shukrani — 'thanks, gratitude'.

Wimbo wa Taifa la Tanzania.

Mungu ibariki Afrika
Wabariki viongozi wake
Hekima, umoja na amani
Hizi ni ngao zetu
Afrika na watu wake.

Ibariki Afrika
Ibariki Afrika
Tubariki watoto wa Afrika.

Mungu ibariki Tanzania
Dumisha uhuru na umoja
Wake kwa waume na watoto
Mungu ibariki
Tanzania na watu wake.

Ibariki Tanzania
Ibariki Tanzania
Tubariki watoto wa Tanzania.

ibariki — 'bless it', *-bariki* 'bless', cf. *baraka* 'blessing'
viongozi — 'leaders', *-ongoza* 'lead aright'
hekima — 'wisdom'
-dumisha — 'make lasting', *-dumu* 'last'
wake kwa waume — 'women as well as men, women and men as a
  group'.

II

(i) The copula stem *-wa* 'be, become', is used in three distinct ways. In the
text it functions alone as a predicator in:
   tuwe tayari 'let us be ready'
   Haki iwe ngao 'let Right be (our) shield'
We could also say, e.g.
   alikuwa mwalimu 'he was a teacher'
   hatakuwa mwalimu 'he will not be a teacher'.
In many respects, e.g. in having subject prefixes, tense and negative
markers, this stem is structured like a verb. It cannot have an object
prefix, however.

-wa also functions as a tense-carrier for other copulas which cannot
themselves have tense prefixes. For example, *-na* (as in *nina* 'I have',
etc.) cannot be marked for tense. If we wish to express the past tense
with *-na* we have to use *-wa* also, e.g.
   zamani nilikuwa nina pesa nyingi 'formerly I had a lot of money'
When *-na* is used with *-wa*, the subject prefix may be omitted from the
-na as in the text we have:
   tuwe na shukrani lit. 'let us have thanks', i.e. 'be thankful, give thanks'.

The negative would normally be on the *-na*, e.g.
   nilikuwa sina pesa 'I had no money'.

But there is the possibility of a subtle distinction in the placement of the negative. For example, you might warn someone that if he went on the way he was doing:

    utakuwa huna pesa
or, *hutakuwa na pesa.*

The first would mean 'you will be without money' (perhaps you will lose or waste any you may now have); the second would mean 'you won't have any money' (perhaps you haven't any now and you won't get any either).

-wa is similarly used with *-po, -ko, -mo* as in:
    alikuwa yuko nyumbani 'he was at home'.
The negative would normally be on the *-ko*, e.g.
    alikuwa hayuko nyumbani 'he was not at home'.

If the copula is not followed by a place noun, a sort of combined form is generally used, especially in the positive, e.g.
    Bi. Maw alikuwa yuko shuleni jana? Ndiyo, *alikuwako.*
                     or, Siyo, *hakuwako/*alikuwa hayuko.

The third use of *-wa* is as an 'auxiliary' in combination with a lexical verb. The function here is to form compound tenses, so we could say:
    alikuwa anasoma 'he was reading'
    alikuwa amesoma 'he had read'
    atakuwa anasoma 'he will be reading'.
Again there is choice for the placement of the negative, but it is usually on the main verb, e.g.
    alikuwa hasomi 'he was not reading'.

III

(b)   *Chemsha Ubongo* 'Boil (your) brain'

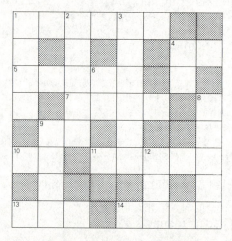

Kulia

1 Bi. Maw ni _____ ya Bw. Harris
4 Rafiki yangu _____ mrefu sana
5 _____ na Bibi Smith
7 Mbili na tatu
9 Watoto _____ Bw. Hasani ni
   wazuri sana
10 Kalamu _____ Sandra iko wapi?
11 Do!
13 _____ pesa! (Imp.)
14 _____ mwenyewe

Chini

1 Saa tano kasa _____ ni saa tano
   kasoro dakika kumi na tano
2 Njoo nyuma! (Imp.)
3 Kwako ni mbali na _____
4 Mimi _____ wewe
6 Ni __ taka bia sasa
8 Si kwa ubishi
9 Watoto _____ wapi?
12 Mbuyu ni _____ mkubwa
Bi. Hasthorpe

....

(c)

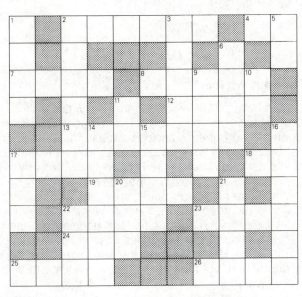

Kulia

2 neg. cl. 17, plus
4 hasha!
7 O.K.
8 kitu cha kufagilia
12 cl. 16, plus
13 swali (3, 4)
17 kuoa, (noun)
18 liko bustanini
19 1st. sing., plus
22 swali, mahali
23 mno
24 Mume wa binti wa Mtume
25 mahali pa haja
26 baba wa baba

Chini

1 saza!
2 neg. 3rd sing. place 17
3 swali, kiasi
5 ama
6 swali, wakati
9 swali, aina
10 tazama 17 kulia, (imperative)
11 Daudi ni mpwa _____ Bi. Maw
14 3rd. pl., plus, cl. 5
15 swali, mtu
16 tazama 13 kulia, jibu (noun)
17 madhumuni
20 swali, cl. 9
21 mwana, wingi*
22 3rd pl. pronoun

* plural

(d) Invent a crossword puzzle for yourself; if with a group, try each others' puzzles.

(e) Complete the paradigm:

Mwaka jana nilikuwa sisemi Kiswahili, lakini sasa nimesoma kidogo. (*mwaka jana* — 'last year')

(f) Answer the questions using *kuwa* to form future tenses, e.g.

Bibi Maw yuko shuleni leo? Siyo, atakuwako kesho, lakini leo hayuko.

Tutakula keki hii leo? Siyo, _____
Bi. Maw anafundisha Kiswahili leo? Siyo, _____
Mama yuko jikoni sasa? Siyo, _____
Mfukoni mna pesa? Siyo, _____.

IV

Swahili in East Africa.

Most countries have problems of national unity, and countries in which Swahili is spoken are no exception. The national boundaries of many African countries sometimes coincide with natural features or with traditional tribal boundaries, but in most cases are such that the peoples comprising a present-day nation are very diverse. The early migrations of different groups of peoples on the continent can now only be traced by a comparison of archaeological remains, artefacts, and linguistic evidence. Coming towards recorded history there have also been movements of Arabic-speakers, and, later, Europeans and people from the Indian subcontinent. The coming of independence to East African countries, even coupled with the exodus of numbers of people of non-African ethnic origin, still left the rulers of these countries with the problem of a population with very divided loyalties. It is sometimes difficult for Europeans to appreciate the great diversity of cultural tradition (and language group) found in Africa. To take East Africa alone, the Swahili, though much influenced by Islam, belong to the large Bantu-speaking group of peoples probably originating in N.E. Zaire or Uganda, and today with main branches throughout Central, Eastern and Southern Africa. The Bantu peoples are mainly agriculturalists. Another large group of peoples are those speaking Nilotic languages, mainly in parts of Kenya and Uganda. Many of the peoples in this group are traditionally cattle-keeping pastoralists. The third large group of peoples are those speaking Cushitic languages, living mainly in the North, and with affinities in North Africa. While in towns there is a considerable mixture of peoples, in the rural areas each ethnic/linguistic group has a traditional 'homeland', and quite large areas are still relatively homogeneous.

One of the means of encouraging national unity amid all this linguistic and cultural diversity is the concept of a national language. Swahili has been chosen as the national language of Tanzania, and it has gained acceptance firstly because it was widely used as the language of administration and as the medium of instruction in primary schools as far back as the German administration, and secondly because, although Swahili is not the first language of the majority of the population, there are no large groups of speakers of any one language to offer a viable alternative.

The situation in Kenya is that Swahili is one of two official languages (the other being English), but it has not the status of national language, although there are moves in that direction. However, other vernacular languages have large numbers of speakers (especially Kikuyu and Luo), and Swahili is perceived by many people to be either a lingua franca with inferior status, of less international use than English, or as the language of a group of people once powerful but now of considerably reduced political and economic influence. Counterbalancing these feelings are admiration of the long literary tradition of the Swahili of Kenya, and the fact that Swahili, since it is no longer associated with power, does not pose a threat to members of other language-groups. It is plain that it would be very expensive to convert the whole education system in Kenya (at present using several vernacular languages for primary education and English, the latter especially in secondary and further education) to using Swahili. Nevertheless there is much encouragement to use the language, and its use is spreading. Newspapers in Swahili, and its use on the radio and in pop culture assist this movement.

Swahili is also spoken as a lingua franca to some extent in Uganda, and from time to time it has been proposed as a national language there, but without success. The same is true of Zaire.

The concepts of nation-building, a national language, unity and so on do of course raise the problems of the clash between 'tradition' and 'progress'. Life in East African countries is changing too rapidly for some individuals; not rapidly enough for others. The processes of change and adaptation are painful in any case, and language is always an emotive issue. Shaaban Robert, great Swahili writer, has written with reference to language:

Titi la mama li tamu, hata la mbwa.

'Mother's breast is sweet(est), even to a dog.' (literally '. . . even a dog's.') One needs to understand the great aversion to dogs felt by Muslims to comprehend the strength of this statement.

Unit 23   Fungu la ishirini na tatu
Ajali — An accident

I

▷ (a) Bw. Harris: Hodi!
Professor Athumani: Hodi!
Bw.H.:   Hodi hodi!
Pr.A.:   Karibu, karibu Stuart.
Bw.H.:   Starehe, Badi, starehe.
     (continue greetings)
Pr.A.:   Habari zaidi?
Bw.H.:   Sina habari nyingi, ila nimepatwa na ajali tu.
Pr.A.:   Ala! Pole sana. Ajali ya namna gani?
Bw.H.:   Asante, nimeshapoa. Ajali ya gari.
Pr.A.:   Lo! Lini, bwana?
Bw.H.:   Jana tu, saa nne ya usiku.
Pr.A.:   Do! Pole bwana. Hukuumizwa, lakini?
Bw.H.:   Ndiyo, sikuumizwa, Alhamdulillahi.
Pr.A.:   Kweli, Mungu yupo.
Bw.H.:   Yupo tu.
Pr.A.:   Ulikuwa peke yako?
Bw.H.:   Siyo. Nilikuwa pamoja na Bi. Joan na Bw. Philip.
Pr.A.:   Do! Habari zao? Hawajambo?
Bw.H.:   Hawajambo kidogo. Lakini Bwana Philip alikatwa
          mguu na Bibi Joan aliumizwa kichwa.
Pr.A.:   Aliumizwa kichwa! Vipi? Kwenye kioo cha mbele?
Bw.H.:   Siyo. Yaani, Bwana Philip alikaa nyuma yake,
          akasukumwa mbele, akamwuma Bibi Joan
          kichwani kwa meno yake!
Pr.A.:   Kumbe! Alitoka damu?
Bw.H.:   Walitoka damu wote wawili. Sasa Bibi Joan
          anaumwa kichwa na Bwana Philip anaumwa meno.
Pr.A.:   Bahati mbaya sana. Lakini afadhali nusu shari
          kuliko shari kamili!
Bw.H.:   Ee. kweli.
Pr.A.:   Lakini ajali yenyewe ilitokeaje hasa?
Bw.H.:   Inaonekana mpira ulipasuka. Gari iliteleza kutoka
          njiani, tukagongana na mti, basi.
Pr.A.:   Nimesikitika sana. Na gari, je?
Bw.H.:   Gari imeharibika kabisa.
Pr.A.:   Pole sana. Ninakumbuka siku moja nilikwenda
          Mombasa pamoja na Bibi Joan, kwa gari yangu,
          tukapata pancha tatu mfululizo! Lakini kwa bahati
          nzuri hatukuumizwa. Tena gari zima. Lakini gari ni
          kama maua.
Bw.H.:   Ee, kweli. Haya, nakwenda sasa.

ila — 'except'
nimepatwa — 'I have been overcome' 'I have had'
-umizwa — 'be hurt'
-katwa — 'be cut'; *alikatwa mguu* 'he was cut on the leg'
kichwa — 'head'
kwenye — 'at', see section II (iii).
kioo — 'glass, mirror'
mbele — 'front'; *kioo cha mbele* — 'windscreen'
-sukumwa — 'be pushed, propelled'; *akasukumwa* — 'and he was
   pushed'
-uma — 'bite', *akamwuma* — 'and he bit her'
kwa — 'with'
-toka — 'go out, give out (inadvertently)'
damu — 'blood'; *-toka damu* 'bleed'
-umwa kichwa — 'have a headache'
shari — 'disaster, ill-luck'
kuliko — 'than'
kamili — 'complete, exact'
ilitokeaje? — 'how did it happen?'
mpira — 'tyre', lit. 'rubber', ('ball')
-pasuka — 'explode'
-teleza — 'skid'
tukagongana — 'and we collided'
-sikitika — 'be sorry'
-haribika — 'be destroyed, ruined' 'a write-off'
-kumbuka — 'remember'
pancha — 'puncture'
mfululizo — 'in a row'
-zima — 'whole, well'
ua/maua — 'flower'
nakwenda — 'I'm off'

II

(i) **-ka- tense**. This 'tense' is much used in narrative, and its meaning is to
express a sequential action, often causally related or naturally arising out
of the first. So in the text, Bwana Harris says *Gari iliteleza kutoka njiani,
tukagongana na mti, basi* 'The car skidded off the road and we collided
with a tree, and that was that'. The collision was seen as a natural pro-
gression after the skid. A story might begin:
   Hapo kale paliondokea mtu; akajenga nyumba, akakaa. 'Once upon a
time there lived (arose) a man; and he built a homestead and settled
down', i.e. building a house and settling down is just what a man might
be expected to do!

The *-ka-* 'tense' can take stress, so there is no need for the insertion of
-ku- before monosyllabic verb stems, e.g. *nikala* 'and I ate'; *akafa* 'and he
died' etc.

The *-ka-* tense frequently follows on the *-li-* tense, but not necessarily.

Another use of it is after an imperative (or subjunctive used for command), with the subjunctive ending, e.g.
nenda ukalete chai 'go and fetch the tea'
where the second action is very much dependent on the first.

In newspaper headlines one may also come across verbs with *ka*- prefixed and no subject prefix. This gives immediacy of effect (and presupposes some knowledge on the part of the reader, or is intended to arouse his curiosity, since the subject is often not given). Comparable devices are used in English, e.g.
(Rais) kafika nyumbani! cf. (President) Home again!

There is no negative equivalent of this tense.

(ii) **Passive**. The passive is formed by adding the extension *-w-* after a verb root ending in a consonant, e.g.
-uma 'bite'   *-umwa* 'be bitten'
Verb roots ending in a vowel normally have extension *-liw-/-lew-* added. The choice of vowel *i* or *e* in the extension follows the vowel harmony rule as set out in Unit 16. So we have:

-nunua 'buy'   *-nunuliwa* 'be bought'
but *-ondoa* 'remove'   *-ondolewa* 'be removed'

If the passive verb is followed by an 'agent' (a person or thing effecting the action of the verb), the agent is 'introduced' by *na*; as in the text we had:
nimepatwa na ajali 'I was overtaken by an accident' 'I had an accident'.
We could say: *mama anawapenda watoto wake*. The passive would be: *watoto wake wanapendwa na mama*. Note that there can be no object prefix in a passive verb.

Some verbs with stems ending in vowels do not follow the rule. There are not many of them but they have to be learned, e.g.
-ua   'kill'   *-uawa*   'be killed'
-ambia 'tell'   *-ambiwa* 'be told'
-tia   'put in'   *-tiwa*   'be put in'.
More will be said about this in Unit 34.

Verbs with one-syllable stems have *-iw-* or *-ew-* as their passive extension. The vowel is not predictable. So we have:
-la   'eat'   *-liwa*   'be eaten'
-pa   'give'   *-pewa*   'be given'
-nywa   'drink'   *-nywewa* 'be drunk'

Verbs of Arabic origin ending in *-i* or *-u* have *-iw-*:
-badili 'change'   *-badiliwa* 'be changed'
-jibu   'answer'   *-jibiwa*   'be answered';

those in *-e* have *-ew-*:

-samehe 'forgive'   *-samehewa* 'be forgiven';
those in *-au* have *-liw-*:
-sahau 'forget'   *-sahauliwa* 'be forgotten'.

If the passive (or active) verb is followed by an 'instrument' (a means by which the action of the verb is effected), the instrument is 'introduced' by *kwa*, as in the text we had:
    alimwuma Bibi Joan kichwani kwa meno yake 'he wounded Joan in the head with his teeth'.
We could have said:
    Bi Joan aliumwa kichwani na Bw. Philip,
although this would suggest a degree of action on the part of Bw. Philip! We could also say:
    Bi. Joan aliumwa kichwani kwa meno yake Bw. Philip.
This suggests that Bw. Philip's teeth did the damage, but not deliberately. The distinction can be seen clearly in contrasting examples, as:
    mtoto alivunja dirisha kwa jiwe 'the child broke the window with a stone' (*jiwe* — 'stone')
    dirisha lilivunjwa na mtoto
    dirisha lilivunjwa kwa jiwe.
One could imagine a situation when driving, for example, if a stone flew up and broke the windscreen one might say:
    kioo kilivunjwa na jiwe
i.e. the stone here is seen as acting as agent of the breaking, not as a mere instrument directed by some other agent.

(iii) **kwenye 'at'**. This consists of the place prefix *kw-* (class 17) plus *-enye* which has some sort of possessive or associative meaning sometimes glossed as 'having'. It is used for expressing an attribute or characterisation, and is followed by a noun, nominal group, or clause. All class agreements can occur; class 16, for example, as in Christian terms:
    mahali penye wafu 'the place of (containing) the dead', i.e. Purgatory. (*-fa* 'die')

Non-place classes can also occur with this form, e.g.
    mtoto mwenye shati jekundu 'the child with the red shirt'
    mtu mwenye umri wa miaka kama ishirini 'a man aged about 20' (*umri* — 'age')
    watu wenye elimu 'people with education', 'educated people'
    wenye kujua mengi 'those who know a lot'
    mwenye mali '(a person) with wealth' 'a wealthy person' (*mali* — 'wealth, property')
    mfuko wenye pesa 'a bag with money (in it)'
    bustani yenye maua 'a garden with flowers, a flowering garden' (*bustani* — 'garden')

The attribution suggested by *-enye* is less close than that of *-a*. So *mama mwenye watoto wengi* means 'a mother with (having) many children' (not necessarily all her own), *mama wa watoto wengi* 'a mother of many children' (born to her). *bustani yenye maua* means 'a garden with flowers in'; *bustani ya maua* means 'a flower-garden', even if they are all dead.

III

(b) Eleza kisa cha ajali kwa maneno yako mwenyewe. Tell the story of the accident in your own words. (-*eleza* 'explain'; *kisa* 'tale'; *neno* 'word')

(c) Give the passive form of the following verbs:

-piga   -ingia
-pika   -funga
-toa   -chukua
-nunua   -kata
-leta   -ondoa.

(d) Change the following sentences into the passive:
Bw. Philip alimwuma Bi. Joan.
Gari itagonga mti ule!
Jiwe lilivunja kioo cha mbele cha gari yangu.
Nani alijenga nyumba hii?
Nimenunua kitabu hicho cha Kiswahili.
Bw. Stuart asafishe vyombo! (-*safisha* 'clean')
Bi. Joan anafua nguo zake. (-*fua* 'wash clothes')
Askari amemwondoa mwizi.
Nani amekunywa bia yote?

(e) Answer using a passive verb, e.g.
Nani amekunywa bia yote? Bia yote imenywewa na Bw. Philip.

Nani amemdanganya Bw. Harris?
Nani alikupiga?
Nani alileta habari hii nzuri?
Nani atamfunga jela mwizi?
Nani amepika chai hii tamu?
Nani ameandika kitabu hiki kikubwa?
Nani ameondoa vyombo vya chai?
Nani amekula biskuti zote?

(f) Give the forms of -*enye* for all classes, e.g.
Class 1 mwenye   2 wenye
      3 wenye   4 yenye

(g) How would you express the following in Swahili:
a house with four windows
a three-legged table
a shirt with small buttons (*kifungo* — 'button')
a cupboard with two doors
a picture-book (*picha*)
a hospital with too many patients
a teacher with forty pupils
two boxes of a dozen eggs
a mosque with a golden roof (*paa* cl. 5)
a poor man with only one leg
(people) who live in glass houses shouldn't throw (-*tupa*) stones.

(h) Answer the following questions, including *-enye* in your answer:

Bibi Maw anawafundisha wanafunzi gani?
Shamba lako lina miti gani?
Unataka kununua koti gani?
Professor Athumani anakaa mahali gani?
Unatumia chai gani?
Watoto wanataka keki gani?
Wamasai wanapenda ng'ombe gani?

IV

For a devout Swahili, God is in charge of our life here on earth, and there are many expressions in common parlance reflecting this traditional viewpoint. *Mungu yupo* 'God's in His heaven' and *Alhamdulillahi* 'thank God' have already been met. *Mungu asifiwe* 'God be praised' is an alternative to *Alhamdulilahi*. Another expression is *shauri la Mungu* 'God's business', used when some incomprehensible situation arises, i.e. God knows what He's doing even if we cannot understand it. On parting one may say *Tutaonana* 'We'll meet again', but must add *Inshallah* or *Mungu akipenda* 'if God wills', or *tukijaliwa* 'if we are spared (blessed)' (sc. by God). If the speaker does not add one of these expressions, the hearer will do so. *Wallahi* 'by God' is an expression of surprise or chagrin, or can be used as an emphatic oath and is not blasphemous. You will notice that many of these expressions contain the Arabic *Allah*; others refer to *Mungu* which can mean 'a god' 'providence' as well as 'God'. (*Mungu*, not *Allah*, is used for God by Christian Swahili-speakers, but nevertheless expressions involving the words *Allah* and *Mungu* are common to all speakers.)

Pious expressions are common, not only at times of stress. *Mungu akuweke* 'God keep you', *Mungu akubariki* 'God bless you', may occur at the ends of letters, or at parting for any length of time. *Maskini wa Mungu* is used to refer to a destitute person, or a cripple.

Apart from expressions mentioning God, the choice of grammatical structure often seems to suggest some outside influence. In the text, Bwana Harris says *nimepatwa na ajali*, lit. 'I was got by an accident', where in English we would say 'I had an accident', or at most 'I was involved in an accident'. It is as if in Swahili the accident happens to the victim without his volition. Also with pain, you will note Bwana Harris says later *Bwana Philip alikatwa mguu na Bibi Joan aliumizwa kichwa* lit. 'Philip was cut leg and Joan was hurt head' — 'Philip had his leg cut open and Joan's head was hurt', where more normal English would be 'Philip cut his leg and Joan hurt her head'. Similarly with illnesses, we may say in Swahili *nimeshikwa na homa/mafua* etc. lit. 'I am gripped by fever/a cold etc.' where English would have 'I've got a fever/cold etc'. In English we even go further and 'catch' a cold! This is not to say that the English consciously think of themselves as going about catching illnesses, nor that the Swahili consciously think of themselves as being chased and caught by illnesses, but the Swahili may have a more resigned attitude of mind to what cannot be helped. Even the expression *namshukuru Mungu* 'I thank God' has a strong element of resignation in it. If you ask someone how they are and they reply *namshukuru Mungu* you know that things are not going very well in fact. (cf. English 'musn' grumble', 'can't complain'.)

Many idioms and proverbs give expression to a fatalism perhaps connected with a feeling of helplessness in the face of nature (or God). So in the text, Professor Athumani says: *gari ni kama maua* 'cars are like flowers', nice but ephemeral. He also quotes a proverb: *afadhali nusu shari kuliko shari kamili* 'part disaster is better than total', disasters must come but there are degrees of disaster! Proverbs figure quite largely in Swahili conversation, bringing a sensation of comfort and familiarity while at the same time the apt choice of proverb shows a skill which is much appreciated.

However, this attitude of fatalism does not mean in practice that people do not take precautions. For example, both Professor Athumani and Bwana Harris mention travelling in company with Bibi Maw. Partly a matter of sharing comes in here, partly the fact that a woman would not normally be expected to travel entirely alone. But also in any case people do not lightly go on a journey alone. (One word for 'friend', *mwenzi* means literally someone who accompanies one, related to the verb *-enda* 'go'.) For journeys by car, the distances are great so an extra driver is always useful. Then in case of any mishap it is an advantage to have help or companionship available. In an environment full of potential dangers, company is valued. There are few 'loners' in Swahili society.

Unit 24 Fungu la ishirini na nne.

Ugonjwa — Illness

I

(a) Bi. Maw: Namna gani, Binti Abdalla? Sijaonana nawe tangu
zamani sana.

Bi. Abdalla: Ndiyo, kwa sababu nilikaa hospitalini siku chache, halafu
nikapumzika nyumbani.

Bi.M.: Vipi, mama! Ulipasuliwa? Nielezee.*

Bi.A.: Ee, nililazwa siku ya Jumatano, tarehe kumi na moja,
tayari kwa operesheni.

Bi.M.: Operesheni gani?

Bi.A.: Yaani, sehemu hii ya juu, kwenye koo, yote ilikuwa
imevimba sana, nikapata taabu sana. Nilizuiwa nisimeze
vizuri. Basi daktari aliniambia lazima zikatwe.
Zisipokatwa, nitapata taabu zaidi.

Bi.M.: Uliogopa?

Bi.A.: Kidogo niliogopa lakini vile vile nilifurahi kuona kwamba,
ugonjwa huu ukiondoka sitapata taabu tena. Basi, kufika
hospitalini, nilipokewa vizuri na sista mwenye zamu,
nikavua nguo zangu, nikalazwa kitandani. Nilikatazwa
nisile cho chote wala nisinywe cho chote. Halafu
nilipimwa homa, kama nilikuwa na homa, na wala sikuwa
na homa. Nikalala . . . siku ile mama alikuja kunitazama.
Tukazungumza, halafu akaja mwuguzi akanipiga sindano,
inaitwa mofya, kunifanyia akili ipotee kidogo. Wakaja
watu kunipeleka kwenye thiata, na baada ya kufika huko,
sikumbuki jambo lo lote.

Bi.M.: Kumbe hujui ilikuwaje?

Bi.A.: Ndiyo sijui, wala sielewi. Baadaye niliamka tu, na kujikuta
niko kitandani kwangu sasa.

Bi.M.: Ajabu! Uliona maumivu?

Bi.A.: Koo ilinikwaruza sana, hasa nikimeza. Nikaletewa chai
baridi, ya rangi tu.

Bi.M.: Chai gani isiwe na sukari tena baridi!

Bi.A.: Tena nilipewa vibonge vidogo vya kumeza pamoja na maji
kidogo, mara tatu kwa siku. Lakini siku ile ile nilitoka
kitandani, na siku yake ya pili nilivaa nguo zangu na kurudi
nyumbani.

Bi.M.: Sasa huna taabu tena?

Bi.A.: Ndiyo, sina. Lakini daktari aliniambia kwamba zile tonseli
zangu zilikuwa kubwa sana, zikapelekwa Dar es Salaam
kama maonyesho, wanafunzi wa udaktari wa huko
wapate kuziona!

Bi.M.: Kumbe wewe ni mtu maarufu sana, bibi.

Bi.A.: Siyo mimi, ila tonseli zangu tu ndiyo maarufu!

* On the tape, the speaker here misreads *nieleze* which means 'let me explain'. The text *nielezee* means 'explain to me'.

Binti Abdalla — 'Miss Abdalla', i.e. daughter of Abdalla. See section note (v)

-pumzika — 'rest'

vipi — literally 'how', here means 'how was that?' 'why?'

-pasuliwa — 'be operated on', *-pasua* — 'split'

nielezee — 'explain (it) to me', *-eleza* 'explain'

-lazwa — 'be put to bed'

sehemu — 'part, section'

juu — 'above, top', *sehemu ya juu* — 'upper section'

koo — 'throat, neck'

-vimba — 'swell'

-meza — 'swallow'

zisipokatwa — 'if they weren't cut out/unless they were cut out'

ugonjwa — 'illness', cf. *mgonjwa*

ukiondoka — 'if it (illness) went'

kufika hospitalini — 'arriving at the hospital'

-pokewa — 'be received, welcomed', *-pokea* — 'receive'

sista mwenye zamu — 'the sister on duty'

-vua — 'take off'

nguo — 'clothes'

-katazwa — 'be forbidden', *-kataza* 'forbid'

-pima — 'weigh, measure, test'

homa — 'fever'

-zungumza — 'chat'

mwuguzi — 'nurse'; *nesi* is also heard.

sindano — 'needle', *-piga sindano* — 'inject'

mofya — 'morphia'

akili — 'intelligence, consciousness'

-potea — 'be lost'

-peleka — 'send, take'

thiata — '(operating) theatre'

-elewa — 'understand', cf. *-eleza* 'explain'

-amka — 'awake'

ajabu — 'amazing'

maumivu — 'pain' cf. *-uma* 'bite, hurt'

-kwaruza — 'be sore' as of throat

-letewa — 'have brought'

nikimeza — 'if/when I swallow(ed)'

rangi — 'colour'; *chai ya rangi* — tea without milk or sugar

kibonge — 'pill' (also *kidonge*)

siku ile ile — 'that very same day'

siku yake ya pili — 'the following day'

tonseli — 'tonsil(s)'

maonyesho — 'exhibition', cf. *-ona* 'see'

udaktari — 'medicine'

maarufu — 'famous'

II

(i) **-ki- and -sipo- 'tenses'**.
The *-ki-* infix can frequently be expressed in English by 'if' as in the example:
ugonjwa huu ukiondoka — 'if this illness goes off';
and in this sort of example, the verb in the following clause usually has the *-ta-* tense, as:
sitapata taabu tena — 'I won't have any more trouble'.

Sometimes the meaning is best rendered in English by 'when' or 'whenever', e.g.
hasa nikimeza — 'especially when swallowing'.

In fact the meaning of this 'tense', though often that of a condition, also expresses an idea of simultaneity, as in e.g.
Nilimkuta mamangu akipika chakula cha jioni — 'I found my mother cooking the evening meal';
Kila nikifika ninamkuta akipika — 'Whenever I arrive I find her cooking'.
Walimsikia akilia — 'They heard her crying'.

When used with *kuwa* as an auxiliary, the meaning is that of continuity, e.g.
Wiki hii nzima nimekuwa nikitaka kukuona — 'All this week I've been wanting to see you', 'I've been wanting to see you for a whole week';
Muda huo wote nilikuwa nikisoma Kiswahili — 'All that time (*muda* — 'space of time') I was learning Swahili'.
or of repetition, e.g.
Zamani nilikuwa nikimwona kila Jumatatu — 'I used to see him every Monday'.

A slightly idiomatic use of *-ki-* is found in the expression: *ukipenda usipende* — 'whether you like (it) or not', 'willy-nilly'.

The -ki- 'tense' can take stress, so the *-ku-* stress-carrier is not inserted before monosyllabic verb stems, e.g.
Bia nikinywa, karibu nitatapika (*-tapika* — 'vomit') — 'If I drink beer, I'm nearly sick'.

The *-sipo-* 'tense' is used as the negative of *-ki-*. It is often rendered in English as 'if . . . not', or 'unless', as in the reported speech in the text:
zisipokatwa nitapata taabu zaidi — 'If they were not cut out I would have more trouble' (direct speech — 'Unless they are cut out I shall have more trouble').

This 'tense', like most others, does require *-ku-* to take the stress before a monosyllabic verb stem, e.g.
Usipokula chakula kizuri, utapatwa na ugonjwa — 'If you don't eat proper food, you will get ill'.

(ii) **Reversive extension (sometimes called 'conversive')**. The meaning of a verb stem may be 'reversed' by the addition of an extension, usually *-u-*. There are not many examples of this extension, but it is operative for some very common verbs, e.g.
-funga 'shut'   *-fungua* 'open'.

In the text we have the verb:
-*vaa* 'put on, wear'   -*vua* 'take off' (clothes)
(it is possible that the first *a* in -*vaa* is itself an extension historically).

If the last vowel in the verb root is *o*, the extension is also -*o*-, e.g.
-*choma* 'stab, pierce'   -*chomoa* 'pull out'.

In a few cases the extension is -*w*-, e.g.
-*cha* 'dawn'   -*chwa* 'set' (of sun)
-*nya* 'urinate'   -*nywa* 'drink'.

The reversive form may convey a pejorative meaning, e.g.
-*zaa* 'bear (child)'   -*zua* 'invent' e.g. a lie.

Verbs exist which look like extended forms, and may even be so histori
cally, but which have no simple corresponding verb. So -*nunua* 'buy'
looks like a reversive, but although a simple verb -*nuna* exists, it means
'sulk' and is not related to -*nunua*. -*bomoa* 'demolish' probably is
historically a reversive, but there is no verb *-*boma*, though a noun
boma 'hedge, fence' does exist. Recall also -*tia* 'put in': -*toa* 'take out'
(there is no stem *-*ta*).

(iii)   Verbs of prohibition, e.g. -*zuia* 'prevent', -*kataza* 'forbid' should be
followed by a negative verb, as in the text:
nilizuiwa nisimeze 'I was prevented from swallowing'
nilikatazwa nisile 'I was forbidden to eat'.

The fact that in these examples the first verb is passive, is immaterial.
We could say:
alinizuia nisiende   'he prevented me from going'
alinikataza nisiende   'he forbade me to go'.

(iv)   **-o -ote**. We have encountered the stem -*ote* meaning 'all, whole'. It
can agree with all classes, e.g. *mwili wote* 'the whole body', *miili yote*
'all the bodies' (*mwili* 'body', class 3). If, however, -*ote* is preceded by a
sort of matching -*o*, it means 'any whatsoever'. So in the text we have
nisile cho chote 'I shouldn't eat any (thing — *kitu, chakula*) at all', and
sikumbuki jambo lo lote 'I don't remember anything (*jambo*) at all'. We
could have examples with other classes, e.g. *nipe kalamu yo yote* 'give
me any pen whatsoever'; *sina vitabu vyo vyote* 'I haven't got any books
at all'. The form for class 1 is *ye yote*, e.g. *mtu ye yote* 'anyone at all'.
Forms for all other classes are with -*o*. (There is no corresponding form
for *sote* 'all of us' or *nyote* 'all of you'.)

(v)   **Binti Abdalla**. Sometimes people are named according to their
relationship to others, e.g. *binti Abdalla* 'daughter (of) Abdalla', *mama
Rehema* 'mother (of) Rehema'. This would usually be the case when the
relative is in some way outstanding, and is a subtle form of flattery. Note
that there is no connecting possessive -*a*.

III

(b) Complete the following sentences. In nos. 7–12 use -ki- or -sipo-'tense':

 1 Usipoangalia magari _____ (-angalia — 'watch (out for)')
 2 Ukivuta sigara nyingi, _____
 3 Mtoto asipokwenda shuleni, _____
 4 Wazee wakitoka wakati wa baridi, _____
 5 Ukitaka kunywa bia, _____
 6 Keki zisipopikwa vizuri, _____
 7 _____ utauawa.
 8 _____ watashtakiwa na mapolisi.
 9 _____ lazima turudi nyumbani.
10 Binti Mohammed anafikiri kwamba _____ ataolewa na mtajiri.
11 _____ utakuwa huna pesa.
12 _____ nitakupiga kweli kweli.

(c) **Methali** (proverbs)

Ukitaka cha mvunguni, lazima uiname.
mvungu — 'space under the bed' (where precious or private possessions are kept)
-inama — 'stoop'
'If you want what's under the bed, you must bend down'.

Uji ukiwa wa moto haupozi kwa ncha ya ulimi.
uji — 'thin porridge, gruel' (cf. *maji*)
-poza — 'make cool' (cf. *-poa*)
ncha — 'tip, point'
'You can't cool hot porridge with the tip of the tongue'

Usipoziba ufa utajenga ukuta.
-ziba — 'stop up'
ufa — 'crack'
'If you don't stop up a crack you will (have to) build a wall'

Kufumba na kufumbua
'To cut a long story short'
-fumba 'close eyes'

Suggest inner meanings for these sayings, and possible parallels in your own language.

(d) Fill in the forms for -ote and -o -ote in your noun class concord chart.

(e) Give the reversive forms of the following verbs, suggesting an English gloss:

-fumba 'close eyes'
-ziba   'stop up'
-tega   'set trap, trap'
-fuma   'knit'
-tata   'tangle'

(f) Draw a human figure and label the parts.

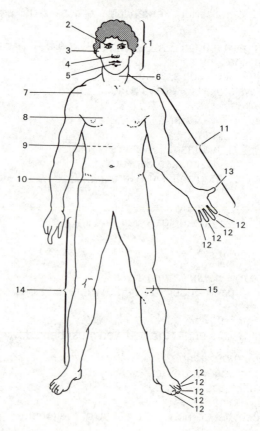

1 kichwa	9 mgongo
2 jicho	10 tumbo
3 sikio	11 mkono
4 pua	12 kidole
5 kinywa	13 kidole gumba
6 koo	14 mguu
7 bega	15 goti
8 kifua	

Give the plurals of these parts of the body.

(g) Answer the questions, looking only at the diagram with numbers.

▷   Unaumwa nini?   Ninaumwa 1 _____
      Unaumwa nini?   Ninaumwa 2 _____
      Unaumwa nini?   Ninaumwa 3 _____
      Unaumwa nini?   Ninaumwa 6 _____
      Una nini?   8 _____ _naniuma
      Una nini?   9 _____ _naniuma
      Una nini?   10 _____ _naniuma
      Una nini?   14 _____ _naniuma
      Una nini?   15 _____ _naniuma.

(h) Write out four consultations between a doctor and his patients, using vocabulary already given, plus the following:

-jeruhi 'wound'
-kohoa 'cough'
-hara 'have diarrhoea'
-funga choo 'be constipated'
-tapika 'vomit'
-vunja 'break'
-anguka 'fall'
-paka 'apply' (ointment etc.)
-tumia 'take' (e.g. medicine)
-vuta pumzi 'breathe in'
-toa pumzi 'breathe out'
mafua 'cold'
dawa 'medicine' (to take or apply)
bendeji 'bandage'
tangu lini? 'since when?'

(i) **Michezo. Maumivu 'pains'.**

One player groans. The rest ask 'Una nini, bwana/bibi?'. He repies, e.g. 'Ninaumwa mkono'. The rest clutch themselves in the part named and repeat the name. Any player to make a mistake is out. (If players are too good, the last to clutch is out.)

As above, but when the first player says what is wrong, he clutches *either* the place he mentions *or* somewhere else. The other players must clutch the correct portion of their anatomy, repeating the name (this is not necessarily the part clutched by the leading player). Any player making a mistake (or the last to move) is out.

IV

Modern medicine has made great strides in East Africa, and the Swahili have not been slow to avail themselves of it. Nevertheless, facilities are limited, medicines are expensive, and human nature being what it is, traditional remedies are also resorted to. Many herbal remedies may have some beneficial effect; others are harmless at least. One nostrum highly prized in the past was *mumiani* 'mummy' — powdered mummy imported from Egypt. However, as an ancient informant in Mombasa told me sadly, after describing the use of some of these traditional remedies, '*Lakini mimi sielewi, lakini tangu kuingia kwa madawa ya kizungu, dawa za kienyeji hazifanyi kazi tena*' 'But I don't know how it is, but since the introduction of European medication, local medicines don't work any more.' There has been recently, especially in Tanzania, some investigation of traditional remedies in the hope of finding inexpensive and efficacious substitutes for imported drugs.

It is not surprising in a country where there is a great variety of tropical and imported diseases, where water is frequently contaminated, where disease-carrying insects abound, and where problems of hygiene and the prevention of infection are imperfectly understood or are difficult to put into practice, that illness is greatly feared and some people will try almost anything for relief. Folk-medicine is universal, and there is no doubt that it can be helpful in some cases. Bone-setters, for example, have traditional skills which they pass on, and may perhaps be compared with osteopaths in Western Europe.

Mental and psychosomatic illnesses are most difficult to deal with in any culture, and here the Swahili have recourse traditionally to *waganga* 'medicine-men' (sing. *mganga*) who may prescribe a variety of medicines and treatment. There is also a considerable belief in the evil eye, and people who have reason to believe they have been bewitched may consult a *mganga*. Many of the *waganga* make use of astrology and passages of the Koran in their diagnoses and suggestions for countering evil. Such *waganga* are concerned with curing or comforting patients, casting horoscopes for people about to undertake difficult enterprises (a journey, marriage, large purchase, etc.), and providing protection, blessing, good spells for the success of love, marriage, crops, cattle and so on. Small children may often be seen wearing an amulet, *hirizi*, round the arm or the neck or ankle. This often contains some lines from the Koran rolled up in a small container, and is there for protection or luck. Much comfort and relief may be obtained from a good *mganga*. Such people often have great insight into the situations and minds of their patients, as well as knowledge of herbal and other remedies.

There is also a strong belief in witchcraft, and those who practise it are *wachawi* 'witches' (sing. *mchawi*) — men or women. These people are believed to have amazing powers and to perform dreadful rituals, encompassing the illness, death or ruin of their victims. Occasional lurid reports of such activities appear in the press.

Unit 25　Fungu la ishirini na tano
Kuazima na kuazimia — Borrowing and lending

I

(a)　Ofisini. Wako Bwana Harris na Bibi Maw.

> Bw.H.:　Joan, kalamu yangu imepotea. Unayo kalamu wewe?
>
> Bi.M.:　Haya, Stuart. Ninazo zangu tatu. Lakini hii moja ndogo sana. Hii ya pili si nzuri. Labda chukua ile ya tatu, yenye raba.
>
> Bw.H.:　Asante sana. Kweli kalamu hii yenye raba itanifaa sana, katika zako zote.
>
> Bi.M.:　Haya, chukua tu.

Anaingia Professor Athumani.

> Pr. A.:　Stuart, sina raba. Unayo raba wewe?
>
> Bw.H.:　Sinayo, lakini chukua hii kalamu yangu yenye raba.
>
> Bi.M.:　Kalamu ile si yako, Stuart, bali ni yangu!
>
> Bw.H.:　Ndiyo kweli. Basi, Badi, chukua hii kalamu yake Joan.

-azima — 'borrow'
-azimia — 'lend'
unayo — 'have you one (pencil)'
ninazo — 'I have some (pencils)'
raba — 'rubber'
katika — here: 'out of'
hii kalamu yake Joan — 'this pencil of Joan's. See section II (i).

(b)　Hotelini. Wako Bibi Maw na rafiki yake Toon.

> Bi.M.:　Toon, gari yetu imeharibika.
>
> Toon:　Pole sana! Gari gani lakini?
>
> Bi.M.:　Kwa kweli ni gari yake Stuart, lakini sisi sote tunaitumia.
>
> Toon:　Bahati mbaya. Ungependa kuazima gari yangu?
>
> Bi.M.:　Gari yako? Ingetufaa sana.
>
> Toon:　Kwa kweli si gari yangu mimi, bali ni gari yake bibi yangu. Tunazo gari zetu mbili.
>
> Bi.M.:　Yaani, Jemima angetuazimia* gari yake?
>
> Toon:　Kweli kabisa. Ngoja kwanza, nitampigia simu mara moja.
>
> Bi.M.:　Kweli wewe na Jemima ni marafiki zetu sana!

ungependa — 'would you like'
ingetufaa — 'it would be useful to us'
gari zetu mbili — 'two cars belonging to us'
angetuazimia — 'would she lend us'
nitampigia simu — 'I shall phone her'

* On the tape the speaker says *-azima* here by mistake.

(c)   Ofisini. Yuko Bwana Harris. Pr. Athumani anaingia.

▷   Pr.A.:   Stuart, naweza kutumia simu yako? Simu yangu haifanyi kazi.
            Bw.H.:   Karibu tu.

      Kiring'-kiring', kiring'-kiring', kiring'-kiring' . . .

            Pr.A.:   Do! Sipati jibu. Hii simu yako inafanya kazi?
            Bw.H.:   Inafanya kazi, lakini mara nyingi hawajibu. Nenda ukajaribu ile
                      ya Bibi Muthama, huko ofisini. Ile yake ni bora zaidi kuliko hii
                      yangu.
            Pr.A.:   Afalek! Watu wengi wanalalamika kwamba simu zao hazifany
                      kazi.
            Bw.H.:   Tena ni kweli.

-tumia — 'use'
naweza — 'I can', 'can I?'. This structure will be dealt with in the next
      Unit.
bora — 'better, best, very good'
afalek — expression of impatience, accompanied by finger-clicking.
-lalamika — 'complain'

II

(i)   **kalamu yake Joan**. *kalamu ya Joan* means 'Joan's pencil (pen)'; to
      use a possessive pronoun plus a possessor is to emphasise the idea of
      possession. This might best be done in English by stress, 'Joan's pencil'
      or by a different grammatical structure 'that pencil of Joan's'. So Toon in
      the second dialogue says:

      gari yake bibi yangu '*my wife*'s car'.

(ii)   **-na plus object relative**. When playing the game *Jamaa* in Unit 17
      we learned that the 3rd person singular object marker *-ye* (plural *-o*) can
      be added to the root *-na*, and indeed must be if the object itself is not
      mentioned or is a living being. So we had the question, e.g. *unaye
      Bwana Bunduki?* and the answer *ninaye* 'I have him' or *sinaye* 'I have
      not got him'. Agreement suffixes of other classes also exist, ending in
      -o. So in the text we have:

      unayo kalamu? 'pencil, have you a pencil?'

      where *-yo* consists of class 9 marker *y-*, plus *-o*. (This *o* is sometimes
      called the '*o* of reference', and will be dealt with further in the next two
      units.) Another example from the text is:

      ninazo tatu 'I have three of them'

      where *z-* is class 10 marker.

      Other class agreements are formed predictably, except that *w-* before
      -o is always elided, as in

      ninao (class 2) 'I have them (people, animals)'

The effect of using this marker with non-animate beings is to emphasise the object, if present, as in

unayo kalamu? 'have you a *pencil*?'

or simply to refer to it, if not present, e.g.

ninayo 'I have one (it)'.

If the object is not present, the agreement *must* be added to *-na-*.

(iii) **'Prepositional' verbs and 'objects'**

As we have seen, in Swahili the prepositional idea is normally expressed in the verb by an extension, e.g.

kusoma	'to read'	*kusomea*	'to read to/for'
kununua	'to buy'	*kununulia*	'to buy for'.

In a clause where both an 'object' and a 'beneficiary' of the action of the verb is present or referred to, the 'beneficiary' has the 'object prefix'. So in the text we had:

angetuazimia gari yake? 'would she lend us her car?'

We could say:

Baba alimnunulia mtoto wake baisikeli 'the father bought his son a bicycle'.

In English grammatical terminology it is common to refer to 'his son' as 'indirect object' and 'a bicycle' as 'direct object'. If these terms are used to describe Swahili, it is important to remember that, as for concord, it is the 'indirect object' which 'agrees'. There can *not* be concord with the 'direct object'. This is true also for verbs with a 'prepositional' meaning, even if they have no prepositional extension, e.g. *-pa* 'give'. We say:

alinipa zawadi 'he gave me a present';

zawadi in this structure can *not* have an object prefix.

The neutral sequence is for the 'beneficiary' to precede the 'object'. Other sequences can occur, but with changes in intonation and concomitant changes in emphasis, e.g.

tulimnunulia mtoto wetu baisikeli 'we bought our child a bicycle'
tulimnunulia baisikeli, mtoto wetu 'we bought our child *a bicycle*'
mtoto wetu, tulimnunulia baisikeli 'we bought *our child* a bicycle'

(iv) **The meanings of 'prepositional' verbs**

Although the form of a 'prepositional', extension to a verb can be predicted, its meaning often can not. It is true that in many cases the meaning of the prepositional form of the verb would in English be expressed by the use of a preposition, as we have seen in Unit 16. But in many other cases the meaning is not so easily linked with the idea of a preposition, although there may be a close relationship. In the text, for example, we have

kuazima 'to borrow/lend' - *kuazimia* 'to lend (to)/(borrow for)

It should also be noted that the simple form of some verbs does convey some prepositional meaning, e.g. *kupa* 'to give (to)', *kulipa* 'to pay/repay'.

In some cases, the use of the object prefix with a simple verb form conveys a prepositional and derogatory meaning, e.g.

-*cheka* 'laugh' - *alinicheka*   'he laughed at me' i.e. ridiculed
-*sema* 'say'   - *alinisema*   'he spoke ill of me'
              - *alinisemea*   'he spoke up for me'

Some simple verbs express motion, and their extended forms express motion towards, e.g.

-*geuka* 'turn (away)'   -*geukia* 'turn towards (on)'
-*fuata* 'follow'   -*fuatia* 'follow up (try to catch up)'
-*hama* 'move house, flit'   -*hamia*   'move in'
-*kimbia* 'run (away)'   -*kimbilia* 'run to'

You will recall that the prepositional extension is also used within a nominal group to express purpose, e.g.

behewa la kulia   'dining-car' (-*la* 'eat')
mawe ya kujengea nyumba   'house-building stones' (-*jenga* 'build')
maji ya kuogea   'washing-water' (-*oga* 'bathe')

A meaning of completeness is sometimes conveyed by the prepositional form, but more often by the double prepositional form, e.g.

-*tupa* 'throw'   -*tupia* 'throw at'   -*tupilia* 'throw away'
-*funga* 'shut'   -*fungia* 'shut for'   -*fungilia* 'lock up'

This use of the double prepositional form is often accompanied by an idiomatic use of the word *mbali* 'far', e.g.

tupilia mbali takataka hii   'throw this rubbish right away'
tutamfungilia mbali mwizi huyo 'we shall lock that thief up for good'

In some cases the meaning, whether suggesting a prepositional idea or not, is hard to predict, e.g. in the text we have:

naweza kutumia simu yako? 'can I use your phone?'

where -*tumia* means 'use'. -*tuma* means 'send'. (Care in use is needed also, since -*tumia* with a living object means 'have sexual intercourse with'.) Some further examples of meanings which are hard for the foreigner to predict are:

-*amka*   'wake up'   -*amkia*   'greet'
-*nuka*   'stink'   -*nukia*   'smell nice'
-*ingia* 'enter'   -*ingilia* 'interrupt'
-*rudi*   'return'   -*rudia*   'punish' 'revise'
-*simama* 'stand'   -*simamia* 'supervise'
-*tembea* 'walk (to)'   -*tembelea* 'visit'
-*vaa*   'put on, wear' -*valia*   'dress up' (esp. with -*ji*-:
                        amejivalia 'he's all dressed up')

(v) **The verb -*piga*** is used in combination with nouns to convey a wide range of meanings. In the previous unit we had -*piga sindano* 'inject'. In this one we have -*piga simu* 'telephone'.
    Here are a few more expressions:
    -*piga pasi*   'iron (clothes etc.)'
    -*piga picha* 'photograph'

-piga teke   'kick'
-piga kelele 'make a noise, shout'
-piga miayo   'yawn'
-piga mtindi 'get drunk, hit the bottle' (*mtindi* lit. 'buttermilk')

Many more can be found in the dictionary under *-piga*.

(vi) Note the verb forms with *-nge-* in the text, meaning 'would'. This will be
    dealt with fully in Unit 28.

III

(d) Jibu maswali hayo mara mbili, (a) kwa kutumia *-azima*,
                              (b) kwa kutumia *-azimia*.

   (Answer the following questions twice, (a) using *-azima*
                              (b) using *-azimia*):

   Bwana Harris alipata wapi raba?
   Professor Athumani alipata wapi raba?
   Bi. Maw na Bw. Harris walipata wapi gari?
   Vipi Professor Athumani alipata kupiga simu?

(e) Jibu kwa maneno yako mwenyewe (Answer in your own words):

   Kwa nini Professor Athumani alitaka kutumia simu ya Bwana Harris?
   Kwa nini Bibi Maw alikuwa hana gari ya kutumia?
   Kwa nini Bwana Harris alichukua kalamu ya Bibi Maw?

(f) Toa maoni yako (Give your own opinion):

   Kwa nini Professor Athumani alitaka kupiga simu?
   Kwa nini Toon aliuliza 'Gari gani lakini?'?
   Bibi yake Toon atasema nini juu ya kuazimia gari yake? (*juu ya* here
      means 'concerning')
   Kwa nini Bwana Harris alisema ati kalamu yenye raba ni yake? (*ati* 'that'
      is used when the reporter wishes to dissociate himself from the
      following statement, or to suggest that it is not true.)

(g) Answer the following questions in the negative, giving an alternative
   owner and stressing the relationship:

   Hiki ni kitabu chako?
   Miti hii ni ya mwalimu?
   Mzee yule ni babako?
   Vyakula hivi ni vya mvua samaki?
   Hiyo ni gari ya Rais?
   Shauri hilo ni lako?

(h) On your concord chart, fill in the object agreements for all classes with
   -na, e.g.

   class 1 *ninaye* 'I have him'
   class 2 *ninao* 'I have them', etc.

(i)   Answer the following questions, omitting the object in your reply, but
      referring to it, e.g.

      Una kalamu yangu? Ndiyo, ninayo. (or, Siyo, sinayo.)

      Una mfuko wangu?
      Bwana Harris ana miavuli yetu?
      Wazee wana nguo za kufaa?
      Mna vibonge vya homa?
      Nyumba yako ina ghorofa? (*ghorofa* 'storey', i.e. 'an upstairs')
      Bustanini mwako mna maua?
      Paka wako ana jina? (*paka* 'cat')
      Philip, una wembe?
      Chupa hii ina kizibo? (*kizibo* 'stopper')

(j)   Give the Swahili for:

      a cooking-pot
      medicine (use -*nywa*)
      ointment
      a bread-knife (*kisu* 'knife')
      a place to live (-*kaa*)

(k)   Rewrite the following sentences, using the prepositional form of the
      verb, e.g.

      Wazee walinunua shati. (mtoto). Wazee walimnunulia mtoto shati.

      Bw. Harris alipiga simu jana. (Bi. Maw)
      Professor Athumani alipeleka barua. (mamake)
      Bw. Philip alifungua mlango. (Pr. Athumani)
      Mtoto analia. (mamake)
      Bw. Philip alitanda kitanda. (Bw. Harris) (-*tanda* 'spread'; -*tanda kitanda*
        'make the bed')
      Bi. Abdalla alitafuta mfuko. (Bi. Maw)
      Wanafunzi wamekasirika. (mwalimu)
      Ondoa vyombo. (bwana)
      Bi. Maw alitia chai. (wageni wake)
      Chagua machungwa makubwa. (mimi)
      Mvuvi ameleta samaki. (sisi) (*mvuvi* 'fisherman')
      Nani alipata kitabu hiki? (wewe)

(l)   Make up sentences using the prepositional forms of the following verbs,
      illustrating their use. Give a gloss for each of your sentences:

      -chukua   -fua
      -uza   -soma.
      -funga

(m)   **Methali — proverb**

      Mtoto akililia kisu, mpe. Translate this proverb and suggest a meaning
      for it.

IV

Ownership.

There is a considerable tradition in many parts of Africa of communal ownership, traditionally of land. Historically this has been the basis of some severe misunderstandings, to put it mildly. Where tribal land is communally owned any individual wishing to cultivate a particular area will ask the chief, and an arrangement will be made, perhaps involving some sort of payment. But the land will never be owned by the individual under this system, it remains the property of the tribe. When Europeans arrived in Kenya, for example, with their concept of individual ownership of land, they frequently thought they had bought a plot, whereas to the local chief they had simply leased it or been allowed to work it. A more recent, poignant example occurred a few years ago in Tanzania when a young Afro-American, no doubt wishing to identify with local people, built himself a hut near a village on land that seemed to him 'waste'. Of course it was tribal land, and the villagers sent for the police who arrested him for squatting. Perhaps he was particularly naive, but it was a sad case, and it arose out of a misunderstanding of the nature of ownership of land.

The Swahili (Muslim) community do have a system of land ownership and inheritance; nevertheless there is much more sharing of possessions, borrowing and lending, than the European might expect. Not only women will lend each other finery. I once commented on the small amount of luggage a Swahili friend of mine had with him for a proposed stay of several weeks abroad. He explained that he was going to stay with a close friend and, as they were roughly the same size, they borrowed each other's clothes quite frequently, and it was very convenient.

This attitude of sharing does also spread to expatriates in Africa. People lend one another cars, for example, fairly frequently, and seem much more hospitable than in Europe. In a country where everyone experiences natural difficulties, such as extremes of climate, widespread disease, lack of amenities and, sometimes, danger from wild animals, there is much more mutual assistance than is called for in normal Western life.

Between Swahili neighbours there is a constant coming and going of child messengers borrowing a cup of sugar here or a little salt there, and it would be thought very churlish to refuse. All the same, there is a sort of running tally kept mentally, of goods and services, and scroungers are the subject of disapproving gossip.

Debt is something which many people live with. Among farmers there may be long gaps between the sale of cash crops, but many of today's desirable commodities can only be obtained for cash. Also it is the custom for all wage-earners to be paid at the end of the month, not weekly, and a small salary may have to stretch round a large family. So most people run up an account at the local shop, and often have very little left from their wages when they have paid off the debt. Borrowing and lending between members of the family and friends is frequent, and of course can lead to trouble. Ingenious schemes abound. For example one small wage-earner

I know agreed with a fellow that they would hold their wages in common, one person taking the lot alternate months. This meant in theory that the one whose turn it was to have both wages would have enough to make some substantial purchase he might need, as well as pay off his debts. It worked for one month; at the end of the second month the man whose turn it was to give up his wage somehow managed to elude the other and spent it all before his friend caught up with him!

Problems arise particularly in inter-racial situations where different systems are in use and where the stranger cannot properly assess the situation. It would be a disgrace for a well-to-do Swahili to refuse to help a friend in dire straits, and generosity is widely regarded as a virtue. On the other hand, nobody would have much sympathy for him if he were taken in by a known scrounger. The foreigner cannot expect to understand this system at once, and may easily feel exploited. Perhaps Westerners put too high a value on money, so that money transactions tend to sour relationships for them. Reactions are different too. In the case of the two Swahili friends who agreed to share wages, the one who was swindled simply went about borrowing from other friends for his immediate needs, and regarded his loss as more or less his own fault for not being outside the door when his friend came out of work with his wage-packet.

The foreigner learning a language must be aware that it is inseparable from the culture of the speakers, and must expect that attitudes to even the most fundamental matters may be very different from those of his own cultural background.

Revision

Render the following into idiomatic Swahili. Use expressions you already know. Do not try to translate, but think of socially equivalent Swahili. For example 'Hello' in English, as the first word of greeting, would be *Hujambo* in Swahili. The second speaker, saying also 'Hello' in English would have to reply *Sijambo* in Swahili, and add *sijui wewe* or some equivalent enquiry.

Hasani: Hello, Philip.
Philip: Hello, Hasani. How are you?
Hasani: I'm fine. How's things with you?
Philip: Alright, but I've got a lot to do.
Hasani: What sort of things?
Philip: Oh, work around the house. What about you?
Hasani: I'm very well. I'm on my way to market. Why don't you come with me?
Philip: Shall I? What are you going to buy? A pig?
Hasani: Don't tease me. I want to buy some oranges.
Philip: Well don't buy bitter ones. My boss was swindled like that* only yesterday.
Hasani: Don't worry, I won't. Come on, let's go.
Philip: O.K.

* like that — *hivyo*

Kwenda Tamarind — Going to the Tamarind

I

(a)   Bibi Maw na Bwana Harris wako Mombasa. Wanastarehe huko.

Bw.H.:   Joan, nimechoka kula chakula katika hoteli hii. Twende
          penginepo leo usiku.
Bi.M.:   Haya, nitafurahi sana. Twende wapi, lakini?
Bw.H.:   Nimesikia Tamarind ni hoteli nzuri. Twende huko.
Bi.M.:   Haya, vizuri. Unajua hoteli yenyewe iko wapi?
Bw.H.:   Sijui, lakini nitapiga simu kuulizia.

          ....

Bw.H.:   Nimepiga simu Tamarind. Tuna meza huko saa mbili na nusu.
Bi.M.:   Nimefurahi sana. Unajua mahali?
Bw.H.:   Wamesema kwamba iko mbele ya daraja la Nyali. Nafikiri
          tutawahi kufika. Unajua daraja liko wapi?
Bi.M.:   Ndiyo, najua.
Bw.H.:   Haya basi, twende.
Bi.M.:   Ngoja kidogo niende kuoga.
Bw.H.:   Usikawie, tuna nusu saa tu kufika huko.
Bi.M.:   Usiwe na wasiwasi, nusu saa itatosha. Kutoka hapa mpaka
          huko ni maili mbili tatu tu.
Bw.H.:   Usichelewe, lakini.

          ....

Kwenye gari.

Bw.H.:   Haya basi, nitaendesha mimi. Wewe utaniongoza niende
          wapi.
Bi.M.:   Vizuri. Fuata kwanza njia hii. Halafu kwenye njia panda, shika
          njia ya kushoto.
Bw.H.:   Haya, twende huyooo!

          ....

Bi.M.:   Kushoto, kushoto! Si nilisema ushike njia ya kushoto?
Bw.H.:   Do, kweli, nami nimepita kulia. Tufanyeje?
Bi.M.:   Haidhuru, endelea tu. Utakapofika bahari, pita njia ya kushoto.

          ....

Bw.H.:   Haya, tumefika bahari. Kushoto sasa, sivyo?
Bi.M.:   Ndivyo. Sasa baada ya jumba la Rais, pita njia ya pili ya
          kushoto.
Bw.H.:   Kushoto tena?
Bi.M.:   Ndiyo.
Bw.H.:   Siyo kulia?
Bi.M.:   Hata!
Bw.H.:   Haya, kushoto tena. Na sasa, je?
Bi.M.:   Sasa kwenye kipilefiti, pita njia ya kulia.
Bw.H.:   Kweli?

Bi.M.:   Kweli kabisa.

Bw.H.:   Nimepotea mimi.

Bi.M.:   Ni sawa tu. Sasa nenda moja kwa moja mpaka daraja.

Bw.H.:   Kweli? Walitaja Digo Road.

Bi.M.:   Hapa ndipo Digo Road. Endelea tu, moja kwa moja.

....

Bw.H.:   Sasa tumekwenda mbali sana. Labda tumepotea. Sioni
         daraja.

Bi.M.:   Endelea tu. Karibu kufika daraja. Umeliona sasa?

Bw.H.:   Naona daraja lakini sioni hoteli. Iko wapi?

Bi.M.:   Sijui hoteli, najua daraja tu.

Bw.H.:   Hakuna daraja jingine?

Bi.M.:   Liko, lakini daraja la Nyali ndilo hili.

Bw.H.:   Lakini hoteli, je?

Bi.M.:   Walisemaje hasa?

Bw.H.:   Walisema mbele ya daraja. Lakini mi naona giza tu.

Bi.M.:   Mimi vile vile. Labda siyo njia hii. Turudi nyuma kidogo na
         kujaribu njia nyingine.

Bw.H.:   Njia ipi?

Bi.M.:   Njia ya kushoto, hakuna nyingine.

....

Bw.H.:   Naona siyo njia hii.

Bi.M.:   Tupite tu, tujaribu.

Bw.H.:   Tazama, hakuna hoteli yo yote hapa. Tena tumechelewa sana.
         Twende wapi sasa?

Bi.M.:   Pita hapa, mkono wa kushoto.

Bw.H.:   Mimi sipendi njia hii. Naona mahali pabaya sana. Tena hakuna
         hoteli.

Bi.M.:   Pita tu, halafu tena njia ya kushoto.

Bw.H.:   Tena? Tunakwenda wapi sasa?

Bi.M.:   Tunarudi tena kwenye daraja. Lazima hoteli iko karibu sana.

Bw.H.:   Sijui wapi, lakini. Tumepotea.

Bi.M.:   Ngoja kwanza, simama hapa. Nitauliza kwenye gereji huko.

Bw.H.:   Haya, uliza tu.

....

Bw.H.:   Walisemaje?

Bi.M.:   Walisema tuvuke daraja, halafu tupite mkono wa kulia.

Bw.H.:   Tuvuke daraja? Lakini watu wa hoteli walisema iko mbele ya
         daraja!

Bi.M.:   Twende tu . . . Tazama huko upande mwingine wa bahari!
         Naona taa nyingi sana. Si hapo Tamarind?

Bw.H.:   Ndiyo kweli. Hapo ndipo Tamarind. Mbona hatukuiona
         kwanza? Tena mbona walisema ati iko mbele ya daraja?

Bi.M.:   Walisema kwa Kiswahili au kwa Kiingereza?

Bw.H.:   Kwa Kiingereza.

Bi.M.:   Na msemaji Mwingereza?

Bw.H.:   Siyo, nafikiri alikuwa ni Mswahili.

Bi.M.:   Basi, bila shaka alijua tutatoka mjini. Alisema hoteli iko mbele
         ya daraja, yaani kwa Kiswahili iko upande mwingine,
         upande wa mbele wa daraja, yaani unapita daraja kwanza.
         Hivyo ndivyo tulivyokosa, sababu sisi bado tunafikiria
         Kiingereza.

Bw.H.:   Kweli Kiswahili kigumu sana!
Bi.M.:   Tena sana! Pita kulia sasa! Tumeshafika.
Bw.H.:   Mungu asifiwe!
Bi.M.:   Amina!

-starehe — 'to have a good time'
kuulizia — 'to make enquiries'
daraja — 'bridge'
-wahi — 'manage'
najua — 'I know'
-oga — 'wash body'
-kawia — 'delay'
wasiwasi — 'nervousness'
-tosha — 'be enough'
kutoka hapa mpaka huko — 'from here to there' (*mpaka* lit. 'boundary')
mbili tatu — 'two or three, a few'
-fuata — 'follow, go along'
njia panda — 'cross-roads, junction'
-shika — 'take' (cf. *-shikilia* 'cling to')
kushoto — 'left'
si nilisema — 'didn't I say'
-pita — 'pass along, turn down'
kulia — 'right' (see note in section II (vi))
-dhuru — 'harm', *haidhuru* — 'it doesn't matter'
utakapofika — 'when you arrive'
bahari — 'sea'
sivyo — 'isn't that so', 'that isn't so'
ndivyo — 'that is so'
jumba — 'palace, large house' (cf. *nyumba* 'house')
hata! — 'not at all!'
moja kwa moja — 'straight ahead', 'without hesitation'
-taja — 'mention'
ndipo — 'is really (place)' see section II (i)
ndilo — 'is really (class 5)' see section II (i)
mi — *mimi* (colloquial)
giza — 'darkness'
siyo — 'is definitely not (class 9)'
-vuka — 'cross water' (by bridge, ship, ferry, jumping, etc.) Also cross
    a road.
upande — 'side'
taa — 'lamp, light'
kwa Kiswahili — 'in Swahili'
msemaji — 'speaker' cf. *-sema* 'speak'
-toka — 'come out/go out'
hivyo ndivyo tulivyokosa — 'this is how we went wrong' (*-kosa* 'make
    a mistake')
tumeshafika — 'here we are' (lit. 'we have already arrived')
Mungu — 'God'
-sifu — 'praise'
Amina — 'Amen'

II

(i) **ndi-**.

In Unit 16 we dealt with *ndi-* plus a personal agreement, e.g.

Bi. Maw ndiye mwalimu wetu 'Bi. Maw *is* our teacher'.

Agreement can also be made with all classes 3–18, with the meaning of a strengthened copula. In the text we have:

hapa ndipo Digo Road ('this (here) is Digo Road'

and:

daraja la Nyali ndilo hili 'this is Nyali Bridge'

(neutral sequence would have been *hili ndilo daraja la Nyali*).

The form of the agreement consists of the class grammatical prefix plus *-o*; just as was seen with *-na-* in Unit 25.

The agreement of class 8 with *ndi-* can be used for nouns, as in e.g.

hivyo ndivyo vitabu vyangu 'those *are* my books',

or also for manner, as in the text:

hivyo ndivyo . . . 'this (manner) is how . . .':

and in:

sivyo? 'isn't it like this?' *ndivyo* 'it is like this'.

(ii) **-vyo- and -po- with verbs**

These agreements can be used as verbal prefixes, following the tense sign. In the text we have:

hivyo ndivyo tulivyokosa 'that is how we went wrong'

We also have:

utakapofika bahari 'when you (future tense) reach the sea'.

These prefixes *-po-* and *-vyo-* can be used with present tense *-na-*, past *-li-* (not *-ta-*). (This future form reflects the fact that historically the future tense prefix is derived from the verb *-taka* 'want'.) e.g.

ninaposoma	'when I am reading'
nilipomwona	'when I saw him'
nitakapoondoka	'when I (shall) leave'
anavyokula	'how he is eating'
alivyoondoka	'how he left'
atakavyoendelea	'how he will go on'

-vyo- and *-po* can also be used without any tense sign in the verb, in which case they come *finally*, and the meaning is one of general application:

(kila) nifikapo, wananikaribisha vizuri '(whenever) I come, they make me welcome'

na afanye apendavyo 'let him do as he likes'

(iii) **Adverbial use of prefixes of class 7/8**.

You will have noticed examples of the prefix *vi-* (and now *vyo*) used adverbially. Unit 12 had *vizuri* 'well' (manner); Unit 20 had *hivi* 'thus', and *vibaya* 'badly'; Unit 18 had *hivyo* 'thus, like that'; and now we have a relative form with *ndi-*: *ndivyo* 'like this is', and a verbal form, e.g. *tulivyopotea* 'how we got lost'. (We could also have *sivyo* 'not like this, not this way'.)

We could sum up by saying that *vi-* with an 'adjectival' stem can have adverbial function, e.g.

Umefanya vizuri 'You have done well (the right thing)'
Walimpiga vibaya 'They knocked him about, roughed him up'
Mamangu alinikaripia vikali 'My mother told me off well and truly'
(*-karipia* — 'scold')

With 'demonstrative' stems, *vi-* has the sense of manner:

Kwa nini alisema hivi? 'Why did he say that sort of thing/talk like that?'
Ninasema hivi: 'This is what I want to convey:'
Aliposikia vile 'When he heard that (how things were)'
kwa vile 'seeing that, since', e.g. *Sitaki kufanya kazi kwa vile nimechoka.*
Usifanye hivyo, fanya hivi 'Don't do (it) like that, do it like this'
vile vile 'likewise' — *Watoto vile vile wanasoma* 'The children too are studying'
Wanafanya vivyo hivyo 'They are doing just the same (as before)'
"Unaendeleaje?" "Hivi hivi tu!" '"How are you getting along?" "So-so!"'

The prefix *ki-* can be used for comparison, e.g. *kitoto* 'like a child', *kiaskari* 'like a soldier'. In this case the stem is usually a nominal one, e.g.

Amevaa kifalme 'He's splendidly dressed' (*mfalme* — 'king')
Anatembea kizungu 'He walks like a European' (i.e. stiffly — the expression is not a compliment!)
mtoto wa kiume/kike 'A male/female child'.

A few examples with adjectival stems are found, e.g.

kidogo 'a little, a small amount', as in *maji kidogo* 'A little water'

but to have adverbial function in a clause, such words need to be preceded by *kwa*, e.g.

Alisema kwa kirefu/kwa kifupi 'He spoke at length/briefly' (*-fupi* 'short').

There is no use of *ki-* with demonstratives, or of *cho* with verb or copula to parallel these uses of *vi-* and *vyo*.

(iv)   ***-a-* tense.**

In the text you will notice several new forms of the verb, e.g.

naona 'I see', 'I can see' 'I feel'
nafikiri 'I think'
najua 'I know'.

In these examples, *n-* represents 1st person singular, class 1; *-a-* is a 'tense' sign connoting a general state. This may be opposed to *-na-* which connotes a continuous or temporary present, e.g.

nakaa Nairobi 'I live in Nairobi' i.e. my permanent home
ninakaa Mombasa 'I am living in Mombasa' (at the moment)

(There is some variation in the use of these two tenses in different dialect areas.) Other persons are as follows:

wajua 'you (sing.) know'
ajua 'he/she knows' (in Mombasa *yuajua* may be heard)
twajua 'we know'
mwajua 'you (pl.) know'
wajua 'they know'

(v) **si**.

Note the form:
   si nilisema . . . 'didn't I say . . .' 'I said . . .'.

si can be used to emphasise as if by opposite, e.g.

   si mzuri huyo! 'how beautiful she is!'
   (cf. English 'she isn't half good-looking!')

(vi) **kulia: kushoto**.

Note that the word for 'right' also is related to the verb 'eat', 'eat with'. *mkono wa kulia* has therefore two inseparable meanings. 'Right hand' is also sometimes *mkono wa kuume* (-*ume* 'male', connotation 'strong'), and left: *mkono wa kuke/kike* (-*ke* 'female', connotation 'weak').

III

(b) Using the text and the map (*ramani*) answer the following questions:

Bibi Maw na Bwana Harris walikaa hoteli gani?
Chora njia yao kutoka hoteli yao mpaka Tamarind. (-*chora* 'draw')
Bibi Maw alitaka kufuata njia gani? Chora katika ramani.

(c) Practise (or write out) the following dialogues, repeating with different vocabulary items:

▷   Mimi: Saa hii ni yako?
     Wewe: Ndiyo, ni yangu.
     Mimi: Ali alisema ati ni yake.
     Wewe: Mtu huyo ni mwongo tu, saa ile ndiyo yangu. (*mwongo* 'liar')

     Mimi: Saa hizi ni zenu?
     Wewe: Ndiyo, ni zetu.
     Mimi: Ali na Hasani walisema ati ni zao.
     Wewe: Watu hao ni waongo tu, zile ndizo saa zetu.

         mfuko; mifuko
         shati; mashati
         kisu; visu
         uma; nyuma

(d) Construct one sentence from each of the following pairs, making the first clause a dependent clause of time, e.g.

Nilifika nyumbani kwake. Mwenzangu alisoma. (*mwenzangu* 'my friend')
Nilipofika nyumbani kwake, mwenzangu alikuwa anasoma.

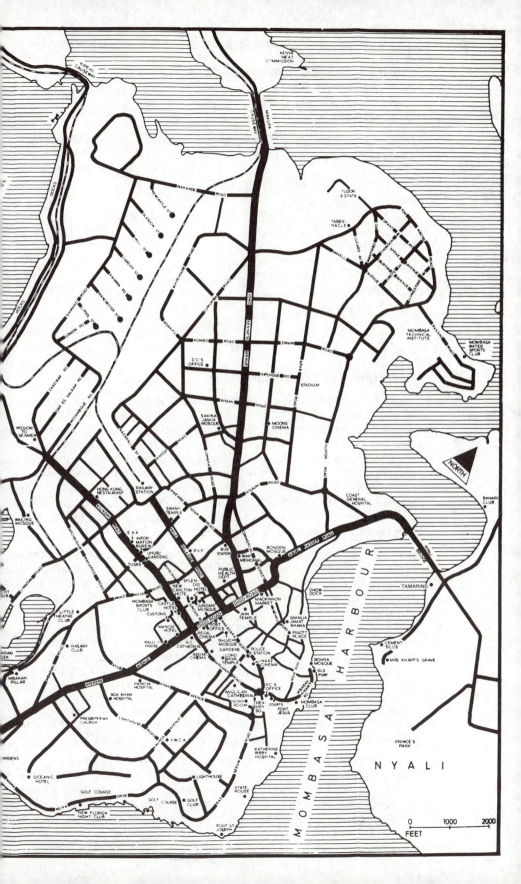

Mjomba wetu alifika. Tulikula chakula.
Wageni wetu waliondoka. Tulifanya kazi.
Tuliondoka nyumbani. Mtoto wetu alilia.
Mlevi alikimbia. Watu walicheka.

Now rewrite your sentences making the *second* clause dependent.
Change the sequence of the clauses.

(e)   Complete the following sentences:
Nilipofika shuleni _____
Mtoto alipovuta sigara _____ (-*vuta* 'pull' 'smoke')
Bi. Maw aliposikia homa _____
Mwivi alipoingia nyumbani kwangu _____
Bw. Harris alipoendesha gari kwa kasi _____ (*kwa kasi* 'fast')
Nitakapopata mapesa mengi sana _____
Kila nifikapo nyumbani _____
Kila nimwonapo mwenzangu _____

IV

Entertainment and festivals.

Apart from European-type hotels and eating-houses, there are everywhere small 'bars' or 'hotels' selling tea, soft drinks, *maandazi* (sort of
doughnuts), and at midday more substantial food, such as rice (*wali*) or
cassava (*muhogo*) with a savoury sauce (*mchuzi*) as a relish (*kitoweo*).
There are also beer dens where huge vats of beer (*pombe*) are brewed
daily and the customers often drink with straws from a communal pot.
Strict Muslims would not patronise these establishments. On the busy
streets there are sellers of coconuts (*madafu* — unripe coconuts full of
sweet water for drinking — very refreshing), fizzy drinks, little packets of
roast nuts, roast cassava or maize cobs.

On the whole it is only men who frequent the 'bars' or 'hotels', dropping
in after work (on the coast many offices work from 8am to 2pm) or in the
evening. Modern girls may sometimes be seen there but in general good
Muslim women stay at home or go out visiting. Swahili professional or
business men may entertain guests in European-type hotels and
restaurants, but these are exceptions to the mass of Swahili society. It is
not really the custom to go out for a meal for pleasure — some light
refreshment, perhaps, but substantial meals are enjoyed at home on the
whole. Nor is it at all the custom for an unmarried woman to go out alone
with a man in the evening, as Bibi Maw and Bwana Harris do in the text.

Quite a lot of entertaining goes on at home, and the Swahili cuisine is
delicious, but cannot be found except in private houses. It is much
influenced by Arabic and perhaps also Indian-style cooking.

Apart from purely social entertaining at home, which is usually informal,
family ceremonies are quite frequent. Within an extended family there is
always someone being born, or married, or dying; and all these
occasions are accompanied by more or less extended ceremonies
involving large numbers of people. Weddings are particular occasions for

celebration, especially by women; and husbands are known to complain about the expense of providing suitable clothes and entertainment. Perhaps in all communities there is an element of rivalry in display; weddings amongst the Swahili are certainly an opportunity for it. Before the wedding traditionally there are processions through the streets to announce it and to invite people. Then not only are there great celebrations at the time of the marriage ceremony itself, but also further parties, often with hired musicians and dancers at the house of the bridegroom's parents. At these receptions the house will be jammed with people, and often the street outside will be taken over as well, curtained off with rugs hung on lines between the houses, and the road covered with more rugs and cushions to sit on. Thus a wedding may last for weeks. Men and women have separate ceremonies as a rule. Wakes are also great occasions for gatherings; so are ceremonies connected with childbirth.

There are also public celebrations of various kinds. Religious feasts among Muslims are quite frequent, and special food is eaten at certain times. Even Ramadan, the month of fasting, takes on a festival air at night. During the daytime, the strict Muslim will not eat or drink, and may not even swallow his saliva, but spits it out. As it is always hot on the coast, going all day without a drink is very tiring, and there is a great impression of lethargy at this time. However, when night falls many stalls appear in the streets, brightly lit, and selling delicious food. People walk about in the cool, and there is an air of relaxation. Special meals are prepared at home, too, and with some people much of the night is taken up with eating and drinking ready for the rigours of the following day. Lethargy during the daytime may be partly attributable to lack of sleep. The end of Ramadan is of course a time of great rejoicing.

Local and national occasions such as trade fairs, or Independence Day, are also times for processions, dancing and feasting. The Swahili do seem to enjoy organising and taking part in celebrations, and not only are great state occasions fully exploited, but also even elections are preceded by weeks of rival processions, songs, slogans, and rallies.

In general it is probably true to say that Swahili entertainment and celebrations are more social and public than private.

Unit 27 Fungu la ishirini na saba
Barua — A letter

I

(a)

Kwa Dr. Maw,

Pokea salamu kutoka kwa Philip na baada ya salamu mimi mzima hofu na mashaka nijuu yako wewe Lakini natumai uhali kadhalika. Baada ya hayo ahsante sana kwa kunikumbuka na post-card iliokuja kupitia kwa Bwana H. Vile vile shukurani sana kwa msaada ulioniletea. Nimefurahi sana kuona umenisaidia bila ya kukuomba, ahsante Mungu akuweke na atupe maisha marefu yenye raha na mafato mema. Amakweli umenifaa sana Sihaba kusema kweli. Sijakusahau mimi mara kwa mara hukukumbuka wewe Rafiki mwema hasa kwa wakati tuliokuwa tukifanya kazi pamoja nyumbani mwa Bwana H. saa zingine tukiongea nahuku tukicheka, Mara roho yangu ikichafuka ndiwe uliokuwa ukinipoza moyo. Basi haya yote ni mengi ambayo sikutaka kuyataja kwavile barua haimalizi maneno hunifanya nitikukumbuka sana. Saa zingine nitiona kila kitabu cha ubighi wa kenya hukukumbuta nakufurahi sana yaani kile uloniachia. Kumbe DR, Maw kitu cha ukumbusho nikizuri hivyo! Nilifurahi sana kufatu kazi ya Posta japo sijajuwa kazi ningali nafunzwa. Lakini njuwa kidogo Huenda baada ya miwe miezi miwili nikaenda shuleni ya mafunzo ya Posta huko mjini Nairobi. Hunitiko Kwale sikubaya, kuna miti mingi sana na hakuna joto kama Sehemu nyinginezo za mkowa wa Pwani.

TFFADHALI ZUNGULA UPANDE NA PILI.

Sijuwi nikwa nini pengine nikwa sababu ya miti. Sijajuwa watu wengi sana lakini kidogo tu, na wenye wilaya hii yakwele hasa ni kabila ya wadigo wele wengine niwao waliokuja kwa kazi. Lakini ajabu nimarafika sana kwa watuwengine. Sina mengi kwaleo Lakini najisikia nikikukusa sana kivyo naona tulionana sijuwa miaka kumi iliopita. ukiona makosa naomba unisamehe kwani sijuwi nimeandika kiamu au nikimvita. Kaa na neema na Mungu akulinde.

Mie, Philip.

Ewe samahani Nisalimie wanao yaani David na ule mwengine sijuwi ndiye nani.

In the following version of the above letter, punctuation is inserted to assist the student, and where non-standard forms are used, the standard variant is given in italics.

Kwa Dr Maw,

     Pokea salamu kutoka kwa Philip; na baada ya salamu, mimi mzima; hofu na mashaka *ni juu* yako wewe. Lakini natumai *u hali* kadhalika. Baada ya hayo, *asante* sana *kwa kunikumbuka* na post-card *iliyokuja* kupitia kwa Bwana H. Vile vile *shukrani* sana kwa msaada ulioniletea. Nimefurahi sana kuona umenisaidia bila ya kukuomba. *Asante.* Mungu akuweke, na akupe maisha marefu yenye raha na mapato mema. *Ama kweli* umenifaa sana, *si haba*, kusema kweli. Sijakusahau; mimi mara kwa mara hukumbuka wewe, rafiki mwema, hasa kwa wakati tuliokuwa tukifanya kazi pamoja nyumbani mwa Bwana H; saa *nyingine* tukiongea na huku tukicheka. Mara roho yangu ikichafuka ndiwe uliyekuwa ukinipoza moyo. Basi haya yote *na mengi* ambayo sikutaka kuyataja *kwa vile* barua haimalizi maneno hunifanya nikikukumbuka sana. Saa *nyingine* nikiona kile kitabu cha *upishi* wa Kenya hukukumbuka *na kufurahi* sana — yaani kile *ulichoniachia*. Kumbe, Dr Maw, kitu *cha ukumbusho ni kizuri* hivyo?

    Nilifurahi sana kupata kazi ya posta japo *sijajua* kazi, ningali nafunzwa. Lakini *najua* kidogo. Huenda baada ya miezi miwili nikaenda shuleni ya mafunzo ya Posta huko mjini Nairobi. *Huku* niliko Kwale *si kubaya*. Kuna miti mingi sana, na hakuna joto kama sehemu nyinginezo za *mkoa* wa Pwani. (Tafadhali zunguka upande wa pili.) *Sijui ni kwa nini*, pengine *ni kwa* sababu ya miti. *Sijajua* watu wengi sana, lakini kidogo tu. Na wenye wilaya hii *ya Kwale* hasa ni kabila ya Wadigo, wale wengine *ni wale* waliokuja kwa kazi. Lakini ajabu, *ni marafiki* sana kwa *watu wengine*.

Sina mengi *kwa leo*, lakini najisikia *nikikugusa* sana, hivyo naona
tulionana sijui miaka kumi *iliyopita*. Ukiona makosa naomba unisamehe
kwani *sijui* nimeandika Kiamu au *ni Kimvita*.

Kaa na neema, na Mungu akulinde.

Miye (Mimi), Philip.

Ewe, samahani, nisalimie wanao, yaani David na *yule mwingine* — siju
ndiye nani.

-pokea — 'receive'
salamu — 'greetings', cf. *salama*
hofu — 'dread, fear, unease'
juu yako — 'concerning you'; *juu* — 'on, above'
-tumai — 'hope, expect'
u hali kadhalika — 'you are in the same state'
iliyokuja — 'which came'
kupitia kwa Bw. H. — 'via Bw. H.', *-pitia* — 'pass by, through, etc.'
shukrani — 'thanks', cf. *-shukuru* 'thank'
msaada — 'help' (usually financial), cf. *-saidia* 'help', verb.
ulioniletea — 'which you sent me' (*-leta* 'bring, deliver')
mapato — noun from *-pata* 'get', so *mapato mema* 'blessings, of a
　　material nature'
-ema — 'good'
ama — here an interjection, 'oh, well'. Can also mean 'or' in the inclusive
　　sense as in 'two or three, several'
haba — 'a little'
hukumbuka — 'I am accustomed to remember'
wakati tuliokuwa tukifanya kazi — 'the time when we were working'
tukiongea — 'we used to chat'
huku — here, 'at the same time'
roho — 'soul, spirit'
-chafuka — 'be in turmoil'
-poza — 'comfort, cool' cf. *poa*
moyo — 'heart'
hunifanya — 'often makes me'
upishi — 'cooking, cookery', cf. *-pika*
hukukumbuka — 'I often think of you'
-achia — 'leave for'
ukumbusho — 'memento', cf. *-kumbuka*
japo — 'although'
ningali — 'I am in the middle of' + verb
-funzwa — 'be taught'
huenda — 'it may be, perhaps'
mafunzo — 'training', cf. *-funzwa* above, also *mwanafunzi*
niliko — 'where I am'
-baya — 'bad'
miti — 'trees', sing. *mti*
joto — 'great heat', cf. *moto*
nyinginezo — 'other suchlike'

mkoa — 'district'
tafadhali — 'please' (used very sparingly, and here from English usage)
-zunguka — 'turn over, round'
wilaya — 'area', cf. *ulaya*
kabila — 'tribe'
Wadigo — 'Digo', a coastal tribe
waliokuja — 'those who came'
sina mengi — 'I haven't much to say'
najisikia — 'I feel myself' (*-sikia* originally means 'hear')
-gusa — 'touch'
miaka kumi iliyopita — 'ten years ago'
-samehe — 'forgive'
Kiamu — Amu dialect
Kimvita — Mombasa dialect
neema — 'plenty, providential blessings'
samahani — 'excuse me', cf. *-samehe*
nisalimie — 'greet for me'
wana — 'children, sons', sing. *mwana*, *wanao* 'your sons', cf.
   mwanafunzi.

For the faint-hearted, a gloss (not a translation) for this letter is provided in the key.

||

(i) Letter-writing

The letter opens *Kwa Dr Maw* 'To Dr Maw', and the writer might equally have dispensed with *kwa*. Some writers these days may begin with *Mpendwa Dr Maw* 'Dear Dr Maw' (from *-penda*). This is the influence of English.

After the opening, it is imperative to greet the correspondent. These greetings are formulaic. An alternative would be *Salaam nyingi sana*. Next, the writer says that he is well; a variation might be *sisi hapa hatujambo sana*; followed by enquiries about the recipient. Only after all these formalities have been completed can the letter proper begin. It would be discourteous to omit them.

Similarly, the letter must end with blessings, and with greetings to the recipient's family, even if (as in this case) the writer does not actually know them. It was indeed a lapse on his part to omit to mention them before signing off.

The most usual final ending these days is *wako* 'yours'; more special-ised is *mimi nikupendaye* 'I who love you' (very informal), or *mtii wako* 'your servant' (highly formal, civil service type).

(ii) Word division and spelling

You will notice in the original text that the writer frequently joins mono-syllabic words to following ones, e.g. *ni+juu, u+hali, si+haba, na+mengi*, etc. This is no doubt because of the strong feeling that a minimal segment of the language (normally a word in lay terms) should have a stress. Monosyllabic words can not have stress in Swahili

because stress is on the penultimate syllable. Therefore this rather
unsophisticated writer joins them to the following word. At one point he
even joins three words *ni+kwa+nini*. He also joins two words in a
nominal group: *watu+wengine*. You will recall that in Unit 17 we
mentioned that in the case of a compound nominal group, only the last
item has stress. The writer is treating this whole group as a single item
presumably because of the single stress.

Some spelling variations are the result of pronunciation, e.g. *asante* is
frequently pronounced with a voiceless velar fricative after the initial *a*
which the writer spells *ahsante*. Occasionally he confuses voiced and
voiceless consonants, e.g. (*ubishi*), *upishi*, (*-kusa*) *-gusa*. This may be
because there is no distinct symbol for *p* or *g* in the Arabic script which
most Swahili children learn at least a smattering of before they go to
primary school. The use of *zingine* is dialectal. Finally, note the somewhat haphazard appearance of semivowels (*w, y*) between vowels, e.g.
sijuwi (*sijui*), *iliokuja* (*iliyokuja*). This again is partly a matter of pronunciation, a glide in any case being present between the vowels, partly a
feeling for the structure of syllables, and partly, as in *iliokuja*, analogy
with similar-sounding forms e.g. *uliokuja* 'you who came', *tuliofika* 'we
who arrived', etc.

(iii) **Relative**

There are two forms of the relative (or relative clause); one is the 'defining' relative and, as its name suggests, it defines the noun to which it
refers, as in a teacher's possible utterance:

"Stand up the boy who did that!"

who did that is a relative clause in English, defining which boy is to stand
up. In Swahili such relatives are normally expressed by a verbal prefix
which follows the tense sign in the verb, e.g.

(mtoto) aliyefanya hivyo '(the child) who did that'

ye has already been used as a suffix marking the object after *-na*
(*ninaye* 'I have him', *sinaye* 'I have got him') (Unit 25). It could equally
well have been described as referring to the object ('I have the person
referred to'). You will recall that with all other classes the equivalent
suffix consists of a class agreement plus *-o*. So referring to a book
(*kitabu*) we would say *ninacho* 'I have it'. (This *o* is sometimes called the
'*o* of reference'.) Such relative particles referring to all classes can be
added to verbs, e.g.

watu waliofika	'*the people who arrived*'
mti ulioanguka	'the tree which fell'
miti iliyoanguka	'the trees which fell'
*jino linaloniuma**	'the tooth which hurts me'
*meno yanayoniuma**	'the teeth which hurt me'
kisu kilichopotea	'the knife which was lost'
visu vilivyopotea	'the knives which were lost'
nyumba itakayobomolewa	'the house which will be knocked down'
nyumba zitakazobomolewa	'the houses which will be knocked down'
uma uliopotea	'the fork which was lost'
kuimba kunakosikika	'the singing which is audible'

mahali panapokalika	'the place which is inhabitable'
mahali kunakokalika	(somewhere about)
mahali mnamokalika	(inside)

*Notice that any object prefix comes *after* the relative prefix.

Just as was seen in Unit 26 with *po* and *vyo* for time and manner respectively, these relative verbs can have the tenses *-na-* (continuous present), *-li-* (past) *-taka-* (future), and also no tense, as in:

    watu wasomao 'people who (habitually) read'

where the relative particle is a *suffix*.

There is one negative form corresponding to these positive relatives, e.g.

    watu wasiosoma 'people who do not read'
    mtu asiyesoma   'a man who does not read'

The relative in the previous paragraphs referred to the subject. It can also refer to the object, as in:

    mwivi niliyemwona   'the thief whom I saw'
    kitabu nilichokinunua 'the book which I bought'

Notice that in these examples the object prefix is also used, in the first case because the object is a living being (*mwivi*), and in the second because it precedes the verb. Except with living beings as objects, however, the object prefix is often omitted after the relative.

When the verb is compound, the relative marker occurs only in the auxiliary verb, e.g. compare

      kitabu ninachokisoma 'the book which I am reading'
with *kitabu nilichokuwa ninakisoma* 'the book which I was reading';

      mtoto ninayemtafuta 'the child (whom) I am seeking'
cf. *mtoto niliyekuwa ninamtafuta* 'the child (whom) I was seeking'.

(Note: you will recall that in the case of a compound verb, the object prefix occurs only in the main verb, in contrast to the relative prefix, which occurs only in the auxiliary.)

Structures will often be heard which involve both a relative verb and a strong copula *ndi-*, e.g.
    hiki ndicho (kitabu) nilichotaka 'this is the book I wanted'.

Even more frequently they involve also a relative demonstrative, as in:

    hicho ndicho (chakula) nitakacho 'that is really the food I want'

(iv) There are also relative forms for copulas. The positive form (corresponding perhaps to *ni*) has a class prefix, *-li-* stem, and a relative suffix, e.g.

    mimi ni mwalimu   *mimi niliye mwalimu* 'I who am a teacher' 'in my capacity as a teacher' and similarly:

> *wewe uliye mwalimu* (sometimes *ulio* is heard)
> *yeye aliye mwalimu*
> *sisi tulio waalimu*
> *nyinyi mlio waalimu*
> *wao walio waalimu.**

Other classes follow suit, e.g.

> *kitabu kilicho changu* 'the book which is mine' etc.

Negative copula has *-si-* where positive has *-li-*, e.g.

> *kitabu kisicho changu* 'the book which is not mine'.

The past tense has *-li-* tense marker and *-kuwa* as stem, e.g.

> *mtu aliyekuwa mwalimu* 'the person who was a teacher'
> *kitabu kilichokuwa changu* 'the book which was mine'

The future tense is formed regularly:

> *wanafunzi watakaokuwa waalimu* 'the students who will become
>   teachers'

*Notice that all relative affixes for singular persons are *ye* and fo
plural *o*.

(v)   The forms for the possessive copula *-na* follow those for the simple
      copula, i.e.

mimi nina watoto	'I have (some) children'
mimi niliye na watoto	'I who have children'
mimi niliyekuwa na watoto	'I who had children'
mimi nitakayekuwa na watoto	'I who will have children'
mimi nisiye (or, *nisiyekuwa*) *na watoto*	'I who have no children'

Notice that if the relative copula with *-na* refers to an object, the concorc
is repeated, e.g.

watoto niliokuwa nao 'the children whom I had'.

(vi) **Place copula**. Here, in the present tense, *-li- (-si-)* is the stem and the
      ko (po, mo) is suffixed, e.g.

mwivi yuko hospitalini	'the thief is in hospital'
mwivi aliyeko hospitalini	'the thief who is in hospital

Other tenses use *-kuwa* as stem:

mwivi aliyekuwako hospitalini	'the thief who was in hospital'
mwivi atakayekuwako hospitalini	'the thief who will be in hospital'
mwivi asiyeko (or, *asiyekuwako*) *hospitalini*	'the thief who is not in hospital'.

Notice in the text we had *hapa nilipo* 'here where I am'.

(vii)   The stem **-ingine** 'other' may also be followed by what looks like a relative agreement, as in the text we have (sehemu) nyinginezo 'other similar places'. *ny-* is class 9/10 agreement and *-zo* is class 10 relative suffix. This form is mostly used in the plural except for class 16. So we can have:

watu wengineo   'other such people'
vitabu vinginevyo   'other similar books'
mahali penginepo   'another similar place'

III

(b)   Study these sayings (*methali*):

Kikulacho kimo nguoni mwako.

Usiache mbachao kwa msala upitao. (*mbacha* — 'old, worn prayer mat' *mbachao*, 'your old . . .'; *msala* '(fine) prayer mat')

Ulacho ndicho chako, kilichobaki ni cha mchimba lindi. (*-baki* 'be left over'; *mchimba lindi* 'grave-digger')

Explanations can be found in the Key. Try to think of near equivalents in your own language.

(c)   How would you say in Swahili:

next week (use *-ja*)
last year (use *-pita*)
the people present
anyone absent
books which have many pictures

(d)   Complete the following dialogues, using the new vocabulary:

Mwuzaji: Saa hii ndiyo utakayo?
Wewe: Ndiyo hiyo.

Mwuzaji: Saa hizi _____?
Wewe:

Mwuzaji: Mfuko _____?
Wewe:

Mwuzaji: Mifuko _____?
Wewe:

Mwuzaji: Shati _____?
Wewe:

Mwuzaji: Mashati _____?
Wewe:

Mwuzaji: Kisu _____?
Wewe:

Mwuzaji: Visu _____?
Wewe:

Mwuzaji: Wembe _____?
Wewe:

Wewe: Mtu _____?
Askari:

Askari: Watu _____?
Jaji:

▷ (e) Complete the following patterns:
kiti hiki ndicho nilichokitaka

viti
meza hii
meza hizi
kabati
makabati
mkeka
mikeka

(f) Combine the following pairs of sentences into single sentences, making
the second clause relative:

Nimenunua kitabu. Kitanifaa sana.
Ninakaa nyumbani. Pana starehe sana.
Umeona mfuko wangu? Ulikuwako mezani.
Tulisikia nyimbo. Zilikuwa nzuri sana.

(g) Combine the following pairs making the first clause relative. You wil
need to change the word order.

Nilinunua kisu. Ni kikali sana.
Nilimwona mtu. Alikuwa ana masikio makubwa.
Tuliwakamata waizi. Ni vijana tu.
Aliona pete nzuri sana. Alitaka kuinunua.
Niliendesha gari. Ni ya Professor Athumani.
Alichukua wembe wa babake. Alijikata kwao.
Tulikwenda mahali. Ndipo penye miti mingi.
Nitakuona kesho. Nitakuwa nimemaliza kazi yangu.
Tulifika jana. Tulikuta shule imefungwa.
Ninataka nazi kubwa. Sizioni.
Aliandika barua. Ndiye Bw. Philip.

Rewrite all except the last 2 pairs, making the second clause relative.

(h) Combine the following pairs making the first a relative clause:

Sitaki viazi. Nitavitupilia mbali.
Watu hawatakiwi. Watapelekwa makwao. (*makwao* 'to their homes')
Vitabu havifai. Vitatupiliwa mbali.

(i) Make the following clauses relative and supply suitable ends:

Wanafunzi hawasomi vizuri _____
Mtu hafanyi kazi _____
Mgonjwa hanywi dawa yake _____
Watu wale si Waislamu _____ (*Mwislamu* — 'Moslem')

(j)   Add a first clause and make the second relative:

_____ chakula si kitamu.
_____ nguo hazinifai.
_____ kisu si kikali.
_____ mwanamume si mwema.

(k)   Combine the following pairs, making the original first sentence a relative clause:

Kitabu kilikuwako mezani. Kiko wapi sasa?
Machungwa yalikuwamo kikapuni. Nani ameyala?
Mwavuli ulikuwapo hapa. Umeuona?
Chupa mbili za pombe zilikuwamo kabatini. Nani amezinywa?
Mlevi alikuwako jela. Ameachwa huru?
Nilikuwa na pete ya dhahabu. Umeiona?
Alikuwa na ng'ombe sita. Umewaona?
Mlikuwa na viazi. Mmeviuza?
Tulikuwa na pesa. Umeziweka wapi?
Walikuwa na mashati mapya. Wameyafua?

(l)   Give the Swahili for:

Other similar

_____

_____

_____

_____

 (*miti*)

_____

(m)   Write a letter to a friend inviting him/her to your house. Suggest a time, tell him/her how to get there, and outline the proposed entertainment (proper!).

IV

(i)   **The client-protector relationship** is a very old one, which survives in most parts of the world, but to a much lesser (or less noticeable) extent in Western Europe than elsewhere. In East Africa it certainly still exists as an alternative to, or extension of family ties. Even slaves in the past — at least household slaves — had a close and well-defined relationship in the Swahili family, with rights as well as duties under Islamic law. After emancipation many slaves stayed where they were, having no other homes; and at the time of writing a few of these old people still exist, cared for in their old age. Wage employment may now have taken the place of slavery, but, except for the cases of large concerns such as factories, the concepts of personal service and reciprocal protection survives, even within large institutions, and especially where there is direct personal contact. An individual who renders service — a messenger, waiter, house servant — of course works for wages, but not only that. To his mind it would be rather insulting to suppose he worked simply for money. He works for his employer (or his representative) and gives a service, takes an interest in his employer's concerns, and expects the employer to reciprocate. The protector (employer) assists the client (employee), but also the client defends his protector's interests against outsiders. That money may pass between them is a fact, but the relationship is far more delicate than that. Ideally it can work very well, and although it is sometimes a cause of irritation when the client feels the protector is deficient or the protector feels the client is too demanding, it can also give both parties a sense of security and mutual support.

(ii)   Note **tafadhali** 'please'. This word is not used a great deal in Swahili and should not be used for 'Yes, please', as in situations in English where one e.g. is being offered refreshment. In English 'Would you like some tea?' could elicit the response 'Please!'. In Swahili 'Nikupe chai?' elicits 'Ee', or 'Haya'. *Tafadhali* in this situation would suggest 'About time too', 'I thought you'd never offer' etc.

Unit 28   Fungu la ishirini na nane
Malaika — Angel

I

(a) Learn the words of this popular song, *Malaika* :

Malaika, nakupenda Malaika,	Angel, I love you Angel,
Malaika, nakupenda Malaika,	
Nami nifanyeje, kijana mwenzio,	What shall I do, your boy-friend,
Nashindwa na mali sina, we,	I'm broke, I've no money, you,
Ningekuoa Malaika.	I would marry you, Angel.
Nashindwa na mali sina, we,	
Ningekuoa Malaika.	
Kidege, hukuwaza kidege,	Birdie, I'm always dreaming of you,
Kidege, hukuwaza kidege,	
Nami nifanyeje, kijana mwenzio,	
Nashindwa na mali sina, we,	
Ningekuoa kidege	
Nashindwa na mali sina, we,	
Ningekuoa kidege	

As with poetry and song texts in all languages, the grammar used is more free than in prose.

kijana — 'youth, lad'
mwenzio — *mwenzi*, from *-enda*, plus *-o* — 'your companion' (standard form. *mwenzako*)
kidege — 'little bird' (*ndege* — 'bird')
hukuwaza — 'I'm always dreaming of you'

II

(i) *mwenzi*. We had in unit 26 *mwenzangu* 'my friend'. All persons can have a friend, i.e.

mwenzangu	'my friend' pl. *wenzangu* 'my friends'
mwenzako or *mwenzio*	'your friend' pl. *wenzako/wenzio*
mwenzake or *mwenziwe*	'his/her friend' pl. *wenzake/wenziwe*
mwenzetu or *mwenzi wetu*	'our friend' pl. *wenzetu*
mwenzi wenu	'your (pl.) friend'
mwenzi wao	'their friend'

Plural:
wenzangu etc.

These forms are alternatives to *mwenzi wangu* etc. To use the amalga-mated form perhaps expresses a greater degree of closeness of relationship.

(ii)   **-nge-**. This 'tense' normally occurs twice in a sentence. The suggestion in the song is:

ningekuwa na mali, ningekuoa, Malaika. 'If I were wealthy, I would marry you, Angel.'

In English the two clauses 'If I *were* wealthy' and 'I *would* marry you' have different verb forms. In Swahili they are the same. In theory the Swahili sentence above *could* mean

'If I married you, I would be wealthy'.

But in practice there is normally no problem of understanding what is meant in the context. If an ambiguity should arise, one can use *kama* 'if' e.g.

Kama ningekuwa na mali, ningekuoa 'If I had wealth . . .
or *Ningekuwa na mali kama ningekuoa* . . . if I married you'

Normally *kama* is not needed, however, as the sense is obvious. Usually the *'if'* clause comes first.

The negative of this 'tense' has *-si-* before the *-nge-*, e.g.

nisingekuoa 'I would not marry you/if I did not marry you'.

Sometimes a form of the negative with prefix *h-/ha-* can be heard:

nisingekwenda   or, singekwenda
usingekwenda   or, hungekwenda
asingekwenda   or, hangekwenda
tusingekwenda   or, hatungekwenda
msingekwenda   or, hamngekwenda
wasingekwenda   or, hawangekwenda.

The first form is the standard.

(iii)   **hu-**. This is usually called a 'tense', but the meaning is one of characteristic or habitual action. It comes first in a verb and is not preceded by a subject marker. So in the text we have:

hukuwaza, glossed as 'I dream of you (all the time)'.

In another text it might mean 'he dreams of you', or refer to any other subject. It is normally used for some characteristic action, e.g.

Waislamu huamini Mungu 'Muslims believe in God'

and in the song *Malaika* it is used somewhat in a spirit of poetic exaggeration. It is often used in traditional sayings, e.g.

haba na haba hujaza kibaba 'a little and a little fills the *kibaba* (large measure)'
ubishi mwingi huleta mateto '(too) much jesting brings quarrelling'
mla mbuzi hulipa ng'ombe 'the person who eats a goat pays a cow'

mwivi hushikwa na mwivi mwenziwe 'a thief is caught by a similar thief'.

It goes without saying that the *hu-* 'tense' must be preceded by its subject. When it is used for persons, the personal pronoun is often used with it to make the meaning clear.

There is no negative equivalent to this 'tense'.

III

(b)   Write out the paradigm for all persons:
Ningekuwapo nyumbani ningefurahi sana.

(c)   Write suitable second clauses for the following:
Ungefika mapema _____
Ningekuwa na pesa nyingi _____
Ningeona nyoka _____   (*nyoka* — 'snake')
Mtoto angeanguka _____
Kaka yangu angekunywa bia sita _____
Tungekwenda Mombasa _____
Ingepiga theluji _____   (*theluji* — 'snow')
Ungekuwa ni mtu mwema _____
Sh. Yahya asingevaa kofia _____
Nisingekuwako kazini _____
Tusingesoma Kiswahili _____
Tungefanya kazi kwa bidii _____   (*bidii* — 'diligence')

(d)   If working in a group, write the first halves of sentences with *-nge-* and pass them round for completion. A further variation is to play consequences, using the names of members of the group or other well-known figures. Write the first half of the sentence on a strip of paper; fold it over and pass it on for completion.

(e)   Write a reply to your invitation in Unit 27, as if you were the recipient. Thank the writer for the invitation and explain why you are unable to accept.

(f)   Study the sayings in Section II (iii), and try to work out what they mean. Are there traditional sayings with similar meanings in your own language?

(g)   Here are the words of another song to learn:

Hakuna Mwingine

Hakuna mwingine zaidi yako
Ni wewe ni wewe wa maisha
Moyo wangu na mapenzi yangu
Nimekuachia.

Unavyonichekea ni wewe pekee
Najivuna kwa maringo mengi
Najiona kama niko ahera
Pamoja na weye.

Basi fanya twende kwetu nyumbani
Mama na baba wakakuone
Ati kule kwetu kuna raha nyingi
Hata wewe bebi utapapenda.

Gloss:

There is no other

There is no other above you
It's you, it's you all my life
My heart and my love
I've saved for you.

The way you smile at me, only you do
I strut around proudly
I feel as if I were in heaven
When I'm with you.

So let's go to my place
Let my parents meet you
Well, at our place it's so very comfortable
That you will like it, baby.

pekee — 'alone', cf. *peke yako* 'by yourself'
-jivuna — 'boast, show off', from *-vuna* 'reap, harvest'
maringo — 'airs, graces', from *-ringa* 'swagger'
ahera — 'the next world'

Note in the last line the use of the object prefix for 'place', *-pa-*, in *utapapenda* 'you will like (it) there'.

Note also in the last two lines an example of how to say 'so . . . that', 'so comfortable that you will like it'. We could say, e.g. *Machungwa haya ghali mno hata siwezi kuyanunua*, 'These oranges are so expensive that I'm not going to buy them' '. . . too expensive for me to buy'. *Nimechoka hata sijui la kufanya* 'I'm so tired that I don't know what to do'.

IV

Music

Music plays a large part in Swahili life, and the forms of it are varied. Perhaps *Ta'arabu* has most prestige. This is performed by a small group of two or three musicians, a player of the *gambusi*, a stringed instrument rather like a mandolin, or the *zeze*, something like a guitar, and one or more singers. Ta'arabu music shows considerable Arabic influence, and is much in demand at weddings and other ceremonies. Nowadays there are some recordings of this music available, and individual performers may become locally quite famous. One of the best known earlier this century was Siti binti Saad, a woman from Zanzibar, whose biography was written by Shaaban Robert, the first well-known Swahili prose writer. Ta'arabu musicians are also composers and improvisers.

A quite different tradition is that of work-songs. These are associated with particular trades or crafts, especially fishing and sea-faring. Other traditional songs are such as lullabies and children's songs and rhymes.

Robust popular music springs up all the time. At one period in Mombasa there was a vogue for bands modelled on the British army bands seen during the 1939-45 war. Especially admired were Scottish bands, and groups were formed, paraded, clothed in kilts at great expense, and took part in processions at festivals, to huge enjoyment. The line between imitation and parody is very fine. Bands of professional and semi-professional musicians are always in demand, and songs are composed for all occasions — elections, official visits — and on subjects of general interest in the public eye. Some indeed may be quite scurrilous, and are often extremely cleverly worded, seemingly innocuous, but with hidden meanings for those in the know.

'Pop' music springs out of all these traditions, and is somewhat influenced by the West, but more so by music from Zaire, which seems to have a strong appeal. Electric guitars and some other accoutrements of Western popular music are found, but the music itself retains a distinctly local flavour.

Unit 29   Fungu la ishirini na tisa
Kukata umeme — Electricity cut off

I

(a)   Bibi Maw na Bwana Philip wako nje ya nyumba ya Bwana Harris, pamoja na vyombo vingi — meza, viti, na kadhalika.

▷   Mtu wa Umeme: Hodi!
    Bi. Maw: Hodi!
          n.k.
    Mtu: Hii ni nyumba ya Bwana Harris?
    Bi.M.: Ndiyo nyumba yake, lakini mwenyewe hayupo.
    Mtu: Yuko wapi?
    Bi.M.: Amekwenda Ulaya; atarudi baada ya wiki mbili hivi.
    Mtu: Basi, bibi, nimekuja kukata umeme.
    Bi.M.: Kukata umeme! Kwa nini?
    Mtu: Kwa sababu bwana hajalipa hesabu yake ya mwezi wa Juni.
    Bi.M.: Bila shaka hajapata hesabu. Angaliipata angalilipa. Au labda amelipa, lakini sijui anaweka wapi risiti zake.
    Mtu: Angalilipa nisingaliambiwa nije kukata umeme.
    Bi.M.: Lakini bwana, ungeukata ningepika vipi chakula?
    Mtu: Sijui. Si shauri langu. Mimi simo. Lakini umeme ungekatwa lazima angelipa shilingi mia tano zaidi kuuunganisha tena!
    Bi.M.: Kumbe, pesa nyingi sana! Na hesabu yenyewe ni shilingi ngapi?
    Mtu: Shilingi mia tisa na hamsini.
    Bi.M.: Lakini bwana, inasikitisha sana, lakini huwezi kuingia nyumbani. Tunasafisha zulia, na unavyoona vyombo vyote viko mbele ya mlango. Haupitiki.
    Mtu: Hayo ni kweli. Lakini hesabu, je?
    Bi.M.: Mimi mwenyewe nitalipa.
    Mtu: Lazima uende ofisini, basi.
    Bi.M.: Ofisi yenyewe iko wapi?
    Mtu: Iko katika Jumba la Umeme. Unajua jumba lilipo?
    Bi.M.: Sijui.
    Mtu: Basi unajua Bunge?
    Bi.M.: Hata.
    Mtu: Unajua Hoteli ya Hilton?
    Bi.M.: Ee.
    Mtu: Basi, kutoka Hilton kuelekea reli unapita Benki Kuu ya Kenya mkono wa kushoto, halafu kupita duka la dawa upande wa kulia, na utaona Jumba la Umeme liko jirani yake. Uingiapo, panda daraja, yaani unalipa kwenye ghorofa ya kwanza.

Bi.M.:   Haya bwana, asante sana. Nitakwenda leo hii.
Mtu: Haya mama. Lakini Bwana Harris angalilipa
          usingalipata taabu hii.
Bi.M.:   Kweli, lakini nilivyosema kwanza, angalipata hesabu
          bila shaka angalilipa.
Mtu: Labda. Haya mama, kwa heri.
                              n.k.

umeme — lit. 'lightning'. Here used for 'electricity'
nje — 'outside'
vyombo — here, 'furniture'
n.k. — *na kadhalika* — 'and so on', *kadhalika* — 'suchlike'
mwenyewe — here, 'the owner'
wiki mbili hivi — 'two weeks or so'
hesabu — 'account, sum' (verb 'to add')
angaliipata — 'if he had got it'
angalilipa — 'he would have paid'
risiti — 'receipt'
nisingaliambiwa — 'I would not have been told'
-unganisha — 'join'
-sikitisha — 'make sorry'
-safisha — 'clean'
zulia — 'carpet(s)' esp. Persian type
-pitika — 'be passable'
Bunge — 'parliament building'
-elekea — 'go/face towards'
-kuu — 'important, great', *Benki Kuu ya Kenya* — 'Kenya National Bank'
jirani — 'next' 'neighbour'
-panda — 'climb'
daraja — here, 'staircase, steps'
leo hii — 'this very day'

II

(i) *-ngali-*. The *-ngali-* 'tense' (or 'aspect') behaves similarly to the *-nge-*
'tense' in that it normally appears twice in a sentence. It *may* be thought
of as further back in conceptual 'time' than *-nge-*; compare:

   Ningemwona ningemwalika 'If I saw him I would invite him'
and *Ningalimwona ningalimwalika* 'If I had seen him I would have
   invited him'.

But there is also the suggestion of non-fulfilment, i.e. 'If I had seen him
(but I didn't) I would have invited him (but I didn't/couldn't).

The negative is formed similarly to *-nge-*, i.e.
   Nisingalikwenda Mombasa nisingalimwona 'If I had not gone to
   Mombasa (but I did) I would not have seen him (but I did).

(As for the *-nge-* 'tense', there is also a parallel form of the negative with
h-/ha- prefix, e.g.
   asingalifika   : hangalifika
   tusingalikwenda : hatungalikwenda etc.)

(ii) It may be useful here to remind you that there are two main* negativ
      forms for verbs, one with *h-* or *ha-* as prefix (except for 1st persc
      singular), and the other with *-si-* following the subject prefix.

      The *h-*, *ha-* prefix is used with:
      (a) general negative (plus *-i* suffix), e.g.
           h-u-fik-i 'you do not come/go/arrive'
           ha-tu-fik-i 'we do not come/go/arrive'

      (b) future, e.g.
           h-u-ta-fika 'you won't arrive'
           ha-tu-ta-fika 'we won't arrive'

      (c) past (plus *-ku-* prefix) e.g.
           h-u-ku-fika 'you did not arrive'
           ha-tu-ku-fika 'we did not arrive.

      (Remember that 1st person singular negative with these forms is alway
      simply *si-*, e.g. *si-fik-i* 'I don't come' (sc. 'I won't'), *si-ta-fika* 'I wor
      come' (future); *si-ku-fika* 'I didn't come'.

      The *-si-* following the subject prefix is used with:
      (a) subjunctive e.g.
           ni-si-fike 'let me not come, lest I come'
           u-si-fike 'don't come/go, lest you come'

      (b) *-nge-* tense, e.g.
           ni-si-nge-fika 'if I did not arrive/I would not arrive'
           tu-si-nge-fika 'if we did not arrive/we would not arrive'

      (c) *-ngali-* tense, e.g.
           ni-si-ngali-fika 'if I had not arrived/I would not have arrived'
           a-si-ngali-fika 'if he had not arrived/he would not have arrived'

      (d) relative (no tense), e.g.
           a-si-ye-fika 'he who does not arrive/whoever does not arrive'

      * The negative infinite is formed with *-to-* following the class 15 pref
      ku-, e.g.
           kutofika 'not arriving'
           kutonipiga 'not hitting me'

III

(b) Finish the following sentences:
     Tusingalimjua Sh. Yahya _____
     Bi. Maw angalikatwa nywele _____
     Bi. Jemima asingaliolewa na mume wake _____
     Usingaliendesha gari ovyo _____ (*ovyo* — 'carelessly, anyhow')
     Wazee wangalilazwa hospitalini _____
     Laiti ningalikaa kwa mama _____ (*laiti* — 'alas, if only', only use
       with *-nge-* or *-ngali-* 'tenses').

(c) Set half-sentences using *-ngali-* for a friend to finish.

(d) On the map p. 214, mark in the *Jumba la Umeme* and *duka la dawa* mentioned in the text.

(e) Complete the following conversations and find or mark in the relevant places on the map.

Bibi Fulani: Una nini, bwana? (*fulani* — 'so-and-so')
Mgeni: Oooh, oooh!
Bwana F.:   _____
Mgeni: La, la, sitaki, ooh, ooh!
Bwana F.:   _____
Bibi F.:   Yuko daktari kwenye kona, karibu na Jumba la Rais.
Mgeni: La, _____ ooh, ooh!
Bwana F.:   Labda _____ _____
Bibi F.:   Yuko daktari wa meno pale pale, jirani ya daktari.
Mgeni: _____ ooh, ooh!
Bibi F.:   Basi tumpelekee duka la dawa. Liko wapi?
Bwana F.:   _____
Bibi F.:   Lakini _____
Bwana F.:   Liko jingine jirani ya duka la mvinyo, kwenye barabara.
            (*barabara* — 'main road, highway')
Mengi: _____ ooh, ooh, ninachotaka ndicho choo!
Bwana F.:   _____
Bibi F.:   Vuka njia kwenye kivuko karibu na kinyozi, na utakuta vyoo
            vya watu viko kule kule. Lakini wewe, bwana,
            lazima uende naye. Mimi mwanamke siwezi kuingia huko.
Bwana F.:   _____
Mgeni: _____

Bi. Maw: Jemima, ninataka kutengenezewa nywele, lakini _____
            (*-tengenezewa nywele* — 'have hair done')
Bi. Jemima: Nasikia yuko mtengenezaji _____
Bi.M.:   Hilton hotel! Siwezi kwenda huko maana _____
Bi.J.:   Basi, yuko mwingine karibu sana na chuo kikuu.
Bi.M.:   _____
Bi.J.:   Unajua duka kubwa la redio?
Bi.M.:   _____
Bi.J.:   Basi unajua gereji la Vic Preston?
Bi.M.:   _____
Bi.J.:   Basi, jirani yake, kuelekea stesheni polisi.
Bi.M.:   Kutoka Norfolk hotel, _____?
Bi.J.:   Karibu sana, itachukua mwendo wa _____ (*mwendo* —
            'journey on foot', *-enda*)
Bi.M.:   _____

Wewe: Mimi mgeni hapa. Nipate wapi vyakula?
Mimi: _____

Wewe: A'a, nimesikia jina lake. Uchumi wapi! Wanaochuma ndio
            wenyewe, siyo sisi wananchi! (-*chuma* 'harvest')
Mimi: Basi liko duka la vyakula jirani ya duka la vitabu. Huko wanauza
            kwa jumla, kwa hiyo _____ (*jumla* 'bulk')
Wewe: A'a, siwezi kwenda huko, maanake mbali sana, tena _____
Mimi: _____

(f) Using the map on page 215 and the following extra vocabulary, wri
      and/or practise conversations asking for and giving directions. Places c
      map whose names you may not know:

kiwanja cha ndege	airport
jumba la simu	telephone exchange
duka la mvinyo	wine-shop
'Uchumi'	'Economic' (a general store)
	(-*chuma* 'harvest')
kituo cha basi	bus stop
kivuko	crossing
kinyozi	barber
duka la nyama	butcher's shop (*nyama* 'meat')
magazeti	newspapers
Chuo kikuu	University
Ubalozi	Consulate, High Commission
kutoka — mpaka	'from — to'
fuata njia ile	follow that road
-shika	take
-pita	turn down
-vuka	cross
moja kwa moja	straight ahead
upande wa kushoto	on the left
upande wa kulia	on the right
karibu (na)	near (to)
mbali	far
nyumba hii kwa hii	houses right next door
baina ya	between
mbele (ya)	in front (of)
nyuma (ya)	behind
kabla ya	before
baada ya	after
njia panda	cross road
-panda	climb (into)
-shuka	descend
Naweza kufika kwa miguu?	Afadhali upande teksi/basi/matatu*
Duka lenyewe liko umbali gani?	Liko umbali wa maili . . . (Umbali
	'distance')
Kufika huko kutachukua	
muda gani?	Ni mwendo wa dakika . . .

matatu See note in Unit 15 section III.

(g) Mchezo. Wachezaji wawili. (*mchezaji* 'player')
Mchezaji A ana ramani page 215 na B ana ramani page 216. A yuko
stesheni, naye anamwuliza B njia ya kufika mahali fulani. Kwa mfano
(e.g.)

Mchezaji A: *Samahani bwana, unaweza kuniambia liko wapi duka la*
dawa? Nimepotea hapa Nairobi.
Mchezaji B anamweleza, Mchezaji A anafuata katika ramani yake, na
kuchora mahali. Akifaulu (-*faulu* 'succeed'), wachezaji wabadilishane
(-*badilishana* 'exchange') ramani, na kucheza tena.

Mahali:

Jumba la umeme	Electricity House
Duka la dawa(2)	Chemist
Ubalozi	Consulate
Mpiga picha	Photographer
Kiwanda	Factory
Duka la redio	
Daktari wa meno	Dentist
Daktari	
Maktaba	Library (cf. *kitabu*)
Vyoo	Toilets (*choo cha wanawake**/ *wanaume* 'ladies/gents')
Mshonaji	Tailor, dressmaker
Mtengenezaji nywele	Hairdresser
Gereza	Gaol
Duka la vyakula	Grocer's
Nyumba ya Professor Athumani	
Nyumba ya Bwana Harris	
Nyumba ya Toon na Jemima	
Hoteli anapokaa Bi. Maw	
Bustani la nyoka	
Westlands	

* sing. *mwanamke* 'woman', *mwanamume* 'man'

IV

(i) **Urbanisation**.

The Swahili themselves have long been accustomed to town life, as is
historically attested from outside sources. Many present-day towns are
on ancient sites, and at least one long-abandoned town, Gedi, some 35
miles north of Mombasa, has been partly excavated and is well worth a
visit. The remains of large mosques, a 'palace' and private houses built
of coral with walls remaining to a considerable height can be seen. A
complex system of wells and water-courses dealt with sanitation;
indeed it is thought that the failure of the water-supply for some reason
was probably what caused the site to be abandoned. Traditionally the
Swahili lived from their estates inland and from trading inland, up and
down the coast, and overseas to the countries of Arabia. Many of these
occupations have now gone, and the Swahili have declined economically.

Towns, however, have grown, and new towns such as Nairobi have bee founded. Apart from the intrinsic attraction of towns, seen as places o opportunity, in Tanzania there has been a deliberate policy of 'village isation', settling of previously nomadic or scattered people in village and small towns, with at the same time a discouragement of imm gration into Dar es Salaam. Practical and social problems attend thes changes. Around the larger towns, shanty towns spring up, occasional razed by the authorities not only for their illegality but also for the reputation of harbouring thieves, disease and so on. But even in th legitimate areas of building there is much overcrowding, and the mun cipal services — water supply, sewerage, electricity, telephones, police fire services, hospitals, schools, transport — are badly overstretched an can hardly cope with the ever-increasing demand.

Social problems also arise particularly out of the fact that people are no living in close proximity who were previously apart. In fact in th residential areas of large towns there tend to be enclaves of particul tribes, since people arriving from the country go to known relatives o acquaintances and settle near them if they can. There also tends to be similar division at work. In Kenya the police and army have been main staffed by Kalenjin and Luyia; the railway by Luo, and so on. This may giv a sense of security to the individual looking for friends in an otherwis impersonal environment, but it does nothing to allay mutual suspicion between tribal groups, and at times of stress these mutual fears are ver evident. Even where people are of the same ethnic background but no live close together where previously they were scattered, problem arise. For example in some of the villages in Tanzania, where farmer who had previously lived on isolated homesteads were brought togethe with the promise of better services, the strains of living close togethe especially problems connected with mingling of the sexes, are not eas to deal with.

Added to these are the usual, universal rivalries between town an country. Times of social change from a rural agricultural population to a urban industrial one inevitably bring unrest and disillusion as well a opportunity and hope.

(ii) **Housewarming**.

It may seem odd to the student that Bibi Maw is living in Bwana Harri house. In East Africa there are problems about accommodation. Hotel are expensive and cater mainly for tourists. Housing for foreigners is als expensive and in short supply. Overseas people on contracts usual have housing provided, but there is often a waiting-list. Also, when suc people do have accommodation they may go on leave, and do not like t leave their houses or flats empty. So there is often a shifting populatio of people 'housewarming' while owners are away. For example, when go to East Africa it is normally for several months, for research work, an I generally manage to 'housewarm' for at least some part of the time There is also an accommodation problem for local people, so that th customs of sharing and lending mentioned earlier in connection wit possessions, also come into play with housing, not always happily, o course; but of necessity.

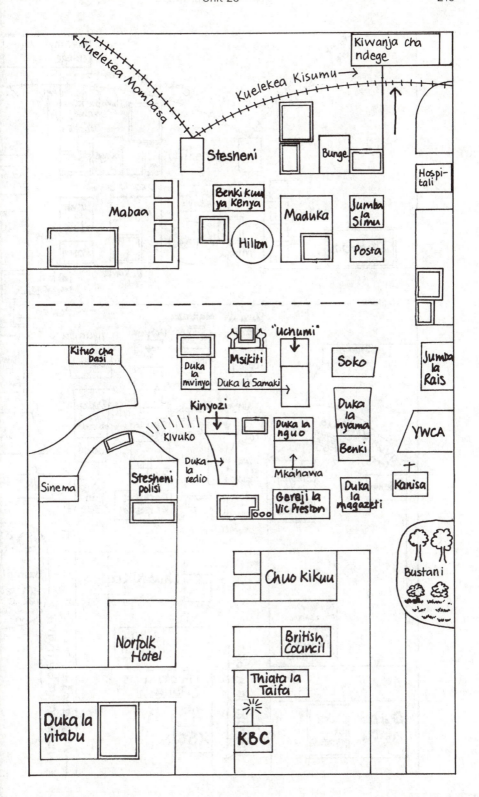

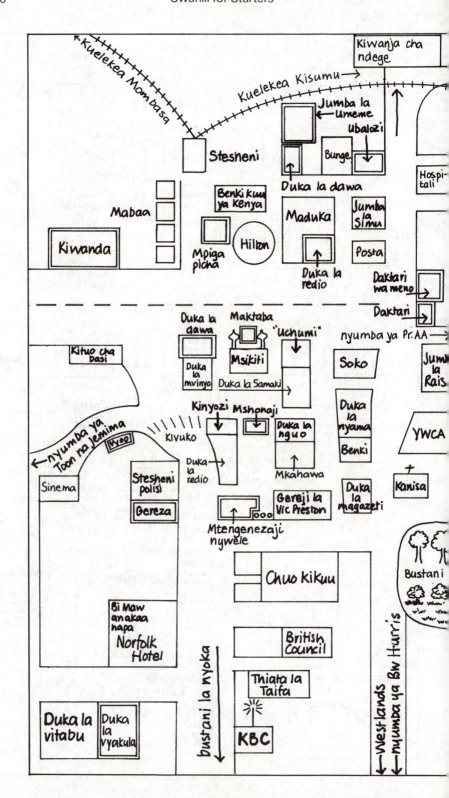

Revision

Take the map of Mombasa from Unit 26. Each player prepares a route from one place to another on the map. Using the vocabulary from Unit 26 and from this Unit, he describes the route to the other players, telling them only the starting-point. After describing the route, he then asks, 'Uko wapi?' This is not such an easy exercise as it seems!

Unit 30   Fungu la thelathini
Haraka haraka haina baraka —
(More haste less speed)

I

(a)   Bi. Maw na Bwana Harris wanakwenda Nairobi kutoka Mombasa, kwa
gari.

▷   Bi.M.:   Sasa Stuart, umeendesha gari kwa muda wa saa tatu nzima.
Lazima umechoka. Kuendesha gari wakati wa joto
kunachosha sana.

Bw.H.:   Ee, kweli nimechoka kidogo.

Bi.M.:   Basi, karibu tutafika Voi. Mbona tusisimame huko? Tutaweza
kujaza petroli na labda kunywa chai kidogo.

Bw.H.:   Haya.

Bi.M.:   Basi, punguza mwendo kidogo, Stuart. Nafikiri tuko karibu.
Tazama huko, upande wa kulia. Pita ndani.

Bw.H.:   Haya, tumeshafika. Nikuteremshe hapa uagize chai, wakati
mimi nitakapojaza petroli. Halafu tutakunywa chai pamoja.

....

Mwuza petroli: Nikutilie petroli kiasi gani, bwana?

Bw.H.:   Jaza tu.

M.P.:   Haya Bwana, tengi imejaa sasa.

....

Baada ya kunywa chai, marafiki hao wanarudi kwenye gari.

Bw.H.:   Joan, kwa kweli nimechoka sana. Labda ungeendesha
wewe kidogo.

Bi.M.:   Kweli? Niendeshe mimi gari lako jipya? Nitafurahi sana, lakini
sijazoea.

Bw.H.:   Utajizoea upesi. Njoo tubadilishe nafasi.

Bi.M.:   Haya, lakini lazima ueleze kila kitu.

Bw.H.:   Nitakuonyesha. Tubadilishane tu.

Bi.M.:   Nimekubali, lakini wewe kwanza rudisha gari barabarani.
Halafu nitaendesha mimi.

....

Kufika barabarani, wanabadilishana nafasi.

Bi.M.:   Basi, niwashe moto?

Bw.H.:   Washa tu.

Bi.M.:   Nionyeshe, niingize wapi ufunguo?

Bw.H.:   Pale pale, karibu na steling'.

Bi.M.:   Ee, ndiyo; lakini kwanza niingize gea. Ziko nne, sivyo?

Bw.H.:   Ndiyo.

Bi.M.:   Na kurudisha? Nionyeshe.

Bw.H.:   Kurudisha unabonyeza mtaimbo, halafu kuusukuma mbele.

Bi.M.:   Hivyo?

Bw.H.:   Ngoja nijaribu. A'a, hujabonyeza kwanza. Jaribu tena.

Bi.M.:   Hivyo?
Bw.H.:   Hivyo barabara. Sasa twende. Lakini kwanza pitisha
         wale watu!

....

Bw.H.:   Joan, unaendesha vizuri, lakini pole pole sana. Ongeza
         mwendo kidogo.
Bi.M.:   Nionavyo mimi, ninaendesha kwa kasi. Tazama, nina kilomita
         themanini kwa saa.
Bw.H.:   Hakuna hatari. Ongeza mwendo. Au unaogopa nini?
Bi.M.:   Siogopi kitu, hakuna la kuogofya. Lakini gari lako li jipya.
Bw.H.:   Si kitu. Ongeza tu. Au unaogopa kuteleza?
Bi.M.:   Siogopi kuteleza wala kitu cho chote. Lakini mbona
         unaniharakisha? Hakuna haraka, au sivyo?
Bw.H.:   Sikuharakishi, lakini hata hivyo ningependa kufika Nairobi
         kabla ya usiku.
Bi.M.:   Nitakufikisha salama, bwana, hata tukichelewa kidogo.
Bw.H.:   Lakini kwa kweli sitaki kucheleweshwa sana. Maanake
         nimealikwa nje, nile chakula cha usiku kwa Professor
         Dobbin.
Bi.M.:   Basi, nimefahamu sasa. Mbona hukunieleza kwanza kwamba
         umealikwa nje? Nitaendesha kwa kasi sana. Shika vizuri!
         Jishikishe! . . . Mwendo wa kilomita mia moja na ishirini
         unatosha? Umetosheka, Stuart?
Bw.H.:   Ee, ndiyo, mwendo huo unatosha. Nimetosheka. Endelea tu.

....

Bw.H.:   Tazama huko mbele. Ziko gari nyingi sana zimesimamishwa.
         Labda kuna ajali. Punguza mwendo.
Bi.M.:   Nimepunguza. Tazama, wako mapolisi wengi huko.
Bw.H.:   Wanataka kukusimamisha. Simamisha gari. Labda wanataka
         msaada.

....

Bi.M.:   Hujambo afisa.
Afisa: Sijambo bibi. Ulikuwa unaendesha kwa kasi sana.
Bi.M.:   Ndiyo. Tunaona haraka sana kwa sababu bwana anataka
         kufika Nairobi kabla ya usiku kuingia.
Afisa: Hivyo. Lakini mama, hujui kwamba ni marufuku kuendesha
         kwa kasi hiyo? Uliendesha zaidi kuliko kilomita mia moja na
         ishirini kwa saa.
Bi.M.:   Hayo ni kweli. Nisamehe bwana, sikujua kwamba kuna sheria
         ya mwendo. Ningetumia spidi gani?
Afisa: Sharti usizidishe kilomita themanini kwa saa.
Bi.M.:   Do! Kumbe nimekosa sana. Lakini mimi mgeni wa Mungu,
         nimetoka Uingereza na kufika hapa Kenya tangu wiki tatu tu.
         Tena gari jipya kabisa. Samahani sana bwana.
Afisa: Basi nitakusamehe mara hii, lakini usiendeshe hivyo tena.
Bi.M.:   Ahsante sana afisa, nitaendesha pole pole.
Afisa: Haya basi, endelea!
Bi.M.:   Kwa heri, bwana.
Afisa: Kwa heri mama.

....

Bi.M.: Wewe Stuart, u mjanja sana. Hukusema neno, na ndiyo wewe
        uliyenilazimisha niendeshe kwa kasi!

Bw.H.: Ndiyo, lakini ulimbembeleza polisi vizuri sana. Niliona afadhali
        ninyamaze. Sikutaka kujiingiza! Lakini namna gani
        alikuamini uliposema kwamba wewe u mgeni, na hali
        ulisema Kiswahili?

Bi.M.: Hata mimi sijui. Labda kwa vile gari jipya. Lakini walijuaje
        kwamba nilizidisha spidi? Sikuona dalili ya mtego.

Bw.H.: Hata mimi. Sielewi. Walibahatisha labda.

Bi.M.: Lakini walifahamu hasa mwendo wangu.

Bw.H.: Kweli, lakini si kitu. Usijali. Ongeza mwendo, tutachelewa.

Bi.M.: Siwezi kuuongeza tena Stuart, hata usemavyo. Sitaki
        kushtakiwa tena na mapolisi. Labda mara ya pili tutatiwa
        ndani. Ukitaka tuzidishe spidi, lazima uendeshe wewe
        mwenyewe. Mtu asipoona, hata akionywa, haoni.

Bw.H.: Basi, Joan, labda una haki. Haraka haraka haina baraka.
        Nitajilaza sasa, endesha upendavyo. Lakini
        usinicheleweshe!

Bi.M.: Nitakufikisha salama, bwana, basi.

haraka — 'haste, hurry'
baraka — 'blessing'
saa tatu nzima — 'three solid hours, three hours on end'
wakati wa joto — 'when it's hot'
-chosha — 'make tired'
pita ndani — 'go in'. Also used when showing a friend into your house.
-agiza — 'order (something)'
tengi — 'tank'
-jaa — 'be full'
-badilisha — 'change'; *badilisha nafasi* — 'change places'
-badilishana — 'exchange'
-kubali — 'agree'
-rudisha — 'return (something); reverse'
-washa — 'fire, light'; *washa moto* here means 'start engine'
-ingiza — 'put in'
steling' — 'steering (wheel)'
gea — 'gear'
-bonyeza — 'push in, depress'
mtaimbo — 'metal rod, crowbar, lever' here, 'gear lever'
sukuma — 'push'
barábara — 'right, proper' (dist. *barabára* 'main road')
-pitisha — 'let pass'
kasi — 'high speed'
li — 'it is'. See note (ii) in section II
wala — 'nor'
-harakisha — 'make (someone) hurry'
hata hivyo — 'all the same, in spite of that'
kabla — 'before'
-fikisha — 'make (someone) arrive'
-cheleweshwa — 'be made late'
-fahamu — 'understand', with intellect
-shika vizuri — 'hold on tight'

-jishikisha — 'fasten oneself (in), make oneself fast'
-simamishwa — 'be stopped'
-simamisha — 'make (sth., someone) stop'
usiku kuingia — 'night falls'. See note (iii) in section II.
marufuku — 'forbidden'
sheria — 'law'
sharti — 'by law', 'of necessity'
-zidisha — 'exceed'
mgeni wa Mungu — 'poor wretched foreigner'
u — 'you are'. See note (ii) in section II.
-janja — 'tricky', 'sly'.
-lazimisha — 'force'
-bembeleza — 'coax, get round someone'
-nyamaza — 'be quiet'
-jiingiza — 'interfere'
namna gani — 'how can it be (that)?'
hali — 'state'; here 'at the same time'. See note (ii) in section II.
dalili — 'sign, evidence'
si kitu — 'it doesn't matter'
hata usemavyo — 'whatever you say'
-shtakiwa — 'be accused'
-onywa — 'be made to see; be warned' See section II note (iv).
haki — 'right, legal right, justice'
-jilaza — 'stretch oneself out'
-chelewesha — 'make late'

II

(i) **Causative extension**

Many verbs used in the text in Section I have a 'causative' meaning, grammatically expressed by a verbal extension. For example, compare:

-jaa 'be full'   *-jaza* 'fill'
tengi imejaa 'the tank is full' : *nimejaza tengi* 'I have filled the tank'
-ingia 'enter'   *-ingiza* 'put in'
ameingia nyumbani 'he has gone into the house'
ameingiza vyombo nyumbani 'he has put furniture into the house'.

In the above examples, *-z-* is added after the root, before the final vowel of the verb. This is the usual case when a Bantu verb root ends in a vowel. Other examples are:

-pungua 'get less'   *-punguza* 'reduce'
-zoea 'be used to'   *-zoeza* 'get used to'
-elea 'be clear'   *-eleza* 'explain, make clear'
-agia 'agree'   *-agiza* 'order, commission'
-bonyea 'be dented'   *-bonyeza* 'press in, dent'.

Verbs whose roots end in *-l* have the *l* replaced by *z* to form the causative, e.g.

-lala 'lie down, sleep': *-laza* 'put to bed/sleep'

(It may be recalled that historically in many cases where two vowels are adjacent an l/r phoneme has been lost between them.)

Verbs whose roots end in voiceless plosive consonants (i.e. *p, t, k*) normally form the causative by replacing the final consonant with a fricative, or fricative plus *y*, as follows:

p	fy	-ogopa	'fear'	-ogofya	'frighten'

t	sh	-pata	'get'	-pasha	'cause to get'
		-pita	'pass'	-pisha	'let pass'
	s	-takata	'be clean'	-takasa	'clean'

k	sh	-choka	'be tired'	-chosha	'tire, make tired'
		-teremka	'get down'	-teremsha	'put (e.g. passenger) down'
		-waka	'burn'	-washa	'set light to, light'

Verbs with roots ending in *-w* also replace it by a fricative plus *y*, e.g.
-lewa 'be drunk'   *-levya* 'make drunk'

Verbs with roots ending in *-n* replace it by *ny*, e.g.
-ona 'see'   *-onya* 'warn'

Verbs with roots ending in any other consonants normally form their causative by adding *-ish-* or *-esh-* according to the rules for vowel harmony, e.g.

-fika   'arrive'   *-fikisha*   'get (someone) there'
-enda   'go'   *-endesha*   'drive' (make go)
-simama   'stand, stop'   *-simamisha*   'stop (someone or something)'

Verbs of non-Bantu origin also take *-ish-* or *-esh-*, e.g.
-badili 'change (oneself)'   *-badilisha* 'change (something)'
-rudi 'return'   *-rudisha* 'give back'
zidi 'get larger'   *-zidisha* 'make larger, greater'

Causative verbs can also be formed from roots which are not verbal, especially from loan-words, e.g.
bahati 'luck'   *-bahatisha* 'guess'
haraka 'haste'   *-harakisha* 'make (someone) hurry'
lazima 'necessary'   *-lazimisha* 'force'

A few verbs are irregular in their formation of the causative. Some of the most common exceptions to the rules as above are:

-fanya 'do'   *-fanyiza*   (or *-fanza*) 'make do'
-lipa 'pay'   *-lipiza*   'exact' (e.g. revenge)
-penda 'like'   *-pendeza*   'please'
-shika 'grasp'   *-shikisha* 'make firm'
-weka 'put'   *-wekesha*   'cause to put'

(*-chelewa* 'be late': *-chelewesha* 'make late' looks like an exception, but the *w* is historically a passive extension, not a stem-final consonant.)

Some verbs have two causative forms with distinct meanings, e.g.

-pita 'pass', 'pass along'

-pisha 'let through' *watu walimpisha mgeni* 'the people let the visitor through'

-pitisha 'cause to pass' *dereva alimpitisha mzee* 'the driver let the old man past' (e.g. waving him on etc.)

-lewa 'be drunk'

-levya 'make drunk' *pombe ilimlevya* 'the beer made him drunk'

-lewesha 'get (someone) drunk': *rafiki yake alimlewesha (pombe)* 'his friend made him drunk (with beer)' (*pombe* 'native beer')

Although in most cases the meaning of a verb with a causative extension is that of causation, in some cases it may be that of intensification, e.g.

-bemba	'wheedle'	*-bembeleza*	'coax', 'bamboozle'
-funga	'close'	*-fungisha*	'fasten tightly, imprison'
-nyamaa	'be quiet'	*-nyamaza*	'be totally silent'
-sikia	'hear'	*-sikiza*	'listen intently'
		(*-sikiliza*	'listen')
-telea	'descend'	*-teleza*	'slide, skid, fall by slipping'

There are also a few instances where the meaning of a causative form is specialised, in which case another form may be used for the meaning of causation, e.g.

-ona 'see'   *-onya* 'warn'

                -onyesha 'show'

(*-onyesha* is a 'double causative' form).

(ii) **Agreement copula**

Something which looks like the subject prefix as used with place copulas (*niko, uko, yuko*, etc.), but standing alone, functions as a copula itself. Its use is to express a state, as in the text:

gari lako li jipya   'your car is new'

wewe, Stuart, u mjanja sana 'you, Stuart, are very sly'.

The forms for persons are:

1st person singular	*ni*	'I am'	1st person plural	*tu*	'we are'
2nd person singular	*u*	'you are'	2nd person plural	*m*	'you are'
3rd person singular	*yu*	'he/she is'	3rd person plural	*wa*	'they are'

(In fact the 3rd person plural form is very rarely used.)

Forms for the other classes are predictable, e.g.

Class 3	*u*	'it is'
Class 4	*i*	'they are'
Class 5	*li*	'it is'
Class 6	*ya*	'they are',
etc.		

This copula is not very frequent in use; more frequently there is no copula (e.g. *gari lako (li) jipya; wewe (u) mjanja*). But its meaning is distinct from that of using *ni* for all classes, as in *Sheikh Yahya ni mwalimu* 'Sh. Yahya is a teacher'. Here the copula *ni* is equating Sh. Yahya as a teacher. It would be possible to say:

Sheikh Yahya yu mwalimu,

where we would be inferring that Sh. Yahya was characteristically a teacher, and a 'real' teacher at that! We might contrast:

alikuwa ni mwalimu 'he was a teacher (at that time)'

with *alikuwa yu mwalimu* 'he used to be a teacher (when he was alive)'.

Also, it would be possible to say:

mwalimu (wangu) ni Sh. Yahya '(my) teacher is Sh. Yahya'

but NOT:

*mwalimu (wangu) yu Sh. Yahya,

NOR:

*mjanja u wewe,

though we *could* say:

mjanja ni wewe 'the sly person is *you*', 'you are the one who is sly'.

Although this copula is not very often heard, there is one context in which it is common. The word *hali* 'state', 'condition' has been encountered. A frequent, polite enquiry after the initial greeting, is:

U hali gani? 'How are you?'

and the response:

Ni hali njema. 'I am well'.

One can also enquire about a third person, e.g.

Baba yu hali gani? (Response: *Yu hali njema*)

and to more than one person:

M hali gani? (Response: *Tu hali njema*).

Note also the expressions: *yu hai* 'he is alive' (cf. *amekufa* 'he is dead'), *yu macho* 'he is awake, aware' (cf. *amelala* 'he is asleep')

Even more rarely encountered are the negative forms:

(1st person singular   *si*)
2nd person singular   *hu*
3rd person singular   *hayu*
1st person plural   *hatu*
2nd person plural   *ham*
3rd person plural   *hawa*

Class 3   *hau*
Class 4   *hai* etc.

(iii) The nouns *kabla* 'before' and *baada* 'after' almost always occur in a nominal group structure, followed by *-a* plus another nominal word or group, e.g. *kabla ya hayo* 'before that (those things)'. Thus verbs have to occur in the infinitive (verbal noun) form, e.g.

kabla ya kusoma   'before reading'
kabla ya kufanya kazi   'before working'

There can sometimes be structural ambiguity, as in:

kabla ya kufika kwake   'before his arrival'
                             or 'before arriving at his place'

Normally the context will make the meaning clear, though it is also possible to follow *kabla* by a verb with the *-ja-* tense, e.g.

kabla hajafika   'before he arrived'.

In the text, *kabla ya* was followed by a clause with its own subject:

kabla ya usiku kuingia   'before night-fall'.

baada functions like *kabla*, but without the possibility of being followed by a verb with the *-ja-* or any other tense, e.g.

baada ya kusoma   'after reading'
baada ya kufika kwake   'after his arrival' etc.

There is also the form *baadaye* (from *baada yake*) meaning 'afterwards', which has already been used (Unit 12). You may deduce from the agreement *ya* that *baada* and *kabla* function as class 9 nouns.

wakati takes part in similar structures, with the meaning 'time when', as in:

wakati wa joto   'during the heat', 'when it's hot'.

We could also say:

wakati wa kufanya kazi   'while working'

(although this would more likely mean 'work-time', but context would show the distinction). You will deduce from the agreement *wa* that *wakati* is a class 11 noun. Indeed it may sometimes have a plural *nyakati* 'times', as in:

nyakati zile za zamani   '(in) the old days'.

(iv) **Methali**: Mtu asipoona, hata akionywa, haoni, 'if a person can't see, even if he's warned (or, made to see), he won't (doesn't) see'. *-onya* is causative of *-ona* 'see' (vid. section (i)), and 'ought' to mean 'make (someone) see', but usually has the meaning 'warn'. The proverb means something like: it's no good telling a person, he has to experience it for himself. Or cf. the English proverb 'You can lead a horse to water but you can't make it drink'.

III

(b) Rewrite the following sentences, using a causative verb, e.g.

Maji yamechemka.   Bibi amechemsha maji apike chai.

Nazi ilianguka.

Watoto wanaimba wimbo wa Taifa.

Mwizi anakimbia.
Nilisikitika sana niliposikia habari ya kufa kwake. (-*fa* 'die')
Watoto wako tayari?
Mwanafunzi yule amesoma vitabu vingi.

(c)   Give the causative forms of the following:

-amka
-fahamu
karibu
-nawa (wash hands and face)
-potea
-ruka
-samehe
-weza

Invent a Swahili sentence for each causative form, and give an Englis
gloss for each sentence.

(d)   Give the agreement (state) copulas for classes 7 to 18.

(e)   How would you say in Swahili:

How is your mother? (use *hali*)
We are all well. (use *hali*)
Working in the cold is very tiring.
After you've gone (use -*ondoka*) I shall be very sad.
Your going will make me sad.
Before the Europeans came to East Africa, the *Arabs* did.* (use -*fika*)

     * Notice that in Swahili there is no verb like 'do' in English which ca
substitute for anything (e.g. 'I like sweets and so *does* my brother';
went to Mombasa in the holidays and so *did* a lot of other people). I
Swahili it is usually necessary to repeat the verb, e.g.

Ninapenda sana peremende, na kaka yangu vile vile (anazipenda).
     (peremende 'sweet(s)' from 'peppermint')
Nilikwenda Mombasa wakati wa likizo, na watu wengine wengi
     walikwenda huko vile vile. (*likizo* — 'leave')

(f)   Translate the last paragraph of the conversation in section I into collc
quial English. (If English is not your first language, translate it into you
mother-tongue.)

IV

(i)   **Attitude to time**

haraka haraka haina baraka, literally: 'hurry hurry has no blessing', whic
I have glossed as 'More haste less speed', but of course the correspor
dence is not exact. Another Swahili saying is *kawia ufike; kukawia*
means 'to delay, loiter, be late', so the proverb can be translated literall
something like 'delay so that you may arrive', i.e. 'take it easy', 'don

rush your fences' etc. Many English sayings in fact exhort one to hurry or be on time, e.g.

time and tide wait for no man
punctuality is the courtesy of kings
a stitch in time saves nine
ripeness is all.

Few Swahili sayings do that, and this may reflect a more relaxed attitude to life. You may also like:

pole pole ndio mwendo 'slowly is (the right way to) travel',

even going slowly is progress. Not quite the same as 'slow and steady wins the race', but comparable. What other proverbs and sayings related to time can you find in your own language?

(ii) **'Being'**

It may be as well to reiterate that where in English we have a single verb 'to be', in Swahili different concepts of 'being' are expressed differently grammatically. For example, we can say:

He is in bed   (place)
He is alive   (state)
He is a thief (equivalence)

These three are different in Swahili and have different grammatical expressions, viz:

Yuko kitandani
Yu hai
Ni mwizi.

(iii) **Authority**

The Swahili have always had their version of Islamic law (*sheria*) with its systems of rights and duties, guarded by the *kadhi* (judges). Other groups of people have had their customary laws enforced by systems of elders and chiefs. These legal systems still stand and are upheld to cover certain situations. At the same time there is also an overall centralised system of law and administration in the countries of East Africa, based on the British system. At times of social change and mobility, traditional checks and balances are weakened, while new forms of authority do not yet command the same respect as the old.

(iv) **Necessity**

Different kinds of necessity or compulsion are perceived in Swahili. In English we might say to someone 'You must help your mother'. In Swahili there are a number of ways of saying this, with different implications. For example:

Afadhali umsaidie mamako. You must help your mother, it would be a good thing (sarcasm), why haven't you done so?

afadhali ('better') is used in situations where you are trying to persuade a person to do something, perhaps in order to avoid trouble. (A related word, *tafadhali* 'please', is extremely polite, and is normally only used to

equals or superiors, e.g. not to children. See note on this word in Un
27.)

Lazima umsaidie mamako. You must help your mother because I (or
some other outside agency) will make you do so.

lazima suggests you'll have to, *ukitaka usitake* 'like it or not'. *lazima* ma
also be used followed by the future tense, e.g. *lazima utatoa* 'you'll hav
to pay up'. A related verb, *-lazimu*, is normally used impersonally, e.g
Inanilazimu nimsaidie (or, *kumsaidia*) *mamangu* 'I'll have to help m
mother'; and in the causative form means to force someone else, e.g.
alinilazimisha nimsaidie 'he made me help him'. The passive extension
may also follow, e.g. *nililazimishwa kumsaidia* 'I was forced to help him'

Sharti umsaidie mamako. You must help your mother, it is part of the
system of Islamic law that you so do, in order to preserve the relation
ship.

sharti suggests a condition, in order to achieve some other aim, e.g
Huwezi kufika kule, sharti upite huku 'You can't get through that way
you'll have to go this way round'. *sharti* can also function as a noun
(class 9/10) meaning 'condition', e.g. *Huwezi kumwoa binti huyo mpak*
utimize sharti zake kwanza 'You won't be able to marry that girl unless
you first fulfil the conditions'. There is a verb form in the causative
-shurutisha 'to force someone to do something', as for example a *kadh*
(Islamic judge) might rule. A passive can also be added, *-shurutishw*
'be made to do something'. *sharti* conveys a stronger necessity than
lazima, with more moral force. *lazima* could involve brute force.

Huna budi kumsaidia mamako. You must help your mother becaus
there is no alternative. (Perhaps there is nobody else available, etc.)

budi suggests no possible alternative. It is normally used with the
negative *-na*, as here. But the word can occur otherwise, as e.g.: *Kun*
budi gani? 'What alternative is there? A verb form *-bidi* exists, usuall
used impersonally, as in *inanibidi* 'I must'. This has less force than *sin*
budi, and is more like *inanilazimu* in strength of meaning.

Inakupasa kumsaidia mamako. You must help your mother, it is prope
for you to do so.

-pasa is derived form *-pata* 'get', but has the special meaning of 't
befit'. It is normally used impersonally, as here.

Ni wajibu wako kumsaidia mamako. You must help your mother, it i
your moral duty.

wajibu is normally used as a noun, meaning moral obligation, and ha
more force than the verb *-pasa*.

Ni juu yako kumsaidia mamako. You must help your mother, it is up t
you.

juu plus a possessive (*juu yangu, juu ya mwalimu*) suggests 'concern
business, obligation'. It has less moral force than *wajibu* and has les
appeal to self-respect than *-pasa*. It is simply 'your affair'.

(Note the use of the subjunctive in the first three examples.)

Unit 31 Fungu la thelathini na moja
Kuibiwa — A robbery

I

(a) Askari Polisi: Sasa Bibi Maw, tuelezee hasa yaliyotokea.
Bibi Maw: Haya. Basi, nilitoka nyumbani saa mbili na robo kwenda Mombasa, kufanya kazi yangu.
Askari Polisi: Ulikwenda peke yako?
Bibi Maw: Ndiyo. Nilikwenda kwa gari, yaani gari ya rafiki yangu Bwana Harris. Kuondoka tu, niliona watu wawili wafanya kazi wa majirani, tukasalimiana. Halafu nikaendelea kuelekea njia kuu. Baada ya kitambo kidogo, wakati nilipokuwa bado kwenye njia ndogo — unajua njia hiyo inapindapinda — kupita kona moja niliona mtawi umeanguka njiani. Nilidhani ulikuwa umeanguka sasa hivi, maanake majani yake yalikuwa bado yametikisika. Njia ilikuwa haipitiki kabisa. Nilisimamisha gari nikatazama kila upande. Nikaona mti uliokauka kidogo uko karibu na njia nikadhani labda mtawi huo umeuvunjikia, lakini kwa kweli sikuyaamini. Hata hivyo sikumwona mtu ye yote. Ilikuwa haiwezekani kuendesha mbele, tena gari haigeukiki kwa vile njia nyembamba sana, tena yako mashimo pande zote mbili. Nikaona afadhali nishuke niondoe mtawi.
Askari Polisi: Ingalikuwa afadhali usingalishuka.
Bibi Maw: Basi ningalifanyeje? Tena nilikuwa si mbali sana kutoka nyumbani. Hatari haikufikirika. Basi nilishuka garini nikakaribia mtawi ulioanguka na kujaribu kuuondoa. Mara moja akatokea mtu, kutoka porini. Alikuwa ameshika panga mkononi, nikadhani kwanza ni mkata kuni. Nikamwambia, 'Kumbe ni wewe, bwana', akaitika, 'Ndiyo ni mimi,' akanishika mikono. Akadai mapesa, nikakataa. Nikamwambia, 'Ni aibu unayonifanyia', akajibu 'Sisi maskini tu.' Papo hapo akatokea mwenzake, mwenye kisu mkononi. Huyo alijaribu kufungua milango ya gari, lakini ilikuwa haifunguki, imefungika*, isipokuwa ule wa dereva. Akaufungua huo akachukua mfuko wangu kutoka kiti cha pili. Wa kwanza akasema, 'Kitu kingine', nikamwambia, 'Sina kitu kingine'. Akasema, 'Wajua tunaweza kukuua,' nikajibu, 'Ndiyo, nayajua'. Akatazama kwenye kioo akaona tepu rikoda kwenye kiti cha nyuma, akainyakua. Mwenzake akaichukua akaondoka hali ameshika mfuko wangu na tepu rikoda pia. Tepu rikoda hiyo ni nzito sana, karibu haichukuliki. Ilikuwa ni jambo la kuchekesha kuona jinsi mwizi

alivyojaribu kukimbia akilemewa nayo. Sikucheka lakir
Halafu yule wa kwanza akasema tena, 'Kitu kingine!'
Nikamwambia kwamba 'Sina kitu kingine cho chote.'
Akatazama akaona saa yangu ya mkono akaifungua n
kukimbia nayo. Sawia nikaruka upesi ndani ya gari
nikairudisha mbiombio mpaka nyumbani kwangu, na
kuwaarifu majirani. Wakashtuka sana. Halafu tukaja
kwenu. Hivyo ndivyo yalivyotokea.

Askari Polisi: Majambazi hao, walikuwa ni watu gani?
Bibi Maw: Mmoja alikuwa ni kijana tu, mwenye umri wa labda
                miaka ishirini; wa pili alikuwa mwenye umri zaidi,
                labda kama miaka thelathini na tano hivi. Yeye alikuwa
                amefunikwa kichwa kwa kilemba kilichoraruka.
Askari Polisi: Zaidi ya hayo, walivaa nini?
Bibi Maw: Siwezi kusema, sikutazama vizuri.
Askari Polisi: Aliyekushika amevaa shati gani? La rangi gani?
Bibi Maw: Labda la buluu, sijui.
Askari Polisi: Walikuwa wa kabila gani?
Bibi Maw: Sijui. Walisema Kiswahili. Nafikiri yule mmoja hayu
                Mdigo, lakini sijui hasa. Mimi si mwenyeji wa hapa.
Askari Polisi: Utawatambua tena?
Bibi Maw: Sijui, labda pengine nikiwaona tena watatambulikana,
                lakini sioni hakika.
Askari Polisi: Haya.
Bibi Maw: Majirani wameniambia afadhali ningalipiga honi,
                ingalisikika, lakini walipotokea watu hao honi ilikuwa
                haipigiki maanake yule wa kwanza amenishikilia. Tena
                ningalipiga kelele labda wangalitishika wangalinipiga
                ninyamaze.
Askari Polisi: Ee. Basi Bibi Maw, karani ataandika ulivyosema,
                utasoma maandishi yake na ukikubali kwamba ndivyo
                ulivyosema utatia sahihi.
Bibi Maw: Haya. Unadhani majambazi hao watapatikana?
Askari Polisi: Tutajaribu kila tuwezavyo kuwapata. Labda watapatikika.
                Utakaa hapa mpaka lini?
Bibi Maw: Mpaka wiki ijayo, halafu nitarudi Ulaya.
Askari Polisi: Nimesikitika sana, lakini tutafanya kila iwezekanavyo.
Bibi Maw: Haya, asante sana bwana.

* On the tape the speaker says '*imefungwa*' by mistake.

-iba — 'steal' (*mwivi* — 'thief' is derived from this verb stem)
-tokea — 'happen'
kuondoka tu — 'as (soon as) I set off'
wafanya kazi — 'workers, employees'
-salimu — 'greet'; *-salimiana* 'greet one another' (cf. *salama*)
kitambo — 'a short time'
-pinda — 'bend', *-pindapinda* — 'twist, wind'
mtawi — 'branch'
-dhani — 'think, consider'
sasa hivi — 'just now, very recently'
majani — 'leaves, greenstuff'
-tikisika — 'be shaking'; *-tikisa* 'shake'

haipitiki — 'it is impassable' (from *-pita*)
-kauka — 'be dried up'
haigeukiki — 'it can not be turned round', '. . . changed'
-embamba — 'narrow, thin'
shimo — 'hole, pit'
-shuka — 'get down, descend'
pori — 'bush, scrub, uncultivated land' (class 5/6)
panga — 'cutlass, large agricultural knife'
kuni — 'firewood', *mkata kuni* — 'woodcutter'
-itika — 'respond to a greeting' (from *-ita* — 'call')
-kataa — 'refuse'
aibu — 'shame, disgrace'
papo hapo — 'there and then, at that moment'
haifunguki — 'they could not be opened'
imefungika — 'they were locked'
isipokuwa — 'except'
tepu rikoda — 'tape recorder'
-nyakua — 'snatch'
pia — 'also, as well'
-zito — 'heavy'
haichukuliki — 'it is impossible to carry' (from *-chukua*)
-chekesha — 'make laugh' (from *-cheka*)
jinsi — 'how, in what manner' followed by *-vyo-* in the verb
-lemewa — 'be burdened, hampered' (*-lemea* 'burden, oppress')
sawia — 'at once' (cf. *sawa*)
-ruka — 'jump, fly'
mbio — 'quickly', *mbiombio* 'hastily'
-arifu — 'inform'
-shtuka — 'be shocked, startled'
jambazi — 'villain, terrorist' (class 5/6)
-funika — 'cover'
kilemba — 'turban'
-raruka — 'be torn, tattered' (*-rarua* — 'tear')
buluu — 'blue'
Mdigo — 'a Digo' (coastal tribe)
-tambua — 'recognise'
pengine — 'perhaps', *labda pengine* 'possibly'
-tambulikana — 'be recognisable'
hakika — 'certainty'
-piga honi — 'sound the horn'
-sikika — 'be audible'
-pigika — 'be soundable, strikable'
-shikilia — 'hold firmly'
maandishi — 'writings, thing written' (from *-andika*)
sahihi — 'signature'
-patikana — 'be obtainable' (from *-pata*)
-patikika — 'be obtainable with difficulty'

II

(i) Stative extension

The stative extension, as its name implies, normally is used to express state of affairs. It is formed by the addition of a morpheme including *k* t the verb root. If the root ends in a consonant, the stative morpheme *-ik-* or *-ek-* according to the rules of vowel harmony, e.g.

-funga 'close'	*-fungika* 'be shut'
-choma 'pierce'	*-chomeka* 'be pierced'.

Where the verb root ends in a vowel, the extension is generally *-lik-* *-lek-* according to vowel harmony, e.g.

-nunua 'buy'	*-nunulika* 'be bought'
ng'oa 'uproot'	*-ng'oleka* 'be uprooted'.

But frequently even here the extension is simply *-k-*. This possibly arise by analogy, since many cases of verbs with apparent stem-final vowel are actually already extended, e.g.

simple	stative	reversive	stative of reversive
-funga	*-fungika*	*-fungua*	*-funguka*.

Verbs of foreign origin (mainly Arabic) as usual behave as if the fin. vowel were a stem vowel for the purposes of vowel harmony, e.g.

-pasi	'pass (ball in football)'	*-pasika*
-shutumu	'abuse'	*-shutumika*
-samehe	'forgive'	*-sameheka*
-sahau	'forget'	*-sahaulika*.

Stative verb stems can also be formed from nominal and other stem: e.g.

shughuli 'business affairs'	*-shughulika* 'be busy'
ana shughuli nyingi	'he has a lot of business on hand'
ameshughulika sana	'he is very busy'.
-zee 'old'	*amezeeka* 'he has aged'

In Swahili there is a clear grammatical distinction between a state and passive, which is by no means always so clear in other languages. Fc instance in Swahili we may say:

	mlango umefungwa	'the door has been shut (by someone)'
or:	*mlango umefungika*	'the door is shut' (no implication of agent)
	alitishwa (na nyoka)	'he was frightened (by a snake')'
or:	*alitishika*	'he was afraid/frightened' (no agent).

Although the distinction *can* be made in English, as in the abov examples, it is not normally made clear. But in Swahili there is a clea choice between the passive and the stative, and one of them *must* b chosen; there is no neutral or ambiguous form.

It should be noted that with this meaning of 'state', the stative form i not normally used with other than the *-me-* tense, e.g.

mtawi umeanguka 'a branch has fallen'
milango (ilikuwa) imefungika 'the doors (were) locked'.

or with aspect (e.g. subjunctive), or relative, e.g.

nishuke 'I should get down'
mti uliokauka 'a dry tree' (dead).

The stative form is also used, however, to express potentiality, when it may be associated with other tenses and verb forms, e.g.

hatari haikufikirika 'danger was unthinkable'
karibu haichukuliki 'it is almost impossible to carry'.

In many cases the potential is expressed by the stative extension plus *-an-*, as in:

-weza 'be able'   *-wezekana* 'be possible'
-ilikuwa haiwezekani kuendesha mbele 'it was impossible to drive forward'
-pata 'get'   *-patikana* 'be obtainable'
Unadhani majambazi hao watapatikana? 'Do you think those villains can be caught?'

There may thus be a contrast:

-tambua 'recognise'   *-tambulika* 'be well known'   *-tambulikana* 'be recognisable'.

Sometimes a double stative form may be used to express the idea of potentiality but with difficulty. In the text we have:

Unadhani . . . watapatikana?   'Do you think . . . they will be caught?'
. . . Labda watapatikika.   'Perhaps they may be caught'.

There are also, as with other extensions, cases where the meaning of the stative form is not entirely predictable, e.g.

-ondoa 'take away'   *-ondoka* 'go away'
-ita 'call'   *-itika* 'respond'.

It is axiomatic that a clause containing a stative functioning as a stative or potential cannot have a complement (object), nor can the verb itself have an object prefix, i.e. we can say:

    mwalimu amefunga mlango
    (where *mwalimu* is subject and *mlango* is complement)

or: *mwalimu ameufunga*
    (where *-u-* is the object marker before the verb stem)

but: *mlango umefungika*
    (*mlango* is subject and there can be no complement).

III

(b) Eleza jinsi majambazi walivyotega mtego wao. (*-tega* 'set', *mtego* 'trap').

(c) Baada ya kuondoka, waizi watafanya nini?

(d) Unafikiri Bibi Maw alionaje, baada ya kushambuliwa hivi? (-*shambulia* 'set on', 'attack').

(e) Make a list of the stative verbs in the text and give where possible their corresponding simple, prepositional, passive, and causative forms. Use your dictionary if necessary. e.g.

simple	stative	prepositional	passive	causative
-*toa*	-*toka*	-*tolea*	-*tolewa*	-*toza*.

▷   (f) Write or speak sentences on the patterns given:

Angua nazi! Zimeanguka. Uliziangua wewe? Siyo, zimeanguka tu.
Funga mlango!
Fungua madirisha!
Ondoa mbwa! (*mbwa* — 'dog')
Usivunje vyombo!

(g) Write responses, using negative potential verbs.

Unasikia ndege yule? Siyo, hasikiki kwa sababu _____
Bwana Harris atapita njia ya Waa? Siyo, _____
Daktari wa meno alikung'oa magego? (*magego* — 'molars')
Mwivi alichukua redio yako?
Jaji alimsamehe mwuaji? (*mwuaji* — 'murderer', from -*ua*)
Wageni wanakula chakula alichokipika Bwana Harris?
Bibi Maw amewasahau majambazi waliomwibia?

(h) Make sentences on the pattern given, contrasting stative, potential, and passive extensions, e.g.

Tubomoe nyumba hii?
Siyo, hatuwezi kubomoa nyumba hiyo, haibomoki.
Nyumba ile imebomoka lakini.
Ndiyo, ile ilibomolewa na serikali.

Bwana Philip apike mizizi hii? (*mzizi* — 'root')
Siyo, hawezi kupika mizizi hiyo _____

Nikate mkate huu?

Mwalimu ajibu swali hili?

Bibi Maw alisema maneno haya?

Waizi walivunja benki hii? (-*vunja* here means 'break into')

Wanahewa wamefika nyota zile? (*mwanahewa* 'astronaut', *hewa* — 'atmosphere'; *nyota* — 'star(s)')

(i) Give the stative form of the following verbs and make up a sentence for each, giving them a negative potential meaning. Give a gloss for each of your sentences.

-shika   -nunua
-fika   -hesabu
-maliza

(You may like the expression *kazi haimaliziki* 'work never ends!')

(j) Wewe mwenyewe umepata kushambuliwa, au kuibiwa, au kutishika?
     Eleza yaliyotokea.

IV

Crime and sin.

While there may be certain actions which most people would agree
were wrong, the concept of what constitutes a crime or a sin depends
very much on what a particular society has agreed to derogate as such.
Moreover the two (crime and sin) may not coincide, and they may have a
different relative importance in different societies. In a pluralistic society
there are bound to be different standards, and when attempts are made
to impose standardisation, people find new ways difficult to accept, and
many simply ignore the law where it seems to them unacceptable. This
phenomenon is universal, but because of the great diversity of peoples
and customs and the rapidity of change in East Africa, the problems are
more obvious. For example, some years ago the Tanzanian government
attempted to introduce new legislation to remedy what seemed to be an
anomalous situation whereby Muslims and pagans could have more
than one wife but Christians could not. A tremendous outcry ensued,
perhaps inevitable when legislators seem to be intervening in what
people consider to be their private affairs.

Even attitudes to property may differ. I recall a young Swahili friend
pointing out to me an old man in the street, and saying, "You see that old
man? Well nobody likes him." "Why not?" I asked, on cue. "Oh well," he
said, "once he was walking along and a Greek* passed him on a bicycle.
This Greek had a café and he was going home with the takings in bags
on the back of his bike. One bag fell off into the ditch and the Greek
didn't notice. The old man hid it. After a while the Greek came back and
asked him if he'd seen a bag of money. The old man handed it over; the
Greek gave him a shilling, and said '*You*'ll never be rich!' Now nobody
likes that old man." I was puzzled and asked, "But surely he was honest,
why don't people like him?" "Oh well," said my friend, "he might have
been honest, but don't you see, *God* sent him that money. And he
spurned it. It doesn't do to spurn God's gifts. That's why people don't like
that old man." Whether this anecdote was apocryphal or not, it does
demonstrate an attitude of mind.

Whether the level of crime and violence in East Africa is rising or not,
whether it is or is not worse than elsewhere, there is no doubt that
people are afraid of it. Everywhere homes are made as secure as
possible, with iron bars and shutters at the windows, and strong door
bolts. People expect mainly to have to look after themselves and each
other, and in residential areas strangers are noted. In central Nairobi
people do not walk about the streets at night. In Mombasa they do. In
Mombasa there are very few streets which are not at least backing on to
residential areas. But the centre of Nairobi seems impersonal, with
hotels, banks, shops, cinemas and no residents keeping an eye open.

*The story was told me near Tanga, and there were at that time many
Greek businessmen in the town.

Swahili friends expressed great concern at the ambushing of Bi. Mav
They suggested she stayed with them in town where they felt she woul
be safe, rather than on the coast which they regarded with towns
people's distrust as 'bush'. They expressed relief and considerabl
surprise that she had not been physically harmed, and while som
admired what they saw as her 'bravery' and 'self-defence', other
suggested that the best thing to do would be to give attackers every
thing one had at once and beg them not to kill one. There was conside
able feeling that 'in the old days' such things did not happen. Eve
making allowances for rosy views of the past, it is probably true that in
rapidly growing and changing society there is more opportunity fc
getting away with crime and therefore more incentive to try it.

Unit 32 Fungu la thelathini na mbili
Ziara — A visit

I

(a) Bi. Maw: Yahya, ningependa niende kuwaamkia akina Mazrui, lakini sijui niende lini.
Sh. Yahya: Mazrui gani?
Bi.M.: Wale walionialika nihudhurie arusi ya binti yao, mwaka uliopita. Unakumbuka.
Sh.Y.: Ee, ndiyo, wale wanaokaa Ndia Kuu.
Bi.M.: Ndio wao. Nilifanya urafiki na binti arusi, ambaye sasa amehama, pamoja na mumewe. Lakini hata hivyo ningependa kwenda kuwaamkia mabibi wengine, ambao walinipokea vizuri, wakati huo.
Sh.Y.: Haya basi, nenda tu.
Bi.M.: Sijui niende lini, wala sina mtu wa kumtuma, kuwaarifu kwanza.
Sh.Y.: Basi labda dada yangu, ambaye anajuana nao sana, angefuatana nawe.
Bi.M.: Akikubali nitafurahi sana.
....

Bi. Arafa: Nimempeleka mtoto mmoja ambaye angewaarifu akina Mazrui kwamba tutafika saa kumi na moja. Basi tunaweza kwenda. Ngoja kwanza nivae buibui.
....

Bi.M.: Si tumeshapita nyumba yenyewe?
Bi.A.: Do, ndiyo, nilikuwa sifikiri. Basi, tupite hapa mkono wa kulia.
Bi.M.: Lakini hii si nyumba ambayo nilikuwa nikifika zamani.
Bi.A.: Labda wewe uliingia mlango wa mbele.
Bi.M.: Ee, kweli, mlango uleeee.
Bi.A.: Basi mimi desturi yangu huingia mlango wa nyuma. Lakini tunaweza kutumia ule wa mbele ukipenda zaidi.
Bi.M.: Siyo, tufanye kama desturi yako. Nilishangaa tu kuona tumeshapita mlango ambao zamani nilikuwa nikiugonga.
Bi.A.: Haya, basi, twende tu.
Hodi!
n.k.
Darajani.
Bi.M.: Lakini wajua, hii si nyumba ambayo nilikuwa nikizuru zamani.
Bi.A.: Hii ni nyumba ya Mazrui. Lazima hapa ndipo mahali ulipofika zamani. Huss, tuingie tu.
Hujambo bibi!
n.k.
Basi, bibi, nimekuletea Bi. Maw ambaye alikuwako hapa mwaka uliopita, wakati wa arusi. Unamkumbuka.

Bibi wa nyumbani: Karibu bibi, karibu. Tumepata habari kwamba
                     mtafika. Lakini kwa bahati mbaya rafiki yako
                     hayuko sasa. Amekwenda hospitalini, ambapo
                     mama yake amelazwa na kupasuliwa jana.
Bi.A.:   Do, vipi! Tunakaa mtaa mmoja na mimi sijasikia
                     habari hii.
Bibi wa nyumbani: Ndivyo mambo yalivyo. Ee, amelazwa tangu wiki
                     mbili.
Bi.M.:   Basi naona tusikae, bibi, nilitaka kuwaamkieni tu,
                     sitaki kuwasumbua.
Bibi wa ny.:   Lakini mbona sikukumbuki, bibi?
Bi.M.:   Sijui, lakini walikuwako watu wengi sana mwaka
                     jana.
Bibi wa ny.:   Bila shaka hii ndiyo sababu.
Bi.M.:   Ee. Basi bibi, lazima niende, maanake usiku karibu
                     kuingia, na nyumba ninapokaa iko mbali sana.
Bibi wa ny.:   Ee, si vizuri kutembea usiku, ambapo watu wabaya
                     wanapotembea. Lakini rafiki yako atasikitika sana
                     kuona kwamba amekukosa.
Bi.M.:   Hata mimi nimesikitika sana. Nimsalimie sana.
Bibi wa ny.:   Haya, nitamwambia.
....

Sh.Y.:   Ilikuwaje, ziara yako ya jana, Joan?
Bi.M.:   Kwa bahati mbaya tulikosa nyumba, lakini dada yako alikuwa
         na hakika, hata niliona haya kumwambia kwamba amekosa
         kabisa! Na yule bibi ambaye ningemjua, bila shaka
         asingalinitambua. Kwa bahati niliwahi kumwepuka. Watu wa
         nyumbani walitupokea vizuri, lakini hata hivyo lazima
         walishangaa sana! Adabu ni kitu cha ajabu, bwana.
Sh.Y.:   Kweli kabisa!

-amkia — here means 'call on'
-hudhuria — 'be present' at some function
arusi — 'wedding'
Ndia Kuu — a street in the Old Town area of Mombasa. Ndia — njia.
urafiki — 'friendship' (cf. rafiki)
binti arusi — 'bride' (bwana arusi — 'bridegroom')
ambaye — 'who' (relative)
hata hivyo — 'nevertheless'
-arifu — 'inform'
buibui — black enveloping outer garment worn out of doors by Muslim
   women in East Africa.
ambayo — 'which', referring to nyumba
-shangaa — 'be surprised, amazed'
ambao — 'which' referring to mlango
daraja — here 'staircase'
-zuru — 'visit' (usually formal) cf. ziara
huss — 'ssh'
ambapo — 'where' (relative) referring to hospitalini
mtaa — 'district' (of a town)
-sumbua — 'disturb'
usiku karibu kuingia — 'it's nearly nightfall'

ambapo — 'when' (relative)
haya — 'embarrassment, shyness'
-epuka — 'avoid'
adabu — 'good manners'

II

(i) **amba-**

Relative clauses are of two kinds. The first kind, dealt with in Unit 27, serve to define the item to which they refer, are often called 'defining' relatives, and in Swahili are normally expressed by a relative affix to the verb. In the text in section I, Bibi Maw responds to Sh. Yahya's question as to which branch of the Mazrui family she means by saying:

Wale walionialika nihudhurie arusi ya binti wao — 'Those who invited me to their daughter's wedding',

thus defining or identifying by means of a clause containing a relative verb, which particular people are referred to.

The second kind of relative clause merely gives further information about the item to which it refers, but does not uniquely identify it. These clauses are sometimes called 'non-defining' relative; or 'continuative' as opposed to 'restrictive'. In Swahili they are normally introduced by *amba-* plus agreement. So in the text, Bibi Maw refers to the bride:

Nilifanya urafiki na binti arusi, ambaye sasa amehama, . . .

'I made friends with the bride, who has now moved away, . . .' i.e. the relative clause 'who has now moved away' is not identifying *which* bride Bi. Maw made friends with, but is merely giving more information about her. It would be possible, by contrast, to imagine a situation where one was discussing a number of friends (or even brides) and identifying or distinguishing one of them as the one who moved away. In this case a relative form of the verb *-hama* would be used, e.g. *yule aliyehama* 'the one who moved away'.

The distinction between defining and non-defining relatives is not always very clear to native speakers of English and other languages where there are not two distinct grammatical forms for them. In fact, in English, the distinction is made by intonation in the spoken language, and by punctuation in the written. Consider:

Students who don't work don't pass their examinations.

Without commas, this sentence means that those of the student body who don't work, those identified by this characteristic, don't pass. In Swahili a relative verb would be used, viz:

Wanafunzi wasiosoma hawafaulu mitihani. (*mtihani* — 'exam')

But in the sentence:

Students, who don't work these days, often fail their exams

the relative clause is not picking out some students from the rest, but is making a general statement about the supposed nature of all students. In English this 'non-defining' relative is distinguished only by the

commas round the clause (reflecting the intonation). In Swahili we would
use *amba-*; viz:

Wanafunzi ambao hawasomi siku hizi, mara nyingi huanguka mitihani.

In form, *amba-* is always completed by the relative agreement appropriate to the class of the item to which it refers. So in the text we have:

binti arusi ambaye . . .   'the bride who . . .'
nyumba ambayo . . .   'the house which . . .'
mlango ambao . . .   'the door (at) which . . .'
hospitalini ambapo . . .   'at the hospital where . . .'

and also the idea of time:

usiku ambapo . . .   '(at) night when . . .'.

Agreements for the other classes are regular. There is no difference in
form between subject and object, e.g.

binti arusi ambaye amehama   'the bride, who has moved away'
binti arusi ambaye nimemwona 'the bride, whom I saw'.

Historically, *amba-* is related to the verb for 'to say', now represented by
kuambia 'to tell', and *kwamba* 'that' (introducing reported speech).

Notwithstanding the importance of the fundamental distinction between
'defining' and 'non-defining' relatives, with 'defining' normally expressed
in Swahili through a relative affix in a verb, and 'non-defining' by the use
of *amba-*, there are circumstances where *amba-* is used even though
the relative may be 'defining'. These circumstances are as follows:

1 When the tense (positive or negative) which is required is not one
which can co-exist in the verb with a relative marker. We have seen (Unit
27) that the relative verb can have only the tenses *-li-*, *-taka-*, *-na-* or no
tense in the positive, e.g.

watu waliofika   'the people who arrived'
watu watakaofika   'the people who will arrive'
watu wanaofika   'people who are arriving'
watu wafikao   'people who arrive',

and only a general negative, e.g.

watu wasiofika 'people who do not arrive'.

If any other tense, positive or negative is required, *amba-* must be used
e.g.

watu ambao wangaliondoka 'the people who would have left'
watu ambao hawakuondoka jana 'the people who did not leave
  yesterday'
watu ambao nimewajua tangu zamani 'people whom I have known for
  a long time'.

In the text we have the example:

yule bibi ambaye ningemjua 'the lady whom I was supposed to know'.

In such cases (as in English) the context usually shows whether 'defining' or 'non-defining' relative is meant. Intonation in Swahili can also be
used to make the distinction.

2 *amba-* is also used when other languages have a relative in an 'oblique' case (genitive, dative, ablative). In English these cases are represented by prepositions. So a group such as 'to whom', 'of which', etc. will be expressed by *amba-*, e.g.

mtu ambaye tulizungumza habari zake 'the man about whom we were talking'
mtu ambaye nilikwenda sinema naye 'the person with whom I went to the cinema'
mtu ambaye nilimwuzia gari yangu 'the person to whom I sold my car'
sanduku ambalo aliweka pesa zake ndani yake 'the box in which he kept his cash'.

In the text there is an example of this usage:

mlango ambao nilikuwa nikiugonga 'the door at which I used to knock'.

3 Occasionally both forms of the relative will be found, as in the text:

si vizuri kutembea usiku, ambapo watu wabaya wanapotembea

'it's not a good thing to go around at night, when bad characters are about'.

This is usually for emphasis, i.e. *'that's when* bad characters are about'.

III

(b)   Write out all the forms of *amba-* for all classes.

(c)   Each of the following sentences contains a relative clause. Say whether the clause is defining or non-defining.

Yesterday I saw two men *who were breaking into a shop*.
Yesterday I saw the two men *who broke into the shop*.
People *who live in glass houses* shouldn't throw stones.
The British *who are known to be perfidious* have broken yet another treaty.
The British team *which climbed Everest* has now returned to London.
Irish girls *who are famous for their complexions* are a pleasure to see.
Women *who are pregnant* are entitled to six months' leave.
His father *who was self-controlled* / Bade all the children round attend/ To James' miserable end.
This is the house *that Jack built*.
They *that live by the sword* shall die by the sword.
The barge *she sat in*, like a burnished throne/ Burned on the water.
I know a bank *whereon the wild thyme blows*.
The four prison officers were made to take off their uniforms *which were put on by the escaping prisoners*.

(d)   In each of the following sentences, a clause with *amba-* is used. Say why, in each case.

Kitabu *ambacho kimeandikwa na mwalimu* hakifai kabisa.
Gari *ambalo ningefika kwalo* limeharibika.
Mtoto *ambaye nilimpa mapesa* ametoweka. (*-toweka* 'disappear')

Meza *ambayo uliweka birika juu yake* imeharibika. (*birika* 'kettle')
Malkia *ambaye anaonekana amechoka kidogo* anatoka katika ndege.
   (*malkia* 'queen')

(e) Write the following sentences in Swahili:

The thief, who did not see the policeman, tried to snatch a woman's
   handbag. (*-nyang'anya* — 'snatch')
Where is the man to whom you sold your car?
Armstrong and Aldrin got to the moon where they collected (*-kusanya*
   'collect') stones and dust. (*vumbi* 'dust')
The witch's house, which is roofed with corrugated iron, is near the river
   (*mchawi* 'witch, wizard'; *-ezeka* 'roof'; *mabati* 'corrugated iron
   sheets'; *mto* 'river')
The box that my mother keeps her rings in has been stolen.
Some students whose names I won't mention have not done their work.
Yesterday I saw a dress which I would have bought, but the shop was
   shut.
Some girls marry men whom they have never seen.

You should have used *amba-* in all sentences. Give the reason(s) in eac
case for using *amba-* rather than a relative verb.

IV

(i) **Community relations** are very important to the town-dwellin
   Swahili. Mutual help and assistance is expected from neighbours, and
   lively interest is taken in all the goings-on. Births, weddings, illnesses
   funerals are all discussed and attended with appropriate visits an
   congratulations or sympathy. This close-knit system not only supplie
   support and security; it also implies a degree of social control, since nc
   much happens that neighbours do not know about, and social approva
   or at least tolerance is necessary for the individual to survive. Of cours
   this social control and interest of the neighbours can be irksome, espe
   cially to the young who may see it as a curb on their individuality, bu
   conversely it is generally tolerant of the disadvantaged in society — th
   old, the very poor, the crippled, the mentally unstable. Without senti
   mentality, such people are afforded their place in society, accepting thei
   disabilities as somehow part of God's plan. In the street, people gree
   not only the smart and the sheikhs, but also the grubby children and th
   cripples, even the mad woman shouting at her doorway. They may sa
   to you 'She's mad, she shouts all the time', or 'Those children are neve
   washed'; but they accept them. I am not suggesting that Swahili societ
   is necessarily ideal, but it is very varied and close-knit.

(ii) **'Face'** It is always necessary to spare other people embarrassment in
   civilised community. The farcical situation in section I arose an
   developed from an original misunderstanding which was impossible t
   correct without loss of face on someone's part, once other peopl
   became involved; and it developed amid general puzzlement but wit
   everyone preserving everyone else's face! Fortunately it ended withou
   the confrontation that would have forced a break-down. Probably such

complication would not have arisen if Bibi Maw had not been simultaneously a) an ignorant foreigner and b) a guest! *heshima* 'respect' 'dignity' is a most important concept to the Swahili. To say of someone, *'Hana heshima'* 'He has no respect (for others)' or 'He has no self-respect' is a dreadful indictment.

Unit 33   Fungu la thelathini na tatu.

Nyota — Your stars

I

(a)

★ ★ ★ **NYOTA STARS** ★ ★ ★ **NYOTA STARS** ★ ★ ★

AQUARIUS

(Januari 20 — Februari 20)

WAKATI huu waweza kuwa na matata na jamaa zako, lakini mambo yataweza kuwa mema na kurudia maisha ya kawaida. Katikati ya mwezi utakuwa na bahati njema na mafanikio mema kazini mwako. Mpenzi wako atakufurahisha wakati huu. Waweza kufanya safari mwezi huu.

PISCES

(Feb. 21 — Machi 20)

Utakuwa na furaha kubwa kwa sababu jamaa zako wote watakuwa tayari kukusaidia kwa shida ungekuwa nayo. Hakuna mabadiliko utakayo kuwa nayo katika afya yako na maisha yako ya kawaida, isipokuwa pengine waweza kusumbuliwa na kuumwa na kichwa. Usijaribu kufanya uamuzi wo wote mpaka katikati ya mwezi ujao.

ARIES

(Machi 21 — Apr. 20)

Utakuwa mtu wa manufaa sana kwa watu wengi kwa sababu watategemea msaada wako. Usiwaepuke. Wiki ya kwanza utaweza kukutana na watu wengi wanaotaka uwasaidie na uwe na shughuli nyingi sana. Haifai wakati huu uhudhurie sherehe ama mambo mengine ambayo yangekuletea shughuli nyingi mpaka tarehe 24, mwezi huu.

TAURUS

(Apr. 21 — Mei 20)

Huu ni mwezi mzuri sana kwako kwenda likizoni. Baada ya tarehe 4, utaweza kuwa na mambo mengi ya kufurahisha. Kama ukiwa hutaenda mahali po pote ukiwa nyumbani kwako, marafiki zako na watu mashuhuri watakutembelea na mtazungumza nao mambo ya kupendeza. Huu ni mwezi mwema kwako kununua kitu ulichokusudia kununua hapo zamani.

GEMINI

(Mei 21 — Juni 20)

Jambo ambalo ulikuwa ukiliepuka kama miezi minane iliyopita laweza kukumbana nawe wakati huu. Yafaa uwe ukifanya mambo kwa busara hasa kuwaepuka watu wenye tabia mbaya. Mpenzi wako ama bibi yako atakuwa mtu wa kukusaidia sana kwa shida zako. Afya yako ni njema mwezi huu.

CANCER

(Juni 21 — Julai 20)

Watu waliozaliwa chini ya nyota hii wana bahati sana kwa sababu watakuwa na majalio mema na kufaidika rohoni zao na kwa jamaa zao. Ikiwa unataka kwenda kuwatembelea marafiki zako walio mbali fanya wakati huu. Kama unataka kununua kitu cha maana kama motakaa, hii ni bahati yako.

LEO

(Julai 21 — Ago. 20)

Una matumizi mengi ya pesa mwezi huu, yafaa ufanye mpango unaofaa na utumie pesa zako kwa busara. Ikiwa unakusudia kumtafuta mpenzi ambaye mngeoana hii ni bahati yako, fanya pilka pilka mitaani, utamkuta amekungojea. Tumia pesa zako kwa busara, kwani hutaweza kuwa na kutosha.

VIRGO

(Ago. 21 — Sep. 20)

Fanya kazi yako kwa bidii mkubwa wako anafurahiwa na utumishi wako; huenda akakupandisha madaraka ama uongezewe mshahara. Nyumbani kwako mambo si mema sana, jamaa zako wanategemea msaada wako; utumie pesa zako kwa busara. Walio wasio na wapenzi, wafanye uangalifu, marafiki wabaya wataweza kukuharibia maisha yako.

LIBRA

(Sep. 21 — Okt. 20)

Jaribu kufikiria mambo yote uliyofanya mwaka jana. Utashangaa kwa kuona vile Mungu amekusaidia na kukuletea mafanikio mema; mshukuru. Utaendelea kuwa na mafanikio mema, ukiwa utakuwa ukiwasaidia watu wote. Marafiki zako wako tayari kusaidia.

SCORPIO

(Okt. 21 — Nov. 20)

Utaalikwa karamu na sherehe nyingi. Tangu leo mpaka tarehe 4 utaendelea kuwa na furaha na ikiwa unakusudia kufanya jambo ama kununua kitu, huu ni wakati unaofaa kwako. Jamaa zako watakusumbua kwa mambo kadhaa, lakini yote utaweza kuyaepuka kwa urahisi. Wiki ya mwisho wa mwezi utaweza kupata zawadi.

SAGITTARIUS

(Nov. 21 — Des. 20)

Mara ufanyapo kazi kwa bidii ndio utazidi kupata pesa nyingi. Kufaulu kwako mwezi huu kutakuletea furaha ambayo umekuwa unatazamia kwa muda mrefu. Utampata yule uliyekuwa ukimpenda. Ikiwa una bibi atakutaka umsaidie sana kwa kazi za nyumbani. Afya yako ni njema, waweza kusumbuliwa na meno ama kuumwa na kichwa.

CAPRICORN

(Des. 21 — Jan. 20)

Jamaa na wakwe zako watakusumbua sana mwezi huu. Utakuwa na mawazo mengi lakini kaza moyo. Wiki ya pili ya mwezi huu mambo hayo yatapoa na kurudia maisha ya kawaida. Uwe mwangalifu kwa mpenzi wako kwa mambo ungemwambia, sababu aweza kukuacha. Wiki ya mwisho wa mwezi utapata pesa za kutosha matumizi yako na kuzidi. Afya yako ni njema.

waweza — sc. 'you may' (*-weza* 'be able')
matata — 'problems, difficulties', cf. *-tata* 'tangle'
kawaida — 'normal'
katikati — 'middle', cf. *katika* 'in'
mafanikio — 'success'
mpenzi — 'sweetheart', cf. *-penda* 'like, love'

shida — 'lack, shortage, need'
mabadiliko — 'changes', cf. *-badili* 'change'
afya — 'health'
uamuzi — 'decision', cf. *-amua* 'arbitrate'

manufaa — 'profit, advantage'
shughuli — 'preoccupation, activity'; *-shughulika* 'be busy'
sherehe — 'celebration'

mashuhuri — 'well-known, famous'
-kusudia — 'intend'

-kumbana — 'come up against'; *-kumba* 'shove'
yafaa — 'it would be sensible'; *-faa*
busara — 'common sense, wisdom'
tabia — 'character'

-zaa — 'bear (a child)', *-zaliwa* 'be born'
majalio — 'blessings, gifts, good happenings (from God)', cf. *-jaa* 'be full'
kufaidika — 'to get advantage, satisfaction', cf. *-faa*

matumizi — 'expenditure', cf. *-tumia* 'spend'
mpango — 'plan', cf. *-panga* 'organise'
-tumia — 'spend', cf. *-tuma* 'use, send'
pilkapilka — 'hurry-skurry'

utumishi — 'service', cf. *-tuma*
madaraka — 'position'
mshahara — 'wage, salary'
uangalifu — 'care', cf. *-angalia* 'look out'
-haribia — 'ruin for', cf. *-haribu, -haribika*

-shukuru — 'thank', cf. *shukrani* 'thank you'

tangu . . . mpaka — 'from . . . to'
kadhaa — 'various, a fair number'
urahisi — 'ease', cf. *rahisi*

mara — here 'as soon as'
-letea, cf. *-leta* 'bring'
-tazamia — 'expect', cf. *-tazama* 'look, gaze'

wakwe — 'in-laws' (sing. *mkwe*)
mawazo — 'ideas', cf. *-waza* 'daydream, think'
kaza moyo — 'take courage', *-kaza* causative from *-kaa* 'stay, stop'
-poa — 'get better', cf. *pole*
mwangalifu — 'a cautious, careful person', cf. *-angalia* 'look out'
-acha — 'leave'

II

(i) **Style**. (Popular Journalese) The Swahili of this passage exemplifies
rather simple journalistic style, written for a mass readership, for most of
whom Swahili is the second language. The style is also possibl
influenced by English, and is certainly constrained by the subject-matter

Examples of 'pop' style are:

1 The use of -weza for 'may', e.g.

Aquarius: *waweza kuwa na matata* 'you may have problems'
Leo: *hutaweza kuwa na kutosha* 'you may not have enough'

This is almost certainly the influence of English structure. A more typica
Swahili usage would be to use a conjunction, such as *labda* 'perhaps
pengine 'maybe', e.g.

labda utapata matata
pengine hutakuwa na kutosha.

2 Omission of relatives, e.g.

Pisces: *shida ungekuwa nayo* 'difficulties you might have'
             (for: *shida ambayo ungekuwa nayo*)
             mabadiliko utakuwa nayo 'changes you will experience'
             (for: *mabadiliko utakayokuwa nayo*)
Sagittarius: *mara ufanyapo kazi kwa bidii ndio utazidi . . .*
             'as soon as you start working hard you will get much
             more . . .'
             (for: *mara ufanyapo kazi . . . ndipo utakapozidi . . .*)

3 Excessive use of *kama* and *ikiwa* for 'if', e.g.

Taurus: *kama ukiwa hutaenda* 'if you don't go'
        (for: *usipokwenda*)
Cancer: *kama unataka* 'if you want'
        (for: *ukitaka*)
Leo: *ikiwa unakusudia* 'if you intend'
        (for: *ukikusudia*)

4 Excessive use of *kwa* as a preposition, e.g.

Gemini: *kukusaidia kwa shida zako* 'to help you in your difficulties'
          (omit *kwa*)
Cancer: *kwa jamaa zao* 'by/with respect to their families'
          (for: *kuhusu . . .*)
Capricorn: *kwa mpenzi wako kwa mambo . . .* 'with your loved one
          in what you say'
          (for something like: *angalia unaposema na mpenzi wako*)

This usage is almost certainly the influence of English.

5 Non-locative agreement:

Cancer: *rohoni zao* 'in their minds'
        (for: *rohoni mwao*)

6 Excessive use of *-fanya* for English 'do', e.g.

Cancer: *fanya wakati huu* 'do it now'
        (for: *nenda . . .*)

Leo: *ufanye mpango* 'make a plan'
         (for: *upange mpango*)

These points should not be emulated by the student aiming at the highest style; but they may indicate a popular trend in areas where Swahili is not the first language.

(ii) **Noun classes**. It is possible to ascribe certain general meanings to the noun classes in Swahili, although by no means all nouns in a particular class will be seen to conform. This is partly because Swahili has a very rich vocabulary, with a large number of 'loan' words. (Loans will be dealt with in Unit 35.) We can say that:

Classes 1 and 2 contain most words referring to people, e.g.
   mtoto, mzee, mwanamke;
Classes 3 and 4 contain most names of plants and trees, e.g.
   mti, mkahawa 'coffee plant'; also nouns with a meaning of extension
   or spreading, e.g. *mto, mkono, mguu*;
Classes 5 and 6 contain names of persons with reference to their
   function or relationship, e.g. *fundi* 'specialist', *bibi*; items in pairs, e.g.
   sikio, jicho; parts of trees and plants, e.g. *tawi/matawi* 'branch(es)',
   tunda/matunda, chungwa/machungwa; multiples and collectives, in
   class 6, e.g. *mapesa* 'small change', *marafiki* 'circle of friends',
   manyasi 'grass', *manyoya* 'hair, fur, feathers'; also liquids, e.g. *maji,
   maziwa*. Classes 5 and 6 are also used for 'amplicatives' (see below).
   Many loan words are found in these classes, especially those
   referring to professions, e.g. *daktari*; and large objects, e.g. *gari la
   moshi*;
Classes 7 and 8 contain inanimate objects, e.g. *kiti*; and also diminutives
   (see below);
Classes 9 and 10 contain animals, e.g. *ng'ombe, paka*. Many objects are
   also found in these classes, and most loan words, e.g. *meza*;
Class 11/14 contain abstractions, e.g. *uzuri* 'beauty'; names of
   countries, e.g. *Uganda*; and some mass nouns, e.g. *uji* 'porridge';
Class 15 contains verbal nouns (gerunds) e.g. *kuimba* 'singing';
Classes 16, 17 and 18 have only the one noun *mahali*; but refer to the
   three aspects of place.

(iii) **Derivation of nouns**. A noun — or perhaps we should here speak of a 'nominal stem' — may 'belong' basically to a particular class, and indeed may be found in the dictionary under that form. But the same stem may appear with a different prefix, and have a different, related meaning. We could take *nyumba* 'house' class 9/10. If we put the stem -*umba* with another class prefix, say class 5, we get *jumba*, and this has an 'amplicative' effect. *jumba* means 'palace' (plural *majumba*). On the other hand we could put it in class 7/8 with 'diminutive' effect: *chumba* 'room' (plural *vyumba*). If we use prefixes 7/8 with 5 we get a pejorative effect: *kijijumba* 'wretched hovel' (pl. *vijijumba*). We can also form a class 1 noun from *chumba* and get *mchumba* 'lover'.

As is the case with all living languages, it is not possible always to predict what forms will occur and what their exact meaning will be. A few more examples may be of interest, but the student should use his dictionary to find related words to any new item, and thus enrich his vocabulary.

mtu 'person', *utu* 'humanity', *kitu* 'thing', *jitu* 'giant', *kijitu* 'dwarf' *mwana* 'child', *kijana* 'teenager, hobbledehoy', *ujane* 'batchelorhood' *mji* 'town', *kijiji* 'village' (less desirable), *Ujiji* name of a town.

Nouns may be formed from adjectival stems, mainly by the use of class 1/2 or 11/14 prefixes, e.g. *mrefu* 'a tall person', *urefu* 'length'. In the text we have *urahisi* 'ease' from *rahisi* 'easy, cheap'.

The most fruitful source for the formation of nouns, however, is verbs. The text in section I provides a number of examples:

-*tata* 'tangle' : *matata* 'trouble, confusion' (class 6)
-*penda* 'love' : *mpenzi* 'sweetheart' (class 1)
-*badili* 'change' : *mabadiliko* 'changes' (class 6)
-*amua* 'decide, arbitrate' : *uamuzi* 'decision' (class 11/14)
-*panga* 'arrange' : *mpango* 'plan' (class 3)
-*tuma* 'send' : *utumishi* 'service' (class 11/14)
                     matumizi 'expense' (class 6)
-*angalia* 'watch' : *uangalifu* 'care' (class 11/14)
                     mwangalifu 'cautious, careful person' (class 1)
-*waza* 'dream' : *mawazo* 'ideas' (class 6).

Nouns may be found in all classes 1 to 11/14 derived from verbs. It will be noted that some of the above examples are derived from simple verbs (e.g. -*panga*: *mpango*) and others from extended forms (e.g. -*badili*: -*badilika*: *mabadiliko*). i.e. Nouns may be formed from simple or extended verbs.

Final vowels. It will be noted that a variety of final vowels appears in these nouns formed from verbs (sometimes called 'deverbatives'), e.g.

-a   *matata*
-i   *mpenzi*
-o   *mpango*
-fu   *mwangalifu* (this ending is sometimes -*vu*).

We could also have:

-e   *pete* 'ring' (-*peta* 'bend')
-aji   *msomaji* 'reader'.

These endings may also be said to convey some vague 'meaning', such as:

-i   doer of action, agent
-aji   habitual doer of action
-fu/vu   state
-o   instrument or result of action
-e   passive agent, receptor of action
-a   not clear. Infrequent, normally requires another noun, e.g.
           mchunga mbuzi 'goat-herd'.

Thus the meaning of any one deverbative noun will be a combination of the lexical meaning of the root, plus the meaning of the class prefix and that of the deverbative suffix. So *mpango* has the idea of arranging, plus 'extension', plus the result of the verbal action, i.e. a plan. *mpenzi* has the idea of love, plus causation (-z-) plus person (m-), plus doer of action (-i) i.e. 'a person who causes (someone else) to love'. *mwangalifu* is 'a person who is characteristically careful'. *pete* is 'a thing which has been bent'. *uamuzi* is 'an arbitration in the abstract'.

It follows from this, as a practical point, therefore, that when looking up words of Bantu origin in the dictionary, you may find many nouns under verb stems.

Again, however, a note of caution is needed, as not all possible forms are necessarily realised, nor is the meaning of any one form necessarily predictable. A few examples are given:

-soma 'read, study': *somo/masomo* 'lesson(s)': *msomaji* 'regular reader'
-la 'eat': *mlo* 'food, fodder': *chakula* 'food' (from *kitu cha kula* 'something to eat'): *mla* plus noun 'devourer', e.g. *mla watu* 'cannibal': *simba mla watu* 'man-eating lion'.
Proverb: *mlaji ni mla leo, mla jana kalani?* (*kalani? = amekula nini?*)
'The eater is the one who eats today; he who ate yesterday, what did he eat?' i.e. Never mind about yesterday, it's today that matters, or, You can't have your cake and eat it.

In some cases a large number of derivative nouns may be found from a single verb with its extensions, e.g.

> *-pinda* 'bend'; *-pindua* 'overturn'
> *pindi* 'a bend, twist' (also used for 'when/if')
> *kipindi* 'a space of time'
> *kipindo* 'wrapper, fold of cloth used for a purse'
> *pindo* 'selvedge, hem'
> *pindu* 'somersault'
> *upinde* 'bow' (weapon)
> *mpindani* 'person bent by disease etc.'
> *pinduo* 'change'
> *pindupindu* 'convulsions'
> *mapinduzi* 'revolution'

> *shinda* 'defeat'; *-shindana* 'compete'
> *mshinda, mshindi, mshindaji* 'victor'
> *ushindi* 'victory/point of dispute'
> *ushinde* 'defeat'
> *mshinde* 'loser'
> *shinda* (class 5) 'residue'
> *mshindo* 'shock, din, (orgasm)'
> *mashindano* 'competition'
> *mshindani* 'competitor'
> *ushindani* 'rivalry'.

(iv) **Other derivations**. Verbs are sometimes formed from adjectival stems, e.g.

-refu 'long'   *-refuka* 'be lengthened'
-fupi 'short'   *-fupisha* 'shorten'

rahisi 'easy'   *-rahisisha* 'make easy, cheap'
-nene 'fat'   *-nenepa* 'get fat' (obsolete extension *-p-*, 'inceptive')

Occasional verbs are also formed from nouns, e.g.

shughuli 'business, affairs': *-shughulika* 'be busy'
taifa 'nation': *-taifisha* 'nationalise'

(v) **Arabic derivation**. Words of Arabic origin are sometimes related by vowel changes. This is the influence of Arabic, though the meanings and forms are not always consistent, e.g.

-safiri   'travel'   *safari*   'a journey'
-badili   'change'   *badala (ya)* 'instead (of)'
-shukuru   'thank'   *shukrani*   'thank-you'
-hubiri   'inform'   *habari*   'news'
-saidia   'help'   *msaada*   'assistance'

When looking up an Arabic loan word in the Swahili dictionary, therefore, try switching the vowels if you do not find the word where you think it should be. Arabic words may often be recognised because they

(a) may contain sounds which are not Bantu, e.g. *gh*; (*shughuli*) (Unit 14)
(b) may contain consonant clusters which are not Bantu,
     e.g. *kr* (*shukrani*) (See Unit 35)
(c) normally have three consonants in their stems/roots. (Bantu words normally have two or less, not counting extensions.) e.g. b-d-l (*badala, -badili*), s-f-r (*safari, -safiri*).

See also Unit 34.

III

(b) Make a chart for deverbative Bantu nouns, showing the classes along one axis and the deverbative suffixes along the other, e.g.

	-a	-aji	-e
1 m-	mla	msomaji	mshinde
2 wa-			
3 m-			
4 mi-			

etc.

Try to find words to fill in all the spaces. Some are more frequent than others.

(c) Make amplicative nouns from the following words:

nyoka
mto
moto

mwana
kisu

Suggest meanings for your new forms.

(d) Make diminutives from the following words, and suggest meanings:

mtoto
njia
mlima (mountain)
uvuli (shade) cf. *mwavuli* 'in the shade' i.e. 'sunshade, umbrella'

(e) Make derogatory forms from the following, and suggest meanings:

kitabu   mbuzi
mto   mtoto
duka   mti

(f) Choose your own birth prediction from section I and render it into appropriately journalese English (or your own first language).

(g) Who do you think are the readers at whom the predictions in section I are aimed? How do you know? Are such newspaper predictions aimed at the same audience in your own culture?

Some preoccupations are universal — health, wealth, relationships. What differences (if any) do you observe in the treatment of these subjects from what might be found in your own culture? Can you explain the differences?

Are there any points in the text which might not occur in such texts in your own language? Are there any matters omitted which you might have expected from your own background?

IV

Contemporary preoccupations

Although the form of the predictions here presented (from a popular magazine) is much influenced by English publications, interest in astrology and prediction is not new in Swahili life. Some of the problems here hinted at reflect the society at which they are aimed, however. For example, health is mentioned several times. Everyone worries about their health at some time, but in East Africa medical services are not so freely available as in Europe. Specific problems mentioned are toothache (dentists are even more rare than doctors, and teeth are apt to be neglected), and headache. This latter is most likely to occur, since malaria is endemic.

Finance is another general worry. Notice here that readers are exhorted to be careful with their money, and buy things or expect presents at the end of the month. This reflects the fact that all wages are paid at the end of the month, and most people find it very hard to budget properly. Requests for help from friends and relations are anticipated, reflecting the same inability to budget on their part.

Indeed relatives figure quite largely, reflecting the extended family commitments. Also, those earning enough cash to be able to buy magazines are probably working in towns and are very likely to be applied to for cash help by country cousins. These relatives, however, also help (see e.g. Gemini), as indeed country folk do by providing food at times of difficulty. Quite often the man will work in town and the wife look after the *shamba* in the country.

Travel and visiting are also mentioned. People constantly call on each other and go to visit relatives, often at a considerable distance. These visits seem to be regarded as a good thing. On the other hand, readers are warned against 'parties' and 'bad friends' — in other words the temptations of the big city. Girl friends are not far away, but you have to treat them properly. In fact Swahili women on the whole are strong-minded, and have their own ways of asserting their rights.

The mention of God (though only once) suggests that the readership is not totally secularised.

You will notice that these predictions are aimed at *men*. Not that women are not interested in the future, but on the whole it is men who are sufficiently educated and have the spare cash to buy magazines. Similarly, most of the letters written to Agony Aunties are from men. Perhaps the rapid changes in society causing anxiety affect men first.

Unit 34   Fungu la thelathini na nne
Mwanasesere — The doll

I

(a) **Mwanasesere**

Ninakumbuka siku moja ya Sikukuu, baba yetu alituchukua dukani
kutununulia michezo: Nadya upesi alichagua mtoto wa sanamu mkubwa
na aliye mzuri kuliko wote hapo, na ndiyo baadaye na miye nikaweza
kuchagua katika waliobakia. Tulipofika nyumbani, Nadya alimgonga
mtoto wake, akameguka kidogo sana kidole cha gumba cha mguu. Hapo
Nadya aligaragara chini na vilio visivyokuwa vidogo, akipiga kelele,
'Simtaki, simtaki tena mtoto huyo mbovu'. Baba alimbembeleza, na
kumwambia kwa taratibu, 'Si mbovu, kwani ni kidogo tu amemeguka;
mchezee, na siku za mbele nitakununulia mwengine'. Lakini Nadya
aliendelea kusema, 'Simtaki tena huyu. Ninamtaka huyo mdogo wa
Shadya—ndiye ninayempenda. Mwambie tubadilishane.'
    Hapo baba alistaajabu, na kumuuliza, 'Lakini ilikuwaje Nadya? Huyu
mtoto umemchagua mwenyewe, tena mwanzo kabla ya Shadya
kumchagua wake; na vipi sasa amekuwa si mzuri?' Ghadhabu zilimzidi
Nadya, na alisema kwa kelele, 'Mimi hayo siyajui, ila mwambie Shadya
tubadilishane, au nitalitupa, nilivunjilie mbali toto hili'. Baba alimjibu kwa
taratibu ingawa uso wake ulionesha umewiva kwa hamaki, 'Mvunje;
lakini jua hutompata mtoto wa Shadya wala ye yote mwengine
sitokununulia'. Kwa hivyo, Nadya alizidi kupiga makelele ya vilio, na
kumtupa kwa nguvu mtoto wake juu ya sakafu, akavunjika vipande
vipande. Mama aliyekuwa juu, alishuka kwa haraka, akauliza, 'Kuna nini
tena jamani? Nadya mwanangu, mbona unalia? Njoo mwanangu
nikupakate; njoo mpenzi wangu.' Baba alimweleza mama yote
yalivyokuwa, na akamaliza kwa kumuomba, 'Bibie, mwachie aliye
mwisho atanyamaza'. Lakini mama alinena, 'Eh jamani, na nyinyi
mnapenda makelele—hamumpi huyo mtoto ampendaye?' Na tena
alinigeukia mimi, na kuniambia, 'Shadya mwanangu, hebu mridhi mdogo
wako—umpe huyo mtoto. Wake ndiyo keshamvunja kwa hamaki, na
alivyo mkaidi? Namjua Nadya hanyamazi mpaka apewe anachotaka.'
Hapo baba kwa sauti ya tashtiti aliuliza. 'Alaa? Ndivyo ulivyomzoelesha,
Bibie? Ni uzuri uliyoeleza, nikapata kujua. Lakini bibie kwa leo hii inafaa
ufahamu wewe na yeye Nadya, kwamba kilio chake hakitosaidia kupata
anayoyataka, hata akilia kutwa na kucha. Nadya lazima ajifunze kwamba
si yote ayatakayo duniani lazima ayapate ijapokuwa si kwa njia nzuri
ifaayo. Tena lazima ajifunze kuwafikiria wenzake, siyo nafsi yake tu,
kama mnyama. Na la mwisho, ijapokuwa ni mwanzo, yeye aliposema
kuwa anampenda na anamtaka mtoto wa Shadya, kwa nini hakujua
mbele kama huyo ndiye amtakaye? Mbona hajamchagua tangu
mwanzo? Lakini miye sasa nimekwishajua wapi anapopotelea Nadya, na
kwa hivyo, Bibie, sitokuwachia uzidi kumpoteza.'

'Lakini Bwana, Nadya bado mdogo—atajifunza yote hayo wakati wake ukiwadia,' Mama alijibu. 'Wakati wake ndio huu wa kujifunza; ni wakati udongo uli maji, siyo ukisha kauka.' Baba alisema.

NAILA S. KHARUSI: *Usinisahau, Swahili*, 36/2 Septemba 1966

sesere, mwanasesere — 'doll' (traditionally made of grass)
sanamu — 'image'; *mtoto wa sanamu* — 'doll'
-bakia — 'leave behind', cf. *-baki* — 'be left over'
-meguka — 'be chipped', from *-mega* 'nibble'
kidole cha gumba cha mguu — 'big toe'
-garagara — 'roll about' (sometimes *-gaagaa*)
vilio — 'cries', from *-lia* 'cry'
-bovu — 'rotten' (literally and metaphorically)
taratibu — 'gentleness'
kwani — 'for'
siku za mbele — 'someday' (in the future)
tena — here, 'any more'
-badilishana — 'exchange, swap', from *-badili* 'change'
-staajabu — 'be amazed', cf. *-ajabu* 'something surprising'
-chagua — 'choose'
mwanzo — 'first, at first', from *-anza* 'begin'
ghadhabu — 'rage'
-zidi — 'increase', cf. *zaidi* 'more'. Note structure *ghadhabu zilimzidi*
  Nadya –– 'Nadya's rage increased', 'Nadya was overcome with rage',
  'beside herself with rage'
-vunjilia — 'smash', from *-vunja* 'break'; *-vunjilia mbali* 'smash up'
toto — amplicative from *mtoto* — 'monstrous, ugly doll'
-jibu — 'reply'
ingawa — 'although', 'even though'
-wiva (or *-iva*) — 'get dark'; literally, 'ripen'
hamaki — 'temper, vexation'
hutompata — here and elsewhere in this text, *-to-* is used for standard
  Swahili *-ta-* future tense marker. This is a feature of Zanzibar Swahili.
sakafu — 'hard (concrete) floor'; can also refer to ceiling (floor of upper
  storey)
kipande — 'small piece'; *vipande vipande* 'scattered fragments'
jamani — 'folk', used in address, cf. *jamaa* 'family'
-pakata — 'hold on lap or shoulder' esp. a child; from *-paka* 'apply'
-omba — 'ask a favour, beg'
bibie — *-e* is often added to a term used in address 'O bibi'
-nena — 'declare'; *neno* 'word' is derived from this verb
hamumpi — here and elsewhere *mu-* is used for 1st person subject
  prefix where standard Swahili would write *m-*.
hebu — 'well then', used in expostulation or slight reproof
-ridhi — 'satisfy, please'; note expression *niwie radhi* 'be pleased with
  me', i.e. 'forgive/excuse me'
-kaidi — 'disobedient, obstinate'
sauti — 'voice, sound'
tashiti — 'provocative, sarcastic'
-zoelesha — 'train up', from *-zoea* 'be accustomed'
uzuri — 'well', from *-zuri* 'good'

kutwa na kucha — 'day and night' (lit. to dawn and to set); often found
   as *kutwa kucha* without *na*
-funza — 'teach'; cf. *-fundisha* 'teach', *fundi* 'craftsman', *mwanafunzi*
   'pupil'; *-jifunza* 'learn for oneself'
dunia — 'world'; this world as opposed to the next
nafsi — 'self'
mnyama — 'animal', cf. *nyama* 'meat'
mwisho — 'end', 'finally'; from *-isha* 'come to an end'
ijapokuwa — 'although', 'even if'
miye — *mimi*, dialect form
-potelea — 'go wrong', from *-potea* 'be lost'
-poteza — 'ruin', lit. 'lose', from *-potea* as above
-wadia — 'be fully time'; *wakati wake ukiwadia* 'when her time is ripe'
udongo — 'clay, earth'; *wakati udongo uli maji* 'while the clay is soft',
   siyo ukisha kauka 'not when it's already dried out'

II

(i) Style; Loan words from Arabic

The passage in section I is an example of modern prose style, not too
difficult, since the work it comes from is a piece of fiction, intended to
entertain as well as instruct. The story is set on the coast of East Africa
and the Swahili has some features typical of Zanzibar Swahili. The
vocabulary includes a fair number of recognisably Arabic loan-words,
which is normal in a literary style. Words have been taken from Arabic
into Swahili in the areas of Islam (including Islamic law), and intellectual
and artistic pursuits. They can be recognised by:

(a) containing three consonants in the stem, e.g. *haraka*;
(b) containing consonants or consonant clusters not found in words of
   Bantu origin, e.g. *ghadhabu; tashtiti*;
(c) having two vowels in the stem, without an intervening consonant
   (though this can also occur in Bantu words where an *r* or *l* is lost),
   e.g. *sauti, -kaidi*. (In general in such words, the consonant — a glottal
   stop — has been lost in the shift from Arabic to Roman spelling of
   Swahili. It is sometimes still pronounced, however);
(d) in verbs, having a vowel suffix other than *-a*, e.g. *-fahamu, -zidi*;
(e) initial *ta-*, representing a frequent Arabic prefix, e.g. *taratibu*.

Sometimes, of course, loan words may be completely assimilated into
the language and may not be recognised as such except by scholars.

(ii) Verbs with multiple extensions

We have seen that verbs can be 'extended', and that these 'extensions'
have grammatical meaning. For example, if we take the verb *-funga*
'shut', we can have the following extensions:

Prepositional   *-fungia* 'shut for' (Units 16 and 25)
Reciprocal   *-fungana* 'tie together' (Unit 17)
Passive   *-fungwa* 'be shut (by someone)' (Unit 23)
Reversive   *-fungua* 'open' (Unit 24)

Causative   -fungisha 'cause to shut' (Unit 30)
Stative   -fungika 'be shut' (Unit 31)

(There are in fact a few more extensions, but they are not very produc-
tive: 'Durative' -a-, -tanda 'spread', -tandaa 'spread out wide'
'Static' -m-, -gandama 'coagulate', -ganda 'set';
'Tenacious' -t-, -pakata 'hold child on knee or shoulder', -paka 'apply,
smear';
'Inceptive' -p-, -nenepa 'get fat' -nene 'fat'.)

You may have noticed (e.g. in Unit 17 and elsewhere), however, some
examples of verbs with more than one extension. In the text in Section I,
for example, we have:
-meguka 'be chipped' from -mega 'nibble'. This has Reversive (pejorative) -u-, plus Stative -k- extensions.
-badilishana 'exchange, swap', from -badili 'change (oneself)'. This has
Causative -sh- and Reciprocal -an- extensions.
-vunjilia 'smash', from -vunja 'break'. This form was mentioned in Unit
25; a 'double prepositional' extension, meaning 'completely'
-zoelesha 'train up', from -zoea 'be accustomed'. This has Prepositional
-le- plus Causative -sh- extensions.

It is quite common for a verb to have two extensions, and three or more
is not unknown. One of the most common (and useful) combinations is
of the prepositional plus passive extensions. We have in fact had an
example of this in Unit 24, when Bibi Abdalla said nikaletewa chai baridi
'I was brought some cold tea'. -letewa is a passive form, and is derived
from -letea 'bring to/for', which itself is prepositional and derived from
-leta 'bring'. So we could say:

active	passive
alileta chai	chai ililetwa (naye)
'he brought some tea'	'tea was brought (by him)'
prepositional active	prepositional passive
aliniletea chai	nililetewa chai (naye)
'he brought me some tea'	'I was brought some tea (by him)'

The choice of which form to use depends on the 'topic' of the clause
(sentence), which usually comes first. So:

(a) Bwana Harris alipiga simu 'Mr. Harris made a phone call'
(b) Bwana Harris alimpigia Bibi Maw simu 'Mr. Harris phoned (up) Miss
Maw'
    — in both these utterances, Bwana Harris is the topic. But if Bibi
Maw is to be the topic, we would say:
(c) Bibi Maw alipigiwa simu na Bwana Harris 'Miss Maw was phoned
    (up) by Mr. Harris'.

Notice that although we could say alimpigia simu Bibi Maw (i.e. reverse
the order of objects in (b)) the word order in (c), is fixed.

As with other extensions, the meaning of the prepositional passive is not
always obvious, e.g. kucha 'to dawn'; kuchelewa 'to be late' (lit. to be
dawned on).

(iii) **Reduplication**

We have seen (Unit 13) that repeating a demonstrative has the effect of intensifying its meaning, e.g. *hapa* 'here', *hapa hapa* 'right here'; *pale* 'there', *pale pale* 'right there'; *hapo* 'there we know of', *hapo hapo* 'that very place'. Demonstratives qualifying nouns can also be reduplicated, e.g. *nyumba hii* 'this house', *nyumba hii hii* 'this very house'; *nyumba ile* 'that house', *nyumba ile ile* 'that very house'. It will be recalled that *vile vile* has a special meaning of 'likewise', but could also be used as a qualifier, e.g. *vitabu vile vile* 'those very books'. Context would show which meaning was intended. Variant forms for the near and referential demonstratives of place, time and manner are heard: *papa hapa* 'right here', *papo hapo* 'right there', 'there and then'; *humu humu* 'right in here', *mumo humo* 'right in there'; *vivi hivi* 'just like this', *vivyo hivyo* 'just like that'. Similarly constructed forms for the noun classes could occur, but are very rarely heard.

We have also seen repeated forms used for a 'distributive' meaning, e.g. *shilingi mbili mbili* 'two shillings each' (Unit 14). A somewhat similar meaning is found in the text in section II, where the doll was broken *vipande vipande* 'into scattered pieces' 'shattered'.

Verb stems may be repeated, usually to express a repeated action, as in the text (section I) *Nadya aligaragara chini* 'Nadya rolled about on the floor'. Further examples:

-lia	'cry'	-lialia	'whimper, grizzle'
-tanga	'go to and fro'	-tangatanga	'hang about'
-kanyaga	'tread'	-kanyagakanyaga	'trample'
-piga	'hit'	-pigapiga	'batter'
-omba	'beg'	-ombaomba	'pester'.

Proverb: *kulegalega si kuanguka*, lit. 'tottering is not falling'; used for example in response to an enquiry about how one is getting on — 'I'm not done for yet', 'I'm still struggling on'.

Some verbs have a first syllable repeated, which may be a form of reduplication that has happened earlier in the history of the language, e.g.

-*tetemeka* 'tremble'
-*papasa* 'grope about, pat'.

III

(b) What extensions are present in the following verbs? Give a meaning for each verb, and put it into a sentence.

-onyeshana	-cheleweshwa
-tupiana	-pitishwa
-julishana	-tozwa
-ogofyana	-funganishwa
-funguliana	

(c) Make causative reciprocal forms of the following verbs, and suggest
     meaning for each:

     -ongoa   -kimbia
     -kataa   -sema
     -jaa   -lala

(d) Make sentences using the prepositional and prepositional passive form
     of the verb, on the pattern of 1:
     1 (a) Wazee walinunua shati
        (b) (mtoto) Wazee walimunulia mtoto shati
        (c) Mtoto alinunuliwa shati na wazee.
     2 (a) Bw. Harris alipiga simu jana.
        (b) (Professor Athumani) Bwana Harris _____
        (c) Professor Athumani _____
     3 (a) Professor Athumani alipeleka barua. (mamake)
     4 (a) Bwana Harris alifungua mlango. (Bibi Maw)
     5 (a) Bwana Philip alitanda kitanda. (Bwana Harris) (-tanda kitanda
             'make bed')
     6 (a) Binti Abdalla alitafuta kanga. (Bi. Maw) (kanga — two pieces of
             printed cloth worn by women, one tied round the body under
             the armpits and the other draped over the head.)
     7 (a) Bi. Maw anashona shati. (Bw. Harris)
     8 (a) Wanafunzi wataandika insha. (Sh. Yahya) (insha — 'essay')
     9 (a) Bibi Maw alitia chai? (Sh. Yahya)
     10 (a) Wanafunzi wamekasirika? (mwalimu)
     11 (a) Mtoto analia. (mamake)
     12 (a) Chagua machungwa makubwa. (1st person singular)

(e) Make up sentences using the prepositional passive forms of the follow-
     ing verbs, illustrating their use. Give a gloss for each of your sentences:

     -tengeneza   -pata
     -imba   -soma
     -funga   -toa
     -chukua   -endesha

(f) Make a chart showing all the possible morphemes in the structure of the
     verb. Make a list of restrictions on the co-occurrence of any morpheme
     — e.g. the negative morpheme can occur initially (generally as h- or ha-
     or medially (as -si-). Devise some means of showing when the different
     forms occur, and any other restrictions you can think of.

(g) Make a list of the Arabic words in the text in section I. In each case say
     how you recognise the word as Arabic. (Use the dictionary to help you if
     necessary.)

IV

Swahili literature

The earliest written Swahili literature is poetry. The oldest known manuscript is dated 1728, but the style and language of that poem suggest

that it has behind it a long history of poetry. The earliest poets seem to have lived in the towns on the Northern Coast of Kenya and to have composed in one of the Northern dialects of Swahili. Manuscripts were written in Arabic script. All this early poetry (or all that has survived) was concerned with Islam. It consists mostly of long narrative poems (*tendi/tenzi*, sing. *utendi/utenzi*) concerned with episodes in the life of the Prophet.

The first nationalist poet, Muyaka, lived in Mombasa in the early nineteenth century. He perfected the quatrain (*shairi*, pl. *mashairi*), the other main form of Swahili verse. The subjects of his poems are varied; much of it is love poetry; some of it is political.

From Mombasa the verse tradition spread to Pemba, where it flourished during the late nineteenth century and into this. It also spread to Tanga in the early twentieth century.

In fact the verse/poetic tradition is still very much alive in Swahili. New poets emerge regularly and some have had their works published by the East African Literature Bureau. But perhaps more surprising to the European, many Swahili write verse easily, and most Swahili newspapers have regular pages of contributors' verses, most on contemporary topics. Political comment is not absent, either, sometimes subtly expressed so that the inner meaning is only clear to those with insight.

Swahili prose has a much more recent history, dating back really only to the beginning of this century. The late Shaaban Robert of Tanga is the best-known author, but as more interest develops with the spread of Swahili in schools and in higher education, more books and stories are being written. Short novels are the favourite form, many of them dealing with the problems of a changing society, emancipation of women, and so on, and generally point a moral. A few detective novels are found; and, most recently, a few plays. Swahili prose writing is still in its infancy, but is certainly growing.

LAITI SIWELE NYUNI

Verse (i) Lai*t*i siwele nyuni haruk'a haja uliko[1]
               Tukangia faraghani hapungua siki*t*iko
               Hakupa yangu lisani nawe ukanipa yako[2]
               Na*t*amani kuja kwako lakini sina idhini.

       (ii) *D*alili ya ku*t*amani nawe waifahamia
               Uningizile moyoni siwezi kuvumilia[3]
               Ndipo hafanya huzuni shughuli ikaningia
               Kwako na*t*amani kuya lakini sina idhini[4]

(i) 1 Siwele nyuni = St. ningekuwa ndege.
     2 Lisani = St. maneno.

(ii) 3 Uningizile = St. umeningia.
      4 Kuya = St. kuja.

LONGING TO SEE HIS BELOVED

Verse (i) *I wish I were a little bird who could fly to where you are,*
And we'd be by ourselves so that we could chase away
this sadness,
So that we could communicate our innermost feelings,
I to you;
I long to come to you but approval is not yet given!

(ii) *The signs of longing are very clear to you.*
You occupy my mind so much, I can no longer bear it.
That's why I am so unhappy and disturbed—
I long to come to you but approval is not yet given.

from *Muyaka*, ed. M. H. Abdulaziz, (K.L.B., 1979) pp. 328/9

This poem by Muyaka is not in the standard dialect, and is included here merely as an example of the genre. A few conventions may be noted apart from the assistance given by the editor.

(i) *ha-* before a verb stem, sc. *nika-*, e.g. in l.1 *haruka = nikaruka*. This is a dialectal form.
(ii) vowels may coalesce, e.g. in l.2, *tukangia = tukaingia*; l.7, *ikaningia = ikaniingia*. This device is usually for the sake of scansion.
(iii) Possessives may precede the noun they qualify, e.g. l.3, *yangu lisani = lisani yangu*. This is a poetic convention.
(iv) Italic *t* and *d* represent dental pronunciation in the Mombassa dialect.

With these aids, and the help of a dictionary, the student can no doubt work out a literal meaning. The feeling of the poem, the effect of the choice of words, is something that can only come with a longer acquaintance with the language, which I hope those who have persevered so far through this course will go on to obtain.

Unit 35   Fungu la thelathini na tano
Mpira — Football

I

(a) *N.F.A.: Express yalambwa*

B.A.T. ilibwaga Express kwa mabao 2-1 kwenye pointi za kupambania N.F.A. katika uwanja wa Kadeni juzi.

Timu ya Express ilitangulia kushambulia mlango wa B.A.T. wakati akina Aswani, Mutili na Caleb Okutu walipotawala laini yote ya mbele. Walipata bao la kwanza kutokana na penalti ilipopimwa na Aswani ambaye hakufanya makosa.

Muda si muda, mechi ilichezwa kwa vikali na katika muda wa dakika 28 hivi B.A.T. ikawahi kujibu kwa lile lake ambalo lilibaki la mwisho.

S. Bureka aliyengojea karibu na goli ya Express alipata mpira na kuondoa shuti kali ambayo kipa hakuona mahali alipopitia hadi wavuni.

Kipindi cha kwanza kilimalizika timu zote zikiongozana kwa mabao 1-1. Kipindi cha pili kilipoanza, timu ya B.A.T. ilijaribu iwezavyo kuzuia upande wake ili mabao mengine yasiingizwe na ikatawala upande wa mbele.

Mechi hii iliendelea kwa utaratibu na kila mwanasoka alinuia kupata boli tu bila kushambuliana kwa njia ya rafu. Ikiwa imebakia dakika chache mechi imalizike, Edodio alipata mpira naye bila kupeana pasi akaenda moja kwa moja na kuangusha dhoruba kali kimiani.

Ilifikiriwa kuwa ushindi wa B.A.T. ulitokana na wale mafowadi wake. Kwa maana walikuwa na ule mtindo wao mpya wa kupasiana mpira yaani kupata boli na bila kusinzia unampatia mwenzako — ili kwamba wapinzani waonekane kama wanaotangatanga uwanjani.

Mechi ilipokaribia kumalizika wale madume wa Express walionekana wakitumia staili zao mpya za 4-2-4 lakini muda hakuweza kuwahurumia. Kwa hivyo, filimbi ilipopulizwa wachezaji wake waliondoka uwanjani wakiangalia chini kwa vile walikuwa wamechoka zaidi.

N.F.A. — National Football Association
-lamba — 'lick', 'stick out tongue' (gesture of derision)
-bwaga — 'throw off/down' e.g. a burden
bao — lit. 'board', here = 'goal', presumably from scoreboard.
pointi — 'point(s)'
-pambana — 'jostle, collide'
uwanja — 'open space, clearing', here, 'pitch'
timu — 'team'
-tangulia — 'go first, precede'
mlango — here, 'goal-mouth'
-tawala — 'rule, control'
laini — 'line'

penalti — 'penalty'

-pima — lit. 'measure', here something like 'carefully place'

muda si muda — 'in a short time'

mechi — 'match'

hivi — 'or thereabouts'

goli — 'goal'

mpira — lit. 'rubber'; used here for 'ball', also for 'football (soccer)'

shuti — 'shoot, shot'

kipa — '(goal)keeper'

hadi — 'as far as'

wavu — 'net', originally 'fishing-net'

timu — 'team(s)'

-ongozana — 'leading each other', 'struggling'

iwezavyo — 'every way possible'

-zuia — here 'defend'

mwanasoka — 'soccer-player'

-nuia — 'intend'

boli — 'ball'

rafu — 'rough (play)'

pasi — 'pass'

dhoruba — 'hurricane'

kimia — 'net' (lit. a circular casting-net)

mafowadi — 'forwards'

mtindo — 'style, fashion'

-pasiana — 'pass to one another'

-sinzia — 'doze'

mpinzani — from -pinga 'oppose'

madume — 'big lads', 'hulking brutes'; from -ume 'male', cf. mume,
   kiume etc. dume is used for male animals, e.g. ng'ombe dume 'bull',
   paka dume 'tom-cat'; the prefix ma- is amplicative. A slang
   expression.

staili — 'style'

-hurumia — 'take pity on', from huruma 'pity'

filimbi — 'a whistle, flute'

-puliza — 'blow' (with mouth)

chini — 'down'; chini ya 'below'

(b) Mara Spurs yafundisha Prizon soka

Mbele ya umati mkubwa uliojazana katika uwanja wa Musoma, madume
wa Prizon walitwangwa mabao 3-1 na majogoo wa Mara Spurs hiv
majuzi.

Ilikuwa timu ya Prizon iliyojipatia bao la kwanza. Romard alipopata mpira
na kuona ameachia difensi ya upinzani wake yadi nyingi, alienda moja
kwa moja na kuondoa shuti kali hadi wavuni. Baada ya mpira kuwekwa
katikati ya uwanja na filimbi kupulizwa, Mtaki aliyecheza laini ya mbele ya
Spurs alipata boli naye akapeana pasi kwa Juma ambaye alifanya chenga
nyingi na kuingiza lao la kusawazisha.

Kipindi cha pili kilipoanza, huku Spurs iliongoza kwa mabao 2-1, Prizon
ilionekana imemalizika zaidi. Kwa hivyo wanasoka wa Spurs waliamua
kutoingiza haraka haraka, bali walifanya chenga za kuzidi kiasi za
kuchokesha wapinzani wake.

Walipozidi kutumia mitindo hiyo, Prizon ilipoteza matumaini yake ya kujipatia bao lingine. Na katika muda mfupi hivi, baadhi ya wachezaji wake wakaanza kuponyoka uwanjani wakienda zao kabla mechi kumalizika.

umati — 'crowd'
-twanga — lit. 'pound grain'; 'hammered'?
majogoo — *jogoo* 'cockerel', implications of skill (as well as maleness);
    ma- amplicative prefix; 'clever Dicks'?
hivi majuzi — 'recently'
difensi — 'defence'
yadi — 'yard' (measure)
chenga — 'dribble'
-sawazisha — 'equalise', from *sawa* 'the same, equal, O.K.'
tumaini — 'hope', also verb; cf. *-tumai*.
baadhi — 'some, several'
-ponyoka — 'slip away', from *-poa*

II

(i) **Style**

Association football (soccer) is very popular in East Africa. Being a recent import from Europe it is a fresh subject which requires new language to describe it. In some cases old words are given new meanings, e.g.
    mpira 'rubber', for 'ball; football game'
    wavu, kimia, different kinds of fishing net, for 'football net'.

In other cases words are taken over from English, with certain changes, described in (ii). Many team names are reflections of European names, e.g. Spurs, Express. The language used is also colloquial and racy, with considerable use of metaphor, e.g. *madume, majogoo*, for different types of players; *-twangwa, -lambwa*, for 'defeated'. The game is described in exaggerated and somewhat emotional terms, e.g. *muda hakuweza kuwahurumia* 'time refused to pity them'; *Mara Spurs yafundisha Prizon soka* 'Quick Spurs (Hotspurs?) teach Prison soccer'. This is a kind of teenager, with-it Swahili, subject to rapid fashion changes, amusing, lively, and in details ephemeral. It plays an increasing part in the popular media.

(ii) **Loan words from English**.

Loan words from English into Swahili are found mainly in areas of technology and aspects of life adopted from European models. Such words are adapted, more or less, as they come into Swahili, to fit into the patterns of existing Swahili word-structure, from the point of view of spelling, sound (phonetics), structure, and, sometimes, syntax.

Spelling. On the whole, in Swahili, there is one symbol for one sound. The letter *k* is always pronounced 'hard', as in English 'kick'. Letter *c* in Swahili only occurs with *h* as *ch*. So the *k* spelling in *soka* 'soccer' is an example of Swahili spelling. You will have noticed also *sinema* for English 'cinema'. In *rafu* 'rough' we have *f* because spelling *gh* in

Swahili has a different sound. In *penalti* we have *-i*, because letter *y* Swahili is used for a consonant (as in *haya*), never for a vowel sound.

Vowels. There are a large number (at least 20) of vowel sound (phonemes) in English and only five in Swahili. In some cases, tw English vowel sounds will give one in Swahili, e.g. the *i* in *kipa* 'keepe and in *penalti* in English are two different sounds. Similarly *u* in *shu* 'shoot' and in *futi* 'foot (measure)' reflects two different English vowel *o* in Swahili covers at least three vowel sounds in English, as in *bo* 'ball', *goli* 'goal' and *lori* 'lorry'. The unstressed English vowel as in th first syllable of 'about' or the last syllable of 'soccer', 'forward', is usua represented in Swahili as *a* (*soka, fowadi*), as also are the vowels 'pass', *pasi*, and 'rough', *rafu*. The English vowel in 'match', however, heard more as *e* to a Swahili ear, therefore we get *mechi*.

English diphthongs (vowels whose quality changes; often represente by two vowel letters, as in 'scout', 'coal', 'pear', 'point', or indicated by final *-e*, as in 'bite' cf. 'bit', 'made' cf. 'mad') are sometimes represente by two vowels in Swahili, e.g. *pointi, staili* 'style', and sometimes simpl fied, as in *goli* 'goal', *keki* 'cake'.

A full list of English vowels and their equivalents in loan words int Swahili is found as Chart IV.

Consonants. Double consonants in English are simplified in Swahi e.g. *soka* 'soccer'. Consonant clusters in Swahili roots consist on of *mb, nd, nj, ng*, or a few consonants followed by *w* or *y*. Whe morphemes come together, some further juxtapositions may occu as in *mbwa* 'dog' (*m+bwa*), *mpya* 'new' (*m+pya*), *walimpend* 'they loved him' (*wa+li+m+pend+a*), *alipendwa* 'he was loved (*a+li+pend+w+a*), etc. But in general Swahili word stems have a alternate consonant-vowel structure. Consonant clusters in Englis words which do not fit into Swahili structure are *sometimes* accepted as in *penalti, pointi*, but more often separated by having a vowe inserted, as in *baisikeli* 'bicycle'. Sometimes one consonant is droppe as in *gofu* 'golf'.

Final vowel. All Swahili words end in a vowel; English loans have vowe added, e.g. *goli* 'goal', *timu* 'team'. Generally the vowel added is *-i*, b after a labial consonant (*f, v, p, b, m*) it is usually *-u*.

Class prefixes. Many loans go into class 9/10, but some into class 5/6, which case there will be a plural prefix, e.g. *mafowadi* 'forwards'. some cases a loan word will appear to have a prefix, e.g. *kilabu* 'clu (social)', and then will have an appropriate plural *vilabu* 'clubs'. Some times analogy may go further, and we get *madigadi* 'mudguards singular, *digadi*.

Verbs. Most loan words are nouns, but occasional verb forms are seer as in *kupasiana* 'to pass to one another'. This appears to be treated as verb root *-pas-*, with prepositional and reciprocal extensions.

Other changes may occur, such as only part of a word being taken ove e.g. *refa* 'referee'; or two words being amalgamated, as in *pikap* 'pickup (truck)'.

New formations. You will have noticed the coining *mwanasoka* 'soccer-player', on the analogy of *mwanafunzi, mwanahewa* 'astronaut', *mwanasiasa* 'politician' (*siasa* 'politics'). Combined expressions may also occur, e.g. *mtoto shoo* 'show-girl'.

Word order. Loan words may have to conform to Swahili word order, even when more than one loan word is involved, as in *freni mai* 'my friend', the title of a former popular song.

Meanings. The meanings of loan words may be restricted or may change in the new environment, e.g. *tebo* 'table (mathematical)', *buku*, pl. *mabuku* '(holy) book', *laifu* 'life' in *kupiga laifu* 'to live it up', *stimu* 'electricity' (from 'steam').

When reading newspapers, then, it is as well to bear some of these rules in mind, otherwise much time can be wasted looking for puzzling words in the dictionary. On the whole, such possibly ephemeral vocabulary is not to be found there.

III

(c) Make a list of the loan words from English in texts (a) and (b). Point out the changes that have taken place in each word.

(d) Guess the English from which the following words are derived:

supu	pancha
stempu	lokapu
trekita	leseni
kona	hafubeki
kipilefiti	taipuraita
koleji	waya
ukoloni	tineja
yunifomu	wingi raiti
stoo	ching'oda

(e) Translate passage (a) into idiomatic English.

IV

Gestures

Strong feelings can not always be expressed fully in words, sometimes they overflow into gestures. These gestures may be comprehensible in a situation, but they are culture-specific. A few Swahili gestures are described here.

Annoyance with oneself may be expressed by extending the forefinger of the right hand and biting it from the side, at the same time grimacing with the teeth bared, and making the sound of a glottal stop.

Annoyance with another, especially a child, plus threat, may be shown by extending the left hand, fist downwards, and making a twisting gesture of knife-sharpening, as if the right hand were a knife, on the left forearm.

Dismissal of some annoying idea is expressed by blowing (lips rounded and thrust forward) and simultaneously flapping the right hand (fore finger to the lips) across the mouth, making a fricative 'wh' sound.

Exultation (such as when a favourite player gets a goal) is expressed by clapping the hands above the head, and possibly simultaneously capering.

It may be thought fitting that our language course ends where language ends, or where it began!

P.S. What now?

You are now equipped to read anything in Standard Swahili, with the aid of a dictionary at times, and using some ingenuity to recognise loan-words — especially when reading newspapers. Poetry will require further study. You should also be able to understand an everyday conversation, and hold your own, if haltingly at first. Fluency in speaking always comes last, after recognition, but it will come with practice. And Swahili speakers are always so pleased when foreigners make the effort, and never laugh at us for our mistakes — though if the mistake were truly funny, they would like to share the joke with us!

In this course I have avoided the use of translation, and especially from English into Swahili. Translation is a special skill, and to my mind the effort to translate hinders learning at the early stages, not least because it inevitably produces mistakes, which is disheartening, or clumsy expressions which, while not ungrammatical, are not Swahili. However, for those who feel the need, I append a few conversations which may be *rendered* into Swahili, i.e. not *translated*. The student should try to comprehend the situation, and put Swahili equivalents, which have been encountered in the course, in place of the English expressions. I also append a few extra selected passages for reading in Swahili. But the student should proceed to full texts as soon as possible.

For the rest, I envy you who are about to go from these humble beginnings and meet a whole new world of thought. *Mwende salama!*

Appendix. Passages for Reading and 'Translation'

The following texts should not be *translated* but *rendered* into colloquial Swahili. Use expressions you know from the course.

1

Ms.F.: Hello Mr. Peake!
Mr.P.: Hello Ms. Ferreira! How are you this morning?
Ms.F.: Fine. How about you?
Mr.P.: I'm alright. Have you seen Ms. Woodhall today?
Ms.F.: No, I haven't seen her for several days. I don't think she's very well.
Mr.P.: I'm sorry to hear it. Are *you* well, however?
Ms.F.: Oh yes, I'm very well health-wise, but I'm in a bad temper.
Mr.P.: Why's that?
Ms.F.: Well I wanted to go to Mombasa by train, but I couldn't get a ticket because the train was full. It costs too much by air. Dr. Maw said she'd take me by car, but then she and Mr Harris had an accident. They crashed into a tree and the car is a write-off.
Mr.P.: Goodness! Were they hurt?
Ms.F.: Oh no, they're alright apart from a few aches and pains. But it means I'm stuck here in Nairobi.
Mr.P.: I was thinking of going to Mombasa myself by bus, tomorrow. Would you like to come with me? You'd have to get up early, though.
Ms.F.: Oh, yes, I'd love to. I wouldn't like to go by bus on my own. You never know who's going to sit next to you, and if you don't like them, you can't get away from them as you can on a train. What time must we leave?
Mr.P.: We'll have to be at the bus station by seven-thirty. I'll call for you at quarter to six. O.K.?
Ms.F.: Alright, I'll be ready, and thanks a lot.
Mr.P.: Don't mention it; it's a pleasure.

2

Mother: Hurry up, hurry up. Do you know what time it is?
Child: No, I don't. What time is it, then?
M: Half past seven. You should be at school at eight. Get dressed, I'll pour you some tea.
C: Where are my socks? I can't find them.
M: Where did you leave them last night? That's where they'll be now.
C: I don't know where I left them. Help me to look for them. I'll be late.

M: Here they are. Get them on and drink your tea.
C: I can't, it's too hot. Is there any bread?
M: Take this. Don't eat so fast, you'll be sick.
C: Where's my school bag? I can't find my Swahili books. Where
        have you put them?
M: I haven't touched them. They're probably still in your bag. I don't
        think you did any Swahili revision last night, did you? Look in
        your bag.
C: Oh no, I didn't. They're in there.
M: Get off then, don't hang about.
C: Right. Goodbye mother.
M: Goodbye love. Take care on the road!

3

Y.:   Hello Tim. How are you?
T.:   I'm fine. What about you, Yewa?
Y.:   Oh, I'm alright. How's things at home?
T.:   Fine. Are your folks alright? Haven't seen you for ages.
Y.:   Yes, they're all flourishing. But you look fed up. What's the matter?
T.:   Well, yes, I've got this awful cold, my head aches something chronic,
        and I can't sleep at night for coughing. Then I'm too tired next day
        to work at Swahili, and once or twice I've even missed a class.
Y.:   I'm very sorry to hear it. You seem to need some help. Have you
        been to a doctor?
T.:   Oh I don't believe in doctors. They just give you some useless
        medicine and tell you to pull yourself together. I would pull myself
        together if I could.
Y.:   Perhaps you ought to stay in bed for a few days. That's really the
        best way to get rid of a cold.
T.:   I suppose you're right, but it's very boring. I like to go out and enjoy
        myself at night. Life's too short for staying in bed.
Y.:   It'll be shorter still if you get pneumonia and die! Still, it's up to you.
        Anyhow, let me buy you a cup of tea in that caff over there. That'll
        warm you up.
T.:   Thanks very much. But I'd rather have a beer.
Y.:   Just like a man! Come on then.
T.:   O.K.

4

Policeman: Stop, you, stop!
Thief: Who, me?
P: Yes, you. What's your name?
T: My name? Why?
P: Never mind why. What is it?
T: David Hassan.
P: Right, David Hassan, what are you doing here?
T: Just passing.
P: Passing, eh? Where have you come from?

T: From home, in Eastleigh.
P: And where do you think you're going?
T: Well, I was going to the pictures.
P: Which cinema?
T: The Odeon, in Kijabe Street.
P: This isn't on the way to Kijabe Street.
T: No, well, I was going to call for a friend on the way, he
              works at a big house near here, but he wasn't in, so I . .
Householder: Officer, stop that man, I think he's the one who just broke
              into my house!*
P: What!
H: Yes, I was sitting having supper and I heard a noise in the
              bedroom. I went in and someone was just climbing out of
              the window. It looks like him.
P: Had he taken anything?
H: I didn't have time to look properly, but the clock was missing
              from my bedside table.
P: Here, you, what's in the bag?
T: Just a few things of mine.
P: You'd better come along to the police station and we'll see.
              You come too sir.
H: Thank you, officer.
T: You're making a mistake.
P: We'll see. Let's go.

*to break into a house — *kuvunja nyumba*.

5

Ms.K.: Hullo Mr Huggins!
Mr.H.: Hullo Ms Kamara. How are you?
Ms.K.: I'm fine, what about you?
Mr.H.: Great! How are the kids?
Ms.K.: All well, thank goodness. What about your folks?
Mr.H.: Oh they're all O.K. What's new?
Ms.K.: Nothing much. I hear you've had some trouble with the police.
Mr.H.: Not trouble exactly, just I got stopped the other day for speeding.
Ms.K.: Bad luck. Are they going to prosecute you?
Mr.H.: No. Luckily I had Dr Maw with me and she persuaded them
        that I was just a poor foreigner, so they let me off with a
        caution.
Ms.K.: You were lucky. Last year I was stopped and I was fined two
        thousand shillings.
Mr.H.: Good God, I couldn't pay that sort of money! You must be very
        rich!
Ms.K.: What do you mean rich, I'm broke!
Mr.H.: Well, come and have a beer with me. I'll pay, to celebrate my
        good luck.
Ms.K.: Thanks, I'd like to.
Mr.H.: Let's go, then.
Ms.K.: Right.

6

Mwanafunzi:	Good morning, Sh. Yahya.
Sh.Y.:	Good morning to you.
Mw.:	How have you been this long time?
Sh.Y.:	Very well, thank you. How about you?
Mw.:	Well enough, but I've got too much work.
Sh.Y.:	What a pity! Have you heard from your friend Justin?
Mw.:	No, I haven't heard a word since the end of term. He was to get a job for a while and then go to Kenya in September. Lucky thing!
Sh.Y.:	Do you think he's gone, then?
Mw.:	I don't know. I hear there was some trouble in Kenya last month so perhaps his father would try to stop him going. Parents are always nervous about their children's safety!
Sh.Y.:	It's understandable, though. Wouldn't *you* be anxious about *yours*?
Mw.:	How should I know? I haven't got any yet. Perhaps I'd be glad to get rid of them, nasty little brats!
Sh.Y.:	You might think that now, but I can tell you that when the time comes you'll be even more anxious than most. You're that sort of person.
Mw.:	Maybe. I'm certainly anxious about my exams next week.
Sh.Y.:	Don't worry, God's in His Heaven.
Mw.:	I hope so.
Sh.Y.:	Definitely!

To be nervous, anxious — *kuona wasiwasi*.

The following texts are for reading. If you wish to translate them, aim for a suitable style in your own language.

1

Maoni ya kitoto

Siku moja baba alikuwa hana kazi yoyote akasema twende huko ambako alizaliwa, mji wa Kaloleni, Giryama, maili ishirini na sita kaskazini ya Mombasa. Basi mimi nilikuwa sijui kama baba ni kabila ya Mgiryama kabisa. Basi tulipofika huko mimi niliona ajabu sana kuona watu wa kike huko kwao wavaa mahando ya chawa na waume wavaa shuka chafu sana. Niliona ajabu sana kwa vile yeye huvalia suti nzuri nzuri, kumbe kwao namna hii. Basi baba akaongea nao hao Wagiryama wenziwe huku kwachinjwa mbuzi wa karamu yetu. Basi mimi nilikuwa sitaki wanisogelee karibu yangu kabisa. Walipokuwa hao kina baba wanaongea, pakaja jamaa mmoja. We! Niliogopa kwa kuwa alikuwa na mdomo mrefu sana, kumbe hivyo ni kaka yake baba. Nilizidi kustaajabu sana.

'Karibu kila mtu hupendelea kutumia lugha yake ya kimama saa fulani ya kila siku.' Mimi ndivyo nipendavyo, kwani siku hiyo nilikuwa sisemi na

mtu yeyote, ila mama tu. Kwani nilikuwa kama nikisikiliza Kigiryama
chasemwa na sielewi wasemayo. Mimi na mama tukawa twaongea
Kiswahili tu. Muda si muda tu, pakaletwa chakula juu ya meza. Hapa basi
nilijua hawa ni Wagiryama kweli, kwani nilizidi kustaajabu sana nilipoona
hicho chakula kimeletwa katika mvure. Basi mimi nilikuwa sikuzoea hivi
hata sikula hicho chakula kabisa, nilikunywa chai ya ndugu yangu mdogo

JAMES KATANA RODGERS

2

Uchunguzi

Uangalifu mwingi hufanywa kumfunza mtoto kuwa mchunguzi hodari wa
kuweza kuhesabu vitu kwa kuangalia tu bila kuhesabu kimoja kimoja
hasa kondoo, mbuzi, ng'ombe au watu, kwani inafikiriwa mwiko, *mugiro*
kwa Gikuyu, kuhesabu kitu kimoja kimoja, na ni jambo ambalo laweza
kuleta mabaya kwa watu au wanyama. Kwa mfano, mtu mwenye
ng'ombe mia moja, kondoo na mbuzi, humfunza mtoto wake kuwajua
kwa rangi zao tu au ukubwa na aina ya pembe, hali kila mmoja ana jina
lake.

Ili kujaribu uwezo wa mtoto huyo wa kukumbuka au kuangalia
makundi mawili au matatu ya wanyama kutoka makao mbali mba
huchanganywa, na mtoto akaulizwa kutenga wao akimchagua kila
mmoja. Wakati mwingine baadhi ya kondoo au mbuzi wao huwe
wamefichwa, na mbuzi au kondoo wanapopumzika mchana, mtoto
huulizwa kuangalia, *guthurima*, kama wote wako, atoe ripoti yake. Ripoti
yake huangaliwa sana na wale wanaomfunza. Akikosa, hawezi
kulaumiwa kwa njia kali, lakini huulizwa kwa upole kukagua tena taratibu
aonyeshe kondoo au mbuzi fulani aliyekuwa amefichwa makusudi. Kwa
kurudia ukaguzi wake mara ya pili hugundua makosa yake mara moja
Yule mwalimu wake humwuliza ajaribu kukumbuka ni mahali gani na
wakati gani tangu alipomwona mara ya mwisho mnyama
anayekosekana. Kwa njia hii pale anapoonekana dhaifu katika fikira zake
husahihishwa. Kwa mwindaji, mazoezi haya ni mengi mno, kwa ajili ya
vijia vingi vya msitu na shida ya kufuata nyayo za wanyama, inahita
kutumia akili nyingi kabisa. Wakati wa utoto wangu, kazi yangu katika
jamaa ilikuwa kuwachunga kondoo, mbuzi na ng'ombe. Kwa hivyo
nilijifunza mambo haya na baadaye nikawafunza ndugu zangu.

JOMO KENYATTA: *NAUSHANGILIA MLIMA WA KENYA*

3

Unadhifu

Nywele hukamilisha uzuri wa mwanamke. Bibi wa kisasa anapenda
kuonekana nadhifu na wa kuvutia kila anapokuwa katika kundi la watu
ofisini, karamuni, sokoni, nyumbani kwake na mahali pengine po pote.
    Mavazi mazuri na ukwatuaji wa nyuso kwa njia ya kufaa humfanya
mwana mama apendeze lakini kama akizisahau nywele zake, yote hayo

ni bure. Nywele zikiwa matimu timu zinaondoa urembo na umaridadi wote.

Mabibi wa Kiafrika wamepewa nywele nzuri ambazo wanaweza kuzichana au kuzisuka. Wengine wanalalamika kwamba nywele zao ni za aina ya 'kipilipili'. Hakuna haja ya kulalamika maana zikitunzwa vizuri matokeo yake yatakuwa mema.

Usukaji wa nywele kwa mabibi wa Kiafrika si jambo geni. Mtindo huu umekuwapo tangu zamani. Mabibi wa Kiafrika wanayo mitindo mingi ya kuzisokota nywele zao. Wengine hutumia kamba nyeusi na wengine hutumia tu ufundi wa kuzisuka. Nywele zinazosukwa, kupakwa mafuta ya kufaa, na kusafishwa kwa uangalifu huwa ndefu na laini kwa kuchana. Hata zile za kipilipili zinazowaudhi wengi huweza kuwa za kuvutia sana.

Nywele za kipilipili haziwatishi walio nazo katika ulimwengu wa siku hizi. Akina mama wamerahisishiwa kazi hiyo. Wengi sasa wanatumia vitana vidogo badala ya machanuo ya miti.

Zimeingia dawa za kunyoshea nywele, na pia wengine hutumia vitana vya moto ambavyo hunyosha nywele na kuwapa akina mama nywele nzuri ambazo mara nyingi akina baba wameziita 'Singa za Bandia'. Matokeo yake kwa wale walio waangalifu daima yamekuwa ni mazuri. Kwa wale wasiofuata masharti matokeo yake yamekuwa mabaya sana.

Akina mama si wageni wa mambo haya.

HILDA KUNDYA: *Nchi Yetu*, Septemba 1966

4

Simba Mla Watu Stesheni Kima

Historia ya ujenzi wa njia ya reli toka Mombasa hadi Uganda, haitokamilika bila kutajwa kwa simba mla watu katika stesheni ya Kima iliyoko maili 260 kutoka Mombasa na maili 69 kutoka Nairobi.

Kifo cha Bw. C. H. Ryall, aliyekuwa mkuu wa Uganda Railway Police kilichotokea 1900 alipouawa na simba mla watu hapo stesheni ya Kima pia kinatajwa kwenye vitabu vya historia ya relwe. . . .

Wakati mmoja mkuu wa usafirishaji wa Idara ya Relwe wakati huo alipigiwa simu kueleza kifo cha Mwafrika mmoja wa kundi la kutengeneza reli, na kabla ya hatua kuchukuliwa akapatwa na nyingine kumweleza kifo cha wafanyi kazi wengine kwenye stesheni hii. Ukatili wa wanyama hawa ulizidi kuongezeka muda baada ya mwengine.

Makundi ya Idara ya Relwe yalisafiri hadi Kima ili kumuwinda mnyama huyu, lakini hawakufaulu. Ryall siku moja alilazimika kwenda Nairobi kutoka Mombasa kwa kazi fulani. Yeye ni muwindaji hodari. Alipofika Kima aliamua kubaki humo usiku huo ili aweze kupambana na simba wala watu.

Kwenye stesheni hii, Ryall alitaka behewa lake liwekwe kando kwenye reli nyingine. Wote watatu, Ryall, Parenti na Hueber walisafiri katika behewa moja, likiwa na mlango kila upande. Pia alikuwako Mhindi aliyekuwa akibeba mizigo ya Ryall.

Ryall alifanya mpango kwamba usiku huo kila mmoja ashike zamu kungojea simba afike. Wenzake walikubali kufanya hivyo. Wa kwanza kushika zamu alikuwa Parenti, Balozi wa Italia naye Ryall angeshika zamu kuanzia usiku wa manane na baadaye ashike zamu Hueber mpaka chee, kuanzia saa tisa za usiku.

Kabla ya Ryall kushika zamu, alimwambia Parenti kuwa aliona mng'a wa macho ya wanyama kwa mbali ambayo yalionekana kama macho ya panya waliokuwa wakicheza kwenye giza.

Kutokana na nyayo zilizoonekana baada ya kifo cha Ryall ilikuwa dhahiri mnyama huyo alikuwa karibu sana na behewa kabla ya Ryall kushika zamu.

Hapana budi, simba alinyemelea wakati alipoona ukimya na taa zimezimwa kwenye behewa; akapanda kingazi kilichokuwa kwenye mlango wa nyuma ya behewa hadi ndani.

Parenti na Hueber wakati huo walikuwa wamelala; pengine Ryall naye alikuwa amechukuliwa na usingizi kidogo na kwa hivyo hakumsikia simba akipanda ngazi za behewa hilo.

Simba alipoingia tu kwenye behewa hakusita bali alimrukia Ryall kwa miguu yake ya nyuma ikiwa imemkanyaga Parenti. Kukanyagwa huku kulimfanya Parenti kuamka, kwani aliwahi kuhadithia kishindo kilichokuwamo wakati simba alipomkamata Ryall, lakini hapakuwa na sauti yo yote iliyotoka kwa Ryall kupiga makelele.

Parenti alijaribu kujikokota kwa kifudifudi lakini kwa kuwa alijawa na hofu kubwa na harufu ya kuchefuka kwa mnyama huyo hakuweza kufanya lo lote.

Parenti alisema baada ya mnyama akiwa amembeba kupata fahamu kwamba aliona Ryall katika kichwa chake huku akijishindilia kwenye dirisha lililokuwa karibu na mlango.

Parenti alipoona simba ameondoka na maiti ya Ryall, alipitia dirisha akikimbilia chumba cha stesheni. Hueber aliyekuwa amejificha kwenye behewa alishinda humo ndani pamoja na watumishi Wahindi wa Ryall waliokuwa humo ndani kabla ya maafa hayo ya Ryall.

KWOME KHASITO: *Nyota*, Machi 196

5

Freyyoh

Huyo kijana mgeni aliyesemwa, alikuwa kijana wa Kiarabu mweupe wa rangi na mzuri wa sura. Nyusi zake zilikaa kwa namna ya kupendeza juu ya macho yake manene, na chini ya pua yake palikuwa na msta mwembamba mweusi ulioonyesha kimaji maji alama ya masharubu madogo. Alipokuwa akicheka, Bwana Msa aliona meno yake meupe yamepangana sawasawa; na nywele zake za singa zilikuwa zimelala kichwani kwa mafuta ya nywele na zinang'ara katika jua.

'Basi yule ndiye Freyyoh, mgeni kutoka Kongo', aliwaza Najum, 'Kafika hapa inapata mwezi unusu sasa, kafikia hapo Vuga, nyumba ya Bwana Rashid, ile iliyo jirani na Ahmed, rafiki yetu. Mwenyewe Bwan-Rashid hayupo kasafiri kenda bara na kampa funguo na ruhusa yule kijana kutumia nyumba yake marefu kwa mapana kwa muda atakokuwapo hapa.'

'Bwana-Rashid kafanya vizuri', alitia lake Bwana Msa, 'hii ndiyo sifa ya watu wa Unguja—wao na nchi yao—hodari kwa kupokea wageni.'

'Basi ndio hivyo,' aliwaza tena Najum, 'na inasemekana kuwa yeye tajiri sana huko kwao. Nasikia karithi zaidi ya laki sita—na inaonesha! Haiwi hiyo gari yake tu aliyokuja nayo kutoka kwao Kongo makusudi ya kutembelea kwa siku hizo atakazokuwapo—hapana mfano wake hapa kwetu! Haiwi hizo nguo alizonazo, zote za thamani kubwa kubwa, anabadilisha kutwa—sijui mara ngapi!'

'Pahala pake,' Bwana Msa alisema, 'hata mimi, kama ningalirithi kama yeye, ningefanya hivyo hivyo.'

Najum alikohoa kidogo halafu akaendelea kusema, 'Lakini ninaloona ajabu mimi, ni kuwa, ingawa kafikia katika nyumba jirani na Ahmed, kama unavyojua—nyumba hii kwa hii—lakini hawakuunga urafiki ila siku hizi za mwisho tu—kama nilivyokwambia, kiasi labda mwezi mmoja tu sasa, na urafiki wao ukastawi kwa ghafla namna hii. Imekuwa wanakwenda sinema pamoja, na pengine pamoja na mkewe Ahmed, watatu wao tu. Vile vile, nastaajabu namna Ahmed alivyosabilia urafiki huu—yeye mwenyewe na kilicho chake, hata mkewe!'

'Hata mkewe?' Bwana Msa aliuliza.

MUHAMMED SAID ABDULLA: Uchafu Wenye Jina

6

Ujamaa si Ubaguzi

Msingi wa Ujamaa ni kuamini umoja wa binadamu, na kwamba katika historia ya binadamu watu huinuka pamoja na huanguka pamoja. Ndiyo kusema kwamba msingi wa Ujamaa ni usawa wa binadamu.

Kukubaliwa kwa msingi huu ni jambo la maana kabisa kwa Ujamaa. Haja ya kuwa na Ujamaa inakuwako kwa sababu ya Binadamu; si kwa sababu ya nchi, wala bendera. Ujamaa haujengwi kwa faida ya watu weusi, au watu weupe, rangi ya kahawia, au manjano. Shabaha ya kujenga Ujamaa ni kuwafaidia Binadamu bila ya kujali rangi yao, kimo chao, umbo lao, ufundi wao, uwezo wao, ama kitu kingine cho chote. Na vyombo vya uchumi vya Ujamaa, kama vile tunavyoviunda sasa kutokana na Azimio la Arusha, shabaha yake ni kumsaidia binadamu aliyeko miongoni mwetu. Mahali ambapo watu walio wengi ni weusi, basi wengi watakaofaidika kutokana na Ujamaa watakuwa weusi. Lakini kufaidika huko hakutokani na weusi wao; kunatokana tu na ubinadamu wao.

Miaka michache iliyopita nilisema kuwa utawala wa nguvu na ubaguzi vinaweza kuendeshwa pamoja, lakini ubaguzi na Ujamaa havipatani hata kidogo. Sababu yake ni rahisi kuelewa. Utawala wa nguvu ndiyo ukatili wa mwisho wa mtu kumnyonya mtu mwingine: unaendeshwa kwa kuwagawa binadamu makusudi, ili kundi moja la watu ligombane na kundi jingine. . . .

Lakini mtu anayewachukia 'Wayahudi', au 'Wahindi', au 'Wazungu', au hata 'Wazungu wa Magharibi na Marekani', si mtu wa Ujamaa. Anajaribu kuwagawa binadamu katika vikundi, na anawalinganisha watu kufuatana na rangi ya ngozi yao au umbo walilopewa na Mwenyezi Mungu. Au anawagawa watu kwa kufuata mipaka ya mataifa yao. Kwa vyo vyote vile, anauharibu udugu na usawa wa binadamu.

Bila ya kukubali usawa wa binadamu hakuwezi kuwako Ujamaa.

J. K. NYERERE: Ujamaa

Chart I Noun class agreements.

noun[2]		possessive	epithet[2]	demonstrative			numeral[2]	copula (place)		
				-le	h-	h -o		-ko	-po	-mo
1. m mzee mw mwana mwingereza mu Muumba		wangu wako wake wetu wenu wao	mzuri mwekundu	yule	huyu	huyo	mmoja	niko uko yuko	nipo upo yupo	nimo umo yumo
2. wa wazee w wana waingereza		wangu etc	wazuri wekundu	wale	hawa	hao	wawili watatu wanne watano wanane	tuko mko wako	tupo mpo wapo	tumo mmo wam
3. m mfuko mw mwavuli		wangu etc	mzuri mwekundu	ule	huu	huo	mmoja	uko	upo	umo
4. mi mifuko (my) myavuli miavuli		yangu etc	mizuri myekundu	ile	hii	hiyo	miwili mitatu etc	iko	ipo	imo
5. ji jicho j jino ø ua		langu etc	zuri jekundu	lile	hili	hilo	moja	liko	lipo	limo
6. ma macho m meno maua		yangu etc	mazuri mekundu	yale	haya	hayo	mawili matatu etc	yako	yapo	yamo
7. ki kitabu ch choo		changu etc	kizuri chekundu	kile	hiki	hicho	kimoja	kiko	kipo	kimo
8. vi vitabu vy vyoo		vyangu etc	vizuri vyekundu	vile	hivi	hivyo	viwili vitatu etc	viko	vipo	vimo
9. N¹. nyumba ø kalamu		yangu etc	nzuri nyekundu	ile	hii	hiyo	moja	iko	ipo	imo
10. N¹. nyumba ø kalamu		zangu etc	nzuri nyekundu	zile	hizi	hizo	mbili tatu nne tano nane	ziko	zipo	zimo
11/ u ufunguo 14. uzuri w wembe		wangu etc	mzuri³ mwekundu³	ule	huu	huo	mmoja	uko	upo	umo
15. ku kuimba kufika		kwangu etc	kuzuri	kule	huku	huko	kumoja⁴			
16. pa mahali		pangu etc	pazuri	pale	hapa	hapo	pamoja etc			
17. ku nyumbani		kwangu etc	kuzuri	kule	huku	huko	kumoja⁴ etc			
18. mu etc.		mwangu etc	mzuri	mle	humu	humo	mmoja⁴			

¹ N stands for a nasal prefix
² take 'adjectival' prefix
³ If noun is abstract, may take u-/w- prefix
⁴ very rare occurrence
⁵ items in brackets only before -a tense

copula	verb		prefix	relative	whole/all	any	'many'[2]	'other'[2]			
ndi-	s		o		-ote	-o -ote	-ingi	-ingine	-a	-enye	na-
ndimi ndiwe ndiye	1 ni(n) 2 u(w) 3 a	ni ku m/mw		ye		ye yote		mwingine	wa	mwenye	nami nawe naye
ndisi ndinyi ndio	1 tu(tw) 2 m(mw) 3 wa(w)	tu wa(+-ni) wa		o	sote nyote wote	wo wote	wengi	wengine	wa	wenye	nasi nanyi nao
ndio	u(w)		o		wote	wo wote		mwingine	wa	wenye	nao
ndiyo	i(y)		yo		yote	yo yote	mingi	mingine	ya	yenye	nayo
ndilo	li(l)		lo		lote	lo lote		jingine	la	lenye	nalo
ndiyo	ya(y)		yo		yote	yo yote	mengi	mengine	ya	yenye	nayo
ndicho	ki(ch)		cho		chote	cho chote		kingine	cha	chenye	nacho
ndivyo	vi(vy)		vyo		vyote	vyo vyote	vingi	vingine	vya	vyenye	navyo
ndiyo	i(y)		yo		yote	yo yote		nyingine	ya	yenye	nayo
ndizo	zi(z)		zo		zote	zo zote	nyingi	nyingine (zingine)	za	zenye	nazo
ndio	u(w)		o		wote	wo wote		mwingine	wa	wenye	nao
ndiko	ku(kw)		ko		kote	ko kote		kwingine	kwa	kwenye	nako
ndipo	pa(p)		po		pote	po pote	pengi	pengine	pa	penye	napo
ndiko	ku(kw)		ko		kote	ko kote		kwingine	kwa	kwenye	nako
ndimo	m(mu)		mo		mwote				mwa	mwenye	namo

Chart II Verbs.

Class	Negative Subject	Subject	Neg./tense	Relative	Object prefix	Root	Extensions[6]	Suffix	Relative[9]
1st pers. sing.	si	/ ni	si[3]	ye	ni	-pend-	passive (w)	a	ye
2nd pers. sing.	h[1]	u	na	ye	ku	-som-	causative (sh/z)	i[7]	etc
3rd pers. sing.	ha[2]	a	a	ye	m	etc.	stative (k)	e[8]	
1st pers. pl.		tu	me	o	tu		prepositional (i/e)		
2nd pers. pl.		m	*ki	o	wa		reciprocal (n)		
3rd pers. pl.		wa	nge	o	wa		reversive (u)		
3		u	ngali	o	u				
4		i	*ka	yo	i				
5		li	*ja[4]	lo	li				
6		ya	(sipo)	yo	ya				
7		ki	*hu[5]	cho	ki				
8		vi		vyo	vi				
9		i		yo	i				
10		zi		zo	zi				
11/14		u		o	u				
15	kuto	/ ku		ko	ku				
16		pa		po	pa				
17		ku		ko	ku				
18		mu		mo	mu				

[1] Before vowel
[2] Before consonant
[3] With subjunctive, or relative & no tense, or nge, ngali
[4] Only with negative
[5] Without subject or negative
[6] Any number combined
[7] Only with 'general' negative
[8] Subjunctive
[9] When no tense present, in positive.

Chart III Nouns derived from verbs

	-i	-e	-a	-o	-fu/vu/u	-aji
Class 1/2	mwokozi	mshinde	mwoga	mrembo	mtakatifu	msomaji
3/4	mtoki	mkate	mmea	msemo	mnyevu	mtambaaji
5/6	vazi	kombe	kosa	neno	pumu	paji
7/8	kizazi	kiumbe	kinywa	kielezo	kikaufu	kinywaji
9/10	mboni	pete	ndoa	ndoto	mbinu	
11	ugomvi	ushinde	ushinda	wimbo	wokovu	ujengaji

Chart IV English vowels in loan-words into Swahili.

English example	English vowel symbol	Swahili vowel	Loan-word example
bead	iː	i	timu (team)
bid	i	i	picha (picture)
bed	e	e	difensi (defence)
bad	a	e	mechi (match)
		a	bangili (bangle)
bard	aː	a	pasi (pass)
bod	o	a	daktari (doctor)
		o	lori (lorry)
board*	oː	o	boli (ball)
good	u	u	futi (foot)
booed	uː	u	shuti (shoot)
bud	ʌ	a	basi (bus)
bird	əː	a	shati (shirt)
about	ə	a	fowadi (forward)
bidder			kipa (keeper)
bide	ai	ai	laini (line)
bayed	ei	e	keki (cake)
bough	au	au	skauti (scout)
bode	ou	o	goli (goal)
boy	oi	oi	pointi (point)
beard	iə	ia	bia (beer)
bared	eə	ea	ripea (repair)
		eya	skweya (square)
bored*	oə	oo	droo (drawer)
boor	uə	uwa	pyuwa (pure)

* For some English speakers, these two vowels are the same.

Key to Exercises

Unit 1, section III

(k) Hujambo, mzee.
Hamjambo, wanafunzi.
Hujambo, bwana.
Hujambo, mama.
Hamjambo, watoto.

Sijambo, bibi.
Sijambo, baba.
Sijambo, mwalimu.
Sijambo, Bibi Maw.

Baba hajambo?
Mama hajambo?
Bwana hajambo?
Watoto hawajambo?
Mzee hajambo?
Wanafunzi hawajambo?

(m) sijambo, hajambo?, hatujambo, hawajambo, hamjambo?, hujambo?

(n) Mimi sijambo, sijui wewe. (or, *wewe, je?*)
Yeye hajambo, sijui wao. (or, *wao, je?*)
Sisi hatujambo, nyinyi, je? (or, *sijui nyinyi*.)

(o) before; last, or may come first; the same as statements, or *je?* may be used.

Unit 2 section III

(i) Habari za mchana?
Habari za siku nyingi?
Habari za asubuhi?
Habari za leo?
Habari za usiku?
Habari za tangu juzi?

Habari za safari?
Habari za nyumbani?
Habari za kazi?
Habari za baba? or, Baba hajambo?

Nzuri (tu).
Salama (tu).

(j)   After.

(k)   Habari za mzee?
Habari za watoto?
Habari za mama?
Habari za baba?
Habari za wanafunzi?
Habari za mwalimu?
Habari za bibi?
Habari za bwana?

Unit 3 section III

(k)   Kwa herini, wanafunzi.
Kwa heri, mwalimu.
Kwa heri, Bwana Harris.
Kwa heri, Bwana Philip.

Kwa heri ya kuonana!
Pole (sana), bwana!
Ndiyo maisha!
Haya!
Kazi nyingi sana! or, Kazi kubwa sana!
Mvua kubwa sana!
Habari nzuri sana!
Kweli!
Habari zako wewe?
Baba hajambo sana!
Safari nzuri sana!
Nimeshapoa!
Kusoma Kiswahili (kweli) (ndiyo) kazi kubwa sana.
Mwalimu ndiyo mkali sana!

(n)   *kazi nyingi* — 'a lot of work', 'a number of jobs'; *kazi kubwa* — 'a huge task'.
mvua nyingi — 'a lot of rain'; *mvua kubwa* — 'heavy rain'.

(o)   *ee; ndiyo; kweli*.

(p)   *ku-*.

Revision exercises, Units 1, 2, 3

(a)   6, 1, 3; 2, 5, 4.

(b)   4, 9, 1; 6, 2, 3; 5, 8, 7.

Unit 5, III

(e) bwana   ndio   gani   hujambo etc.
     bibi   je?
     baba   sijui
     habari   juzi
     asubuhi
     nyumbani
     kubwa

Unit 6, III

(g) bar, station, cinema, post-office, police station, bank, jail.

(h) Maskini yuko wapi? Yuko _____
     Mwizi yuko wapi? Yuko _____
     Mlevi yuko wapi? Yuko _____
     Askari yuko wapi? Yuko _____

(i) Baba yuko kazini.
     Mama hayuko nyumbani, yuko safarini.

Unit 7, III

(e) Nani yuko hospitalini?
     Bwana na bibi wako wapi hasa? *or*, Wako wapi hasa bwana na bibi?
     Sijui mwizi yuko wapi.
     Mwizi yuko jela na askari vilevile yuko.
     Labda mwalimu yuko kazini leo.

(g) nipo   sipo   nimo   simo
     upo   hupo   umo   humo
     yupo   hayupo   yumo   hayumo
     tupo   hatupo   tumo   hatumo
     mpo   hampo   mmo   hammo
     wapo   hawapo   wamo   hawamo

Revision exercises, Units 6 and 7

(a) Baba yuko wapi? Yuko kanisani.
     Mzee yuko wapi? Yuko sokoni.
     Bwana yuko wapi? Yuko hotelini.
     Mama yuko wapi? Yuko mezani.
     Mwalimu yuko wapi? Yuko hospitalini.
     Bibi yuko wapi? Yuko dukani.

(c)   Watoto wako wapi? Wako kitandani, Alhamdulillahi!
      Twende Afrika ya Mashariki.
      Mama, bado niko taabani.
      Baba, mimi na bwana/bibi bado tuko hapa Uingereza.

Unit 10, section III

(f)   ishirini na moja, thelathini na mbili, arobaini na tatu, hamsini na nne,
      sitini na tano, sabini na sita, themanini na saba, tisini na nane, mia
      moja na tisa, elfu moja mia mbili.

(g)   Mwezi wa Disemba
      Mwezi wa Machi au Aprili
      Mwezi wa Januari
      Mwezi wa Februari
      Mwezi wa Mei

(h)   Mwaka wa elfu moja sitini na sita.
      Mwaka wa elfu moja mia tisa kumi na nane
      Mwaka wa elfu moja mia tisa thelathini na tisa
      Mwaka wa elfu moja mia saba themanini na tisa
      Mwaka wa elfu moja mia tisa themanini na tano

(j)   mtu   watu
      mgonjwa   wagonjwa
      mvuvi   wavuvi
      mkulima   wakulima
      mzungu   wazungu
      mwarabu   wa(a)rabu

(k)   Sina pesa.
      Sijui, sina saa.
      Siyo, hatuna watoto (bado).
      Siyo, watoto hawana pesa.
      Siyo, hatuna wanafunzi sasa.
      Siyo, wanafunzi hawana kazi nyingi.
      Mwalimu hana watoto (bado).

Unit 12, section III

(i)   Ndiyo, pika tu.
      Ndiyo, chemsha tu.
      Ndiyo, ondoa tu.
      Ndiyo, tia tu.
      Ndiyo, kunywa tu. (or, unywe tu)
      Ndiyo, koroga tu.
      Ndiyo, kula tu. (or, ule tu)

(j)   A'a, usitie chai, tia maziwa tu.
      A'a, usile mahindi, kula (or, ule) keki tu.

A'a, usipike kahawa, pika chai tu.
A'a, usiondoe maziwa, ondoa maji tu.
A'a, kupika chai usitie maji baridi, tia maji ya moto tu.
A'a, mwalimu asisomeshe Kiswahili, asomeshe Kiingereza tu.
A'a, tusile mchele, tule mahindi tu.
A'a, wanafunzi wasinywe bia, wanywe _____ tu.
A'a, watoto wasile sukari, wale _____ tu.
A'a, Bi. Maw asitie sukari, atie _____ tu.
A'a, Bw. Philip asitie maziwa ya moto, atie _____ tu.
A'a, Bw. Harris asiende Lamu, aende _____ tu.

(k)
nichemshe	nile
uchemshe	ule
achemshe	ale
tuchemshe	tule
mchemshe	mle
wachemshe	wale

nisikoroge	nisinywe
usikoroge	usinywe
asikoroge	asinywe
tusikoroge	tusinywe
msikoroge	msinywe
wasikoroge	wasinywe

(l)
-chemsh-	kuchemsha	chemsha	chemsheni	nichemshe	nisichemshe
-end-	kwenda*	nenda*	nendeni*	niende	nisiende
-fik-	kufika	fika	fikeni	nifike	nisifike
-ka-	kukaa	kaa	kaeni	nikae	nisikae
-kat-	kukata	kata	kateni	nikate	nisikate
-korog-	kukoroga	koroga	korogeni	nikoroge	nisikoroge
-l-	kula	kula/ule	kuleni	nile	nisile
-let-	kuleta	lete*	leteni	nilete	nisilete
-maliz-	kumaliza	maliza	malizeni	nimalize	nisimalize
-nyw-	kunywa/	kunywa/	kunyweni	ninywe	nisinywe
		unywe			
-ondo-	kuondoa	ondoa	ondoeni	niondoe	nisiondoe
-ongez-	kuongeza	ongeza	ongezeni	niongeze	nisiongeze
-pik-	kupika	pika	pikeni	nipike	nisipike
-shib-	kushiba	shiba	shibeni	nishibe	nisishibe
-ti-	kutia	tia	tieni	nitie	nisitie
-tumi-	kutumia	tumia	tumieni	nitumie	nisitumie

* irregular forms

Unit 13, section III

(b)   1 Bibi Maw asimame sokoni.
      2 Bwana Philip anataka kununua mahindi.
      3 Bwana Harris anakwenda na Philip.

4 Wanakwenda kununua mahindi. (kujaribu kununua mahindi)
5 Kuna mahindi, lakini hakuna (mahindi) ya kufaa.
6 Pili wanakwenda soko la wananchi.
7 Bibi Maw anataka kurudi nyumbani kwa sababu amechoka, tena
  jua kali sana.
8 Philip anataka kununua nazi tena.
9 Kuna nazi, lakini hakuna (nazi) za kufaa.
10 Mahindi tele yako kikapuni (karibu nao).
11 Ndiyo, mwishoni Bwana Philip ananunua mahindi.

(c) Kumbe hakuna tena? ('You mean to say there still aren't any?')
     Twende zetu. ('Let's be off')
     Kwa nini sasa? ('What for now?')
     Kumbe tunataka nazi? ('What do we want with coconuts?')
     Basi, na mwende tu. ('Well get on then')
     Si mahindi tele hapa? ('What's this but a huge heap of maize?!')
     Hapa hapa ('Right here, under your nose')
     Alhamdulillahi! (God be praised!)

(d) 1 Watu wanasimama dukani.
     2 Mtoto anakunywa maziwa.
     3 Mama ananunua mahindi.
     4 Ninakwenda sokoni.
     5 Bibi Maw anakula keki.
     6 Ninatia sukari.
     7 Wanafunzi wanataka chai.
     8 Mwalimu anasomesha Kiswahili.
     9 Tunatazama msikiti.
     10 Ninakwenda Nairobi na mama.

(g) -choka
     -endesha
     -faa
     -fanya
     -fika
     -jaribu
     -ngoja
     -nunua
     -ondoka
     -rudi
     -simama
     -taka
     -tazama

ninarudi nyumbani	'I am going back home'
unarudi nyumbani	'you are going back home'
anarudi nyumbani	'he/she is going back home'
tunarudi nyumbani	'we are going back home'
mnarudi nyumbani	'you (pl) are going back home'
wanarudi nyumbani	'they are going back home'

Unit 14, section III

(e) sichukui   sinywi
     huchukui   hunywi
     hachukui   hanywi
     hatuchukui   hatunywi
     hamchukui   hamnywi
     hawachukui   hawanywi

(f) Siyo, siuzi machungwa leo.
     Siyo, mama hanunui ndizi.
     Siyo, watoto hawataki kufanya kazi.
     Siyo, wanafunzi hawasomi Kiingereza.
     Siyo, hatupiki keki.
     Siyo, siwezi kuvunja noti ya shilingi kumi.

(g) Siyo, hatuuzi nazi, bali tunauza _____.
     Siyo, siendi dukani, bali ninakwenda sokoni.
     Siyo, Bibi Maw hapiki chai, bali anapika kahawa.
     Siyo, wanafunzi hawanywi maziwa, bali wanakunywa bia.
     Siyo, watoto hawali keki, bali wanakula mkate.
     Siyo, sitaki kwenda sinema, bali ninataka kwenda nyumbani.

Revision exercises, Unit 14

(a) _____ apike chai.
     Wanafunzi wale _____.
     Twende _____ sasa. (or, *Mwende* _____)
     Nunua (or, *ununue*) _____ leo.
     Watoto waende _____.
     Ndiyo, soma (or, *usome*) Kiswahili leo.
     _____ sasa.

(b) Nani anapika chai?
     Wanafunzi wanakula nini?
     Tunakwenda wapi sasa?
     (Ninanunua nini leo?)
     Watoto wanakwenda wapi?
     (Ninasoma Kiswahili leo?)
     (Tunafanya nini sasa?)

(c) _____ anapika chai.
     Wanafunzi wanakula _____.
     Tunakwenda _____ sasa. (or, *Mnakwenda* _____)
     (Unanunua _____ leo.)
     Watoto wanakwenda _____.
     (Ndiyo, unasoma Kiswahili leo.)

(d) Siyo, wanafunzi wasisome Kiswahili kwa sababu _____.
     Siyo, tusinunue viazi kwa sababu _____.
     Siyo, tusiende nyumbani kwa sababu _____.

Siyo, mwalimu asisomeshe Kiswahili kwa sababu _____.
Siyo, wazee wasiende kanisani kwa sababu _____.
Siyo, usipike kahawa sasa kwa sababu _____.
Siyo, usinunue sukari nyingi kwa sababu _____.
Siyo, mama asikate keki kwa sababu _____.
Siyo, tusinywe chai sasa kwa sababu _____.

Unit 15, section III

(b) Bwana Harris aende Mombasa kuchukua gari (yake).
Aende Mombasa kwa reli.
Bibi Maw aende stesheni kununua tikiti (ya kwenda Mombasa).
Bibi Maw anunue tikiti ya kilasi ya kwanza.
Nauli ya kwenda Mombasa (ni) shilingi elfu mbili mia saba na hamsini.
Nauli ya kwenda Mombasa na kurudi Nairobi (ni) shilingi elfu tano mia
tano.
Siyo, Bwana Harris na Bibi Maw wasirudi Nairobi kwa reli, warudi kwa
gari ya Bwana Harris.
Wapate godoro na mablanketi katika behewa.
Treni inachukua saa kumi na tatu na nusu kufika Mombasa.

(c) Kwenda Nairobi kutoka London uende kwa ndege.
Kwenda Mombasa kutoka Lamu wananchi waende kwa boti.
Kufika stesheni polisi kutoka British Council Bwana Harris aende kwa
miguu.
Kufika Hurlingham kutoka posta watu waende kwa basi.
Polisi waende njiani kwa gari.
Bwana Philip afike kazini kwa baisikeli.
Watu waende Kisumu kutoka Nairobi kwa gari la moshi/treni/reli.
Wananchi maskini waende kazini kwa lori.

(d) Bwana Philip anataka kununua mahindi.
Bwana Harris anataka Bibi Maw apike/anywe/atie chai.
Tunataka kwenda hospitalini.
Tunataka mwende msikitini.
Ninategemea kufika usiku.
Ninategemea uje saa kumi na moja na nusu.
Mwalimu anataka kusoma Kiswahili.
Mwalimu anataka wanafunzi wasome Kiingereza.

(e) Nini nauli ya kwenda Kisumu?
     Nauli ya kwenda Kisumu ni shilingi elfu mbili mia sita.
Treni ya kwenda Kisumu inaondoka saa ngapi?
     Inaondoka saa tatu ya asubuhi.
Nipate wapi godoro?
     Upate godoro katika behewa.
Nini bei ya tikiti mbili ya kwenda Kisumu na kurudi?
     Shilingi elfu tano mia mbili.
Nini bei ya godoro na mablanketi pamoja?
     Shilingi tisini.

(f) Ninataka tikiti tatu.
Siyo, sitaki kwenda leo, ninataka kwenda kesho.
Siyo, hakuna nafasi leo, lakini kuna nafasi kesho.
Gari la moshi linafika Mombasa saa mbili ya asubuhi kila siku.
Jina langu _____

(g) boti, reli, tikiti, stesheni, ofisi, kilasi, nambari, mablanketi, steward, treni, basi, baisikeli, lori.

Unit 16, section III

(b) 1 Katika behewa la Bi. Maw yuko mtu mmoja kwanza: Bi. Maw.
  2 Bw. Harris hataki kukaa katika behewa lake la kwanza kwa sababu wako watu wengi huko.
  3 Wanavuta sigara na kunywa bia.
  4 Kandakta anaingia kwanza kutazama tikiti za Bw. Harris na Bi. Maw.
  5 Halafu kandakta anakwenda kumpatia Bw. Harris nafasi penginepo
  6 Ndiyo, behewa la C 20 liko mbali sana, kupita behewa la kulia, halafu behewa la tatu.
  7 Bw. Harris hataki kandakta achukulie mizigo kwa sababu anataka kukaa katika behewa la Bi. Maw.
  8 Bw. Harris anaacha kitabu chake katika behewa lake la kwanza.
  9 Anaacha kitabu chake huko kwa sababu ndiyo kiti chake.
  10 Bw. Harris anapenda behewa la Bi. Maw kwa sababu pana starehe huko. (kwa sababu yuko Bi. Maw?)
  11 Kandakta hataki Bw. Harris akae katika behewa la Bi. Maw kwa sababu anashikilia desturi za zamani.

(c) 1 Ninaingia behewa langu
Unaingia behewa lako
Anaingia behewa lake
Tunaingia behewa letu
Mnaingia behewa lenu
Wanaingia behewa lao.

  2 Ninanunua kitabu changu
Unanunua kitabu chako
Ananunua kitabu chake
Tunanunua kitabu chetu/vitabu vyetu
Mnanunua kitabu chenu/vitabu vyenu
Wananunua kitabu chao/vitabu vyao.

  3 Nina bahati yangu
Una bahati yako
Ana bahati yake
Tuna bahati yetu
Mna bahati yenu
Wana bahati yao.

  4 Ninataka kwenda zangu
Unataka kwenda zako

Anataka kwenda zake
Tunataka kwenda zetu
Mnataka kwenda zenu
Wanataka kwenda zao.

5 Ninamkaribisha mama kwangu
Unamkaribisha mama kwako
Anamkaribisha mama kwake
Tunamkaribisha mama kwetu
Mnamkaribisha mama kwenu
Wanamkaribisha mama kwao.

(d) Lete blanketi langu.
Ondoa vitu vyake.
Tazama vitabu vyako.
Pika chai yetu.
Ule biskuti zetu.
Tengeneza kitanda chako.
Lete mablanketi yao.

(e) magodoro yenu
vitu vyao
kitabu chake
kahawa yako
majina yangu
behewa letu
keki zako.

(f)

kuandika	kuandikia
kufanya	kufanyia
kufika	kufikia
kugonga	kugongea
kuja	kujia
kujaribu	kujaribia
kukaa	kukalia
kuleta	kuletea
kulipa	kulipia
kungoja	kungojea
kununua	kununulia
kunywa	kunywea
kuongeza	kuongezea
kupika	kupikia
kupita	kupitia
kupunguza	kupunguzia
kusema	kusemea
kusimama	kusimamia
kutaka	kutakia
kutengeneza	kutengenezea
kutia	kutilia
kutoa	kutolea
kuuza	kuuzia.

Unit 17, section III

(c)   Wazee wako bado wako nyumbani?
      Mtoto wako bado yuko hospitalini?
      Mwalimu wako bado yuko safarini?
      Ng'ombe zako bado wako shambani?

(d)   Nani ana nazi ya mzee?
      Nani ana viazi vya maskini?
      Nani ana nyanya za bibi?
      Nani ana chungwa la mtoto?
      Nani ana mahindi ya baba?
      Nani ana kitabu cha mwalimu?

(e)   Watoto wako wako wapi? Wako nyumbani kwa mama.
      Bwana Harris yuko wapi? Yumo garini mwake.
      Mwanafunzi wetu yuko wapi hasa? Yupo shambani pa askari.
      Wazee wangu wanakwenda dukani kwa Mhindi.
      Ng'ombe zenu wanakaa wapi? Wanakaa shambani kwetu.

(f)   -pendana   -patana
      -juana   -pitana
      -someshana   -gongana

(g)   -nunuliana
      -tiliana
      -leteana
      -patiana
      -ngojeana
      -uziana
      -pikiana

(i)   Bwana Yahya ana watoto wanne.
      Bw. Hamadi ana watoto sita.
      Bi. Aisha ana watoto watatu.
      Bi. Salma ana watoto watatu.
      Bw. Hamisi ana watoto wawili.
      Bi. Hawaa ana watoto watano.
      Bi. Esta ana watoto watatu.
      Bi. Hadija ana wajukuu saba.
      Bw. Hamadi ana wajukuu wanane.
      Bi. Salma ana wajukuu watatu.
      Bw. Hamisi ana ndugu watatu, wawili wa kiume na mmoja wa kike.
      Bi. Hawaa ana binti wawili na watoto wa kiume watatu.
      Hasani ana dada wawili.
      Naila ana kaka wawili.

      Bw. Yahya ni mume wa Bi. Hadija.
      Bi. Hadija ni mama wa Bi. Mariamu.
      Bi. Hafida ni mke wa Bw. Hamisi.
      Bw. Hamisi ni baba mdogo wa Omari.
      Bi. Mariamu ni shangazi ya (la) Ali. (or, *wa*)

Bw. Juma ni mjomba wa Hasani.
Bahati ni binamu wa Hasani.
Bi. Salma ni mama wa kambo wa Bi. Tatu.
Bw. Hamadi ni babu ya Naila. (or, *wa*)
Bi. Salma ni nyanya/bibi ya Sulemani. (or, *wa*)
Bi. Tatu ni mama mdogo wa Kibibi.

1 Mimi ni Tatu.
2 Mimi ni Kibibi.
3 Mimi ni Mariamu.

Unit 18, section III

(b)   Siyo, Bwana Philip hamwogopi nguruwe, Bwana Hasani anamwogopa.

Bwana Philip anaendesha baisikeli.
Bwana Hasani anakaa nyuma.
Bwana Hasani anatazama nyuma/msituni.
Siyo, nguruwe hatafuni mtu.
Bwana Philip na Bwana Hasani hawaanguki, lakini karibu wanaanguka.
Bwana Hasani anatetemeka kwa sababu anamwogopa nguruwe.
Inaonekana Bwana Hasani ni mwoga, pengine.
Bwana Philip anamtania Bwana Hasani.
Bwana Philip anaeleza habari ya nguruwe.
Ndiyo, pengine nguruwe ni mkali.

(c)   Bwana Harris anamsaidia Bi. Maw.
Bw. Philip anamwona Daudi.
Tunakuona.
Bw. Harris na Bi. Maw wanampenda Bw. Philip.
Ninamtazama mpwa wangu.
Unawapa Bi. Maw na Bw. Harris chai.
Bw. Harris anamchukulia mzee mizigo.
Sheikh Yahya anawasaidia/anawasaidieni.
Mnatupa chakula.
Daudi ananipa pesa.

Bw. Harris hamsaidii Bi. Maw.
Bw. Philip hamwoni Daudi.
Hatukuoni.
Bw. Harris ni Bi. Maw hawampendi Bw. Philip.
Simtazami mpwa wangu.
Huwapi Bi. Maw na Bw. Harris chai.
Bw. Harris hamchukulii mzee mizigo.
Sheikh Yahya hawasaidii.
Hamtupi chakula.
Daudi hanipi pesa.

Bw. Harris amsaidie Bi. Maw.
Bw. Philip amwone Daudi.
Tukuone.

Bw. Harris na Bi. Maw wampende Bw. Philip.
Nimtazame mpwa wangu.
Uwape Bi. Maw na Bw. Harris chai.
Bw. Harris amchukulie mzee mizigo.
Sh. Yahya awasaidie.
Mtupe chakula.
Daudi anipe pesa.

Bw. Harris asimsaidie Bi. Maw.
Bw. Philip asimwone Daudi.
Tusikuone.
Bw. Harris na Bi. Maw wasimpende Bw. Philip.
Nisimtazame mpwa wangu.
Usiwape Bi. Maw na Bw. Harris chai.
Bw. Harris asimchukulie mzee mizigo.
Sh. Yahya asiwasaidie.
Msitupe chakula.
Daudi asinipe pesa.

(d) Ndiyo, ninawaona, bali hawanioni mimi.
Ndiyo, mwalimu anampenda mtoto, bali mtoto hampendi mwalimu.
Ndiyo, mwizi anatutazama, bali hatumtazami yeye.
Ndiyo, mwizi anawaona askari, bali hawamwoni yeye.
Ndiyo, askari wanamtazama mlevi, bali mlevi hawatazami wao.
Ndiyo, tunawapenda, bali hamtupendi sisi.
Ndiyo, mvua samaki anatufundisha kuvua samaki, bali hatumfundishi
     yeye.
Ndiyo, mwuzaji anakudanganya, bali humdanganyi yeye.
Ndiyo, tunamjua Bwana Harris, bali hatujui sisi.

(e) Vitabu vyangu vimepotea. Umeviona? Siyo, bado sijaviona.
Mtoto wangu amepotea. Umemwona? Siyo, bado sijamwona.
Nguruwe zangu wamepotea. Umewaona? Siyo, bado sijawaona.
Bibi yangu amepotea. Umemwona? Siyo, bado sijamwona.
Gari yangu imepotea. Umeiona? Siyo, bado sijaiona.

(f) Viti vya wanafunzi viko wapi?/Viko wapi viti vya wanafunzi?
Machungwa ya wanafunzi yako wapi?
Wazee wa wanafunzi wako wapi?
Nyumba za wanafunzi ziko wapi?
Chai ya wanafunzi iko wapi?
Mabasi ya wanafunzi yako wapi?

(g) Nguruwe wa mlevi yuko wapi?/Yuko wapi nguruwe wa mlevi?
Bia ya mlevi iko wapi?
Chupa ya mlevi iko wapi? (chupa is class 9/10.)
Gari ya mlevi iko wapi?
Mtoto wa mlevi yuko wapi?

(h) Siyo, babake bado hajafika nyumbani.
Siyo, dada yangu bado hajakwenda sokoni.
Siyo, mjomba wangu bado hajaingia hospitalini.

Siyo, bado sijamwona ng'ombe wako.
Siyo, mtoto bado hajalala./hajalala bado.
Siyo, wanafunzi bado hawajamaliza kazi.
Siyo, bado hatujakwenda Dar es Salaam.

(i) Ndiyo, nimekiona.
Ndiyo, ninataka kuvinunua.
Ndiyo, ninapenda kuzila. (*or* kuila)
Ndiyo, nimeliandika.
Ndiyo, nimezila (zote).
Ndiyo, nimeipika.
Ndiyo, nimevitengeneza.
Ndiyo, nimeyauza (yote).

Siyo, bado sijakiona.
Siyo, sitaki kuvinunua bado.
Siyo, sipendi kuzila bado. (*or* kuila)
Siyo, bado sijaliandika.
Siyo, bado sijazila zote.
Siyo, bado sijaipika.
Siyo, bado sijavitengeneza.
Siyo, bado sijayauza yote.

(k) Sijavinunua kwa sababu _____.
Baba mdogo hajazileta kwa sababu _____.
Bibi Maw hajaipika kwa sababu _____.
Hatujakijua kwa sababu _____.
Wagonjwa hawajainywa kwa sababu _____.

Unit 19, section III

(b) Bi. Maw na Bw. Harris waende nyumbani kula lanchi.
Waende nyumbani kwa Bw. Harris.
Waende kwanza sokoni kununua vyakula.
Bw. Harris anataka kununua mikate, jibini, nyanya na matunda.
Soko lenyewe liko karibu na nyumba ya Bw. Harris.
Bw. Harris ananunua mikate miwili.
Mwuzaji amekata chungwa moja tu.
Bw. Harris ananunua matunda kwa shilingi thelathini na tano.
Bw. Harris ananunua mfuko mmoja wa matunda.
Siyo, Bw. Harris hanunui machungwa matamu.
Siyo, hamna machungwa mfukoni, mna madanzi tu.
Mwuzaji ni 'mwizi'.
Bw. Harris anafikiri amenunua machungwa kwa sababu ameona
chungwa moja zuri, na anafikiri yote ni sawa.

(c)

mchana	'daytime'	(plural not used)
mchele	'rice'	(plural not often used)
mfuko	'bag'	mifuko
mguu	'leg'	miguu
mkate	'loaf'	mikate

mkono   'arm'   mikono
mlango 'door'   milango
moto   'fire'   mioto
msikiti 'mosque'   misikiti
msitu   'forest'   misitu
mtego   'trap'   mitego
mwaka   'year'   miaka
mwezi   'month'   miezi

(d) nyuso nzuri
     nyuso mbaya
     nyuso kali
     nyuso nyingi
     nyuso nyekundu
     nyuso ndefu

(e) shauri   mashauri
     tunda   matunda
     mkono   mikono
     mguu   miguu
     danzi   madanzi
     mwavuli   miavuli
     upepo   pepo
     ushanga   shanga

(f) Ninataka kununua kitabu _____
     etc.

(g) e.g. 1 Mzee mrefu tena mkali.
          2 Wazee warefu tena wakali.
             etc.

(h) Mkebe wangu uko wapi?
     Shanga zangu ziko wapi?
     Uma wangu uko wapi?
     Mifuko yangu iko wapi?
     Mwavuli wangu uko wapi?
     Funguo zangu ziko wapi?

(i) Usinunue machungwa madogo, nunua makubwa.
     Usinipe chai baridi, nipe ya moto.
     Usilete keki chache, lete zote.
     Usiuze viazi vizuri, uza vibaya.
     Usiibe mfuko mmoja, iba mingi.
     Usinywe bia kidogo, kunywa (or, *unywe*) nyingi (or, *tele*).

(j) Mfuko wake mzuri sana. Unaupenda? Siyo, siupendi, ninapenda
        zaidi mfuko wa _____
     Kuimba kwake kuzuri sana. Unakupenda? Siyo, sikupendi, ninapenda
        zaidi kuimba kwa _____
     Malimau yake mazuri sana. Unayapenda? Siyo, siyapendi, ninapenda
        zaidi malimau ya _____

Ng'ombe zake wazuri sana. Unawapenda? Siyo, siwapendi, ninapenda
  zaidi ng'ombe za _____
Kitanda chake kizuri sana. Unakipenda? Siyo, sikipendi, ninapenda
  zaidi kitanda cha _____
Nyumba yake nzuri sana. Unaipenda? Siyo, siipendi, ninapenda zaidi
  nyumba ya _____
Jina lake zuri sana. Unalipenda? Siyo, silipendi, ninapenda zaidi jina
  la _____
Viti vyake vizuri sana. Unavipenda? Siyo, sivipendi, ninapenda zaidi
  viti vya _____
Dada yake mzuri sana. Unampenda? Siyo, simpendi, ninampenda zaidi
  dada wa _____

(k)   Siyo, hakuna nazi sokoni, kuna _____
      Siyo, hamna waizi katika jela, mna _____
      Siyo, hakuna watu wengi nyumbani, kuna _____
      Siyo, hapana hapa wanafunzi wa Bi. Maw, pana _____
      Siyo, hamna nyanya nzuri kikapuni, mna _____

Unit 20, section III

(b)   Philip anataka kununua nazi kwa wingi pwani kwa sababu hakuna nazi
        Nairobi.
      Ninafikiri anataka kuziuza Nairobi kwa bei kubwa.
      Philip hataki kuzinunua zile za kwanza kwa sababu anaona ni ghali
        sana.
      _____
      Bwana Harris na Bibi Maw wanakwenda gereji kununua petroli na
        vilevile kumpa Philip nafasi ya kununua nazi kwa urahisi.
      Bwana Harris amekasirika kwa sababu Philip amechelewa/amechoka
        kumngojea Philip/amepata joto.
      Bwana Philip hasemi sana kwa sababu anajua amekosa/hataki Bw.
        Harris akasirike.

(d)   Mwalimu yupi?
      Wanafunzi wepi?
      Nyanya zipi?
      Shamba lipi?
      Viazi vipi?
      Kitanda kipi?
      Nazi ipi?
      Msikiti upi?
      Mahindi yapi?

(e)   Vitabu vile ni vyako? Ndiyo, ni vyangu.
      Unasoma kitabu cha mwalimu? Ndiyo ninakisoma, ni kizuri sana.
      Kiti hiki kinafaa? Siyo, hakifai, ni cha zamani sana.
      Ninunue nazi hii? A'a, usiinunue, haifai.
      Unapenda kula keki zile? A'a, sizipendi zile, zina sukari mno; ninapenda
        zaidi hizo, zina matunda kidogo.
      Ufunguo wako uko wapi? Umo mfukoni mwangu.

Ushanga wangu wa dhahabu uko wapi? Sijui, sijauona.
Wako watu wengi katika darasa lako? Siyo, hawako wengi, wako
     _____ tu.
Koti langu zuri liko wapi? Limo kabatini mle.
Kwa nini unanunua kalamu ile ghali? Kwa sababu ninaipenda, tena
    siku yangu ya kuzaliwa.
Mnakula chakula cha usiku saa ngapi? Tunakila saa _____
Mti huu una matunda mengi? Siyo, hayana (or, *hauna*) mengi lakini
    mazuri.
Yako maji ya moto katika birika? Ndiyo, yako mengi.

(f)   Siyo, lile ni l-_____.
       Siyo, kile ni ch-_____.
       Siyo, ile ni y-_____.
       Siyo, ile ni y-_____.
       Siyo, zile ni z-_____.
       Siyo, ile ni y-_____.
       Siyo, ule ni w-_____.
       Siyo, kile ni ch-_____.
       Siyo, ile ni y-_____.
       Samaki zile ni z-_____.

(g)   Mtoto yupi ni wa mwalimu? _____.
       Unataka kununua shanga zipi? _____.
       Nyumba ipi ni ya mtajiri? _____.
       Kalamu zipi ni za Bwana Philip? _____.
       Viti vipi ni vya shule? _____.
       Mama amekupa mfuko upi? _____.
       Bwana Harris amenunua matunda yapi? _____.
       Bwana Philip amekula chungwa lipi? _____.
       Bwana Harris amampa Bwana Philip ufunguo upi? _____.

(h)   kufika - kutofika, _____.
       kunywa - kutokunywa, _____.
       kununua - kutonunua, _____.

Unit 21, section III

(c)   Nilimwona mamangu jana.
       Ulimwona mamako jana.
       Alimwona mamake jana.
       Tulimwona mama yetu jana.
       Mlimwona mama yenu jana.
       Walimwona mama yao jana.

(d)   Sikufika nyumbani kwangu jana.
       Hukufika nyumbani kwako jana.
       Hakufika nyumbani kwake jana.
       Hatukufika nyumbani kwetu jana.

Hamkufika nyumbani kwenu jana.
Hawakufika nyumbani kwao jana.

(e) Nitakutana na rafiki yangu kesho kutwa.
Utakutana na rafiki yako kesho kutwa.
Atakutana na rafiki yake kesho kutwa.
Tutakutana na marafiki zetu kesho kutwa. (or, *rafiki yetu*)
Mtakutana na marafiki zenu (or, *rafiki yenu*) kesho kutwa.
Watakutana na marafiki zao (or, *rafiki yao*) kesho kutwa.

(f) Sitaonana na mtoto wangu tena.
Hutaonana na mtoto wako tena.
Hataonana na mtoto wake tena.
Hatutaonana na watoto (or, *mtoto*) wetu tena.
Hamtaonana na watoto (or, *mtoto*) wenu tena.
Hawataonana na watoto (or, *mtoto*) wao tena.

(h) Siyo, Bwana Hasani na Bwana Philip hawakuanguka baisikeli.
Siyo, Bwana Philip hakumwogopa nguruwe.
Siyo, Bwana Harris hakununua machungwa matamu.
Siyo, Bwana Philip hakununua nazi chache, alinunua nazi nyingi.
Siyo, Bibi Maw hakuenda Ghana, Professor Athumani alikwenda huko.

(i) Siyo, sitasoma Kiswahili sikukuu, bali _____.
Siyo, watu hawatakaa nyumbani siku ya mwaka mpya, bali _____.
Siyo, hatutamaliza kazi zetu mapema, bali _____.
Siyo, sitamsaidia mamangu nyumbani kidogo siku ya Krismasi,
bali _____.

Unit 22, section III

(b)

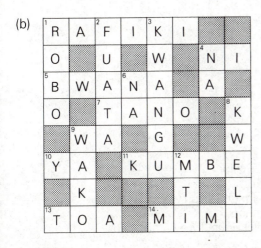

(c)

¹A		²H	A	K	U	³N	A		⁴L	⁵A
C		A			G		⁶L			U
⁷H	A	Y	A		⁸F	⁹A	G	I	¹⁰O	
A	U		¹¹W		¹²P	A	N	A		
		¹³K	¹⁴W	A	¹⁵N	I	N	I		¹⁶S
¹⁷N	D	O	A		A		I		¹⁸U	A
I			¹⁹N	²⁰I	N	A		²¹W		B
A		²²W	A	P	I		²³S	A	N	A
		²⁴A	L	I				N		B
²⁵C	H	O	O			²⁶B	A	B	U	

(e) Mwaka jana nilikuwa sisemi Kiswahili, lakini sasa nimesoma kidogo.
Mwaka jana ulikuwa husemi Kiswahili, lakini sasa umesoma kidogo.
Mwaka jana alikuwa hasemi Kiswahili, lakini sasa amesoma kidogo.
Mwaka jana tulikuwa hatusemi Kiswahili, lakini sasa tumesoma kidogo
Mwaka jana mlikuwa hamsemi Kiswahili, lakini sasa mmesoma kidogo
Mwaka jana walikuwa hawasemi Kiswahili, lakini sasa wamesoma
    kidogo.

(f) Siyo, tutakuwa tunaila _____ lakini leo hatutaila.
Siyo, atakuwa anakifundisha _____ lakini leo hafundishi.
Siyo, atakuwako _____ lakini sasa hayuko.
Siyo, mfukoni mtakuwa nazo _____, lakini sasa hamna.

Unit 23, section III

(c)
-piga	-pigwa
-pika	-pikwa
-toa	-tolewa
-nunua	-nunuliwa
-leta	-letwa
-ingia	-ingiliwa/-ingiwa
-funga	-fungwa
-chukua	-chukuliwa
-kata	-katwa
-ondoa	-ondolewa

(d) Bi. Joan aliumwa na Bw. Philip.
Mti ule utagongwa na gari!
Kioo cha mbele cha gari yangu kilivunjwa na jiwe.
Nyumba hii ilijengwa na nani?
Kitabu hicho cha Kiswahili kilinunuliwa nami.

Vyombo visafishwe na Bw. Stuart!
Nguo zake zinafuliwa na Bi. Joan.
Mwizi ameondolewa na askari.
Bia yote imenywewa na nani?

(e) Bw. Harris amedanganywa na _____.
Nilipigwa na _____.
Habari hii nzuri ililetwa na _____.
Mwizi atafungwa jela na _____.
Chai ile tamu imepikwa na _____.
Kitabu kile kikubwa kimeandikwa na _____.
Vyombo vya chai vimeondolewa na _____.
Biskuti zote zimeliwa na _____.

(f)   5 lenye   6 yenye
       7 chenye   8 vyenye
       9 yenye   10 zenye
           11/14 wenye
           15   kwenye
           16   penye
           17   kwenye
           18   mwenye

(g) Nyumba yenye madirisha manne.
Meza yenye miguu mitatu.
Shati lenye vifungo vidogo.
Kabati lenye milango miwili.
Kitabu chenye picha.
Hospitali yenye wagonjwa wengi mno.
Mwalimu mwenye wanafunzi arobaini.
Masanduku mawili yenye mayai kumi na mawili.
Msikiti wenye paa la dhahabu.
Maskini mwenye mguu mmoja tu.
Wenye kukaa katika nyumba za kioo wasitupe mawe.

Unit 24, section III

(e) -fumba   -fumbua   'open eyes'
     -ziba   -zibua   'unstop', 'uncork'
     -tega   -tegua   'spring trap'
     -fuma   -fumua   'unravel'
     -tata   -tatua   'untangle'

(f) kichwa   vichwa
     jicho   macho
     sikio   masikio
     pua   pua
     kinywa   vinywa
     koo   koo
     bega   mabega
     kifua   vifua

mgongo	migongo
tumbo	tumbo (*matumbo* — 'intestines')
mkono	mikono
kidole	vidole
kidole gumba	vidole gumba
mguu	miguu
goti	magoti

▷ (g) Ninaumwa kichwa.
        Ninaumwa jicho.
        Ninaumwa sikio.
        Ninaumwa koo.

        Kifua kinaniuma.
        Mgongo unaniuma.
        Tumbo inaniuma.
        Mguu unaniuma.
        Goti linaniuma.

Unit 25, section III

(d) Bwana Harris aliazima raba (kutoka) kwa Bi. Maw.
     Bibi Maw alimwazimia Bwana Harris raba.

     Professor Athumani aliazima raba (kutoka) kwa Bwana Harris.
     Bwana Harris alimwazimia Professor Athumani kalamu yenye raba.

     Bi. Maw na Bw. Harris waliazima gari kwa mkewe Toon.
     Toon aliwaazimima Bi. Maw na Bw. Harris gari ya bibi yake.

     Professor Athumani alipata kupiga simu kwa kuazima simu ya Bibi
         Muthama
     Bibi Muthama alimwazimia Professor Athumani simu yake.

(g) e.g. Siyo, kile si changu, ni kitabu chake rafiki yangu.

(h)   3 ninayo
      4 ninao
      5 ninalo
      6 ninayo
      7 ninacho
      8 ninavyo
      9 ninayo
     10 ninazo
     11 ninao
     15 ninako
     16 ninapo
     17 ninako
     19 ninamo

(i) Ndiyo, ninao. / Siyo, sinao.
     Ndiyo, anayo. / Siyo, hanayo.
     Ndiyo, wanazo. / Siyo, hawanazo.

Ndiyo, tunavyo. / Siyo, hatunavyo.
Ndiyo, inayo. / Siyo, hainayo.
Ndiyo, mnayo. / Siyo, hamnayo.
Ndiyo, analo. / Siyo, hanalo.
Ndiyo, ninao. / Siyo, sinao.
Ndiyo, inacho. / Siyo, hainacho.

(j) Chombo cha kupikia.
Dawa ya kunywa.
Dawa ya kupakia.
Kisu cha kukatia mkate.
Mahali pa kukalia.

(k) Bw. Harris alimpigia Bi. Maw simu jana.
Professor Athumani alimpelekea mamake barua.
Bw. Philip alimfungulia Professor Athumani mlango.
Mtoto anamlilia mamake.
Bw. Philip alimtandia kitanda Bwana Harris.
Bi. Abdalla alimtafutia Bi. Maw mfuko.
Wanafunzi wamemkasirikia mwalimu.
Mwondolee bwana vyombo.
Bi. Maw aliwatilia chai wageni wake. (or, *wageni wake chai*)
Nichagulie machungwa makubwa.
Mvuvi ametuletea samaki.
Nani alikupatia kitabu hiki?

(l) -chukua   -chukulia
-uza   -uzia
-funga   -fungia
-fua   -fulia
-soma   -somea

(m) If a child cries for a knife, give him one, i.e. let him learn.

Unit 25, Revision exercise.

Note that this is a suggested equivalent; if you have written something
different it may be perfectly correct. If possible check your version
against earlier texts, or with a teacher.

Hasani: Hujambo, Bwana Philip.
Philip: Sijambo, Bwana Hasani. Sijui wewe.
Hasani: Mimi sijambo. Habari gani?
Philip: Nzuri, lakini nina kazi nyingi.
Hasani: Kazi gani?
Philip: Basi, kazi za nyumbani. Habari zako, je?
Hasani: Nzuri sana. Ninakwenda sokoni. Mbona usije mami?
Philip: Nije? Utanunua nini? Nguruwe?
Hasani: Usinitanie. Ninataka kununua machungwa.
Philip: Basi, usinunue madanzi. Bwana wangu alidanganywa hivyo
         jana tu.

Hasani: Usijali bwana, sitandanganywa. Haya, twende.
Philip: Haya.

Unit 26, section III

(b)   Bi. Maw na Bw. Harris walikaa Oceanic.

▷   (c)   M.:   Mfuko huu ni wako?
W.:   Ndiyo ni wangu.
M.:   Ali alisema ati ni wake.
W.:   Mtu huyo ni mwongo tu, mfuko ule ndio wangu.

M.:   Mifuko hii ni yenu?
W.:   Ndiyo, ni yetu.
M.:   Ali na Hasani walisema ati ni yao.
W.:   Watu hao ni waongo tu, ile ndiyo mifuko yetu.

M.:   Shati hili ni lako?
W.:   Ndiyo, ni langu.
M.:   Ali alisema ati ni lake.
W.:   Mtu huyo ni mwongo tu, shati lile ndilo langu.

M.:   Mashati haya ni yenu?
W.:   Ndiyo, ni yetu.
M.:   Ali na Hasani walisema ati ni yao.
W.:   Watu hao ni waongo tu, yale ndiyo mashati yetu.

M.:   Kisu hiki ni chako?
W.:   Ndiyo, ni changu.
M.:   Ali alisema ati ni chake.
W.:   Mtu huyo ni mwongo tu. Kisu kile ndicho changu.

M.:   Visu hivi ni vyenu?
W.:   Ndiyo ni vyetu.
M.:   Ali na Hasani walisema ati ni vyao.
W.:   Watu hao ni waongo tu, vile ndivyo visu vyetu.

M.:   Uma huu ni wako?
W.:   Ndiyo ni wangu.
M.:   Ali alisema ati ni wake.
W.:   Mtu huyo mwongo tu, uma ule ndio wangu.

M.:   Nyuma hizo ni zenu?
W.:   Ndiyo, ni zetu.
M.:   Ali na Hasani walisema ati ni zao.
W.:   Watu hao ni waongo tu, zile ndizo nyuma zetu.

(d)   Alipofika mjomba wetu, tulikuwa tunakula chakula./Mjomba wetu
     alipofika, . . .
Wageni wetu walipoondoka tulikuwa tunafanya kazi.
Tulipoondoka nyumbani, mtoto wetu alikuwa analia.
Mlevi alipokimbia, watu walikuwa wakicheka.

Mwenzangu alipokuwa anasoma, nilifika nyumbani kwake.
Tulipokuwa tukila chakula, mjomba wetu alifika.

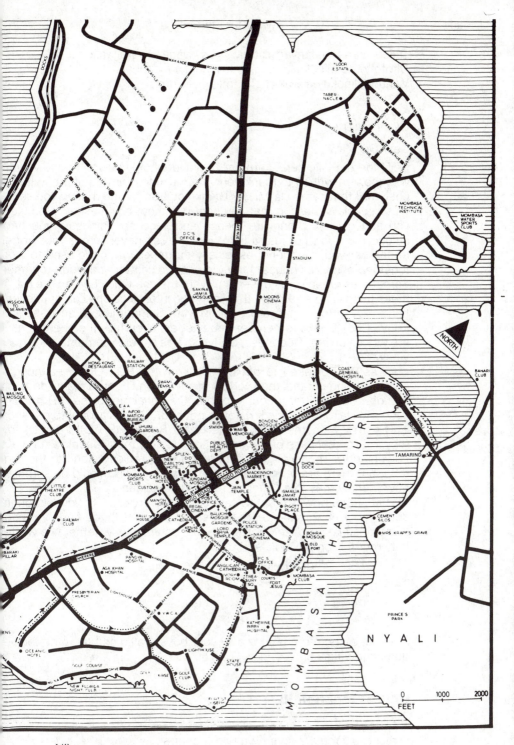

Njia yao . . > . .
Njia ya   Bi. Maw - - > - -

Note. This map is now out of date (1991). The Nyali Bridge (a pontoon bridge) has now been dismantled and a new one built further North.

Tulipokuwa tunafanya/tukifanya kazi, wageni wetu waliondoka.
Mtoto wetu alipokuwa analia, tuliondoka nyumbani.
Watu walipokuwa wakicheka, mlevi alikimbia.

Gloss to letter:

Dear Dr. Maw,

Hello there, Philip here. I am fine; I wonder how you are. I hope you ar
well too. I'm writing to thank you very much for thinking of me, with th
post-card that came via Mr. H. Thank you also for the money you sent.
was especially pleased that you sent it without being asked. God bles
you and give you long life, peace and success. Honestly, you hav
helped me a lot, not just a little, really. I can never forget you; I ofte
remember you, my friend, especially the times when we used to wor
together in Mr. H's house; how we used to chatter and laugh together
Sometimes when I was upset you were the one who cheered me up. A
these things and a lot more that I can't go into, since one can't put every
thing in a letter, make me think of you. Sometimes when I see tha
Kenya Cook Book I remember you and feel cheerful—the one you gav
me when you left. Goodness, Dr. Maw, has a mere memento such goo
vibes?

I was very pleased to get my job with the Post Office—although
don't yet understand the work, I am learning. I can already do a bi
though. Maybe after a couple of months I shall go to the P.O. trainin
school in Nairobi. Here in Kwale it's not bad. There is a lot of forest and
isn't as hot as some parts of the Coast Region. (P.T.O.) I don't know
why, maybe because of the trees. I don't know many people yet but I'r
beginning to. The local people here in Kwale region belong to the Dig
tribe, but there are others who have come for work. You'd be surprise
how friendly they (the Digo) are towards outsiders.

That's it for now, except to say that I feel very close to you, although
don't know how many years it is since we met! If you find I've mad
some mistakes, please forgive me, for I don't know whether I've writte
in Lamu or Mombasa dialect!

All good wishes. God keep you,
Yours,

Philip.

P.S. Oh, sorry, remember me to your boys, David and the other one—
don't know his name.

Unit 27, section III

(b) *Kikulacho kimo nguoni mwako*. Your nearest and dearest annoy you
most; or, You are your own worst enemy.

Usiache mbachao kwa msala upitao. Old friends are best; or, A bird in
the hand is worth two in the bush.

Ulacho ndicho chako, kilichobaki ni cha mchimba lindi. Eat, drink and
be merry, for tomorrow we die; or, You can't take it with you.

(c) Wiki ijayo.
Mwaka uliopita.
Watu waliopo.
Asiyepo.
Vitabu vilivyo na picha nyingi.

(d) Saa hizi ndizo utakazo?
Ndizo hizo.

Mfuko huu ndio utakao?
Ndio huo.

Mifuko hii ndiyo utakayo?
Ndiyo hiyo.

Shati hili ndilo utakalo?
Ndilo hilo.

Mashati haya ndiyo utakayo?
Ndiyo hayo.

Kisu hiki ndicho utakacho?
Ndicho hicho.

Visu hivi ndivyo utakavyo?
Ndivyo hivyo.

Wembe huu ndio utakao?
Ndio huo.

Mtu huyu ndiye umtakaye?
Ndiye huyo.

Watu hawa ndio uwatakao?
Ndio hao.

(e) Viti hivi ndivyo nilivyovitaka.
Meza hii ndiyo niliyoitaka.
Meza hizi ndizo nilizozitaka.
Kabati hili ndilo nililolitaka.
Makabati haya ndiyo niliyoyataka.
Mkeka huu ndio nilioutaka.
Mikeka hii ndiyo niliyoitaka.

(f) Nimenunua kitabu kitakachonifaa sana.
Ninakaa nyumbani panapo starehe sana.
Umeona mfuko wangu uliokuwako mezani?
Tulisikia nyimbo zilizokuwa nzuri sana.

(g) Kisu nilichokinunua ni kikali sana.
Mtu niliyemwona alikuwa ana masikio makubwa.
Waizi tuliowakamata ni vijana tu.
Pete nzuri sana aliyoiona alitaka kuinunua./Alitaka kununua pete . . .
Gari niliyoiendesha ni ya Professor Athumani.
Wembe wa babake aliouchukua alijikata kwao./Alijikata kwa wembe
    wa babake aliouchukua.

Mahali tulipokwenda ndipo penye miti mingi.
Nitakapokuona kesho nitakuwa nimemaliza kazi yangu.
Tulipofika jana tulikuta shule imefungwa.
Sioni nazi kubwa nitakazo.
Aliyeandika barua ndiye Bwana Philip.

Nilinunua kisu kilicho kikali sana.
Nilimwona mtu aliyekuwa na masikio makubwa.
Tuliwakamata waizi walio vijana tu.
Aliona pete nzuri sana aliyotaka kuinunua.
Niliendesha gari lililo la Professor Athumani. (Or, *iliyo ya* . . .)
Alichukua wembe wa babake aliojikata kwao.
Tulikwenda mahali palipo miti mingi.
Nitakuona kesho nitakapokuwa nimemaliza kazi yangu.
Tulifika jana tulipokuta shule imefungwa.

(h) Nitatupilia mbali viazi nisivyovitaka.
Watu wasiotakiwa watapelekwa makwao.
Vitabu visivyofaa vitatupiliwa mbali.

(i) Wanafunzi wasiosoma vizuri _____.
Mtu asiyefanya kazi _____.
Mgonjwa asiyekunywa dawa yake _____.
Watu wale wasio Waislamu _____.

(j) _____ chakula kisicho kitamu.
_____ nguo zisizonifaa.
_____ kisu kisicho kikali.
_____ mwanamume asiye mwema.

(k) Kiko wapi sasa kitabu kilichokuwako mezani?/Kitabu kilichokuwako . .
Nani ameyala machungwa yaliyokuwamo kikapuni?
Umeuona mwavuli uliokuwapo hapa?
Nani amezinywa chupa mbili za pombe zilizokuwamo kabatini?
Mlevi aliyekuwako jela ameachwa huru?
Umeiona pete ya dhahabu niliyokuwa nayo?
Umewaona ng'ombe sita aliokuwa nao?
Mmeviuza viazi mlivyokuwa navyo?
Umeziweka wapi pesa tulizokuwa nazo?
Wameyafua mashati mapya waliyokuwa nayo?

(l) Gari nyinginezo (or, magari mengineyo)
Mahindi mengineyo
Viazi vinginevyo
Watoto wengineo
Ng'ombe wengineo
Miti mingineyo

Unit 28, section III

(c) Ningekuwapo nyumbani ningefurahi sana.
Ungekuwapo nyumbani ungefurahi sana.

Angekuwapo nyumbani angefurahi sana.
Tungekuwapo nyumbani tungefurahi sana.
Mngekuwapo nyumbani mngefurahi sana.
Wangekuwapo nyumbani wangefurahi sana.

Unit 30, section III

(b) -anguka   -angusha
     -imba   -imbisha
     -kimbia   -kimbiza
     -sikitika   -sikitisha
     tayari   -tayarisha
     -soma   -somesha.

(c) -amka   -amsha
     -fahamu   -fahamisha
     karibu   -karibisha
     -nawa   -navya
     -potea   -poteza
     -ruka   -rusha
     -samehe   -samehesha
     -weza   -wezesha

(d) 7   ki
     8   vi
     9   i
     10   zi
     11/14 u
     15   ku
     16   pa
     17   ku
     18   mu

(e) Mamako yu hali gani?
     (Sisi) sote tu hali njema.
     Kufanya kazi wakati wa baridi kunachosha sana.
     Baada ya kuondoka kwako nitasikitika sana.
     Kuondoka kwako kutanisikitisha sana.
     Kabla ya Wazungu kufika Afrika Mashariki, walifika Waarabu.

Unit 31, section III

(e) **simple**	**stative**	**prepositional**	**passive**	**causative**
-ondoa	-ondoka	-ondolea	-ondolewa	-ondosha
-angua	-anguka		-anguliwa	-angusha
-tikisa	-tikisika	-tikisia	-tikiswa	-tikisisha
-pita	-pitika	-pitia	-pitwa	-pitisha
	-kauka	(-kaukia)		-kausha
-vunja	-vunjika	-vunjia	-vunjwa	-vunjisha
-weza	-wezek(an)a		-wezwa	-wezesha

-geua	-geuka	-geulia	-geuliwa	-geuza
-shua	-shuka	-shulia	-shuliwa	-shusha
-fikiri	-fikirika	-fikiria	-fikiriwa	-fikirisha
-ita	-itika	-itia	-itwa	-itisha
-fungua	-funguka	-fungulia	-funguliwa	-funguza
-funga	-fungika	-fungia	-fungwa	-fungisha
-chukua	-chukulika	-chukulia	-chukuliwa	-chukuza
(-ruka	-rukika	-rukia	-rukwa	-rusha)
-shtua	-shtuka			-shtusha
(-funika	-funikika	-funikia	-funikwa	-funikisha)
-rarua	-raruka	-rarulia	-raruliwa	
-tambua	-tambulika	-tambulia	-tambuliwa	-tambulisha
-sikia	-sikika	-sikilia	-sikiliwa	-sikiliza/-sikiza
-piga	-pigika	-pigia	-pigwa	-pigisha
(-andika	-andikika	-andikia	-andikwa	-andikisha)
-pata	-patika	-patia	-patwa	-pasha
	-sikitika			-sikitisha

Note that *-ruka, -funika*, and *-andika* look like stative forms, in that they have *k* before the final vowel, but function like simple verbs.

(f) Funga mlango! Umefungika. Uliufunga wewe? Siyo, umefungika tu.
Fungua madirisha! Yamefunguka. Uliyafungua wewe? Siyo, yamefunguka tu.
Ondoa mbwa! Ameondoka. Ulimwondoa wewe? Siyo, ameondoka tu.
Usivunje vyombo! Vimevunjika. Ulivivunja wewe? Siyo, vimevunjika tu

(g) Siyo, haipitiki _____.
Siyo, hayang'oleki _____.
Siyo, haichukuliki _____.
Siyo, hasameheki _____.
Siyo, hakiliki _____.
Siyo, hawasahauliki _____.

(h) Siyo, hawezi kupika mizizi hayo, hayapikiki.
Mizizi ile imepikika lakini.
Ndiyo, ile ilipikwa _____.

Siyo, huwezi kukata mkate huo, haukatikani.
Mkate ule umekatika, lakini.
Ndiyo, ule umekatwa _____.

Siyo, hawezi kujibu swali hilo, halijibikani.
Swali lile limejibika, lakini.
Ndiyo, lile limejibiwa _____.

Siyo, hawezi kusema maneno hayo, hayasemeki.
Maneno yale yamesemeka, lakini.
Ndiyo, yale yamesemwa _____.

Siyo, hawawezi kuvunja benki hiyo, haivunjiki.
Benki ile imevunjika, lakini.
Ndiyo, ile ilivunjwa _____.

Siyo, hawawezi kufika nyota hizo, hazifikiki.
Mwezi umefikika, lakini.
Ndiyo, mwezi umefikiwa _____.

(i) -shika   -shikika
-fika   -fikika
-maliza   -malizika
-nunua   -nunulika
-hesabu   -hesabika

Unit 32, section III

(b) 1   ambaye
2   ambao
3   ambao
4   ambayo
5   ambalo
6   ambayo
7   ambacho
8   ambavyo
9   ambayo
10   ambazo
11/14 ambao
15   ambako
16   ambapo
17   ambako
18   ambamo

(c) who were breaking . . .   non-defining
who broke . . .   defining
who live . . .   defining
who are known . . .   non-defining
which climbed . . .   defining
who are famous . . .   non-defining
who are pregnant . . .   defining
who was . . .   non-defining
that Jack . . .   defining
that live . . .   defining
she sat in . . .   defining
whereon the . . .   defining
which were put on . . .   non-defining

(d) Kitabu . . .   verb requires -me- tense
Gari . . .   'oblique' relative; -nge- tense
Mtoto . . .   'oblique' relative
Meza . . .   'oblique' relative
Malkia . . .   non-defining relative

(e) Mwizi, ambaye hakumwona askari, alijaribu kumnyang'anya
mwanamke mfuko wake. (kunyang'anya mfuko wa mwanamke).
Non-defining relative; use of past negative.

Yuko wapi mtu ambaye ulimwuzia gari yako? 'Oblique' relative.
Armstrong na Aldrin walifika mwezini ambapo walikusanya mawe na
  vumbi. Non-defining relative.
Nyumba ya mchawi, ambayo imeezekwa mabati, iko karibu na mto.
  Non-defining relative; use of -me- tense.
Sanduku ambalo ndani yake mamangu huweka pete zake limeibiwa.
  'Oblique' relative; use of hu- 'tense'.
Wanafunzi wengine ambao sitataja majina yao, hawajafanya kazi yao.
  Non-defining relative; 'oblique' relative.
Jana niliona gauni ambalo ningalilinunua, lakini duka lilikuwa
  limefungwa. Use of -ngali- tense.
Wasichana wengine huolewa na waume ambao hawajawaona. Use of
  -ja- tense.

Unit 33, section III

(b)   See chart III p. 279.

(c)   joka 'big snake', 'serpent'
      jito 'large river'
      joto 'great heat, a scorcher'
      jana 'big strong child, a buster'
      jisu 'carving-knife, slasher, cleaver'

(d)   kitoto 'baby, weakling'
      kijia/kinjia 'path, track'
      kilima 'hill'
      kivuli 'shadow'

(e)   kijitabu 'insignificant screed'
      kijito 'trickle, rivulet'
      kijiduka 'miserable, grubby shop'
      kijibuzi 'runt' (goat)
      kijitoto 'urchin'
      kijiti 'stick'

Unit 34, section III

(b)   -onyeshana   double causative, reciprocal; 'show one another'
      -tupiana   prepositional, reciprocal; 'throw to (at) one another'
      -julishana   causative, reciprocal; 'let one another know' 'introduce'
      -ogofyana   causative, reciprocal; 'frighten one another'
      -funguliana   reversive, prepositional, reciprocal; 'undo for one another'
      -cheleweshwa   passive, causative, passive; 'be made late'
      -pitishwa   causative, passive; 'be allowed to pass'
      -tozwa   causative, passive. 'be made to pay (give)' e.g. a fine
      -funganishwa   reciprocal, causative, passive; 'be forced to be tied
        together'.

(c)   -ongozana   'lead one another aright'
      -katazana   'forbid one another'

-jazana   'fill one another' 'pack in together'
-kimbizana   'chase each other'
-semezana   'speak seriously together'
-lazana   'put one another to bed', e.g. children when mother is out.

(d)   2 (b) Bwana Harris alimpigia Professor Athumani simu.
          (c) Professor Athumani alipigiwa simu na Bwana Harris.
       3 (b) Professor Athumani alimpelekea mamake barua.
          (c) Mamake alipelekewa barua na Professor Athumani.
       4 (b) Bwana Harris alimfungulia mlango Bibi Maw.
          (c) Bibi Maw alifunguliwa mlango na Bwana Harris.
       5 (b) Bwana Philip alimtandia kitanda Bwana Harris.
          (c) Bwana Harris alitandiwa kitanda na Bwana Philip.
       6 (b) Binti Abdalla alimtafutia Bibi Maw kanga.
          (c) Bibi Maw alitafutiwa kanga na Binti Abdalla.
       7 (b) Bibi Maw anamshonea shati Bwana Harris.
          (c) Bwana Harris anashonewa shati na Bibi Maw.
       8 (b) Wanafunzi watamwandikia Sh. Yahya insha.
          (c) Sh. Yahya ataandikiwa insha na wanafunzi.
       9 (b) Bibi Maw alimtilia Sh. Yahya chai?
          (c) Sh. Yahya alitiliwa chai na Bibi Maw?
      10 (b) Wanafunzi wamemkasirikia mwalimu?
          (c) Mwalimu amkesasirikiwa na wanafunzi?
      11 (b) Mtoto anamlilia mamake.
          (c) Mamake analiliwa na mtoto.
      12 (b) Nichagulie machungwa makubwa.
          (c) Nichaguliwe machungwa makubwa.

(e)   -tengenezewa   -patiwa
      -imbiwa   -somewa
      -fungiwa   -tolewa
      -chukuliwa   -endeshewa.

(f)   See Chart II p. 278.

(g)   Loan words from Arabic, in order of appearance in the text:

      sanamu (1)*   -ridhi (2, 4)
      kelele (1)   -kaidi (3)
      taratibu (1, 5)   sauti (3)
      -badili (1, 4)   tashtiti (1, 2, 5)
      -staajabu (2, 3, 4, (5))   -fahamu (1, 4)
      ghadhabu (1, 2)   -saidia (3)
      -zidi (4)   lazima (1)
      jibu (4)   dunia (3)
      hamaki (1)   -fikiri (1, 4)
      lakini (1)   nafsi (1, 2)
      sakafu (1)   wakati (1)
      haraka (1)   -wadia (3)
      jamaa (3)   sahau (3, 4)
      hebu (2)

      * PTO for explanations of numbers in brackets

1 - three consonants in stem
2 - non-Bantu consonant/consonant cluster
3 - loss of consonant between vowels
4 - non-Bantu verbal suffix
5 - *ta-* prefix.

Unit 35, section III

(c) pointi (4)   boli (1, 2, 4)
     laini (2)   rafu (1, 2, 4)
     penalti (4)   pasi (1, 4)
     mechi (2, 3, 4)   mafowadi (1/2, 4, 5)
     goli (2, 4)   kupasiana (1, 5)
     shuti (2, 4)   staili (2, 4)
     kipa (2)   difensi (1, 2, 4)
     timu (2, 4)   yadi (1/2, 4)
     mwanasoka (1, 2, 3, 6)

1 - consonant spelling changed
2 - vowel changed (spelling/pronunciation)
3 - consonant cluster simplified
4 - final vowel added
5 - noun/verb structure added
6 - new formation

(d) soup
     stamp
     tractor
     corner
     keep left (bollard, roundabout), pl. *vipilefiti*
     college
     colonialism
     uniform
     store
     puncture
     lock-up (gaol)
     licence
     half-back
     typewriter
     wire
     teenager
     right wing
     marching order (pl. *maching'oda*)

(e) This version is an example only, not to be taken as definitive.

N.F.A.: Express lambasted

B.A.T. clobbered Express 2 goals to 1 in an N.F.A. points struggle at th
Kadeni ground recently.

The Express team took the initiative by attacking the B.A.T. goal with th
combination of Aswani, Mutuli and Caleb Okutu dominating the entir

front line. They got their first goal from a nicely judged penalty from Aswani who made no mistake about it.

Almost at once the match hotted up and in the space of about 28 minutes B.A.T. had managed to reply with their goal, which, however, remained their last.

S. Bureka who was waiting near Express's goal got the ball and let off a rocket which the keeper never saw as it passed him by into the net.

The first half ended with both teams level at one-all. When the second half began the B.A.T. team tried every which way to defend their area to prevent any more goals being forced through and to control their forward area.

The match went on admirably with each player simply attempting to get the ball without any rough stuff. When there were only a few minutes left before the end, Edodio got the ball and without any passing went straight ahead and landed a real cracker in the net.

The general opinion was that B.A.T.'s victory was due to their forwards. For they used their new tactic of getting rid of the ball, i.e. you get the ball and immediately pass it on, so that the opponents are left wandering about the field.

When the match was nearly over Express's big lads were observed to be using their new 4-2-4 tactic but time was not on their side. So when the final whistle sounded their players left the field hanging their heads in exhaustion.

Bibliography

Dictionary:

Johnson, F., *A Standard Swahili-English, English-Swahili Dictionary*, 2 vols, Oxford University Press, 1939.

Grammars:

Ashton, E. O., *Swahili Grammar*, Longman, 1944.
Perrott, D. V., *Teach Yourself Swahili*, E.U.P., 1961.
Wilson, P. M., *Simplified Swahili*, East African Literature Bureau, 1970.

Reading:

Abdallah bin Hemedi 'I Ajjemy, *Habari za Wakilindi*, East African Literature Bureau, 1962.
ed. Lyndon Harries, *Swahili Prose Texts*, Oxford University Press, 1965.
James Mbotela, *Uhuru wa Watumwa*, Nelson, 1959.
ed. W. H. Whiteley, *Tippu Tip*, Johari za Kiswahili, 8, East African Literature Bureau, 1966.

Poetry:

M. H. Abdulaziz, *Muyaka*, Kenya Literature Bureau, 1979.
ed. Lyndon Harries, *Swahili Poetry*, Oxford University Press, 1962.

Index

Notes

Notes

Notes

Notes

Notes

Notes

Notes

Notes

Notes

Notes